Also by
Rachel Louise Martin

Hot, Hot Chicken:
A Nashville Story

A MOST TOLERANT LITTLE TOWN

The Explosive Beginning of School Desegregation

RACHEL LOUISE MARTIN

SIMON & SCHUSTER
New York London Toronto
Sydney New Delhi

Simon & Schuster
1230 Avenue of the Americas
New York, NY 10020

First Simon & Schuster hardcover edition June 2023

SIMON & SCHUSTER and colophon are registered trademarks of Simon & Schuster, Inc.

Portions of this book previously appeared in *Narratively*, *Oxford American*, and *US of America*.

For information about special discounts for bulk purchases, please contact Simon & Schuster Special Sales at 1-866-506-1949 or business@simonandschuster.com.

The Simon & Schuster Speakers Bureau can bring authors to your live event. For more information or to book an event, contact the Simon & Schuster Speakers Bureau at 1-866-248-3049 or visit our website at www.simonspeakers.com.

Interior design by Lewelin Polanco

Manufactured in the United States of America

1 3 5 7 9 10 8 6 4 2

Library of Congress Cataloging-in-Publication Data
Names: Martin, Rachel Louise, 1980- author.
Title: A most tolerant little town : the explosive beginning of school desegregation / Rachel Louise Martin.
Description: First Simon & Schuster hardcover edition. | New York : Simon & Schuster, 2023. | Includes bibliographical references and index. | Identifiers: LCCN 2022042647 (print) | LCCN 2022042648 (ebook) | ISBN 9781665905145 (hardcover) | ISBN 9781982186869 (ebook) Subjects: LCSH: Clinton High School (Clinton, Tenn.) | School integration—Tennessee—Clinton—History—20th century. | School integration—Massive resistance movement—Tennessee—Clinton—History—20th century. | Racism in education—Tennessee—Clinton—History. | African American students—Tennessee—Clinton—History—20th century. | African Americans—Education—Tennessee—Clinton—History—20th century. | African Americans—Segregation—Tennessee—Clinton—History—20th century. | Clinton (Tenn.)—Race relations. | Clinton (Tenn.)—Politics and government—20th century. Classification: LCC LC214.23.C63 M37 2023 (print) | LCC LC214.23.C63 (ebook) | DDC 379.2/630976873—dc23/eng/20220928
LC record available at https://lccn.loc.gov/2022042647
LC ebook record available at https://lccn.loc.gov/2022042648

ISBN 978-1-6659-0514-5
ISBN 978-1-9821-8686-9 (ebook)

*Dedicated to the children sent to undo
four hundred years of injustice*

No one knew what was going to happen. Everybody was hoping. Even though Clinton was segregated, it was still one of the most tolerant little towns.

—JO ANN ALLEN BOYCE

CONTENTS

A NOTE ON LANGUAGE

I have decided to include quotations involving racial slurs. I hope this makes readers uncomfortable. I also hope it illustrates how racism infected white American culture in the 1950s and prompts readers to ask what language we use now that illustrates how racial inequality structures white American life today.

Most of the white people in Clinton who used the N-word were church-going folks who considered themselves highly moral. Many of them eschewed alcohol, cards, and other vices. Few of them would say "shit" or "damn" or "fuck," especially not in public. Most would even avoid saying "Lord!" or "God!" unless they were praying. So it's telling how many people—even the supposedly "good" white folks siding with law and order—used profanity to describe the Black children of Clinton and their families. When they called their fellow townspeople the N-word or some other derogatory, racist term, they did it knowingly. The word was considered so offensive that during the court trials over the violence in Clinton, one white substitute teacher broke down on the witness stand because she was appalled by what she had heard her friends saying. The ugliness of racism had sidelined the other ethical and moral strictures that guided their lives.

The original speakers meant their words to be ugly and hurtful and violent. If you read this book aloud, I encourage you to avoid saying the slurs, especially if you are white. There is a difference between documenting such violence and perpetuating it. It is easy to cross from one side of that line to the other. I have tried to stay on the correct side, but it is a choice that worries me. Contemplate where you see the line drawn.

A MOST TOLERANT LITTLE TOWN

Coming to the Clinch, September 2005

The town of Clinton curls into the cup of land formed where the Clinch River turns sharply to meet the Tennessee, a fertile, gently rolling valley that fosters the community of some ten thousand residents. Behind the town square, the hills crack into a series of long, narrow ridges—ancient fold-and-thrust belts formed when the mountains rose up some 480 million years ago. Veins of coal lay pressed between the strata of rocks. When the land stopped shoving upward, sharp peaks pierced the sky, gathering the morning fogs from the valleys around them. Erosion and time have worn the mountaintops into the hills and hollers of Tennessee.

The first people moved to the mountains at least twelve thousand years ago, and possibly much further back than that. From the Clinch, they gathered mollusks and mussels and fish and turtles. They hunted muskrats and geese and otters on the valley floor and stalked raccoons and rabbits and bears and deer and bison on the ridges. Through careful cultivation of the surrounding forests, they grew nuts and berries for food; they harvested vines and canes that they transformed into baskets and clothing. When they wanted to visit neighboring villages, they navigated the Clinch River, but they also carved a path through the mountains that linked them into an intercontinental network of trails, a trading web stretching from Northern Canada to central South America and from the sea islands of the mid-Atlantic to California. Some of them called their home the Ouasioto Mountains. Then about 250 years ago disease and warfare and the American government drove the Indigenous residents away.

White settlers renamed the peaks the Cumberland Mountains, an homage to Prince William Augustus, Duke of Cumberland. They founded

Clinton and made it the seat of the newly created Anderson County. Then they set about extracting wealth from the hills. Coal miners burrowed and blasted and picked tunnels deep into their hearts. Farmers and bankers and textile workers staked lives on their steep sides and verdant vales, the monied along the river basin, and crofters out in the ravines and glens where planting was hard and seasonal storms washed away the topsoil. Since the rugged landscape wasn't good for large-scale plantation-style farming, slavery never took hold in the region the way it did deeper south, but the richest white leaders still bought and sold the enslaved, shoring up their assets and power in human bodies.

After Emancipation, many of the county's five hundred or so newly freed Black residents moved into Clinton, settling on the first ridge overlooking downtown. They worked wage-earning jobs that protected them from the sharecropping system taking hold of the agricultural South but sent them into the white neighborhoods where segregation and racism reigned. To shelter themselves and their families from hate, they built a neighborhood. They erected houses around two churches—one Baptist and one Methodist—and a small primary school. Soon the district had become known as Freedman's Hill, which locals shortened to simply the Hill. (Ninety years on, the journalists who covered Clinton High's desegregation assumed this was the same as Foley Hill, a white enclave a couple miles away, a confusion both Hill communities found distressing.)

Like most other Black neighborhoods around the South, the Hill's population fell during the early twentieth century as its young fled north and east and west seeking better lives and more opportunities. But the area's numbers rebounded in the 1940s thanks to a cluster of federal projects nearby. By the 1950s, the region supported a small Black business district that included a nightclub and a sandwich shop, but the heart of the community was still the school, by then called Green McAdoo Grammar School, which stood on the crest of the Hill, flanked by Asbury Methodist and Mt. Sinai Baptist.

Downtown, postbellum prosperity had transformed the by-water town into a center of commerce. Back then, industry thrived. Railroad cars heaped with coal lumbered through, coasting out of the mountains to fire the nation's power grid. Many local men, both white and Black, worked in the mines. Another quarter of the town's white adults were employed at Magnet Knitting Mills, a brick industrial complex two blocks from the square. A handful harvested and traded freshwater pearls plucked from the oysters that thrived in the Clinch River despite its annual floods.

Two highways intersected at the square. US 25W, or the Dixie Highway, shuttled drivers from Ohio to Florida; though these travelers didn't realize it, they were following the trail originally opened by the county's first residents. SR61 went into the mountains, connecting the coal miners to the rest of the nation. In 1890, the community had erected a two-story Romanesque brick courthouse with a clock tower and covered porticos in the center of the town square to house the Anderson County Court. Offices and restaurants and shops and one hotel popped up on the streets around it, all catering to white customers, of course. White travelers stopped in Clinton to buy food and gas and rent rooms for the night.

Clinton doesn't bustle any longer, although its population today is the largest it's ever been—about triple what the town's size was in 1956. Globalization and the interstate highway system have contracted the community from being a regional hub into a typical small Southern town with a few historic homes, some rows of empty storefronts, and a smattering of modernist monstrosities, all radiating from the town square.

The coal industry left the county when the veins around Clinton played out, devastating the economy. And then Magnet Knitting shut down, its hosiery farmed out to other parts of the world. Over the next four decades, its redbrick buildings crumbled, a reminder of what the town used to be but was no longer. When I-75 replaced the Dixie Highway, travelers stopped trekking downtown for supplies or a place to sleep. Local boosters have turned Market Street's abandoned shops into an antiquing district, but younger generations prefer a more minimal style of decorating. Only a handful of tourists bother to make the drive.

—

I first came to Clinton in September 2005. That year, I was a research fellow at Middle Tennessee State University's Center for Historic Preservation, and I'd been sent to the town to launch an oral history initiative. I was to collect stories about the high school's desegregation—it was the first instance of court-mandated desegregation in the South, one year before Little Rock—so that the community could open a small museum. Though I'd grown up just a few counties away, I had never heard of Clinton High School before that September. That didn't surprise Clinton's then-mayor, Winfred "Little Wimp" Shoopman. What had happened there in 1956 "was swept under the rug for fifty years," he told me. "History, if it was a pie, they were taking a bite out of it every year by not talking about it. Eventually, the pie was going to be eat up and no more story."

That first visit, Clinton's downtown snuck up on me. One stoplight, I was surrounded by car lots and fast-food joints and other architectural detritus left by 1970s-era urban redevelopment. Next, I was peering at the abandoned Magnet Knitting Mills. Then I pulled up alongside Hoskins Drug Store. In another community, this pharmacy/lunch counter/gift shop would have closed decades ago. It would have sat abandoned until some local kid came back to remodel it, replacing its pumpkin-colored vinyl booths with sleek kitsch. The food would have been billed as "home-style" or "haute Southern." But in Clinton, Hoskins has survived by selling its customers—mostly lawyers doing business at the county courthouse— the same lunches they've always ordered: small hamburgers on ready-made buns, grilled cheese sandwiches, malted milkshakes.

Past Hoskins, I saw the recently remodeled Ritz Theater, all art deco curves and sporting its original marquee. In the 1950s, it was the place to be on a Friday or Saturday night. The weekend after the high school de-segregated, the feature film was *The Fastest Gun Alive*, starring Glenn Ford and Jeanne Crain. That Saturday night, the local white boys who usually gathered out front to court local white girls had faced down the Tennessee National Guard under the Ritz's lit sign: two rows of lanky, white teen-agers, most of whom did not yet need a daily shave. One line wore khaki uniforms with lacquered steel pot helmets. The other had rolled jeans and slicked-back hair. The Clinton boys had pressed into the Guards' bayonet-ted muzzles, pushing forward until the weapons had left crisp creases in their starched button-downs.

On the lawn across the street, outside the county courthouse, sat the war memorial where machinist Willard Till announced the formation of the Anderson County White Citizens' Council. Neighbors had queued up to pay their three-dollar membership fee; they leaned on the monument, signing their registration forms on the rock upon which was carved "Lest We Forget." Over 150 joined the group within the first two hours.

Just past the courthouse, I saw the rebuilt high school, though it now housed the city's middle school. There was the stone wall supporting the school's embankment where Clinton High's first twelve Black students turned, climbed the steps, and waded through the crowd of white teenagers. The white kids had simply watched the Black students enter the school on the first day, but soon they were jeering and then heckling and then assaulting their new classmates.

Starting up the Hill, my vehicle juddered over the railroad tracks where segregationists had once set off three sticks of dynamite. I saw the ditches where the Black men and boys had crouched, sipping coffee to stay awake during the long night watches, hand-built squirrel rifles and inherited Winchesters and borrowed Remingtons clutched in their hands. I passed the empty lot where Ronald Hayden had posed for *Life* magazine on his grandmother's front lawn, standing a few steps from where a bomb would explode. He had dressed up for the occasion in a hip white cotton shirt that laced at the collar instead of buttoning. He'd left the brown leather ties undone and then chained a medallion around his neck, maybe a talisman for safety. While the photographer set up the shot, Ronald had cradled his baby sister, perhaps explaining to her what was going on as a way of making sense of it himself. He'd been a serious boy by then, just a skinny fourteen-year-old kid sent out to undo generations of inequality.

Above me loomed Green McAdoo Grammar School where the children of the Hill met to pray before their hopeful and terrifying descent to Clinton High. Most of the old structure was still sound. Before installing the museum, all the town needed to do was peel away five decades of neglect and abuse: reopen the front porch bricked in to create a small, stuffy storage room; reseal the roofing; remove the paneled drop ceiling; refinish the original floors.

Deciding what narrative—or, more accurately, whose narrative—to feature in the exhibits would be more challenging. The battle over the story of Clinton's desegregation is part of an ongoing national struggle over the politics of memory. History, like all things involving power in America today, is seen as a zero-sum game. But our memories are not time machines. They reveal something much deeper and truer and more personal than a simple timeline of events. We choose what we want to remember, and we also choose what we will forget.

I was able to reconstruct these previously unknown stories because the people of Clinton were generous with their memories. My narrators taught me to think of memory as being like music. The basic building blocks are the solos: one voice telling its story. As soon as more voices join in, the music of the past becomes more complex. Some people have held on to perspectives that harmonize, differing only by gradations of nuance, but more often the various voices are in discord and disagreement. This is the most troubling part of memory, but it can also be the most revealing. There is power in the complexity of a community's story, when it clashes like Stravinsky's *Rite of Spring*. If you stand next to only one voice, the rest of the orchestra seems to be in chaos, but if you can step back and listen to the whole of the group, the differing narratives become the melodies, harmonies, and descants of the piece.

As I've learned about the struggle in Clinton, I've been amazed by its erasure from official accounts of the civil rights movement. Midway through this project, I climbed to the fourth floor of the Davis Graduate Library at the University of North Carolina. I studied the call numbers, searching for E185.61.A425 2002, the beginning of the library's main civil rights history section. I reached for the first book, *The Origins of the African American Civil Rights Movement, 1865–1956*, and flipped to its index, looking for any reference to Clinton. Nothing. I checked the next likely book, *The American Civil Rights Movement: Readings and Interpretations*; still no references to Clinton. I continued down the shelf.

What happened in this little town between 1956 and 1958 wasn't a small story at the time. People around the world followed as twelve Black students braved mobs and beatings and bombings for the right to attend high school in their home county. The Associated Press, Reuters, *Life*, *Time*, the *New York Times*, America's three major television networks, even the BBC and the *London Daily Sketch*, all stationed journalists there. Pioneering documentarian Edward R. Murrow filmed two award-winning specials about the school. Evangelist Billy Graham hosted a crusade in the school's gymnasium, urging repentance, healing, and reconciliation.

The events in Clinton challenge how we talk about our civil rights history. Many of the best-known desegregation narratives—Little Rock, New Orleans, Boston, Birmingham—have been told in ways that give us clear-cut heroes and villains. What happened in Clinton is messier than that. It's a tale of how apathy enables hatefulness. It's a story of how discord can balloon into violence. It's an account of how doing the wrong thing gave some people unprecedented power and opportunity. It's a record of how doing the right thing can leave some individuals permanently scarred, physically and mentally. It's a chronicle of how a small Southern town can explode, and then a whole entire country can forget.

On the first day of the 1956–57 school year, however, none of the participants knew any of this was about to happen. They were doing something never before accomplished in American history. Had their success been decisive and immediate—or had local, state, and federal officials shut down dissent and stood up for the court order, calling integration right and fair—where would we be as a nation today? Instead, everyone in power waffled or looked away. Today we are split by many of the same divisions and grievances that splintered Clinton in 1956. How will our leaders respond? And if they, too, continue to abdicate their responsibility, how will we take charge?

—

The process of forgetting an event as important as the desegregation of Clinton High School sounds passive, but it requires an active "correction" of the record. When I started my work in Clinton back in 2005, my first oral history interview was with Margaret Anderson, a white woman who had been the high school's business and typing teacher. She had served as the unofficial guidance counselor for the twelve Black students. Though she had not believed in desegregation when the 1956 school year began, she did believe in obeying the law. The Black students' struggles to remain in Clinton High changed her into a true integrationist. She wrote about desegregation in a series of articles for the *New York Times*, which she later expanded into a memoir, *The Children of the South*. In her narrative, she centered the Black students and castigated many white leaders. Maybe that was why when I was introduced to her by a local white official just old enough to have seen the events for himself, he admonished her. "Now remember, Ms. Anderson, you lied in your book," he said. "You tell Rachel what we agreed had occurred."

After he left, Margaret made me a mug of instant coffee, and we sat down in her parlor to chat. She was nervous. "When I don't want you to record it, could I just raise my hand or something, give you a signal?" she asked me. "That way I feel free. You know what I mean?"

I didn't realize it that morning in Margaret Anderson's kitchen, but I would spend the next eighteen years of my life immersed in the stories the people of Clinton had to share, whether their neighbors wanted them to or not. As each person I spoke with would show me, William Faulkner was right: history wasn't dead; it was barely the past. And I don't just mean that stories told by grandparents and great-grandparents lived on in their descendants' minds. This history was so recent that many of the participants themselves were still alive. When locals looked at the pictures of white rioters around the school, they knew the faces captured on film. These were the people they shopped with at the local Food City or worshiped with at First Baptist Church or traded presents with every Christmas. The people in the pictures had birthed and raised them.

The best way to settle the conflict over desegregation was to let it lie, many white folks said. Or, as one founder of the Tennessee White Youth told me when I asked him for an interview, "Honey, there was a lot of ugliness down at the school that year; best we just move on and forget it."

But though the rest of the world did forget about Clinton High School, the students and teachers and parents and townspeople affected by the story could not. Their experiences had changed them, scarred them, broken them. Some were able to rebuild their lives, but others were not. Two of the people I'd come to admire—complicated individuals with the hamartias necessary for classical heroes—never recovered. Both would die by suicide.

The first lesson of this book is this: History is the story of human be-ings, individuals responding to events already in motion and seldom under their control. Along the way, many of them end up doing things they never expected. Sometimes they act bravely, changing their world for good. At other times they do injury to people they would have called friends.

Very few of us are simply heroes or villains. None of us deserves to be remembered for only the very best or the very worst things we have done. And yet we must be accountable for our damage.

And a lot of damage was caused in those years.

ONE

Descending Freedman's Hill

In the packed schoolyard, the teenagers had divided into their usual clusters and cliques, the layout of Clinton High's social strata mapped so clearly that even the freshmen bused in from the county's rural K–8 schools had already found their people. Wannabe rebels with duck-ass haircuts and cuffed, fraying jeans lurked on the fringes or stood on the stacked stone wall edging the campus. A few sported the black leather jackets that were the uniform of the local gang, creatively named the Black Jackets. Along the sidewalk, a cluster of clear-faced girls with curled ponytails and circle skirts bounced nervously in their bobby socks. Elsewhere, the nerds and the aggies and the cheerleaders had each carved out their respective places. Jocks in black letterman jackets with fuzzy orange *C*s prowled throughout the crowd, establishing their right to police the school. Those who had been part of the Bob Neyland Conference Championship teams had tan footballs stitched onto their coats' right pec.

Yes, on the morning of Monday, August 27, 1956, everything on the lawn looked as it ought to on the first day of school, and yet nothing was right. Where was the din? The bustle? The babble? How could it be that no one, not a single one of the gathered gaggle, was saying a word?

Jo Ann Allen found the silence creepy. She'd prepared carefully for this, her first day in her new school. She'd sorted through the five skirt-and-shirt combinations her grandmother Minnie had sewn for her over the summer, finally settling on her favorite: a prim blouse with cap sleeves that she'd tucked into a dark, full skirt and cinched to her slender frame with a snug black belt. She'd curled her bangs and twisted her ponytail into a ballet bun. Then she'd tucked some small white flowers into her updo.

Maybe, just maybe, the white girls along the sidewalk would see her and recognize a kindred spirit, another good girl looking for friends.

As ready as she could be, Jo Ann had picked up her lunch bag and her notebooks and headed over to Green McAdoo Grammar to meet the nine other Black students from the Hill who would be walking to school with her. The twelve teens who'd be desegregating Clinton High that morning were divided equally between girls and boys, but two of the girls—Jo Ann's best friend, Gail Ann Epps, and Anna Theresser Caswell—did not live on the Hill and would meet them at the school.

Up on the Hill, the ten students held hands and looked toward downtown while Bobby Cain, one of two seniors, prayed for their safety. His prayer echoed the words that the Reverend O. W. Willis, pastor over at Mt. Sinai Baptist Church, had murmured over them the night before. "Help us to love our enemies," the reverend had said, "and send our children down the Hill with peace in their hearts." After the service, had the adults whispered about what the coming day would bring? Yes, the courts were on their side, but what would that mean? Could the Supreme Court's ruling be enforced? Could equality really be won with pretty words on a page?

Maybe all would be well, the Black students thought. After all, in May 1954, a mere week after the Supreme Court announced its first decision overturning segregation in education, administrators in Fayetteville, Arkansas, had announced they'd be desegregating their high school. By the next fall, they'd done so. Now yes, white public outcry had stopped Sheridan, Arkansas, from following suit. But both Hoxie and Charleston, Arkansas, had voluntarily and quietly abolished their segregated schools in the autumn of '55. The trick seemed to be for towns to do it quickly and without public stink. Sure, a couple hundred segregationists had shown up in Hoxie a month and a half after the Black teens had started classes, having been tipped off by *Life* magazine. But when Governor Orval Faubus refused to intervene, the local courts issued a temporary restraining order ending the protests, and that was that. So maybe, the Black students thought, they'd face a few protestors and suffer a couple nasty glances and it would be over. Just maybe. The students must've worried, however, that their reception would be worse. They weren't continuing what the kids in Arkansas had already accomplished. This was the first time desegregation would be forced on a town. And by the feds, no less! If the courts got their way at Clinton High, no segregated school in America would be safe.

They'd all heard the rumors, the ones that said some white folks in Anderson County were organizing, that they'd filled up reams of paper with petitions protesting the Black students' entry. They'd heard about the bill filed in Chancery Court just last Wednesday, the one that would strip Clinton High of state funds if they were allowed to start classes, and they'd seen the advertisement taken out in the *Clinton Courier-News* by the Tennessee Federation for Constitutional Government asking people to join the organization and help prevent "mixed schools." But maybe the white folks would stick to petitions and lawsuits and ads.

It was time to test the segregationists' resolve. Wouldn't do for the Black students to be tardy on the first day of school. As the teens gathered their school supplies and began down the Hill, any family members who could come assembled to see them off. There, spread across Green McAdoo's playground and steps, were Jo Ann Allen's little sister and Bobby Cain's younger siblings and some of the Hayden kids and countless cousins. (After all, wasn't everybody on the Hill somehow related to these groundbreaking souls?) Few of the older folks were around to witness their trek, however. Most of their parents had already left for work, some in Oak Ridge, others in shops and homes around Clinton. Across the county, the adults must've glanced up at the nearest clock and whispered a plea. Perhaps William Turner, janitor at Green McAdoo, stepped out to the school's arched brick entryway to watch his daughter Regina stride forward, notebook and pen in hand, ready for her junior year.

Half brothers Alfred Williams and Maurice Soles walked side by side down the Hill, a senior and a freshman. Their uncle had brought them back to Clinton specifically for this day, uprooting them from their grandmother's house in Alabama and transferring them out of their high school so they could participate in the Clinton High experiment. No matter how the coming year went, they knew they needed to have each other's backs. Neither one was real tall in stature. No, they were about the slightest of the group, but at least they could stick together.

Up until a few weeks before, Alfred and Maurice and the other Black students had paid scant attention to the judicial battle over Clinton High's desegregation. Sure, folks had talked six years earlier when a handful of Black teens had sued for the right to enter Clinton High. There was no Black high school in the county, so the administrators had bused students to a failing high school in LaFollette an hour away and in a totally different county. The students and their lawyers had called the arrangement sepa-rate and unequal. No one was surprised when they'd lost at trial—white students from rural parts of the county were bused at least as far as the Black students were, the judge reasoned—and the case spent years pend-ing in the federal court of appeals. Most felt the lawsuit had accomplished some good, though, because the county transferred the Black kids from failing LaFollette Colored High to the much more academically rigorous Austin High in Knoxville. But then in 1954, the Supreme Court released their first decision ending school segregation. They followed up that rul-ing in 1955, announcing that desegregation needed to happen with "all deliberate speed." Based on that, the judge hearing the Anderson County case had declared that Clinton High would desegregate in the fall of 1956. A handful of other judges mandated a similar timeline for pending cases in Kentucky and Texas, but those schools wouldn't open until after Labor Day.

Even after the ruling, most of the Black teens in Clinton didn't think desegregation would happen, not there. Segregation defined every action off the Hill from shopping to eating to working. Who could imagine life without those strictures? Surely, the white people would find some way to sidestep the court ruling. Separate Black schools were even written into the state's constitution. Any school that refused to abide by segregation was to lose state funding. Who would upend a structure that buttressed an entire culture?

And so when the 1955–56 school year ended in May, they'd made plans to return to Austin High School in Knoxville. Bobby Cain put down a deposit on his senior prom. Regina Turner adjusted her class schedule and hoped the talk of desegregation would disappear. She didn't want to go to Clinton High, didn't want to try to convince the white people she was good enough for their school. Alfred Williams assumed he'd graduate with his friends back in Anniston, Alabama. But then his uncle Steve had told his nephews they'd be coming to live with him in Clinton that year. He and the rest of the teenagers' parents and guardians had agreed that the teens would force Anderson County to follow the court order. These kids would claim the promise of the American dream for all future Black and brown children. They'd prove *Brown v. Board* could be forced upon the South, and it could happen immediately.

The ten students crossed the railroad tracks and followed West Broad Street as it descended toward Hillcrest Street. Jo Ann was surprised and relieved to see that there weren't many protestors awaiting them. According to local gossip, Mayor W. E. Lewallen and Principal D. J. Brittain Jr. and *Clinton Courier-News* editor Horace V. Wells all thought their town was ready to change American history. Looking now at the small group of people awaiting the new students, Jo Ann thought that maybe they were right. Maybe Clinton really was "one of the most tolerant little towns" in America.

No one would later agree on how many protestors had been there that day. Less than a dozen? Thirty? Fifty? Closer to seventy-five? The number depended on who was doing the reporting: a segregationist, a town official, or one of the handful of local journalists covering the event (and it was mostly local reporters for now, plus one stringer from Chicago's Black paper). Let's go with the most likely one, the one Horace Wells printed in the *Clinton Courier-News*. Twenty or so older white men stood, watching the Black students approach. Just past them was a clump of some thirty-odd white protestors, mainly women and a handful of teenage kids. Or perhaps it was thirty teenagers and twenty-five adults. The kids—Jo Ann's classmates?—carried handwritten signs: "We the students of Clinton Hi don't want Negroes in our school" and "Integration? No" and "We don't want to go to school with niggers." Papers fluttered in their hands, pamphlets to be handed out to passersby warning that the fluoride in the water was a secret government mind-control mechanism, Eisenhower was a tyrant, "Race mongrelism is contempt for the Creator," and they should "Destroy the reds. FIGHT RACE HATERS."

One of the teens outside the school that morning was John Carter, a smooth-faced kid with a lanky build and close-cropped, light-colored hair. Lately, he'd been something of a local celebrity. It started the previous March when a rabid fox had attacked his pet dog. Enraged, John had grabbed a shovel and bashed the fox about the head. John won the fight, but before it died the fox bit John on both hands. Testing showed the fox was rabid, so John had to undergo a painful and expensive treatment: twenty-three abdominal inoculations. A few weeks later while still getting shots in his stomach, John stepped back into the local news by winning the district 4-H speaking championship. His address was "Responsibilities of Good Citizenship." And John had lived out his good citizenship: 4-H chapter secretary one year, vice president the next, and now three years as president. He'd also won multiple trophies for his beef cattle projects. And he was a member of the Clinton High football team. For his prowess in composing and delivering his address, the district office awarded him twenty-five dollars and took him to Nashville to compete at the state level.

That August, John should have been starting his junior year at Clinton, ready to thrive as an upperclassman. Instead, he stood on the street outside the school door with a poster strung around his neck: "WE WON'T GO TO SCHOOL WITH NEGROES." For him, this was the next iteration of good citizenship: fighting for the white Southerners' way of life and maintaining the racial order set up by God.

—

Looking at the ragtag assembly—a pitiful sight, really, when you thought that today might be the loss of all that white Southerners supposedly held dear—the assistant police chief told a journalist that the low numbers proved that desegregation wasn't going to be a big thing. Even the ones who had shown up with signs didn't really mean anything by it. "They're just boys from the country come to see the show," he said.

The low numbers were a disappointment to the protest's organizers. "There was supposed to be a lot more of us, but they didn't show up," a picketing teenager told a local reporter. "They just talked big."

The network of segregationists had mobilized the previous January when the federal courts had ruled on Clinton High. They scaffolded their efforts on those begun a year earlier in neighboring Oak Ridge. Built as one of the Manhattan Project's secret cities, Oak Ridge was transformed into a military installation after World War II. Now it was being slowly transitioned to civilian control. It had been subject to the executive orders desegregating the armed services beginning in 1948, but because of the base's peculiar position, the schools had remained untouched until the Supreme Court announced their first *Brown v. Board* verdict. With that decree, the Atomic Energy Commission ordered the community to obey it. The decision to integrate the base's schools, adding eighty-five Black students to Oak Ridge classrooms, had frustrated many white folks, but few were ready to challenge the federal government while living and working on a federal installation. And so the problems had stayed within the high school: a few fistfights, a smattering of hollered slurs, a couple graffiti incidents. Other moments seemed hopeful. Some of the white students even stood up for their Black peers, like when the physics and chemistry classes went on a field trip to the space center in Huntsville, Alabama, and a restaurant refused to serve the one Black student in the group. All the white students walked out alongside him.

Overall, Clinton's white leaders thought, the lesson from Oak Ridge High and the schools in Arkansas was that desegregation was going to happen, at least in the short term, whether they liked it or not. And none of them liked it. But they were balancing their beliefs against other political and professional goals. They would not aid desegregation. They would not plan for it. They would never support it. Neither would they take to the streets against it.

For other white people, however, Oak Ridge taught a different lesson. It showed that segregation was not the foregone establishment they'd assumed it was. Oak Ridge answered to the feds, but if Clinton High desegregated, it would set a precedent for other schools in Tennessee and across the nation. The stakes were too high for them to meekly obey. When the federal judge mandated Clinton High enroll Black students, members of a group calling itself the Tennessee Federation for Constitutional Government assembled a mailing list of sympathizers. Soon chapters had popped up across the state, and the clubs sent money back to Anderson County to fund resistance efforts there. They also sent lobbyists to Tennessee's legislature, asking the representatives to obey the state constitution and pull state funds from any desegregated schools.

One of the local leaders for the Tennessee Federation for Constitutional Government was Oak Ridge machinist Willard Till. The Tills had only been in Anderson County for a couple years, coming from Raleigh,

North Carolina. They'd probably moved because of the amazing career opportunities Oak Ridge offered to inventive machinists. Willard was a tinkerer, always coming up with ways to improve the gadgets around him. In 1948, one of his inventions, "Auxiliary Support for Use with Ironing Boards," had even merited a patent.

A sturdy man—six feet tall with gray eyes and brown hair—Willard had once been a boxer, competing in the local Golden Gloves competitions and making his way to the North Carolina state finals in the light heavy division. In 1940, he'd put his boxing days behind him when he married Frances Amanda Williams in front of a justice of the peace. The young couple was fun and not opposed to a little showboating, so they'd planned an unconventional ceremony performed before a couple thousand barn dancers gathered for a Saturday night hoedown. "That's the biggest audience for a wedding that I have ever seen," their officiant told a reporter for the Raleigh *News and Observer*. They didn't have long to settle into family life. Within a few months, Willard's draft number came up. He enlisted in the Civilian Air Patrol, became a pilot, and was made a lieutenant. Then he helped drive German submarines away from the Eastern United States. When he returned from war, Willard and Frances started on their family, having a daughter in 1946 and a son in 1949.

Willard was a God-fearing, churchgoing man, so as soon as the Tills arrived in Clinton, they'd gotten themselves settled into First Baptist Church. Then they'd stepped on up when asked to take over leadership positions in the congregation. Willard had never smoked and never drank and held no grudges against anybody. Sure, he opposed the mixing of the races in that high school, but it wasn't because he was a hateful man, he told himself as he geared up for the fight ahead. It was because he was a good man, a steadfast man, a man who knew the difference between right and wrong, a white man who was willing to do what was uncomfortable to protect the Southern way of life, that way of life that generations of his forefathers had been willing to die to save because they understood that it was the way God had arranged the world. And being an American meant standing up to tyranny.

—

Racism was an essential ingredient in the potent mix of hatred and activism that was stirring in Clinton's white neighborhoods, but local white people were also sick and tired of the federal government meddling in their lives. They thought desegregation was Clinton's Fourth Reconstruction, the fourth federal incursion into the community. The first happened when the Union Army seized control of the region, freed the slaves, instituted martial law, and disenfranchised unrepentant Confederates. The second occurred in 1936 when the Tennessee Valley Authority (TVA) constructed Norris Dam just seven miles from town. The project created jobs and wired the mountains for electricity, but it also cost local farmers thirty-four thousand acres of rich bottomland, land the federal government confiscated at a questionable rate, forcing many farming families into the textile mills and coal mines. In addition, it killed the Clinch's oysters, ending the pearl trade. What one local historian called "the third invasion of the damn Yankees" came a few years later when President Roosevelt decided to place one of the three Manhattan Project sites seven miles to the other side of Clinton. Oak Ridge ate up another fifty-five thousand acres of farmland. Some farmers were evacuated before they'd even had time to gather up their livestock. The secret city drew in outsiders, all those physicists and secretaries and engineers and administrators with their elite educations and liberal ideas. Many white locals felt dispossessed politically and geographically and economically. Some were about ready to win one of these skirmishes with the feds.

The first step was assessing who was an ally of the segregationist cause. Over the summer of '56, members of the Tennessee Federation for Constitutional Government circulated a petition protesting desegregation. Four hundred and twenty-four local white folks—almost 11 percent of Clinton's total population—signed it, scrawling their names and addresses on the five-by-eight sheets of folded white notepaper. "We (the undersigned) are against Negroes entering Clinton High School or any other White School in Anderson County, Tennessee," someone had typed across the top of all twenty-one pages. They submitted the petition to the local court system on August 12. The judge denied their request. They filed the motion to strip Clinton High of state funds about a week later.

Local white leaders—the mayor, the newspaper editor, the school superintendent, every white pastor in town—also publicly opposed desegregation, but most weren't willing to march for it. Theirs was a pragmatic decision. Over the preceding decades, they had forged valuable relationships in D.C. Their influence was disproportionate to their size. State senators, cabinet members, and other officials now made tours through Anderson County, currying favor with the Clinton politicians who had made the TVA and Oak Ridge possible. In 1956, both presidential candidates would make detours to drive through, delivering speeches. Some local white officials also benefited economically by playing nice with Washington. The federal projects of the Second and Third Reconstructions had made Anderson County the wealthiest county in Southern Appalachia. Local businesses profited off the new residents who came to work at the sites; federal agencies invested money in the county's infrastructure.

And so municipal leaders decided they would obey the letter of the new court ruling but not the spirit of it. They would concede to the federal authorities that the law of the land called for desegregation . . . but they would refuse to help implement it. They would not even set up policies for how a desegregated Clinton High School would function. And they would protect the town's white spaces and white institutions from any trouble that might arise. They were prepared to squash any person who threatened Clinton's good name, people like those rabble-rousers calling themselves the Tennessee Federation for Constitutional Government who had promised to make a scene on the first day of the new school year.

Would the white officials be protecting the Black community, though? Well, they'd stirred all this up for themselves, hadn't they?

—

Though the picketers had been shouting and booing throughout the morning, they stilled when the ten Black students appeared. The phalanx of Black teens also stopped talking as they continued along the concrete sidewalk toward Clinton High. Kinda eerie, Jo Ann thought, this unnatural silence on the first day of school, when everyone who'd been away at camp or on vacation met up with those who'd stayed behind, helping out around the house or watching younger siblings or holding down summer jobs.

Now the Black students had reached the corner of the school's property. Clinton High had been built into the bottom edges of the Hill, and the sidewalk continued on down the embankment for a while before a set of stone steps on the left took visitors up to the building's front doors. At the upper corner of the grounds, the ten Black students were eye level with their new classmates, but every step inched them farther down the Hill until their heads were below the white teens' feet. Had they ever noticed this before, how vulnerable the sidewalk made pedestrians on this stretch of road? Then the ten teenagers turned left and climbed the stone steps up to the schoolyard, toward the building. They walked through the assembled white high schoolers.

Alfred Williams recognized many of his new classmates. Some were nodding acquaintances. A few were fishing buddies. And there were the white boys he'd played football with over the summer, meeting up in the fields and glades around town where segregation wasn't as tight, at least not for kids. The games weren't official, of course, just ad hoc matches put together when teens found themselves with little to do. Now he looked the other boys over. How large some of them were, about like grown people!

As they trudged along the path, Jo Ann saw some of the white kids sneaking looks at her, studying her from behind new notebooks. Others took quick, shy glances, making eye contact, smiling slightly, then turning back to their friends. One group of white boys gathered by the front door, jeans freshly pressed and short-sleeve shirts tucked in, sneered at the Black students as they climbed the final five steps into the building. A young woman in a black sailor dress a size too large stood on the first step, nostrils flaring as though she smelled something unpleasant.

But the Black students—Jo Ann Allen, Bobby Cain, Anna Theresser Caswell, Minnie Ann Dickie, Gail Ann Epps, Ronald Hayden, William Latham, Alvah Jay McSwain, Regina Turner, Maurice Soles, Robert Thacker, and Alfred Williams—had breached the double glass doors of the school without incident. Surely, that alone counted as a success.

TWO

Wynona's Fight

Wynona McSwain fired up the stove at the Anderson County Jail, a two-story, heavy stone building near the courthouse. As she went about her morning chores as cook and cleaner for the two jailers and their inmates, she must've watched the clock, wondering where her daughter was on the journey into Clinton High. Alvah Jay, just a freshman in high school, was the fourth youngest of Wynona's nineteen children. She was such a little thing to send out to change the world, but Wynona had tried to raise her girl to do what was right, stand against those who spread hate, and demand what was her due. She'd taught Alvah her worth, that her value and her potential was so much higher than the world around her recognized.

Wynona had treasured each of her nineteen kids, though by 1956 only twelve were still living. Seven had been lost, mostly to preventable causes, ripped away from Wynona by poverty and racism. Like her son Harrison, who had died in 1936 of diphtheria, a wrenching way for a child to go. At first, Wynona wouldn't have known what was wrong with him. Somewhere between two and five days after he'd contracted the illness, he would have complained he was feeling puny, all tired and achy, and his throat hurt. When she felt his forehead, he would have been running a fever, one high enough to stay home from school but not high enough to alarm her. He probably would have refused to eat, something she might have blamed on his sore throat. What she couldn't have seen, however, was that a bluish membrane the color of a hot flame had colonized his tonsils and was creeping across his larynx. Soon—maybe the next day or the day after that—it would have begun to block Harrison's breathing, causing the air to rasp in and out of his lungs. Then Wynona would've known what the disease was, but what could she do? In this segregated time, was there a doctor who would come see Harrison, a Black child? Could his family have afforded it, even if a physician was willing to climb the Hill? The infection would have progressed. It may have begun to eat through the lining of his throat, the scabbing blood turning the membrane black. A few days later, his neck itself would have swelled, a condition folks called bull neck. Soon he'd have gone pale, his pulse would have raced, and then he would have lost consciousness. He would have been dead within a fortnight.

When Wynona was a child, many American kids died this way, as many as fifteen thousand a year. But then researchers developed an effective vaccine. By the mid-1920s, it was saving lives across the United States. Everyone had heard about the miracle the drug could perform, especially after an outbreak of the disease threatened remote Nome, Alaska, in January 1925. Dog mushers rushed the vaccine across the countryside and saved the town (a trek known then as the Great Race of Mercy or the Great Serum Run that is still commemorated annually as the Iditarod race). Soon, the children of Anderson County lined up for the shot, administered by the local health department at local schools. Or at least at white schools. The campaign did not reach the Black children of the Hill.

For the sake of her surviving children, Wynona had looked for ways to improve their lots. That was why she had launched her campaign to overhaul Black education in Anderson County some sixteen years earlier. And here it was, the moment when segregated education in Clinton ended and her daughter Alvah Jay would finally receive the schooling she deserved. Wynona hoped her child understood why her parents and older siblings had sent her down the Hill. Was the girl worried about her role in what her family had fought for? Did Alvah see how this could benefit her? Or would she resent being sent to that school?

—

Now, Wynona had truck with the education her kids had gotten over at Green McAdoo, a fine enough school where the teachers did their best, though it was just two of them managing as many as ninety students. And yes, they had to cover all classes from kindergarten through eighth grade. Still, the students graduated knowing all the basics. And the building wasn't too bad either, especially since the county had gotten spooked about integration and started upgrading the facilities.

She must've liked, too, that in 1947 the town's white leaders had voted to rename the school for Green McAdoo. Course, to the white townspeople, Green McAdoo was the courthouse janitor who'd served the town for twenty-four years. The Black residents on the Hill, however, knew him as a war hero from a family of war heroes. The tradition had started with his brother John, who during the Civil War had been a member of the United States Colored Troops, enlisting in the First Regiment, Heavy Artillery, as a private. His bravery had earned him a promotion to corporal. Green McAdoo had followed his brother in 1878, joining the ranks of Black men sent west to fight against the tribes who were refusing to cede their land to white settlers. They were nicknamed the Buffalo Soldiers. During his fifteen years of service, Green built and repaired the roads that allowed the United States Army and the white settlers to move between forts. Now, years after his death, he was receiving some recognition.

The spot where Green McAdoo Grammar School now stood had been the site of a series of Black schools. When Emancipation came, the freedpeople who settled the Hill had built a small frame building in the center of their new community. It was a multipurpose space: church on the weekends and school during the week. The teacher was a Northern-born Black woman sent by the Presbyterians. One visitor reported that it was "one of the best buildings, and one of the best schools, taught by one of the best teachers, in this part of the state." The residents of the Hill had prioritized the school because everyone in the South knew education brought freedom. People who could read their work contracts and lease agreements and terms of purchase were harder to control and to trick than those who did not know their rights. And so Clinton's Black residents packed the new schoolhouse with kids during the daylight hours and adults at night after work.

One of the Black residents of Anderson County who was a particular champion for education was Adaline Staples Crozier, Jo Ann Allen's maternal great-great-grandmother. Adaline had been born into slavery in Oliver Springs, a crossroads on the Anderson County/Roane County line. Family tradition held she was actually the daughter of the plantation owner, which might've been the reason she and her brother Isaac had been taught to read and write. Unlike in many other Southern states, literacy wasn't illegal for enslaved people in Tennessee, but it remained rare, especially in the mountains, where only about 10 percent of the people in captivity learned to read and fewer than 2 percent could write. After the Civil War, Isaac had headed to a community eight miles the other side of Clinton, a town then known as Coal Creek that was renamed Lake City after the TVA closed Norris Dam. There he helped build the first Black school in the area. Back in Oliver Springs, Adaline and her husband, Henry Crozier, made their marriage legal, something denied them during slavery days. Then they went about raising their children for freedom. All the Croziers' babies went to school, and then their grandbabies did, right on down to Jo Ann and her generation.

Because education gave the Croziers and other Black families greater control over their own destinies, white Southerners targeted schools like the one on the top of Freedman's Hill. Early on Sunday morning, March 7, 1869, just four years after the end of the Civil War, arsonists set fire to Clinton's Black school/church and burned it to the ground. One of the only surviving relics was a blackboard on which the teacher had scrawled: "Three Cheers for U.S. Grant, President of U. States."

The former Confederates were winning back their political power, too. That same year, Tennessee's Republican governor, who worried he would be unseated by a more radical Republican, gave the right to vote back to most of Tennessee's former Confederates. Conservative white politicians immediately seized control of the statehouse and repealed the law mandating public education for all children across the state. Instead, each county could decide for itself. In 1873, statewide public education was reinstated, but its implementation was still spotty. Then in 1877, the last of the Federal troops withdrew from the South, leaving Black Tennesseans without any protection or recourse.

Segregation wove its way even more deeply into the nation's legal system in 1896. That year, the United States Supreme Court decided *Plessy v. Ferguson*, a case brought by a Black man in Louisiana who bought a first-class train ticket and then demanded to sit in the first-class, white-only car. The Supreme Court ruled for the defense, claiming that as long as segregation was equal, it was constitutional. Southern justices, however, made no effort to guarantee equality. It was expensive to maintain two separate school systems, so white leaders consistently and systematically underfunded Black education, giving white children more resources.

In Clinton, this meant that in 1935 when the town accepted federal funds to build a two-room grammar school for the Black children, the school board did not provide them with the same facilities as they built at the newly erected Clinton Grammar School for white children down the Hill. At Clinton Colored, they refused to construct a cafeteria or a gymnasium. The Black students also had older, rattier textbooks, fewer extracurricular activities, and less equipment.

And while the board was willing to build a new elementary school using state funds, they had no interest in creating a Black secondary school. They declared it was financially impossible because of the small numbers of Black students. In fact, they said, it was illegal. State law mandated high schools for communities that had seventy-five students or more, but the county only had a couple dozen Black teenagers. That didn't *really* make building a secondary school illegal, but it did make it easy to avoid erecting one anytime soon.

Well into the twentieth century, Anderson County provided no high school for its Black youth. Parents who wanted their children to continue past Green McAdoo had to either scrape together the money for a boarding school or ship them off to live with relatives in a community with a Black high school.

———

In 1939, a confederation of Clinton's Black leaders—some of whom were descendants of Green McAdoo, Adaline Crozier, and Isaac Staples—began gathering signatures from the Black families inside Clinton's city limits as well as those scattered across Anderson County whose children attended smaller one-room schools. They wandered from Lake City to Claxton to Wheat, meeting with parents and arguing that if the county refused to build a school for Black teenagers to attend, then they had to provide transportation and tuition to a Black secondary school in a neighboring county. (County property taxes make up the bulk of funding in most school districts, so when a student attends an out-of-county school, their parents essentially pay taxes to two counties.) Hoping to seem reasonable and responsible and economical, the school board eventually agreed to pay for tuition, but it told the families to cover the transportation costs. The board arranged for the students to go to LaFollette Colored High, a failing school about twenty-five miles away with few electives or advanced-level classes.

But a failing school a county away wasn't good enough for Wynona McSwain and her kids. She knew an unaccredited school with only a smattering of college prep courses wouldn't give her children the academic background they needed to thrive in the twentieth century.

As an adolescent, Wynona had read the Pan-Africanist activist Marcus Garvey and dreamed of sailing away to Africa with him on one of the ships in his Black Star Shipping Line, of escaping the injustice of racism in America and building a better, freer world on the continent kidnappers had stolen her ancestors away from. Life for a poor Black Southern girl like Wynona didn't offer many such chances, however. She'd fallen in love with Allen McSwain while still in her early teens and married young just like her momma had before her. She and her husband, Allen, had built a good life for themselves in Clinton, but she hoped her children would have better, would have the more she'd always wanted. She'd even named one of her middle sons Ras Tafari, a nod to her pan-Africanist, liberationist leanings. Thankfully, Allen felt the same. They wouldn't settle for LaFollette Colored High, not for their kids. So in 1942, the McSwains sent Eula, their eldest, to Allen High School in Asheville, North Carolina, a private, accredited boarding school for Black girls that was subsidized and operated by the predominately white Women's Division of Christian Service, a mission of the Methodist church. The school did offer a few vocational classes like hairdressing, but it didn't shuttle the girls into working-class positions. Almost half of its students went on to college.

At some point, the McSwains convinced the county to cough up part of the tuition. After all, if they were cutting and mailing a check to school officials in LaFollette, then they could just as easily send a check to Asheville. Perhaps because of that, Wynona and her husband sent Lela, their second-oldest child, to Allen High as well. Then came a son. They sent him to school in Nashville, where he roomed with Wynona's half sister. She lived about four blocks from Pearl High School, a sprawling art deco building featuring separate labs for biology, physics, and chemistry, extensive athletic facilities, a well-stocked library, and an excellent music program. Perhaps that's where he was enrolled.

By the end of the decade, the McSwains had put three daughters through Allen High and sent their second son off to school. In 1949, however, Wynona got a call at work from her son, Ethridge. He had followed his older brother to Nashville.

Now why was he calling her in the middle of his school day? she demanded.

He wasn't playing hooky, he reassured her. He'd tried to go to class, but the administration had ordered him out of the room. Anderson County hadn't mailed their part of his tuition check.

Alarmed, Wynona rushed over to the county superintendent of education's office half a block down from the jail.

Where is the payment? she asked him.

Well, see, he said, we've cut the check, but we haven't mailed it yet.

Why not? she demanded.

We're not so sure we want to keep paying for your kids to go to these fancy schools, he said. Tell you what, we'll mail this one last check. I'll put it in the post myself tomorrow, but this is it. No more.

Wynona knew he meant it. She'd have to find an alternative. And so the following summer, in August 1950, five Black high school students—among them one of Wynona's middle daughters, Joheather* McSwain—walked into the principal's office in Clinton High. One of the teens had seen an ad in the *Clinton Courier-News* reminding students to register for the upcoming semester. It said "students enroll," he later testified in federal court. "Didn't say white, black, yellow, green, blue." Principal D. J. Brittain Jr. refused to register the high schoolers and sent them to see the

---

* Pronounced joe-HEE-tha.

county's school superintendent, who monitored the various local principals and oversaw finances and had refused to send any more tuition checks to the McSwain kids' chosen schools. The superintendent also turned them down.

It was a risky move. City Attorney William Buford Lewallen (locals called him Buford) warned the school officials that if the Black parents wanted to turn this into a lawsuit, they had a chance of winning. Over the previous decade, Principal D. J. Brittain Jr. had transformed Clinton High School into one of the best schools in the state, far better than that LaFollette Colored High. If the school board wanted to claim that the county's Black pupils were getting an education equal to their white peers, they needed to send them to a better school.

After surveying the nearby options, the county announced they would be transferring the students over to Knoxville's Austin High School. Austin High wasn't as convenient as Clinton High would've been, but it was an academic improvement over LaFollette. The facilities were newer, and many of the teachers had trained at Knoxville College, a Black liberal arts institution founded in 1875 by the United Presbyterian Church. This meant students at Austin had teachers who added cultural stimulation to their lives and modeled what Black education and success looked like. Joheather enrolled in the Knoxville school.

Still, Wynona wasn't satisfied. The limited Greyhound bus schedule and the hour-long ride kept Joheather from joining in extracurricular activities. By being shipped out of the county, Joheather and the other children were missing out on all that a secondary education could offer to them, opportunities they would receive at Clinton High. Clinton's Black teenagers deserved the best education, and the best education wasn't found thirty-nine miles away where they could only be present for the school day itself, where they couldn't participate in drama and music and sports and arts and dances and parties. Jo Ann Allen, a good eight years younger than Joheather, only attended one social event at Austin: the homecoming football game during the fall of her sophomore year. She bought a new coat in celebration. She sat in the stands, feeling so gorgeous, cheering and yelling for her team.

The families also worried about the days when the students couldn't reach school at all. Winters in Appalachia can be unpredictable, and the two-lane highway connecting Clinton and Knoxville ran through a narrow mountain pass. During inclement weather, the twisting road quickly became impassable, washing away or icing over. Sometimes the students were late to class; other times they missed school for days in a row.

Besides, a good education wasn't just about reading, writing, and arithmetic, nor was it only about the clubs joined and the parties attended. The right schooling could bring economic and political freedom. When a Clinton High graduate applied for a job, a prospective employer knew what that meant. No one called their education second-rate the way they did when a kid presented a diploma from a Black school, even one as good as Austin. Knowing they had the same credentials as their white peers would prompt more Black Clintonians to demand their places in the world, some Black parents and educators posited. A kid who sat in a classroom at Clinton High would demand to sit on the first floor of the Ritz Theater rather than in the balcony. They would insist on eating at the Hoskins lunch counter rather than taking their milkshake to go. They would expect to try on hats at the Lewallen-Miller Department Store and ride in any bus seat and work at any job. And the white students who had sat at the desks nearby would be more inclined to loosen racialized constraints.

When the principal and the superintendent turned away Joheather and the others, Wynona went to visit with Knoxville's chapter of the NAACP. The NAACP had a cadre of lawyers prepared to handle Tennessee's civil rights cases, all of whom answered to Thurgood Marshall, executive director of the NAACP's Legal Defense Fund who was implementing the organization's plan to desegregate education. Z. Alexander Looby of Nashville was delegated to head up the lawsuit. A noted civil rights lawyer, Alexander had argued alongside Thurgood for over a decade. Their first case together was the defense of twenty-five Black men accused of attempted murder following a 1946 riot in Columbia, Tennessee. Twenty-four of the twenty-five were acquitted. The NAACP also assigned two Knoxville lawyers to assist on the case: Avon Williams—Thurgood Marshall's first cousin—and Carl Cowan. In addition to fighting for others' civil rights, all three of the attorneys would break color barriers themselves.

In 1951, Z. Alexander Looby would be the first Black Nashvillian elected to the city council since 1911. In 1953, Carl Cowan would become Knox County's first Black district attorney. And in 1969, Avon Williams would become the first Black senator elected in the state.

About twenty years earlier, Thurgood Marshall and his mentor Charles Hamilton Houston had identified education as the place where segregation was weakest, as the part of American culture where government-sponsored separate and unequal was the most obviously illustrated. They had started with professional graduate schools, convincing the courts to rule that sending Black students to other states or to substandard professional schools rather than opening previously all-white state institutions to them was a violation of the students' constitutional rights. Then they chipped away at segregationists' work-arounds, winning rulings that white universities couldn't simply found substandard Black departments on the same campuses, nor could the institutions put Black students in a separate part of the same classroom. And no, they couldn't seat them in the hallway, either. With all those precedents set, by 1950, the lawyers were ready to tackle the nation's public school system.

Now the team of lawyers got to work on behalf of Clinton's Black teens, though the attorneys thought other challenges to segregation more likely to succeed now that the Black high school and the white high school were academically close to equal. Most white leaders likewise assumed the case would die in court, and most white townspeople paid it little attention. Nevertheless, on December 5, 1950, James and William Dickie, Joheather McSwain, and Lillian and Shirley Willis and their parents filed suit against the Anderson County Board of Education and its representatives. (Though the case name would be shortened to bear Joheather's name alone, perhaps in recognition of Wynona's advocacy, all five students were equal plaintiffs.) Sure enough, the Anderson County school board won the first phase of the lawsuit.

Clinton was a consolidated high school, drawing white students from all over the county, Federal Judge Robert Love Taylor explained in his decision. Yes, a few went to Lake City High, and others attended Oliver Springs High, shared with Roane County. But for many, Clinton was the default option. Some of those white teens were coming at least as far as the Black youths were sent, the judge reasoned. That meant education in Clinton was actually separate *and* equal, he concluded.

The Clinton plaintiffs appealed the decision, but in 1952 their case stalled, placed on hold pending the Supreme Court's decision in *Oliver Brown et al. v. Board of Education of Topeka, Shawnee County, Kansas, et al.*, which was itself a consolidation of five different segregation cases from across the country that the Supreme Court chose to hear together. Each of the cases we now know simply as *Brown v. Board* challenged educational segregation from a slightly different angle. Black elementary school students in Topeka, Kansas, weren't permitted to attend the schools nearest their homes. In Delaware, Black kids were being sent to a run-down school in a different town while white children were bused to a much better one. Washington, D.C., had built a new high school for white students, but several of the classrooms sat empty and Black parents wanted their kids to be able to use those facilities. Teens in Virginia had organized a two-week strike protesting their terrible building, an overcrowded tar-paper shack. And parents in South Carolina had originally asked that their children have buses to ride to school. When the county denied their request, they sued for full desegregation.

Because of the number of plaintiffs and defendants involved in the *Brown v. Board* case, the court heard the arguments over the course of several sessions, starting in December of 1952, continuing in October of 1953, and finally issuing their decision in the spring of 1954. The Anderson County school board took those extra years to better local Black education, hoping to placate the families and the courts by adding a gymnasium, cafeteria, and kindergarten to Green McAdoo.

On May 17, 1954, the Supreme Court issued a unanimous opinion in *Brown v. Board* finding that segregated facilities were inherently unjust and did psychological damage to both Black and white children. They placed no time frame on the implementation of their desegregation decision, however. Instead, they asked for desegregation plans from the attorneys general of every state that had segregated educational systems and then held more hearings. A year after their initial decision, the justices issued an order popularly known as *Brown II* mandating that American public schools would desegregate with "all deliberate speed." In many places, white leaders used the vague wording of that dictate to justify decades of dillydallying. Surely they were showing deliberate speed so long as they were debating desegregation? After all, the phrase had evolved from the English chancery, the original phrase being "speed thee slowly," which evolved into "make haste slowly" and then "all convenient speed." Or, as Francis Thompson wrote in an 1893 poem, "But with unhurrying chase / And unperturbed pace / Deliberate speed, majestic instancy . . ."

But the school board in Clinton didn't have that same room to shilly-shally. It was already snarled in a federal case. On June 3, 1954, three weeks after the *Brown* ruling, the federal appeals courts reactivated *McSwain v. Anderson County* and sent it back down to Judge Robert Taylor's bench pending the Supreme Court's decision on *Brown II*. In January 1956, Robert Taylor ruled that in Clinton "all deliberate speed" would mean that Black students must be allowed to attend the high school the following fall.

By August 1956, Joheather McSwain and her cohort had graduated from Austin and were making adult lives for themselves: as shop clerks, as homemakers, as soon-to-be recruits in the United States Army. Their families, however, were still embroiled in the fight for educational equality. Joheather's little sister Alvah Jay was one of the kids walking into Clinton High that August morning. Walking alongside her was Minnie Ann Dickie, younger sister of Joheather's co-plaintiffs James and William.

Not all the Black teenagers and their families thought enrolling at Clinton High sounded like a good idea, however. About thirty or so Black adolescents in Anderson County were of high school age. Half had already started jobs or simply did not want to go to a white high school. Others had trouble getting registered. Eddie Soles was the older brother of Maurice Soles and younger half brother of Alfred Williams; like them, his uncle/guardian Steve Williams had moved Eddie to Clinton specifically so he could attend Clinton High. But while Maurice's and Alfred's transcripts had arrived in Clinton on time, Eddie's never turned up. Steve was an early soldier in the fight for civil rights who felt strongly that his nephews should not attend a Black high school when they were eligible to go to an integrated one. Eddie headed out to find a job. This was the end of his schooling. The fourth Soles/Williams brother, Charlie, had no desire to study at the white school and so enlisted in the armed forces.

Like Steve Williams, the adults who sent their children down to Clinton High knew they were joining the struggle for equality and justice and education. Many had been fighting for generations. Adaline Crozier's descendants had inherited her love of learning. A year earlier, one of Adaline's great-great-granddaughters had been among the eighty-five Black teens to desegregate Oak Ridge High School. Over in Lake City, one of Isaac's granddaughters was using the lawsuit to improve Black education in that town as well. Now it was Jo Ann's turn to take on Adaline's cause.

And of course Alvah Jay McSwain. As Wynona's daughter, she'd never questioned whether she'd enroll at Clinton High when her chance came. She knew it was her right to be there. And now she was doing it, this slim fifteen-year-old girl who'd inherited her mother's narrow face. She was taking up her mother's fight and changing American history. And so as the clock ticked on, Wynona cleaned and cooked and worried. Did Alvah Jay meet up with the other students all right? Had everyone else shown up? Was there any trouble on their way down?

THREE

Behind School Doors

Principal D. J. Brittain Jr. had known this day was coming for six years now, ever since that morning in August 1950 when five Black high school students and their parents had walked into his office and demanded that he enroll them in classes at Clinton High. While most white Clintonians assumed that the courts would defend their segregated educational system—it was enshrined in the state's constitution, after all—D. J. had never believed the county would win. White and Black children had different training and opportunities, and eventually that would make segregated education vulnerable. He'd been right. So now here he stood, just inside the school's doors, greeting the ten Black students who were coming down from the Hill.

A slight and bespectacled man, D. J. favored light gray suits cut a touch too big. The extra fabric folding around him made him look like an adolescent whose frugal mother still expected him to hit a growth spurt. Perhaps his appearance was what made the people around him underestimate his grit, seeing him as more scholar than hero.

D. J. was destined to be an educator. His father was the principal of Oliver Springs High School a scant sixteen miles away, straddling the Anderson County and Roane County lines. (The boundary between the two counties lay so exactly through the middle of Oliver Springs that the two county departments of education—which had enough white students to keep multiple, separate white elementary schools afloat—traded off which county funded the town's only Black elementary school, each one supporting its budget on alternating years.) His mother taught, also. His uncle was the superintendent of schools in neighboring Roane County. And D. J. had married a teacher, Clarice, a home economics instructor.

After earning an M.Ed. from the University of Tennessee, Knoxville, he'd returned to Anderson County to teach and coach football at Clinton High School. Four years later he was appointed principal of nearby Lake City High, and in 1944 he'd been named principal of Clinton, where he used the money provided by increased tax revenues from the Manhattan Project folks to drag the typically troubled Appalachian educational institution up to being one of the best schools in the state. In 1944, the school had needed classroom space, teachers, and supplies. He'd triaged the situation, lobbying the Anderson County school board into adding two classrooms to the building. Then he'd pushed until they'd tacked on a home economics wing, a music department, and a gymnasium seating twenty-five hundred people, or almost two-thirds of Clinton's total population. He found books for the new library, beakers for the chemistry department, and farmers to train the kids studying agriculture.

D. J. also courted energetic, creative young faculty. Since he couldn't pay them what they earned elsewhere, he sold them on the altruistic side of teaching. They could help him rescue the next generation of Appalachian children from poverty and backwardness by demonstrating how to be responsible citizens who thought clearly and objectively; developed "moral, spiritual, and aesthetic values"; built their physical, mental, and emotional health; learned academic skills; prepared for the future; and made "wise use of their leisure time." His plea worked. By the early 1950s, over half of Clinton High's twenty-four faculty members had graduate degrees, and in 1952 the school earned an A-rating from the Tennessee State Department of Education. The following year, it became a member of the Southern Association of Colleges and Secondary Schools, which ranked it as an A-1 school, one of the best high schools in the South.

But Anderson County continued to grow, so Principal D. J. Brittain Jr. kept up his battle to stay ahead of the school's needs. In the spring of '56, he had launched another campaign to lessen the overcrowding at his school, challenging the people of Clinton to build a separate vocational high school for students with lower academic goals. Arguing this institution would help rural students guide their families' farms into the atomic age, siphoning off the vocational-track students would also transform

Clinton High into the academic institution D. J. dreamed of it being. The division of academic from vocational was what many rural parents wanted for their kids, he insisted. To illustrate this, he polled 742 parents who had children enrolled at Clinton High. Forty-one percent of them had never attended high school, D. J. discovered. Only 6 percent were engaged in work D. J. considered professional or semi-professional. He assumed all parents would want their children to follow in their career paths.

For now D. J. was setting aside that fight, however. He was navigating desegregation for the county, and he was doing it mostly on his own. The Anderson County school board—which should have formulated the desegregation plan, perhaps modeling it after one of the Arkansas desegregations—had left D. J. hanging, refusing for seven long months to get involved. ("Bunch of pantywaists," teacher Celdon Medaris Lewallen said.) The board's silence convinced the virulent segregationists that D. J. had a choice, that he could kick out the Black students if he wanted . . . or if he was put under enough pressure. D. J., however, thought his only option was to obey the law whether he agreed with it or not. And if he was going to obey the law, then he would do so with the efficacy with which he did everything else.

When the judge handed down his order, D. J. predicted that "with time, information, and an intelligent plan, the problem would work itself out with fairness to everyone." And yes, he still hoped the problem would solve itself by a federal recommitment to segregation. Maybe a new law from Congress? Or a new segregation strategy approved by the Supreme Court? But just in case that didn't happen, in the spring of 1956 he began discussing the ruling during faculty meetings, encouraging teachers to talk about desegregation with their students. D. J. also reached out to parents for help, attending specially called meetings of the Clinton High School Parent-Teacher Association so white parents could voice their concerns. He said his acquiescence to the law was simply patriotism. "The community should know that we are following the orders of the courts," he told newspaper editor Horace Wells in early August. "Loyal Americans must always do so."

D. J. was a little more honest with his students. They all had to make the best of the situation, he told the football team with fatalism and resignation a few weeks before school started. "When you lose, you lose," he said. "You go ahead and play the game by the new rules."

Every spring, D. J. traveled to Clinton High's feeder schools, meeting the eighth-grade students matriculating in the coming fall. During these visits, he tested the pupils' aptitude and readiness for high school–level classes, and based on their scores, the students joined the school's vocational or college-bound tracks. In May 1956, Principal D. J. Brittain Jr. added a new stop on his tour, going to Green McAdoo to meet with the Black students and their families. He brought with him Margaret Anderson, Clinton High's business and typing teacher. D. J. gave the teens the same test their white peers had taken. A month later, Margaret returned to Green McAdoo to help the students choose classes based on their scores.

While Margaret met with the students, D. J. talked with the parents, laying out just how limited desegregation would be. D. J. had read the order carefully and would maintain segregation wherever he could. He believed the races needed to remain separate socially. Sitting side by side during English or chemistry shouldn't change that. The Black students could come to school, but they'd be sent straight back home again at the end of the day. No sports. No mixers. No sock hops. No clubs. No pep rallies. No parties. Yes, one of the major arguments for the original lawsuit had been that the distance to Austin High kept the Black teens from having their full high school experience. That was not his concern, D. J. warned the parents. The judge had mandated the students get educated, and D. J. would make sure that happened. Nothing more.

Still, he insisted on treating all his students decently, even when he hadn't wanted them there. Based on their scores, several of the Black teens were eligible for entering the college track, so that was where Margaret counseled them to go.

And now the Black students were official Clinton High Dragons. The principal even smiled at them as he ushered them toward the auditorium for their first morning assembly.

As the bell rang, most of the white students followed their new peers through the school's double doors. Across the street, three of the protesting teenagers handed off their signs and picked up their books. Abandoned pamphlets danced across the empty schoolyard. But some of the white students skipped school that day. "We're not going to press them for the first few days at least," D. J. told a local reporter. "And if they don't want to attend our school, that's alright, too."

One of those students was Jerry Hamilton. His parents ordered him to enroll at Lake City High, a smaller school on the eastern edge of Anderson County that was not slated to desegregate. Since both of his parents worked and no county school bus would run him there, Jerry had to catch a ride with a relative who was a bit of a troublemaker. The principal met them at the door and told the two teenagers he didn't really want them in his institution. By the end of the day, Jerry's relative was expelled and Jerry was reenrolled at Clinton High.

—

The mass of white students flowed into the Clinton High auditorium and settled themselves onto wood seats. The teachers shut the school doors on the tumult outside, muffling the voices of the dispersing protestors. The downstairs filled and then the balcony, too, but still no one said anything to the Black students seated together on the ground floor, a spot they couldn't occupy at the Ritz Theater downtown.

As senior Bobby Cain folded himself into one of the chairs and balanced his notebooks on his knees, he caught the eye of a white boy across the aisle. The other teen went oddly still, neither smiling nor looking away. This was a staring contest, Bobby realized. He was fighting for his right to be there by refusing to blink. What a stupid thing, but Bobby had to win. He kept the kid's gaze, eyes burning. Then suddenly it was over. The white boy turned to a friend and started chatting as though nothing had happened. Bobby slumped back, so tired he didn't know what to do. If he was already this exhausted, how would he survive the day?

The welcoming convocation kicked off, predictably unremarkable. The students pledged their allegiance to the American flag and bowed their heads for the school year's christening prayer. They listened as D. J. Brittain Jr. talked about his hopes for the next nine months. This year was a record enrollment. Eight hundred and six students in Clinton High! Then everyone cheered for Jerry Shattuck, incoming student council president/ captain of the football team. They doodled in their notebooks and whispered to their friends and calculated the easiest way to get through the crowd to their homerooms. And then the assembly was over, the kids dispersed, and the twelve Black students were on their own, diffused into a sea of white faces.

Robert Thacker leaned against the two-tone tan wall outside the auditorium, trying to get his bearings. The white students swirling and chatting around him kept a careful distance, averting their gazes as though they'd make him vanish by ignoring him. He curled his shoulders in a bit and scuffed his white buck shoes. Regina Turner and Alvah Jay McSwain walked to their first class together, clutching their books. Each looked past the other as white students jostled by.

But Jo Ann Allen had landed in Eleanor Davis's homeroom. Eleanor, the honors senior English teacher, had been part of the desegregation debate since the first lawsuit back in 1950 when her husband, Sidney, was one of the attorneys arguing against the Black students and their parents. Like D. J. Brittain Jr., however, the Davises would obey the law even when they disagreed with it. This tepid endorsement made Eleanor one of the Black students' strongest allies. Eleanor had a plan: she would begin as she intended to proceed. And she hoped there wouldn't be trouble, but if any started, she would deal with it on her own. She'd never been a teacher who pawned students off on the office. Sending a kid to see the principal was a sign of weakness, a surrender of power.

Eleanor made a big deal out of Jo Ann's first day, welcoming the girl and encouraging other juniors to get to know her. The white kids sitting at the desks around Jo Ann seemed excited to have a new face in their classroom. Then the teacher began her start-of-the-year business. After handing out schedules, she called for nominations. Clinton High's student government was a multilayered representative structure that started in the homerooms. And Carole Peters, a white girl, nominated Jo Ann to be their vice president. Somebody else nominated one of the football players. Jo Ann was elected unanimously.

"It's just that Jo Ann is so pretty and smart," Carole told a reporter. And she "has such a wonderful personality."

A few periods later, Jo Ann was in Clarice Brittain's home economics class when Clarice asked Jo Ann if she'd let the white students ask her a few questions, an interrogation that was supposed to feel welcoming.

What did she like? they asked. And where did she get her cute clothes?

Thankfully, Jo Ann had a reasonable answer to that. She wasn't any richer than her new friends, she told them. She just had a grandmother who sewed.

What an appropriate answer for a home ec class! Clarice bridged into what they'd be learning over the coming year.

All in all, Jo Ann thought, the day had gone swimmingly. Her new school might end up being even better than she'd let herself dream.

She wasn't the only student to think their school year was off to a promising start. The Black students expected the white teachers to use assigned seats to create a miniaturized version of segregation, but none of them—not one!—had been ordered to sit along the wall or in the back or near the door. Not in a single class! Nope, they chose any desk they wanted. Same went in the cafeteria, where seven of the Black teenagers ate at a table near their white peers. Five of them, however, decided not to risk that. No one ate next to white people inside. So those five went off campus to eat. "We don't want to force ourselves socially," Minnie Ann Dickie explained. She and a couple other girls walked over to the jail to eat with Alvah Jay's mother, Wynona.

After that first day, Gail Ann Epps was grinning when she got home. She told her mother, Anna Mae, and Aunt Mattie Bell she loved her new school. Anna Mae's specialty was homemade blackberry jelly. Did she sit her daughter down to eat some jelly on leftover biscuits while Gail Ann told them about her day? Maybe when her aunt Mattie Bell—a woman who loved to talk politics and who had pushed for Gail Ann's inclusion among the twelve—saw Gail Ann's big smile, she breathed a sigh of relief.

When a reporter for the *Chicago Defender*, a Black newspaper, asked Robert Thacker and Alfred Williams about their day, the two boys said everyone was getting along so well that they thought Principal Brittain would change his mind and let them go to the school's social events.

Why, they'd probably get to go to the homecoming dance, they said, though of course they'd "dance with Negro girls only."

Robert Thacker was sanguine about these developments. Though he'd started out in a segregated elementary school in Toccopola, Mississippi, over the course of his seventeen years, he'd attended racially mixed schools in Michigan, Indiana, and Wisconsin, moving often as his parents searched for better jobs and more opportunities. Going to the same school as white kids and playing on their teams? Well, what was the big deal with that? "We are all just people," he said.

Another boy asked to join an intramural basketball team and was told the coach wanted to wait and see what happened, which was much better than hearing a flat no. And Alvah Jay, who played the trumpet, thought she might get to join the Clinton High School Band. She could just see herself all decked out in their military-style uniforms, gold braid shoulder cords glinting as she marched under the football stadium lights.

—

Bobby Cain, however, was not as pleased with his first day at Clinton High. As he was one of two seniors, everyone saw him as a particular threat. If he survived the year, there'd be no going back. Even if the virulent segregationists resegregated the school the following year, Clinton High would always have a Black graduate. Though the classrooms were fine, white boys tried to intimidate him in the halls, bumping into him and blocking his way. When he got back to his house after the dismissal bell rang, he refused to tell his parents about his day. Instead, he slouched in a living room chair and "just kind of trembled for a little while."

Many of the teachers were as hopeful as their new students were, but Margaret Anderson overheard D. J. Brittain Jr. mutter, "If we can get through the first two weeks, we'll be all right." Why was he so apprehensive when the day had been peaceful? But then later that afternoon, the couple dozen protestors who'd stuck around outside threw a glass soft drink bottle at a Black woman walking by. And then they pushed another Black woman down and broke her glasses. And then they forced a Black girl off the sidewalk. And then Fireman Sam Warden found a knife with an illegally long blade on the sidewalk outside the school.

And then that evening, several hundred white spectators gathered on the courthouse lawn for the first of what would become nightly rallies. Most of them were locals, so they treated this like an unexpected midweek festival, milling about as full dark fell, hallooing friends and shaking hands with neighbors. They drew nearer to the courthouse's portico as the activities started, pressing forward to hear speaker after speaker—again mostly locals—urge them to defy the federal court.

Men who cared about protecting their wives and daughters from Black sexual predators, Communists, and "'race mongrelizers'" would resist desegregation, the speakers preached (though they did not yet have a public address system to use, so the audience strained to catch their words). And they'd harass anyone attempting to implement it. "If you had a sheriff, if you have a police chief with any guts, he would arrest the first Negro student and the parents of that student to enter Clinton High School!" one of the men shouted. And don't let them get started on that principal at the school. Didn't he look a bit like a Jew?

That night, Principal D. J. Brittain Jr. received his first round of harassing phone calls. Nothing serious, no actual threats, just a constantly ringing phone with no voice on the other end. For him, there would be no rest nor respite on this long summer's night.

FOUR

A Carpetbagging Troublemaker

Tuesday morning dawned unseasonably cool, edged with a crispness that promised autumn would arrive soon. Again, ten of the Black students met on the crest of the Hill to pray and gossip and walk the third of a mile down to Clinton High. Just over the railroad tracks, they passed a white woman digging in her garden. She threw a spadeful of dirt at the teens.

Unlike the day before, this morning the crowd awaiting them at Clinton High was not silent. There were seventy-five or maybe three hundred protestors. Or maybe it was thirty adults and a herd of children. Anyway, it was enough that the crowd could divide itself. On Monday morning, they'd hugged the sidewalk across from the school, keeping out of the road and away from the approaching teens. Tuesday, some of them broke off, crossed the street, and heckled the ten Black children as they walked down the road. The atmosphere in the schoolyard had also changed. The white students waiting at the top of the stairs stepped a little closer and glared a little more than the group stationed there the day before. The Black teenagers straightened their shoulders and marched through the school doors.

But still, when the bell rang for homeroom and the teachers called their classes to order, many of the people outside the school left. This morning, however, they weren't headed home or to work. They were flooding into the county courthouse a few blocks away. Everyone was anxious to know the outcome of the first case on the morning's docket: the town of Clinton v. John Kasper.

John Kasper was the local segregationist movement's newest and most uncomfortable ally. The charismatic Columbia-educated, tall, clean-shaven man from New Jersey had arrived in Clinton on the previous Saturday's afternoon bus. He had the sort of smallish, regular features that made him approachably handsome, and a few of the local white ladies had taken notice. The leaders of the local white separatist movement didn't know what to make of him. He might be God's answer to their cries for help, or he might be their undoing. With such an unexpected and unknown character, who could guess? (And this was before they learned that John was a man with a spotty past, especially on questions of racial purity.)

John had been a troubled child, unwilling to obey rules and difficult to control, so his parents had shipped him off to a series of military academies. Even these institutions had a hard time containing him. He was expelled from one school when he interrupted a Sunday school meeting, yelling that the church members around him were all "fakes and hypocrites." Following this outburst, his parents took him to Philadelphia for psychological observation. But somehow, John didn't just graduate from high school. He did well enough that he was admitted to Columbia University. There he fixated on the fascist poet Ezra Pound, incarcerated at St. Elizabeths Hospital, a psychiatric facility, so he wouldn't be tried for treason for the four years of radio broadcasts he'd aired during World War II supporting Mussolini, Hitler, and the Holocaust. The summer between his junior and senior year, John traveled to Washington, D.C., to meet Ezra. After that encounter, the two men began a correspondence that would last almost a decade. The poet instructed the student in matters of music, art, politics, and economics. Ezra even chose the younger man's friends.

When John graduated from Columbia in 1951, he attempted to enlist in the armed forces, but the military ruled him unfit for service. He then went back to New York where he opened the Make-It-New Bookshop, named for a 1935 collection of Ezra Pound's essays. Soon he had partnered with another admirer of Ezra's work and philosophies to launch Square $ Books, a publishing house that only chose authors who shared Ezra Pound's fascism and anti-Semitism. John knew what the poet wanted to hear from him. "You know Gramps," he wrote one week. "This city gets me down. . . . God! how it stinks! I sometimes go over to Yorkville on the East side to get a breath of fresh air. That's where the German population of NYC live, and they have managed to keep the Yits out of their lives socially, but not, of course, financially. There are a few Nazis over there still and I enjoy talking to them. They know what is fact and what ain't."

But John struggled to match his mentor's ideological purity. He stocked fascist texts in the bookstore, and one time he piled all the psychology books in the middle of the floor and stuck a sign on them labeling them "'Jewish Muck.'" But John had been the one to stock the books in the first place.

John's social life was even more confused and confusing. While in New York City, he joined the National Renaissance Party—an organization devoted to anti-Semitism and the belief that "what national socialism bestowed upon the German people stands before the world as a monument to all of the Western World"—and he invited the party to use Make-It-New as their meeting space. But he also attended NAACP meetings and distributed their materials in his store. And he helped a mixed-race couple find housing in the city and began a romantic relationship with a young Black woman. And he even brought her to visit Ezra Pound in St. Elizabeths.

About a year before he arrived in Clinton, John's first bookstore closed, probably due to bankruptcy. He moved to Washington, D.C., to be closer to Pound, and he opened a new bookstore there that also specialized in fascist literature. That's when his anti-Semitism morphed into fully developed white supremacy. John met Asa Carter, leader of Alabama's violent white supremacist movement, who told him about what was coming in Clinton. The other towns under a court order had segregationists who were getting organized, but it seemed to Asa all was a little too quiet in the mountains. Plus, the other schools wouldn't be opening until after Labor Day. If the segregationists could shut down Clinton High, it would be even easier to win the other fights that fall. John joined the Seaboard White Citizens' Council, a fringe chapter of the national organization whose motto was "Honor-Pride-Fight: Save the White!" He wrote and published a series of pamphlets to publicize the organization and was soon its self-appointed executive secretary.

Over the summer of '56, John left his new shop in the care of a female friend and began traveling, spreading his message of hate. On June 15 and July 20, he gave speeches in Maryland and Virginia. On August 4, he was arrested for distributing handbills without a license. He held his first rally on August 18 in Charlottesville, Virginia. There he hit on themes that would soon become familiar in Clinton, urging his listeners to fight against school desegregation and to found a White Citizens' Council (under his purview, of course). Four days later, he crashed a local chapter meeting of the Virginia Council on Human Relations, a biracial civil rights group. While he railed against the members of the council, other white supremacists set fire to a cross outside. The following day, John Kasper stepped off a bus and onto the sidewalk in front of Hoskins Drug Store.

—

When John arrived in Clinton, he had nowhere to stay, no friends to support him, and no connections to the local community, but he did have a pocketful of dimes. That afternoon, after checking into the Park Hotel on Main Street, one of two hotels in the town, he stood in a downtown phone booth and called members of the Tennessee Federation for Constitutional Government, presumably from a list supplied by a mutual sympathizer, urging them to come picket the school.

Then he started walking, asking each passing white person, "You know they're going to have to integrate the school system here next Monday?" and "What do you want to do about it?"

News of John's activities got back to the white municipal leaders. At first these were just small-town rumors of a new man around, but then came reports from white folks he'd stopped on the street. This new guy was a wild card in their deck.

At 1:30 on Sunday afternoon, the mayor, police commissioner, sheriff, acting police chief, and newspaper editor held an emergency consultation to plan what they would do if trouble started. Horace Wells's wife interrupted the meeting. John Kasper had rung up the house, asking if he could buy cardboard from the *Clinton Courier-News* to make placards. She told John that Horace would be at the newspaper at three o'clock. The assembled officials hustled over to the newspaper office to ambush the outsider, who arrived accompanied by his first local white ally, Willard Till. Mayor Lewallen asked John to leave. Horace Wells told him to go picket the federal courthouse in Knoxville. The sheriff threatened to arrest him. John thanked them and went right back to his work.

That afternoon, about two dozen white men listened to John give a speech on the courthouse lawn. It was "quite a crowd," the sheriff told a local paper, so on Sunday evening he arrested John on charges of vagrancy and attempting to incite a riot and encouraging citizens to violate the law and urging schoolchildren to refrain from attending school and inciting hatred of duly constituted public officials and circulating literature to cause an affray or breach of the peace. No one came forward to pay John's $5,000 bail. He'd been sitting in jail ever since, awaiting his preliminary hearing.

When there were so few picketers and protestors in Clinton's streets on Monday morning, the municipal leaders said it proved the sheriff's wisdom. Who knows how many John Kasper would have wrangled! Then there'd been the rally Monday night and now more folks were picketing Tuesday morning. Who could they blame for that? Surely, it was still that Yankee's doing.

—

Promptly at 9:00, Judge Leon Elkins called his courtroom to order and invited the parties to make their statements.* The city's lawyers warned against setting John Kasper free to make trouble. City officials testified they'd heard John making plans to concoct havoc, but under cross-examination, they admitted they hadn't seen him doing anything illegal. But they knew he had! The lawyers introduced a piece of evidence, a propaganda pamphlet. The cover was a photo of three Black men and two white women. One of the men was kissing one of the women. "We are an attack program," the flyer read. "We proclaim action as our creed. We are fighting. You must fight with us." Surely, that was an example of John's violent intentions. When they finished, John took the stand in his own defense, his first chance to make a public statement about why he was in

---

* John was defended by Knoxville attorney Roy N. Stansberry, who was openly sympathetic to John's racist cause. A decade earlier, Roy had worked for the state, arguing for the conviction of two Black teenagers accused of drowning a white man. He found twelve white women willing to say the Black boys had chased the white man into the lake. Charges were dismissed when the defense introduced other witnesses who said the boys had dived into the lake to save the white man.

Clinton. He focused on the allegations that he'd been sent to Clinton as part of a larger conspiracy against the city. He wasn't a stooge, he insisted, and he was here of his own accord. The judge dismissed all charges against John Kasper for insufficient evidence. The crowd cheered. John thanked the judge, and the court went to recess. "I will remain here until the Negroes are out," John promised. "I am pleased with the results so far."

When John Kasper left the courthouse, the timeline smudges. Perhaps he went straight to Clinton High, leading a parade of seventy-five followers to the school. When they got there, they joined with the twenty-five or thirty folks who had remained in the street, swelling the number of segregationists to a hundred. Or maybe he only led twenty adults to the high school, but there were already close to a hundred gathered outside. Or it could be he disappeared for a couple hours, doing whatever business needed doing when one hoped to foment an uprising, not arriving at the school until lunchtime.

Here's the next time the accounts agree: by noon, John and an unknown number of segregationists were in place outside the school's doors shouting out and demanding an audience with the man in charge, Principal D. J. Brittain Jr. himself. One of the town's policemen volunteered to act as their spokesperson, and he went into the school and asked D. J. to come out. D. J. agreed. He estimated that the crowd outside included twenty-five or thirty adults along with thirty or forty teenagers, most of whom were his students. John would claim there were three hundred there by this point. No matter the number, D. J. had to be frustrated to see the crowd around Kasper. These people—his current students, his former students, the parents of his pupils—were the ones he'd spent his career fighting for, trying to guarantee their right to a good education.

John spoke first: The principal must resign. That's what the parents wanted.

D. J. repeated what he'd said since the court made its ruling, that he did not agree with desegregation, but he would follow the law.

"Look at this big crowd here," John said. "You can see the citizens of Clinton don't want you as principal of this school."

"Present me with a petition showing fifty-one percent of my parents don't want me," D. J. answered. "I will resign that day."

Apparently, that promise wasn't good enough. "If you keep this up, there is going to be bloodshed," John threatened.

D. J. pointed at the protesting students around him. "I hope the rest of you heard this threat," he said. Then he turned away from John and started talking to individual parents and students, asking them about their frustrations and fears. When D. J. went back into the school, ten or twelve parents followed him. They talked for almost an hour and a half about why he was abiding by the court order.

"Many of them had children in the school that I operate," D. J. explained to a federal court a few days later. "I told these people I hoped that when this all got settled down that we would still have their children in our school."

Did you? the judge asked.

Yes, D. J. answered.

But on this day, John Kasper stayed with the protestors outside, urging them to fight for their "fundamental rights." When he mentioned that he had come to Clinton without any financial support, some fifteen people pressed money into his hand.

"We owe you a lot," one of the men said. "You laid down there in jail."

"The food they serve there is terrible," John joked. "That is something that must be corrected."

He tried to organize another parade around the courthouse, but only a dozen or so people followed him. The march fizzled by the end of the block.

—

Inside the school, the students, both Black and white, heard the confrontation through the open classroom windows. The football team discussed what they would do if the mob invaded. Some of them stood guard in the doorways. Others sat near their Black classmates. A few of the white girls sniffled. Several pointed at the signs the protestors carried and said, "Isn't that disgusting?" and "Such a sorry spectacle." Some of the white students glared at their new classmates. A couple tried to pretend nothing whatsoever was going on. The Black children made sure their frozen expressions never changed, that they never showed any alarm no matter what the noise outside.

That afternoon, D. J. Brittain Jr. called the students into another assembly. He told them that he was going to continue obeying the law, that the school would stay desegregated as long as he was in charge. Then he walked out of the room. No teachers or administrators or other adults were present while the student body voted on the question of whether they wanted to keep their principal. It was a unanimous 614 to 0 in D. J.'s favor, though almost 200 of the 806 students were missing from that count, most because they hadn't turned up at school. That night, the parents conducted their own informal poll using secret ballots. They voted for him 447 to 6. Again the results were in D. J.'s favor, but again many were missing. Either way, it gave D. J. the indication of support he needed. Vindicated, he resolved to stay his course.

But national news organizations sensed a story unfolding in Clinton. Didn't seem either side was like to give in anytime soon, which meant it could be a town on the verge of exploding. They sent staffers, stringers, and freelancers to town, just in case, filling up Clinton's two hotels. While in Clinton, these reporters—mostly white and uniformly men—formed a farcical organization they named the Southern War Correspondents Association. (Someone proposed naming it the Southern War Correspondents Association, Suh, a play on the stereotypical enslaved pronunciation of "sir," but this idea was shot down.) They quickly settled on their motto: "Discretion Is the Better Part of Valor." To that end, the membership cards were two-sided: one labeled "Integrated" and the other "Segregated." The men flipped the card to whatever side they thought might be most palatable to the person asking them for identification.

—

On Tuesday night, two hundred or five hundred or six hundred segregationists gathered on the steps of the Anderson County Courthouse. John Kasper nominated himself as keynote speaker. He stood tall and straight, surrounded by a bevy of young acolytes who clung to his every word, straining to hear him over the tourists and travelers shuttling by on the Dixie Highway.

The local authorities have no guts! he yelled.

His audience applauded.

If the sheriff or the police chief had any guts, the Black students would be in jail along with their parents, he shouted.

The crowd bellowed back their agreement.

If they did have any guts, they would recognize that the people are a higher court than the Supreme Court, John continued. And they would ignore all such court orders.

The crowd cheered.

Then he called them "the hard-working hill-billies [*sic*] of East Tennessee."

The crowd fell silent.

Down with the Communists and the race mongrelizers and the county officials, he called.

The crowd was back with him, thundering their *ayes*.

He would be there, he promised, picketing with them until they got the Black students out of their school.

The crowd hooted their support.

He would be there until Principal Brittain resigned.

Some folks clapped at that statement, but others booed, "No, no, no!"

FIVE

The Hardening

Bobby Cain could hear the ruckus raised by the mob downtown. Their shouts carried, ricocheting off buildings and echoing up Freedman's Hill to the Green McAdoo playground where he waited. He jounced his hands in his pockets nervously, feeling the weight of his little penknife bouncing against his thigh. Once the others arrived, the Black students followed the pattern they'd established that first morning just two days past. First Bobby prayed for strength and safety and perseverance. Then they walked, testing whether God had listened to their plea. There was a certain comfort in having a predictable beginning to the day.

On that Wednesday morning, the crowd outside the school was noticeably larger, Bobby thought. One hundred twenty-five segregationists or maybe two hundred fifty or perhaps as many as three hundred awaited the teens. About fifty or so of them were stay-away students. Many of the should-be pupils carried newly penned signs. Early that morning, John Kasper had asked some boys to go into Hoskins Drug Store and buy poster board and markers, and he'd passed the supplies among the crowd. Now the kids shook their signs at Bobby as they yelled. Bobby looked at the faces they were pulling, distorting themselves in their hate, and he wondered what it would be like to study civics or English with them. Seemed like the white kids were egging each other on to see who could come up with the nastiest insult to shout at the twelve children who dared to demand a better education: "Coon!" and "Go home!" and "Nigger!" and "Get out!" and "Pickaninny!" and "Go back to Africa!"

That one caught Jo Ann Allen's ears. "Go back to Africa?" she thought. "Wait, I've never lived in Africa. Why would I go back there?"

While the crowd outside the school stamped and chanted and jeered, a convoy of ten cars circled the town, creeping around the block from the school to the courthouse and back, blowing their horns. Two of the cars had driven over from Lake City and three had come all the way from Michigan. The remaining five were registered to Clinton residents. The vehicles were each bedecked with their own placards. One of the Clinton cars, a light-colored Chevy with two worn RC Cola bumper stickers, had a sign plastered across the back: "WHY DO WE NEED OUTSIDE CIT-IZENS TO CLEAN OUR 'SCHOOLS,'" perhaps a reference to John Kasper, newly arrived from elsewhere. The back passenger-side window preached: "GIVE 'RASTUS' A SCHOOL FOR 'HIMSELF.'" (Rastus was an insulting name used in minstrelsy and other racist entertainments for a happy-go-lucky Black man.)

Other protestors now threw things at the students. Rotten tomatoes and sulfurous eggs splattered on the sidewalk around them. Jo Ann heard something whistle past her ear. It was a rock! She wanted to look for who was targeting her, but she knew that distraction would be seen as a weakness. She held her neck in place, keeping her head high as she and the others paced evenly toward the school.

This morning, the only protection the Black students had as they pushed their way through the scrum was the town's six police officers. The sheriff and his deputies were out in a crossroads community some eight miles south of town capturing the sheriff's sixty-fourth illegal still. And they wouldn't be rushing back to help with the crowd in Clinton either. In-stead, the officers lingered, watching in case anyone visited the site. Maybe they'd arrest a moonshiner red-handed! No hoocher ever appeared, but the sheriff thought about making an arrest anyway. He had noted a foot-path worn through the underbrush. When he followed it, the trail led to a house where a known bootlegger lived. The evidence was too circumstan-tial. He'd leave the man for the next sheriff to worry about. Still, he and his men stayed out in the field, hoping to net his sixty-fifth still before his two-year term expired that Friday.

Without security, rather than push their way through the angry horde to the front door, Bobby, Jo Ann, and the other Black students slipped into Clinton High through a side entrance. Safely inside, Jo Ann Allen com-forted herself that here everything remained calm even if the hallways felt a little emptier than they had before. And no, she wasn't getting the same friendly smiles she had on Monday, but she was safe and she was learning. As she neared her homeroom, she nodded at a pair of varsity football players standing guard nearby. "How's it going?" one of them asked her. "Everything okay?"

Earlier in the week, these guys had felt uncomfortable in their roles as the Black students' guardians. They'd heard the arguments for law and order from the principal and the mayor and their teachers and a few of their parents. Some of them even agreed. But when Principal D. J. Brittain Jr. had shown up at football practice a few weeks earlier to ask for their help, they thought he was taking things a little too far. Yes, they wanted to step up and keep the peace. But what if people thought they supported this desegregation nonsense? Some might even say they believed in racial equality, maybe even in miscegenation. The team had debated their decision hotly, but in the end, they'd decided to do what their principal and their coach asked of them. Now as they stood at their assigned posts, weren't most of them glad they had! Outside, the rabble-rousers and the hoodlums and the greasers were giving Clinton a bad name, but in the school the football players maintained their turf. This was what it meant to be a man, they thought, shielding the weak who couldn't protect themselves. So yeah, these varsity guys were proud that they were still giving kind smiles to the cute Black girls like Jo Ann. They even gave chin juts to the Black boys when they passed. And they made sure all the other white kids knuckled to, each player staying in his assigned position until the final school bell jangled and classes began.

Today the picketers didn't disperse when the Black students made it inside. They remained downtown, their numbers growing as the morning wore on. With the students out of reach for a few hours, the crowd focused on new targets. Some went to yell at Mayor Lewallen, accusing him of enrolling extra Black students at Clinton High. Sure looked like there were more than twelve of them now. Bet he'd been shuttling them in from nearby Oliver Springs. Others harassed Black passersby. Hearing of the threats, some Black residents armed themselves before going downtown. When a picketer glimpsed Jo Ann White's knife, he grabbed some friends and chased her through Clinton's streets. She was saved by a passing driver who threw open a car door and let her jump in. A few minutes later, police arrested a Black seventeen-year-old who was not enrolled at Clinton High. He had tucked a knife into his belt, a knife the police found because they saw its bulge. His bail was set at $250 (or about six weeks of full-time work, assuming he earned the dollar-an-hour minimum wage).

The fracas outside was not conducive to learning, so the teachers kept their windows closed against it as long as they could. Eventually, though, the heat of the day grew stifling. One by one they opened their windows, and the hate-filled shouts entered the building.

—

Midway through the morning, four of the town's attorneys appeared in D. J. Brittain Jr.'s office doorway. They'd come to campus to check out the situation. All had official reason to be concerned, but two of them—Buford Lewallen and Sidney Davis—were married to English teachers at the school, and they were worried about their wives' safety. After visiting with D. J. in his office, they agreed to join the principal on a foray into the schoolyard to reason with people outside. There, they found some 163 protestors had crossed the street and were standing on the school's property, inside the stone wall. (One of the attorneys, Leo Grant, was a meticulous note taker; we have him to thank for this rare precise count.) When D. J. and his escorts approached the segregationists, a posse of teenage boys ringed them. The youths carried sticks and broken lumber in their hands that they wielded like clubs, striking the improvised batons against their legs and hitting their palms.

D. J. let the team of attorneys lead this time. They saw John Kasper in the group and focused their arguments on him. They told John they'd take the case pro bono if anyone could suggest a new legal tactic for resegregating Clinton High.

There's no legal way, John said, so he was using "social pressure."

"Let's go in and pull those Negroes out and let the Indians loose on the reservation!" a local man named Leo Bolton shouted.

Yeah, Theo Hankins, a former candidate for constable, agreed. They should go into the building and pull the Black teenagers out.

At that, John Kasper began pontificating about Communists on the

Supreme Court and the will of the people trumping the will of the judiciary. "The country is governed by the majority of the people," he said.

"If the law along this road says twenty-five miles an hour and your group feels they can drive thirty, what is your feeling?" one of the lawyers asked him.

John stayed silent, perhaps because that was a rather specious argument.

"There are six thousand people in Anderson County," the lawyer continued. "You have a couple of hundred here. This is the will?"

John again said nothing.

"We are going to get those Negroes and nigger lovers," Leo Bolton piped back up. "Chase them out. Run them back to where they came from. Send them back to their nigger friends!"

The crowd roared.

The students inside heard everything.

—

Come lunchtime, the Black students couldn't decide where to go for food. Earlier in the week, a few of them had braved the cafeteria, but were they really allowed in there? They weren't sure. It was a gray area, somewhere between classes, where they were permitted, and social events, where they were not. On Monday some felt safe to test those boundaries, but by Wednesday their calculations had changed. Since they couldn't eat indoors with white people anywhere else in town, they decided not to chance it. Yet they sure couldn't picnic in the schoolyard, what with the mob and all. The girls made do. Jo Ann and Gail Ann found a quiet corner of the building to hide out in. Alvah Jay and Anna Theresser limped down to jail, where Alvah Jay's mother worked. They moved slowly. Anna Theresser had a leg injury she'd sustained when very young that had never healed properly; a recent surgery to try to fix it had left her on crutches.

The boys, however, wanted to get off campus and have a bit of fun to break the tension of the day. And what Bobby Cain really wanted was a hot dog. Yeah, a hot dog with mustard and chili.

He met up with Alfred Williams, Maurice Soles, and Ronald Hayden. Did they want to come with him to the Richy Kreme, a soda stand? Turned out Maurice was craving an ice-cream swirl. And with that, the boys had their lunch plans. They headed out, walking the two blocks past the courthouse and then turning right onto Main Street. The Richy Kreme was just half a block down.

After lunch, the girls returned to school without trouble, but the crowd got excited when they saw the boys near. Bobby pulled his pocketknife out and tucked it up his sleeve, just in case. He saw Alfred do the same. Then one of the white men bumped Bobby hard enough that he dropped his knife. Bobby and his friends took off running, heading away from Clinton High. The white mob followed them, chasing them past the courthouse and trapping them in front of a doctor's office cattycorner to the school. They knocked Bobby to the ground and began beating him with their fists and with the sticks they'd affixed to their protest posters. As Bobby scrambled, looking for safety, he realized he knew many of his assailants, and not just by sight. Some were boys he'd played sandlot baseball with and kids he was supposed to go to school with. One of them, one of the ringleaders, was Mary Nell Currier, a thirty-three-year-old local school bus driver and mother of a ten-year-old girl. None of them helped him.

Alfred, Maurice, and Ronald weren't as deep in the fray. When some members of the Clinton football team saw what was happening, they plunged into the melee and extricated the other three boys, but even they couldn't reach Bobby. The police had to rescue him—and then they arrested him for fighting, along with John Carter, one of Bobby's most vicious attackers. Both teens were given a $250 bond and told to appear in juvenile court. The rest of the students were ordered back to class. But many of the stay-away students had enjoyed their little spat of violence. They weren't ready to disband, so some seventy-five of them ran into a nearby barbershop and grabbed Eugene Gibson, the shop's Black seventeen-year-old shoeshiner. They beat him until the police also took him into protective custody. This time, the police leveled no charges against anyone.

Principal D. J. Brittain Jr. had been taking a working lunch, eating at his desk while being interviewed by some reporters. He happened to glance out his window as the mob jumped his four charges. Then came the news that Bobby Cain had been carrying a knife. Fast as things were escalating, the principal worried one of the Black kids might die on their way home from school. He decided to sneak them home under police escort. Before they left, however, D. J. met with the Black students to tell them to return to school the next morning. Yes, even Bobby, assuming someone bailed him out of jail. So far, seemed the school was about the safest place for them to be, didn't they think?

Anna Theresser Caswell was in study hall when her school day abruptly ended. As a policeman hustled her toward his waiting car, he instructed her teacher, "Tell her not to look down. Tell her not to look down the street." So of course, she looked. At the other end of the hall, she saw almost five hundred contorted white faces yelling at her, leering through the same door she and Alvah had used on their way back from lunch.

As the police drove the students home, Jo Ann thought she recognized George and Riley in the crowd, white brothers who were also her neighbors and playmates. But surely, she was wrong. They couldn't have been part of the mob, could they? Not after the tomatoes and the cups of sugar traded back and forth across the street over the years.

Not all the twelve went home with the police that day. Gail Ann Epps did not live on the Hill but in her grandmother's house in a mostly white neighborhood. A friend—an anonymous friend—had phoned her aunt Mattie Bell. The rioters "planned to go in and mob those kids in there," the caller warned. Gail Ann's mother, Anna Mae, and aunt Mattie Bell decided to rescue the girl themselves rather than trusting the police to do it. When Anna Mae got out of the car, some of the white men started toward the vehicle. She took off running but fell over a bush, tearing her blue silk dress. A friendly white man caught her and escorted her toward the school door. When she finally made it inside, a teacher asserted Gail Ann would be safer in the school than out of it. "No, ma'am, she won't," Anna Mae replied. She took her daughter home.

—

Back at school, D. J. allowed the Student Council to call for a second student-wide assembly, minus the Black students who'd been taken home already. None of the teachers or administrators attended. In the meeting, the white students again voted to keep D. J. Brittain Jr. as their principal. Again, the vote was unanimously in his favor.

The mayor and other city officials were starting to think the protestors might not be managed by their tiny law enforcement team. "I don't know what we're going to do—" the outgoing sheriff told a Nashville journalist. "I don't know what we're going to do unless we get some outside help." Lawmakers in Nashville promised that the National Guard and the highway patrol would be ready to move in if there was bloodshed.

But Bobby Cain had already been injured, the Black parents must've thought. What constituted bloodshed? Did that mean white people needed to bleed? Or were the state officials waiting for one of their children to die?

Unsatisfied with the governor's pledge of possible aid, a cohort of white Clintonians drove to Knoxville to petition Judge Robert Taylor, the same judge who'd ordered them to enroll the twelve Black students. They asked him for a restraining order against John Kasper and five other local agitators they named as ringleaders. One was Tom Carter, John Carter's father, and another had a son who had been protesting with John all week. Leo Bolton and Ted Hankins were both named, too, probably because they had harassed D. J. and the lawyers. The fifth was Mary Nell Currier. The judge granted the restraining order and added an injunction, announcing that those "who are acting or may act in concert with them be and they are hereby enjoined and prohibited from further hindering, obstructing or in any wise interfering with the carrying out of the aforesaid (integration) order of this court, or from picketing Clinton High School, either by words or otherwise."

U.S. Marshal Frank Quarles was sent to Clinton to execute the orders. But when Frank arrived, no one seemed to know where John Kasper was. The marshal went over to Hoskins Drug Store for a Coca-Cola, waiting for the segregationist to appear.

—

Just about then, Eugene Weaver, Bobby's older brother—well, technically his half brother—bailed him out of jail. Bobby emerged resolved. While sitting in his cell, Bobby had decided he wouldn't be the segregationists' whipping boy. If they tried to hurt him, he would make them regret it. In the days to come, he and Alfred began practicing self-defense. They had always carried pocketknives, but now they wedged toothpicks into the blades so that they could flip the knives open when faced with a surprise attack, like a cowboy pulling his pistol from a holster. Soon Bobby had a network of scars on his thumbs from all the times he had cut himself practicing the move.

Bobby also determined he would stick out the year. He'd spent the past few days riddled with anxiety, wishing he could quit. He'd even begged his parents to let him withdraw from school. They had whispered their arguments late at night, voices tight but low so they wouldn't wake Bobby's younger siblings. His parents had said no, though they hated Bobby was enduring this because of someone else's lawsuit. He'd been happy over at Austin High. But he couldn't go back.

"I had to scuffle to get what little education I got," his mother told him. Sure, they might be able to scrape together enough money to cover his senior year's tuition at Austin, now that the county wouldn't be paying for it. "What about the others in there asleep?" she'd said. "Where are your brothers and sisters going to school if you don't stick?"

It's not just about his brothers and sisters, Bobby's father told him. It's about all the other Black children around the United States struggling to better themselves despite the racist world. So every morning, Bobby had gotten up, met the others, and walked down the Hill.

Now it had come to him for the first time: he had a right to attend Clinton High. The white people were breaking the law, not him. He would finish out the year for himself and not for anybody else—not his siblings, not his parents, not the kids at Green McAdoo, not students in faraway states he'd never visited. Bobby Cain would graduate from Clinton High because he deserved to. He deserved the chance to earn a diploma from one of the best high schools in the South. He deserved to see what more his own future might hold.

—

The nightly rally started at 7:30 just as dusk turned to full dark. That Wednesday, eight hundred or maybe a thousand people gathered to hear the segregationist speakers. A line of white teenagers snake-danced around the courthouse.

The meeting opened with a prayer led by the Reverend Alonzo Bullock, a sometimes pastor who moonlighted as a grocer and carpenter and employee at the Purity Packing Company on the side. He had also once run to be the county court clerk, an election he'd lost soundly. Alonzo had prior personal experience with what happened when the government showed up in your county. Back in 1934, his young family had been one of the many displaced by the TVA's Norris Lake, forced by the federal government to abandon the community where Alonzo was born. The Bullocks had gone along with the government's plans peaceably enough, but they'd seen what relocation had cost their many children. How would they find their spot in the world without their extended families to guide them? Now almost twenty years later, the feds were back, and Alonzo did not feel as resigned, especially since this time the government's plans explicitly involved his youngest children who were still school-aged.

The preacher was fighting back. He raised both hands toward the sky, palms facing the assembly in that ancient posture of a pastor bestowing a blessing on his flock. At six feet and three and a half inches tall, he was a commanding figure in the crowd. Everyone fell silent. After his invocation, the crowd saluted the American flag flying from the flagpole on the right of the square and then intoned, "I pledge allegiance to the flag of the United States of America. . . ."

A few Anderson County white men spoke first; then John Kasper stepped forward. And there on the steps, clustered by his right hand, were three school-aged sisters. Each wore a pearl choker and her fanciest church dress. The taffeta of the middle sister's dress glinted in the spotlight. Behind them, almost hidden by John's gesticulations, was another girl in a sleeveless white shirt tucked into a pleated pencil skirt, and behind her was a blond head sporting a DA haircut secured with a bobby pin. Below was a brunette with looks inspired by Audrey Hepburn's *Roman Holiday* adventure. An older woman, hair pure white and carefully curled, reached toward the brunette's elbow to get her attention.

The reporters coming to town were talking about the radicalized shenanigans of the white men and boys, but Clinton's segregationist movement had women at the core of it. These women and girls weren't transgressive or brazen or rebellious. White supremacy had always depended on white femininity. Sure, the supposed purity of white ladies had served as the excuse for much of the racist violence over the years, but white women's complicity went beyond that. They were more than damsels. In Clinton, they were working alongside the white men as provocateurs and organizers and activists and protestors and assailants. It's what women like them had always done.

With theatrical timing, Frank Quarles, along with three deputy marshals and one local police officer, interrupted John Kasper's harangue to serve him with the court papers. Seeing the marshals, the county clerk opened the door to the courthouse and invited them to use the building. Inside, Frank unfolded the documents and began reading. After he recited the restraining order, he opened the injunction. A few paragraphs in, John said, "If you don't care, I will read it. I can understand it better." He stood there looking at the paper for almost ten minutes before walking back outside.

"The marshal served a temporary injunction on me," John told his listeners. The wording of the injunction had caused confusion. The judge thought he'd barred any and all protesting. John Kasper had decided only the people named in the order were prohibited from acting.

I might have to step back, John continued, but that didn't mean the protests should end. This restraining order would not dampen their movement; it was a sign they were winning. The weak white leaders—those men who were willing to sacrifice anything, even their daughters, for the approval of the feds—were running scared. Now everyone could see who the real men in town were. Keep going, he ordered his audience. "We have almost carried this fight to victory!" he shouted. "Now keep on doing it!"

After the rally ended, John Kasper and a group of men walked to the nearest drugstore, where he chatted with the press, most of whom were beginning to cast him as a wily seducer who was calling the racists down from the mountains.

In Knoxville, a group of white boys declared their solidarity with the Clinton protestors and placed a mock gravestone on their high school's lawn beside a sign asking: "What niggers [sic] next?"

SIX

Judging Justice

Early afternoon sun streamed into the room from the oversize Art Moderne windows behind the Honorable Robert Love Taylor. He put aside his work and sat forward in his leather office chair, resting his arms on the ledgers he'd been consulting, some of the many documents piled on his dining table–sized office desk. As he leaned, he let his sleeves ride up in the August heat, refusing to shoot his cuffs. He also refused to acknowledge the youngish photographer crouched at his feet, snapping his every gesture. This wasn't Bob Taylor's first brush with the national press corps. A couple years earlier, almost five thousand Oak Ridge workers had gone on strike. President Eisenhower had ended it, arguing the protest left the nation's nuclear program unstable. A United Press photographer had captured the moment Robert Taylor read the injunction to local labor leaders.

Today's photographer, though, wasn't the second string who had documented Bob's earlier appearance. Howard Sochurek had served as General Douglas MacArthur's photo assignment officer in Tokyo, and he'd just won a Robert Capa Gold Medal for his coverage of the Indochina War. He also had a photo touring the globe with MoMA's Family of Man exhibition, and he would soon take iconic portraits of Robert Frost, Martin Luther King Jr., Henry Kissinger, and Richard Nixon. The *Life* editors had sent him to Tennessee because they sensed the Clinton High saga was about to be an international cover story.

Howard didn't need Bob's compliance to get his shot. He kept opening his shutter as the judge donned his pleated black judicial robes, wove the hidden straps over his shoulders, and secured the button at the top that held the garment in place. He documented the judge's pause in front of the glass-fronted barrister bookcases holding the court's considerable leather-bound law library. He caught the moment the judge pushed his office door open and started down the hall.

These days, Bob Taylor was an enigma to out-of-town journalists and locals alike. Where *did* he stand on the race question? Prior to 1956, everyone had assumed he was a segregationist. After all, he'd been the judge to rule against the Black students and their families back in 1950 when they'd brought their case. But was that evidence of his convictions or a matter of judicial principle and legal precedent? Because when the Supreme Court changed the law, Bob'd been the one to order Clinton High's rapid desegregation. And his court crier was a Black man, an unusual, even bold, move in the 1950s South. So maybe he was an integrationist, an idea that surprised most folks in Knoxville.

As he heard the speculation and the insults, Bob wished he could speak out, could tell everyone that yes, of course he believed in white supremacy. But the bench was to be above politics and personal convictions. His job was to hand out implacable and judicious interpretations and implementations of the law of the land. He was to enforce the Supreme Court's rulings without comment, keeping his opinions to himself. And that was how he'd landed in this post-*Brown* world, hearing people call him an integrationist. Boy, didn't Bob Taylor have a certain envy of the people who were free to criticize the *Brown* decision (in a kind and friendly manner, of course). He would never have taken to the streets, even if he'd been able to voice his opinion. No sir. If the judge had spoken, he would have told everyone he agreed with the law-and-order white leaders in Clinton: integration might be bad, but lawlessness was worse.

—

Speaking of respect for the courts, that very morning, just twelve hours after Bob Taylor's restraining order had been served to him, John Kasper had joined a couple hundred protestors down at the school. Well, John had started out a few blocks away, posting himself across from the Clinton Police Station. People noticed his absence. Was he in jail again? Had he left town?

I've just relocated because of "this injunction they have against me," he told a search party.

To placate his well-wishers, John walked up the block toward the school, close enough that the crowd could see him; then he returned to his outlying corner. One of the police officers guarding the doors sent word to John that he could come nearer to the school, no reason he couldn't stand with the rest of the crowd. But when John walked to the school, another officer told him to move away, that he had violated the injunction by coming on the property. In the confusion, the bystanders must have wondered: Were the officers misinformed? Supporters of John? Lawmen who hoped he'd finally get locked away?

John Kasper wasn't the only one to violate Bob's rulings that morning. Some students, perhaps assuming the injunction and restraining order didn't apply because they weren't named in it, were back out on the streets. One drove up in a car painted with the slogans "go home coons" and "coon season open" and "keep Negroes out." The police didn't take him in, but they were sure getting sick of these miscreants, out here skipping class and making a scene. The police did arrest other teens. As they moved through the crowd, gathering up offenders, journalists ran behind them, trying to name the kids now in custody. Locals looking on told the reporters the kids were all well known. That one there was sixteen-year-old Jimmy Dale Patmore, a student at Clinton High out on parole for earlier acts of delinquency, and over there was fifteen-year-old L. B. Crawley, picked up for carrying signs and yelling epithets. Both were released with a warning. When Jimmy Ray McGill, a seventeen-year-old senior and a member of the Clinton High football team, saw the arrests, some said they'd heard him shout, "The police are afraid of their jobs; that's why they are arresting us!" The officers took him in for questioning.

Somehow, though, the Black students still believed their year might turn out okay. Some of the girls told a journalist that they liked Clinton High, though they thought Austin was the better school.

No way, Ronald Hayden said. "The studies are harder at Clinton than Austin." And he was at Clinton for a full educational experience. Maybe he'd find a way to go out for football. Maybe next year?

When the school bell rang that morning, Principal D. J. Brittain Jr. called the students into yet another assembly. He thanked them for endorsing him as their leader and praised them for standing up for law and order and against the rioters. But only 472 were in class that day, including all 12 Black students. Over 300 white students had voted with their feet, some because they feared the protestors and others because they wanted to join the crowds outside. During the assembly, D. J. publicly lauded the Black students' bravery, their "great courage" for having "the guts to come to school today." His words may not have had much effect, however. D. J. had been struck down by laryngitis. The strain of the year was already taking its toll on him, and he was only three days in.

—

The events in Clinton had gotten Bob Taylor's dander up. He was ready to do something about this John Kasper, that troublemaking carpetbagger. A few minutes before one o'clock, Bob hustled down the corridor toward his bench, moving as quickly as the dignity of his position would allow; too much haste and his black robes would flap open around his ankles. That wouldn't do, not with *Life* documenting his every step. He shuffled his reading glasses to his right hand, looked away from the camera, and pressed his left hand against the robe's front to ensure it stayed closed.

As he neared the courtroom's door, Court Crier James Smith pounded the gavel three times. This man, a Black man, was one of the most powerful people in the room that day. As the judge's bailiff/messenger/assistant/chauffeur, James announced the beginning and ending to every court session and every recess. He guarded the judge's privacy and was privy to many of the court's private conversations and scandals.

"Hear ye! Hear ye! Hear ye!" he called out in his deep voice, shushing the massing lawyers, spectators, witnesses, and defendants. "The United States District Court for the Eastern District of Tennessee is now open pursuant to adjournment," he continued. "All persons having business with this honorable court, draw near, give attention, and you shall be heard. God save the United States and this honorable court."

Principal D. J. Brittain Jr. was the most compelling witness of the day, but his laryngitis was a problem. John Kasper's lawyer kept objecting he couldn't hear. After a couple interruptions, Bob Taylor invited the opposing counsel to come closer to the witness stand. Perhaps he'd like a chair pulled up by the bench?

"I am sorry, but I just can't do any better," D. J. whispered.

D. J. laid out for the court how he had prepared the students and teachers for desegregation. Right up until the moment school started, his plans for a peaceful semester had seemed possible. "Well, there had certainly been disagreement of opinion," D. J. conceded, "but there had not been any physical disturbance."

The principal walked the court through the first few days of school, though occasionally he mixed up his timeline, combining events that happened on Tuesday with his description of what occurred on Monday, and then merging Wednesday's beating of Bobby Cain with Tuesday's brouhaha. The week had been traumatic for this quiet, intense educator. Picketers had even come into the school, though D. J. had stopped them before they reached the Black students. "In some cases, I have had to call the officers in to ask them to leave," he said.

"Did you see any acts of violence?" City Attorney Sidney Davis asked him.

Over the objections of the defense attorney, D. J. Brittain Jr. described how the mob had swarmed Bobby Cain, not leaving the teen alone even when the police had stepped in, how instead "a large delegation gathered right around the doors of the jail." Everyone in the courtroom would've known the history of white lynch mobs kidnapping and murdering Black boys for supposed crimes much less serious than daring to sit in a classroom next to white girls, though some in the courtroom would've called those lynch mobs justice.

"Were you surprised when that opposition manifested itself when the school did open?" the lead defense attorney, Benjamin Simmons, asked the principal under cross-examination. He needed to prove John Kasper was neither the instigator nor the leader of the violence, that the conflict had begun long before he stepped off the bus the preceding Saturday. If events in Clinton would've transpired much as they did without John's arrival, if other people were the masterminds of the protest, then what was Robert Taylor accusing him of? Exercising his right to free speech?

At first, D. J. seemed to help John's case. "This is a question that has existed since the Civil War," D. J. replied. "I knew that everything would not go absolutely one hundred percent smoothly." Still, the principal had never expected the level of vitriol he'd encountered. "From nine o'clock when I got home Monday night until five o'clock in the morning, I received anonymous telephone calls—"

"Well, I object to that," Benjamin jumped in, over D. J.'s rasping voice.

"Why, of course you do," one of the city attorneys retorted.

But D. J. kept right on talking. "Three of these threatened my life. Now, I have never—"

Benjamin tried again to stop the principal, but D. J. continued on, hoarsely telling his story. "I have never had anything like that happen to me before."

The next several witnesses for the prosecution all said much the same thing as D. J.: They'd seen John Kasper around town, and they believed he'd set the events in motion. It couldn't be a homegrown movement. Their white supremacists couldn't have organized something like this. They didn't have the sophistication for it. But when pressed, none of them could name anything John had actually done that was illegal or stirred up violence. No one could prove the unprecedented events of the last four days were John Kasper's fault. No one showed how an overeducated, unknown Yankee had convinced the notoriously distrustful locals to accept him as their racist guru, especially when he'd spent half his time in Clinton sitting in jail.

—

After a short recess, Benjamin Simmons gave Judge Robert Taylor a way out of the quagmire in Clinton. He could say that through his initial court order the previous January he had done his diligence and followed the Supreme Court's lead, then he could allow Clinton High to resegregate. "This court does not have to be a wet nurse, if Your Honor please, to see that this order is carried through," he said. "Your Honor has done your duty." In fact, the lawyer argued, the judge was moving beyond his jurisdiction. "I say the American people have rights, and those rights should not be lightly thrown away!" Benjamin concluded. "This restraining order should be vacated and set aside."

"The court overrules that motion," Bob Taylor replied. The trial resumed.

Benjamin then summoned John Kasper to the stand. John claimed he had no idea there was a restraining order in place barring him from speaking to the crowd on Wednesday night. He had never read it, he said, and the marshal had failed to read it to him. He had no idea what the paper said until he pulled it out of his pocket at 3:00 Thursday morning, exhausted after a night of protesting and a lengthy interview with a *Life* journalist. He was flabbergasted to learn at that point that the judge had taken away his right to free speech.

The *Brown* decision was like Prohibition, John explained. The federal government had made a new law, a terrible new law, a law that would lead to chaos and moral degradation and violence and crime. When the government did that, the people themselves had to repeal it.

By then, it was 4:30 in the afternoon. The judge cut the questioning off quickly when the lawyer started asking John about his childhood. Robert Taylor did not care what made the outsider tick.

"Gentlemen, I believe we will adjourn until nine o'clock tomorrow morning," Bob told them. He set John Kasper's bond at $10,000. Then he told everyone else to behave. "Anybody who goes on those school grounds, and by words, acts, or deeds who undertakes directly or indirectly to interfere with the orderly operation, anybody who does that, does it at their own risk!" Bob warned. "Whether you agree or whether you disagree, that is the law of this land, and the law of this land has to be obeyed."

At 4:45 p.m., Court Crier James Smith adjourned the assembly. Later that night, Bob Taylor dismissed the charges against the other five defendants. Only John Kasper remained in custody. That was good, John told a reporter for the *Tennessean*. He had the authorities in Clinton running scared. "This is the beginning of the end of the Supreme Court decision," he promised. No one paid his bond.

Despite Judge Taylor's warnings, all was not peaceful in Clinton that night. Midafternoon, there'd been a break in the protests, one that held just long enough for a caravan of eight U.S. senators, twenty U.S. representatives, five governors, two former governors, two senatorial nominees, and five hopeful representatives as well as Democratic nominee for president Adlai E. Stevenson and his running mate, Estes Kefauver, to drive around the city square on their way to a political rally in Oak Ridge. Inside the cars, the passengers strained for a glimpse of the chaos they'd heard about on the evening news. No protestors were in sight, but a few abandoned picket signs still fluttered in yards and on sidewalks around the school.

Peace did not last. A few minutes after the motorcade passed, white adolescents pummeled a Black woman with tomatoes and apples. The police arrested three for that assault, and again the journalists on the scene scrambled to identify them. They were all locals, informants told the reporters. According to onlookers, the oldest was twenty-one-year-old Airman Dewey Hopper, who was charged with throwing tomatoes and violating the court order by carrying a poster that said: "We don't want Clinton High School mixed." He resisted arrest; two police officers dragged him away. Also picked up were John Carter, the fox-bashing white boy arrested a day earlier for beating up Bobby Cain, and Jimmy Patmore, the delinquent released with a warning that very morning. When the crowd at the school heard the three were taken in custody, a hundred protestors marched on the jail and broke out one of its windows. It took both the county deputies and the Clinton police to disperse them.

A few hours later, the white townspeople returned for another rally on the courthouse square. The Reverend Alonzo Bullock again opened the event with prayer, but this time he had competition. While he spoke, a lanky farmer in overalls and a stocky Magnet Mills worker also prayed loudly. The three men drowned each other out. Alonzo gave up first. When the other two men had also wound down, Alonzo led the group in a chorus of "Amazing Grace" before beginning his talk.

"Keep the race white," he urged his audience. "Folks, we're bound to win—we are going to keep the Lord on our side."

Twenty-some speakers followed him. While they talked, a man circulated through the crowd handing out yet another pamphlet, this one called *The Mongrel*, an inflammatory tract written in poetic meter. One man was arrested for public drunkenness.

SEVEN

Victory and Defeat

F riday morning, Jo Ann Allen donned the last of the new togs her grandmother had made for her and styled her usual pony-tail. It was hot and clear, the sort of day when girls needed their hair off their necks, but the forecasters in the newspaper and on the radio were promising a change was due. Soon autumn would come to the mountains, bringing relief from the sweltering summertime heat still pressing down upon Southern Appalachia. Finishing up her primping, Jo Ann grabbed her lunch and balanced one perfect fall-crisp apple on top of the stack of books in her arms, an emergency snack in case she couldn't find a peaceful dining spot.

But when she met up with the other nine students who lived on the Hill, they noted a difference. All week, the tumult at the school had been building, and from their perch on the Hill the students had tracked the ratcheting anger, a harbinger of what their day would hold. This morning, however, was quieter. In fact, there were maybe only fifty people awaiting them, and no one was violating Judge Taylor's injunction. They weren't even carrying a poster board. With so few to corral, the chief of police had reassigned all but two officers.

The Black students must've speculated among themselves. Was this it? Had they won? Well, that hadn't been so bad, all in all! They'd have a few stories to tell their grandkids about how they'd changed their world. They could talk about all the things that might've gone wrong, but they'd persevered and right had come out on top, just like it was supposed to. Amazing!

The Black parents, however, weren't about to trust this sudden seeming peace. School hadn't even started over in Mansfield, Texas, but already a mob of white people had attacked a white assistant district attorney out-side the high school, 150 men chasing him through town. And the Clinton parents had read in the newspapers that the Mansfield superintendent of schools had shared all the entrances and egresses of the building; there were no secret exits or safe escape routes left to the Black kids. And then the white folks had hung a Black effigy from the school flagpole and set it afire, an effigy pinned with the note: "This Negro tried to enter a white school. This would be a terrible way to die." No wonder not a single Black teen in Mansfield had registered for classes. Nope, Clinton's Black parents didn't trust this peace one iota. It might be a trap or a trick, a ruse leading their children into harm. No one would be walking to school. They'd arranged for relatives—anyone who had a car and didn't have to be to work early—to drive their kids down to Clinton High and drop them off at the door.

Inside, the school was too empty. In a normal year, this Friday would have been a raucous day. Teachers would have struggled to maintain order. Jocks in letter jackets would have trash-talked in the halls. Cheerleaders with pom-poms would've run their routines. The uniformed marching band would have reviewed their scores. The entire student body clad in orange and white would have focused on that night's excitement, the event marking the true beginning of the school year: the inaugural football game between the Clinton Dragons and their most hated rival, the Lake City Lakers. But on this Friday morning, only 446 students had shown up for school. And where was everyone else, the missing half of the student body? Some had stayed home because their parents were scared of the mobs. A few snatched a chance to play hooky. A couple probably picked up a shift, eager to earn a few bucks. Perhaps a handful were sick. The rest had car-pooled to Knoxville for the second day of John Kasper's trial.

—

At 9:00 a.m., Court Crier James Smith called the courtroom to order, and John Kasper returned to the stand for City Attorney Buford Lewallen's cross-examination. Perhaps buoyed by his supporters, John showed less re-spect and restraint than he had the day before.

Where do you live? Buford asked, probably to remind everyone John was that worst of all outsiders: a New England, big-city Yankee.

"I reside in the Knoxville County Jail," John replied.

Hadn't the marshals serving the injunction asked John "to kindly come inside" the courthouse so they could read the papers to him? Buford inquired.

"They just said, 'Step in.' There was not any particular kindness about it."

Buford tried another tack: What else could the principal have done to legally prevent desegregation?

John didn't even bother answering that. The reason D. J. Brittain Jr. wasn't protecting the white children of Anderson County was a racial one, John said. He had them all fooled. He wasn't a white Christian at all. "He looks Jewish to me," John said. He must be. Any true white American Christian would be seizing the moment and joining the cause. "This is an important reform movement," John said. "This is a profound movement right here. We are going back to constitutional government. We are destroying a Communist conspiracy and all of the corrupt officials who have played their silent part in it by refusing to stand up for the people themselves."

Federal Judge Robert Love Taylor had heard enough of John Kasper's nonsense. The defense rested after John's testimony, and the judge wasted no time issuing his opinion. Despite his own personal opposition to desegregation, Bob declared that the injunction prohibiting interfering in desegregation would remain in effect until 1:00 p.m. on Friday, September 7, when there would be a follow-up hearing on the permanence of the injunction. He also found John Kasper guilty because he "willfully disregarded and violated" the restraining order. "It is the judgment of this Court," Bob told John, "that you are to be confined to some institution to be designated by the Attorney General of the United States for a period of one year for willful contempt of court."

Benjamin Simmons asked the judge to set bail pending an appeal.

"Well, Mr. Simmons," Bob responded, "I will give you until Tuesday. You can write me your views and I will treat it as a brief, and then I will pass on whether he is entitled to bail." John Kasper went back to his Knoxville cell.

Disgruntled and rumbling about the injustice of John's sentence, the white spectators loaded up and headed back north along US 25W to Clinton. Principal D. J. Brittain Jr. did not go back to Clinton, however. He retreated instead into the mountains, somewhere no one would be able to find him. He was, he explained to a friend, "swelled up" by all that had happened. He needed time away.

—

For a few hours on that Friday night, senior tackle Bob Manning thought the world felt so normal, so right. There he was, back in his pads and jersey, battling it out under the stadium lights. On the sidelines, the cheerleaders woo-hooed Bob and his boys. In the stands, spectators decked out in Dragon orange jumped and clapped and hollered.

In the first quarter, the two teams had seemed evenly matched, both stuck scoreless. Then at the end of the second quarter, Earl Nelson, a 155-pound junior halfback at Clinton High, made a five-yard run for a touchdown. With a score on the board, the offensive line settled into Coach Jody Fisher's T-formation style and began to run the field. The next quarter, quarterback Ronnie Fowler handed off to Earl Nelson, who scored a second touchdown, a thirty-five-yard run. That same period, senior halfback Billy Brown rushed fifty yards, darting and dodging the Lakers and breaking out of tackles, to score a touchdown. The officials negated it with an offsides call on one of his teammates. He tried again, this time rushing thirty yards, only to have that touchdown called back as well because of clipping. Finally, in the fourth quarter, Ronnie Fowler faked and pitched out to Billy, who scored on a twelve-yard end run. Then junior Philip Holbrook made a nine-yard run to end the game. The Lakers never saw it to the end zone, no chance of that with Bob and his boys on their case. The final score was Clinton High 25, Lake City High 0.

But then the game was over, and the normal ended. Without the spectators cheering, Bob Manning could hear the hullabaloo from the courthouse filtering onto the field. By the time the game let out, the folks who'd gone to Knoxville had returned, adding their ire to the crowds gathering in the square. Bob paused just outside the field's gates. Usually he would have strutted over to the sock hop at the rec center next to the football field. There he would've flirted with pretty girls and laughed it up with his boys, reenacting the best moments of the game. This year, though, there were no celebratory events to attend. There was only the growing, growling crowd. One thousand or maybe twelve hundred or perhaps fifteen hundred segregationists had packed into downtown. Some linked arms and marched through the streets chanting, "We want Kasper!" They blocked traffic, snarling the Labor Day plans of travelers traversing US 25W and SR61. The city's six police officers were powerless to stop them.

Bob lived over in North Clinton on the other side of the square. His parents had given him strict instructions to avoid downtown, but how else was he supposed to get home? Plus, he was curious. What harm would come from getting a look-see at the chaos? He joined up with J. T. Mc-Cormick and a few of the other guys who lived near him. They'd tour the square together.

But word had trickled out to the protestors that the football players weren't on their side, that they'd protected the Black students, that they'd helped keep the school open and desegregated. As the lettermen walked through the crowd, noticeable in their school jackets, some of the protestors yelled, "You people are a disgrace to the county!" and "Going to school and playing football while we're out here defending you!" Bob and the others hurried home, swearing not to tell their parents where they'd been.

—

The shouts rose up the Hill. The peace of the morning was gone. In their white bungalow behind Green McAdoo, Jo Ann's mother, Josephine, hurried through her preparations, grabbing extra blankets and a few pillows from the linen closet, pouring a thermos of coffee for her husband, Herbert, checking Jo Ann's homework. As she worked, Josephine must've calculated just how long her small family could continue this quixotic campaign to save America's Black schoolchildren through the sacrifice of her daughter's happiness and equanimity. Josephine and Herbert valued education, and they both resented that it had been denied to them. That's why they'd registered Jo Ann at her new school. Oh, but who could have tabulated the cost of their decision? Somehow the elder Allens needed to improve their children's lot, giving them the opportunities and education Josephine and Herbert never had. But they couldn't rob their children— their bright, idealistic children—of their hope, their joy, and perhaps even their lives. Maybe they should've packed it all in and moved to live with her brother in California after all.

Herbert, the eldest son of tenant farmers and born in a small town some fifty miles due south of Montgomery, had dropped out after elementary school, likely because there was no middle school for him to attend. He'd labored alongside his dad until his parents passed, both dying while he was a teenager. Then he moved in with his grandmother and kept right on working, supporting himself and his siblings as best he could. At nineteen, he married Nove Deans, a local girl, and the couple birthed a daughter the following year. They named the girl Minnie Pearl after Herbert's mother. On July 1, 1932, Nove died, leaving Herbert with a toddler to raise on his own. Within a year of his wife's death, Herbert had moved to Anderson County, Tennessee. Perhaps knowing he'd have a hard time caring for Minnie on his own, he left her behind in Alabama. She lived with her maternal grandmother and even went by her mother's maiden name sometimes.

Though he was trained as a carpenter, when Herbert first came to Clinton he'd worked as a domestic servant for a white doctor. That doctor lived down the street from the white Crenshaws. Josephine was the Crenshaws' cook/housekeeper. When Herbert and Josephine married in 1938, the Crenshaws decided they needed a chauffeur as well as a maid. Herbert moved into the house. And that was a good thing, as the young couple wouldn't have seen much of each other otherwise. They each worked about sixty hours a week to make ends meet.

Though Josephine was the great-granddaughter of Adaline Staples Crozier, she also had ended her education sooner than she wanted despite her family's schooling tradition. After graduating from Oliver Springs Elementary School, she'd become a boarder at Nelson Merry High School, a Black secondary school on the other side of Knoxville with a reputation for producing brilliant musicians and amazing teachers, perfect for the studious and musical Josephine. When she was sixteen, however, her father had fallen ill, and the family lost their land. As the oldest, Josephine knew her duty. She dropped out of school before graduation and moved back to Anderson County to work for the Crenshaw family. Out of her wages, Josephine put her younger sister through Nelson Merry, paid for her undergraduate degree at Knoxville College, and then helped her earn an M.A. in education. Josephine also funded her brother through high school and college. He joined the Tuskegee Airmen and then moved to California to teach. Out there, he earned an M.A. in mathematics from UCLA. Meanwhile, Josephine still labored as a domestic servant.

Herbert quit the Crenshaws and moved his family onto the Hill when Oak Ridge's construction began. The government wasn't hiring Black people to be scientists or administrators, but they needed as many carpenters as they could find. Eventually, he and Josephine bought their little house. It wasn't much, just four rooms in all, but it was a sweet place with enough land out back for the family to keep a few chickens and raise a small garden. Best of all, it was theirs. Lately, though, construction work had dried up, and Herbert had been forced back into contingent labor, sometimes as a carpenter and sometimes as a cafeteria worker and sometimes driving up to Michigan for a job and sometimes as an orderly over at the Oak Ridge Hospital and sometimes as a chauffeur/mechanic and sometimes as a janitor for the library. He'd do whatever paid the bills. His kids, though, they'd have better. That was why when Herbert went in to mop the library floors after hours he'd bring Jo Ann along with him. The building was barred to Black Clintonians during the day, but at night Jo Ann could swish soapy water around, cleaning her way to the edge of the fairy-tale section, where she'd drop her mop and grab a book. He'd leave her there to dream of better, fairer worlds.

—

Early in the week, Herbert Allen and the other Black men of Freedman's Hill had known they had a problem on their hands, soon as the first bands of white men, hot from a rally downtown, drove through their neighborhood, yelling and threatening and making a nuisance. Then not a single police officer or sheriff's deputy had stepped up to help. The men of the Hill figured they were on their own. That was okay by them, they must've said to each other. They knew their land better than any white man did, and they had enough experience among them—many had served in World War II or Korea—to organize their own defense. This was the next step in their "Double V campaign," or the commitment by Black soldiers to take the fight for freedom abroad back to the American homeland. Had they realized their battle for civil rights would be a hot war, not a cold one? Had anyone predicted it would come to their Freedman's Hill?

As the experienced tacticians among them examined the Hill, they realized that in theory, the neighborhood—the town's highest ground—should have been easy to defend. Every house, however, was surrounded by vegetable gardens and outbuildings and trees and overgrown fields, countless divots and copses invaders could use. And then there were the smattering of white families who lived on the Hill itself, potential enemies sleeping in the midst of them. Most of the time, those folks were quite kindly toward their Black neighbors. Just last summer, Josephine Allen had lent Axie Smith, a white lady who lived across the street, a few cups of sugar and Jo Ann had hung out with their three kids. The teens had lounged in the Smiths' backyard garden, feasting on sun-ripe tomatoes.

In the last week, however, relations had changed. Jo Ann had even thought she'd seen the boys down at the protests. "You and your people have been nicer to me than my own relatives," Axie tried to explain to Josephine, "but I just don't believe in mixing of the races in school."

Since the Black families were vulnerable at home, the men decided the women and children should shelter in Mt. Sinai Baptist, a centralized building they could fortify. And so on that Friday night, Josephine and the other mothers laid out pallets on the pews, but no one slept. Jo Ann lay in the darkened nave in anxious silence. This space usually felt so safe. Most times, if she was here on a Friday night, it was because it was an extra-special event like a fish fry, everyone sliding battered trout into spitting-hot oil and sipping on soda with peanuts. This Friday, though, she waited for the signal to flee to the church's basement. That sound would mean danger had penetrated the first line of the men's defense. She wondered whether her church really could serve as a sanctuary now. She comforted herself that the men had a backup plan. They'd parked cars strategically around the Hill so the survivors of an attack could retreat quickly, disappearing onto the mountains' dark, winding, unmarked roads.

Outside, Herbert joined the rest of the men who had crouched in viaducts and behind their family sedans, clutching the shotguns they grabbed from hall closets or borrowed from relatives nearby. He chose a bush outside Bobby Cain's house. Settling in for the night, he struck a match to light his pipe.

Inside the house, Robert Cain Sr. saw the flare of the phosphorous match and reached for his gun, ready to shoot the intruder. His sister-in-law urged him to double-check before he shot.

At least step outside, she said. Don't shoot through the window.

Robert walked onto his front porch and saw Herbert's well-known face. Robert's sister-in-law had saved Herbert's life. But no one had time to worry about what might have happened without her warning. The Cains quickly dispersed, the women to the church and the men to their guard duty.

Since it wasn't a school night, Bobby Cain, Robert Thacker, and Alfred Williams joined their fathers and older brothers keeping watch. Eugene Weaver, the brother who'd bailed Bobby out of jail, refused to let Bobby have a weapon. Bobby could stay, hanging out there with the men, lying and waiting, but he wouldn't be part of any more fights, not if his family had a say in it. Robert Thacker's father felt differently. He handed his son a shotgun. Robert looked at the stock of the weapon, then sat cross-legged by his front porch, staring into the surrounding gardens and fields, alert for any signs of danger.

From their positions around the Hill, the men listened to the rioters downtown, hearing clearly as the white mob shouted, "We're going to get them!" They comforted themselves that they had backup, should actual battle occur. A group of World War II veterans—some of them family and some of them friends and some of them absolute strangers—had pledged to come from Knoxville if they were called. Course, by the time they'd made the hour drive, the Hill might have already been lost, but the Knoxvillians could help rescue the survivors.

"I moved here from Mississippi because of white people; this is as far as I run," one of the locals told a reporter for the *Baltimore Afro-American*. "I'll die with my guns shooting."

"We didn't start it," another man warned, "but if they come to my house, I'll help end it."

—

At about nine o'clock on Friday night, the local speakers ceded the night to a new presenter, a face few folks in Clinton recognized. This man, dressed casually in a black suit but no tie, jacket buttons undone, stood at the top of the courthouse steps.

"I'm Asa Carter!" he called out.

They knew that name. "*Asa! Asa! Asa!*" the folks at the rally cheered.

"I'm from Alabama!"

The crowd roared.

Asa was a leader in the North Alabama White Citizens' Council, a renegade branch of the Alabama White Citizens' Council that had separated when the main state body had asked Asa Carter to tone down his anti-Semitism. He had also founded a paramilitary terrorist group called the Original Ku Klux Klan of the Confederacy.* And he'd been the catalyst for John Kasper's visit to Clinton.

During his hour-long speech, Asa condemned the Supreme Court justices, accused the NAACP of being a Communist front, and badmouthed Robert Taylor, the "carpetbagging judge," an ironic accusation from an outsider about a judge with ties deep in Tennessee's political history. He also spread partial truths and blatant lies. "For every three white men there are seven colored men on this earth," he said at one point. "But you'll find that the Anglo-Saxon races are the only ones that have ever maintained a free government for free men."

"He's right!" yelled some in the crowd.

"Tell 'em, Asa!" shouted others.

Not everyone was paying attention to the Asa Carter show, however. While he spoke, some of the emerging local leaders met on the edge of the crowd. They wanted to get ahead of these outsiders hijacking their movement. They needed to found their own White Citizens' Council before John Kasper or Asa Carter or some other racist celebrity from away could

---

* Asa Carter would also become a speechwriter for George Wallace, reportedly penning Wallace's famous commitment to "segregation today, segregation tomorrow, segregation forever." After George Wallace began to soften his stance on race in the late 1960s, Asa Carter retired from politics and began writing under the pseudonym Forrest Carter. His most famous book, *The Education of Little Tree*, was a *New York Times* bestseller and became required reading for many American schoolchildren.

take control. Holding a quick vote, they elected local machinist Willard Till to preside over the new Anderson County White Citizens' Council. Then they started a membership drive, stacking forms on the town's granite war memorial. One hundred and fifty people signed up that night and paid the three-dollar membership fee.

While the new Citizens' Council organized, other folks in the crowd started devolving the meeting, taking it from a rancorous rally to a riot. Maybe they needed to blow off the hate-filled high Asa's speech had given them. Maybe they had spent all week dreaming of doing something real for segregation, something more than milling about the square. Or maybe a bit of mayhem sounded fun on this hot Friday night. Whatever the reason, a clutch of men turned on some of the assembled news photographers documenting their activities, shouting, "The only picture we want is a picture of a nigger with a noose around his neck!"

Another group, perhaps two hundred strong, splintered off and marched toward the mayor's house. Some in the group had a reputation for rough-housing. Some looked like they might be packing a gun or two under their lightweight summer sports coats. And some were miners, powder monkeys, and shot firers who liked to add a little dynamite to any labor dispute. Realizing where they were headed, police raced up Main Street, cutting the mob off before they could reach the Lewallens. When the rioters returned to the square, they were overheard discussing whether to blow up the courthouse.

Then on the outskirts of the mob, a car pulled up full of Black passengers, folks who must've skipped reading the morning's news. The white crowd converged on the vehicle. They struck it with their fists and kicked at it with their boots, cursing its occupants. Someone leaned on one side of the automobile. Did the movement start at the trunk or at the hood? From the right or from the left? Hard to tell because soon everyone within touching distance of the car had the idea. Hands and knees and shoulders and whole bodies jounced on and off the vehicle, rocking it, straining the shock absorber until it screeched, taxing the bolts holding the engine in place, shifting the hoses and loosening the wires. Somehow, the driver of the car kept his calm and inched forward. Eventually, he made a gap big enough to speed away, but the mob had a new game.

Another car of unsuspecting Black travelers approached. This time, the rioters tore open the auto's doors. Two other vehicles driven by Black drivers were almost turned over, and a third driver escaped on his car's rims. The crowd had cut the tires off. That automobile broke down just outside the city's limits, and the police had to rescue its occupants. Then another car approached, a sedan with stripes painted down its side. Seeing the Black faces inside, a lanky white man with a buzz cut took off his shoe and began pounding at the driver's-side window until the glass fractured in a cobweb of shards. To prolong the fun, some of the younger kids in the audience began shooting fireworks off at vehicles.

—

Two minutes after midnight, Glad Woodward was sworn in as the new Anderson County sheriff. He'd been a policeman in Oak Ridge, where his daughters had attended the desegregated Oak Ridge High School the year before. "I intend to carry out the duties of the office as they have been," the new sheriff said of the events downtown. "Personally, I am opposed to integration, but this is the law of the land and we will abide by it."

After the ceremony, he went to the courthouse, where he saw some rioters attempting to flip a car full of Black passengers. He tried to reason with the offenders, telling them they were hurting the segregationist cause more than helping it. Enough of the men were distracted by the new sheriff's conversation that the car was able to escape. But throughout all the violence and the mayhem and the chaos of the night, neither the police nor the sheriff made any arrests.

Why aren't you intervening? a journalist from the *Tennessean* asked one of the police officers who was standing by watching.

"What can we do?" the officer replied. And what could they do against Lord knows how many hundreds.

—

That night, an FBI agent assigned to the Knoxville field office called up attorney Buford Lewallen to warn him that this rioting was just the beginning. The agent had received a tip: there were plans to burn the courthouse, Clinton High School, and possibly the mayor's house.

"We need either the state highway patrol or the National Guard, and we need them badly," Buford told a journalist from the *Tennessean*.

Buford's father, Mayor W. E. Lewallen, tried to reach Governor Frank Clement to beg for aid, calling in the promise the governor had made a day earlier. Frank did not come to the phone.

Later that night, a convoy of Ku Klux Klan cars paraded through the Hill. The Black men and boys didn't stop the cars. They didn't say a word. They just stood up, holding their guns.

Newly installed Sheriff Glad Woodward warned off another group of white men he saw heading toward the Hill. He'd heard rumors of the defense the men of the Hill had laid out to protect their homes and their families. "If you go up there, I'm going to send body bags," he said.

EIGHT

The Best Defense

William Buford Lewallen woke up Saturday morning determined. No, decided. Nay, obdurate. He was done pussyfooting around. It was time for this nonsense to stop.

Clinton was his city. The scion of one of the town's most prominent families, not only was his father the mayor, but his folks were also half owners of Lewallen-Miller Department Store. His people had been here since sometime around the Revolutionary War, back when it wasn't entirely legal for white folks to be on the west side of the mountains. His wife, English teacher Celdon Medaris Lewallen, came from a lineage with roots every bit as deep as his in Anderson County, and she was also the daughter of a former Clinton mayor.

The two had fallen in love while students at Clinton High, a pairing up of the town's bluebloods that must've thrilled their parents. After graduating from high school, the couple had left Clinton for college in different towns. Buford had gone to the University of Tennessee, Knoxville, while Celdon had enrolled at the prestigious Ward-Belmont College in Nashville, a two-year school. As a student at a women's college, Celdon wasn't supposed to marry until after she'd graduated, but she and Buford were too in love to worry about such dictums. They eloped on July 12, 1939, the summer after Celdon's freshman year. Then she returned to school, resolving not to tell their family and friends until after she'd received her degree. They were not discovered until the summer of 1941. Then Celdon transferred to the University of Tennessee, Knoxville, where she studied English and rushed Delta Delta Delta.

They had planned to return to Clinton as soon as Buford finished his law degree at the University of Tennessee, Knoxville, but World War II intervened. Buford enlisted in 1942, and he was sent to Douglas Airfield in Arizona, where he trained to be a pilot with the Army Air Corps. On Tuesday, December 28, 1943, Buford's instructor asked him to come along on a joy ride. Buford was near the end of his training, and the teacher decided to show off. During one particularly tricky rolling maneuver, the winds off the Chiricahua Mountains caught the wing of the aircraft, and the instructor crashed the plane. Theirs was one of four training planes to go down that day. Douglas's commanding officer sent up thirty search planes to look for the missing men, but the would-be rescuers saw no sign of their downed comrades. Reluctantly, the commander sent word to Celdon that her husband was missing. She'd given birth to their daughter, Ann Dancy, less than a month earlier, so she couldn't go to Douglas. She stayed in Clinton, cared for by her family and in-laws, waiting for a telegram.

On the third day, forest rangers stumbled across Buford's instructor. After the first night spent in the woods, he'd realized none of the search planes would be able to see their location. Buford was too injured to move—right leg broken in two places, facial lacerations so severe the cadet couldn't talk intelligibly, a shattered left kneecap—so the trainer had hobbled his way out of the mountains on a broken ankle, leaning on a makeshift crutch. Following the man's bloody trail, the rangers eventually found Buford. The cadet had just dragged himself back into the canopy of trees, searching for safety after setting fire to his plane, his own method of signaling for help. Buford spent two and a half years in military hospitals recovering. His injuries required six surgeries to repair. Eventually, he learned to walk with crutches, but he never regained full mobility. He was also never again completely pain-free. Buford's instructor was court-martialed and fined for his actions that day, but he served another eighteen years, becoming a lieutenant colonel. They were the lucky ones. None of the other cadets or trainers survived their crashes.

Buford returned home just as the war ended. He was a handsome man in his mid-twenties with dark hair, a widow's peak, large eyes, and a surprisingly weak upper lip. A thin white line—presumably a remnant of his plane crash—bisected the center of his fuller bottom lip and then curved off the left side of his chin. Though almost everyone in Clinton was a Republican, he declared himself a member of the party of Roosevelt, a believer in innovations like the TVA and the Manhattan Project, innovations that had brought other Democrats to the mountains. He decided to enter politics though he had yet to finish his law degree. He was elected to the state House of Representatives in 1946, and a year later he became the youngest Speaker of Tennessee's House of Representatives ever, a distinction he holds to this day. While in Nashville, he became a close friend of Frank Clement, another promising young Democratic politician and former veteran. But then Buford picked a fight with some of the leaders of Anderson County's Democratic Party, accusing the sheriff of owning and operating gambling machines and of being a hidden partner in a Lake City bootlegging operation. The party muckety-mucks couldn't have such a fractious upstart. Buford withdrew from the 1948 election. When his term finished in early 1949, the Lewallens returned to Anderson County. Buford, who earned his degree while in the House, opened a law practice. Celdon started teaching English to Clinton High's seniors.

—

Clinton was Buford's heritage and his inheritance. He would defend his city—well, his part of it, anyway—from any mischief or mayhem the rioters might intend. No Yankee blowhard was going to use his courthouse as a base for rabble-rousing! No bootlegging rednecks would threaten his wife and her students! No hillbilly numbskulls would dynamite his father's home!

The whole situation downtown was absurd, really. The locals were following their racist Pied Piper, but, Buford knew, the people in the streets understood little of what was going on. He'd overheard John Kasper regaling them with talk of eighteenth-century political theorist Sir William Blackstone and nineteenth-century British prime minister Benjamin Disraeli. Why, he bet those mountaineers thought Blackstone was a truck driver and Disraeli was a coal miner. But while the locals might have been nothing but pawns in the game the national white supremacist leaders were playing, Buford knew this game could turn dreadfully expensive for Clinton. The town had gained too much—an increased tax base and better jobs and improved schools and regular visits from the nation's brightest politicians—by being nice to the feds. Buford couldn't let this funny business continue any further.

Buford didn't want integration any more than the next white man did. And he'd helped the town pursue every legal means possible to stop it. He'd been entangled in all this mess about as long as anybody in Clinton, one of three city lawyers who had originally argued against desegregation. He'd lost. Now Buford needed an overwhelming show of force to prove Clinton's leaders had more resources and more power than the mob.

The mayor got the official wheels rolling. (Sometimes it was nice to be the mayor's son.) First thing Saturday morning, W. E. and his Board of Aldermen, a body similar to a city council, declared a state of emergency and formally appealed to Buford's old friend Governor Frank Clement for help. Turned out, the governor couldn't act on a telephone call or even a telegram. But the governor would have no more excuses. The men typed up their request, and an Anderson County sheriff's deputy drove it to Knoxville. There the president of Cherokee Airlines picked up the letter to fly to Nashville with it. Jumping in a car, the airline exec then sped to the Governor's Mansion, where the governor was waiting with eleven top staffers including Tennessee National Guard Adjutant General Joe Henry, the secretary of state, and the state's attorney general.

The assembled men quickly agreed to send the highway patrol to Clinton that night, but they debated who would maintain the peace long term. The highway patrol could be no more than a stopgap measure. Within a day or so, they'd need to be back patrolling the roadways. Who'd take their place? The National Guard?

The Guard could be used to quell uprisings and maintain longer-term law enforcement, but the Guard already had some history in the mountains. The state had used the troops to win the Coal Creek War of the early 1890s, an Anderson County coal miner insurrection that ostensibly overthrew the convict leasing system* but actually led to the state moving convict laborers out of private mines and into state-owned excavations. They'd also come in 1919 when a Black Knoxville man had been arrested, accused of murdering a white woman. The Knoxville sheriff had spirited the alleged murderer away to safety in Chattanooga, a prescient move, because while he was gone, a white mob broke into the jail, looking to lynch the Black man. Enraged that the sheriff had outwitted them, they went on a destructive looting spree. The National Guard had instituted martial law to stop the violence. And the soldiers had squashed the General Textile Strike of 1934, which a few called the Uprising of '34. Course, only a few in Tennessee had participated, but they'd all heard about the violence and the bloodshed that happened in Georgia and Massachusetts and North Carolina and elsewhere when the "flying squadrons" of labor organizers and the protesting workers clashed with the mill owners and their National Guard patrols. Same thing when folks in Indiana and Nebraska struck in '35 and Iowa and Oklahoma in '38. And then there'd been the martial law declared after the race riot when white Texans had looted and burned Beaumont's Black neighborhood in 1943.

Maybe the soldiers should be sent unarmed? someone at the meeting suggested.

This situation is "not sham or pretense," General Joe Henry responded. If his men went to Clinton, they would have all their weapons.

—

While the state politicians worried about the ramifications of intervening in a white supremacist riot, Buford, his father, Horace Wells, and a handful

---

* The state sold jailed men and boys to mines for the duration of their sentences at much lower costs than companies had to pay free laborers and with the guarantee of little state oversight, thus transforming prisons from a drain on state budgets to a profitable enterprise, supplying mining companies with an unlimited pool of workers they could starve, mistreat, beat, and replace, and costing untold thousands of Tennesseans their lives. Researchers estimate as many as eight hundred men are buried outside only one of these prison work camps.

of other local white leaders drove down to Knoxville for a meeting with a local FBI agent and Knoxville's chief of police. Neither agency could send additional manpower, but they loaded up the Anderson County cars with a couple machine guns and the ammunition needed to fire the weapons. After a pit stop in Oak Ridge to pick up some tear gas grenades, the men returned to Clinton. They installed one of the machine guns in the mayor's bedroom. The other they put in the second story of the courthouse. They didn't offer any weapons to their neighbors on the Hill.

But the borrowed weapons were useless without someone to wield them, and the city's police had suspect loyalties. Not only had Buford thought he'd seen at least a few of their relatives among the segregationist crowds, but the police had made no preparations for the coming night. Instead, four of their six officers had spent Saturday afternoon up on the Hill raiding the Chicken Shack, a sandwich joint known to carry homemade hooch. A week earlier, a search had netted the officers six pints of moonshine and five gallons of homemade beer in a washtub. This week, they took nine mason jars of white lightning and a dozen or so home-capped bottles of beer. They staged themselves for a *Clinton Courier-News* photographer, arranging themselves by height: tall man, short man, tall man, short man. On a table in front, they set out their loot.

No, the police weren't reliable, so Buford issued an open call over the local radio stations. Any white man supporting law and order was invited to join an auxiliary police force assembling in downtown Clinton. Volunteers should bring their own rifles, pistols, clubs, or other weapons. Forty-seven responded. They were sworn in by City Judge Paul Horton. They raised their right hands. Some raised them high, confident, like they were getting ready to testify in church. Others barely got their hands to shoulder level. They didn't seem to know where to look. They stared at the judge as he read the words. They looked at each other. They glanced at the *Tennessean's* cameraman. A few stared off into space.

"We, the undersigned, do solemnly swear that we will uphold the Constitution of the United States of America," they pledged, "the statutes of Tennessee and the ordinances of the town of Clinton, Tennessee, and that we will perform the duties incumbent upon us as public officials of the town of Clinton, Tennessee, to the best of our ability, so help me God."

Then they were given a white card to sign, which declared that they had taken an oath to support the defense of the state of Tennessee.

The men hadn't come because they believed in desegregation. Not a single white citizen in Clinton had taken that stand, at least not publicly. "Hell, it ain't a matter of wanting or not wanting niggers in the school," one of the newly sworn-in deputies told a writer from *Time*. "It's a matter of who's going to run the town, the Government or that mob out there. It's not easy to go out there and face maybe your neighbors, but it's got to be done."

Some faces in the group looked about young enough to still be at Clinton High; others were old enough to have grandkids at the school. The ragtag force had no uniforms to differentiate themselves from the rioters, just their own summer-weight button-downs. They didn't even get badges to carry, only the cards issued at their deputization. Most were armed only with their own hunting rifles.

"They were without humor, these trudging volunteers," the *Oak Ridger's* reporter wrote. "They carried weapons to be used possibly against their friends and neighbors."

About fifteen of the deputies headed to the mayor's house to guard the Lewallen family. The rest went downtown where a couple hundred white people were already milling about. Buford, unable to walk easily among the crowd due to his wartime injuries, climbed to the second story of the courthouse. He'd man the Thompson submachine gun. The rest of the volunteers stayed on the courthouse lawn commanded by twenty-eight-year-old former infantry captain turned attorney Leo Grant. A veteran of both World War II and Korea, he had been wounded during the battle of Heartbreak Ridge in '51. Carried off the field riddled with bullets and sliced apart by grenade shards, he'd spent years recovering from his injuries. Now he swung a gun around his neck and got back to war.

Leo wasn't the only veteran returning to combat this evening. Most of his men also had war experience, like auxiliary policeman Harold McAlduff of Boston, who had served in the Army Air Corps during World War II and flown twenty-six missions in North Africa before becoming the personal navigator for Carl Spaatz, commander of the Allies' air forces. Now Harold lived and worked in Oak Ridge and had married into a local family.

But many of the rioters were also decorated war heroes.

Whether they had joined the white Home Guard or the rioting segregationists, these men had seen people killed to protect "the American way of life." Some of them had even taken the lives of other soldiers and combatants and civilians, justifying the deaths by saying it was in defense of the nation and democracy. They'd come back to Clinton and been celebrated for their bravery and their willingness to fight for their culture. They were told their actions were right and moral and just. Now they were again battling it out, defending what they saw as the American dream. And frankly, few things were as fundamental to the American way of life as racism.

Knowing the other side might have the same training and the same battle-hardened nerves he did, Leo Grant gave his men simple instructions: protect yourselves, don't let anyone take away your gun, don't run away, and don't get too close to the mob. "Lock them up if they give you any lip," Leo ordered.

—

As the white guard deployed around the courthouse, a parade of cars screamed through the square, heading up the Hill. At the sound of the approaching vehicles, the men signaled to those staying at the church. The women and children grabbed their blankets and ran down to the basement. One little girl cried, asking her older sister if she would die. But the white supremacists didn't stop. Not this time. As the first cars rushed back downtown to join the gathering mob in the courthouse square, another caravan of cars bedecked in Confederate flags came flying through. The men all shifted forward, ready to engage. These cars also kept moving.

The late-summer humidity pressed down on the men and boys guarding the Hill, trapping the day's heat and slicking their skin with sweat. Local meteorologists had predicted rain showers. Had they come, they would've been a mixed blessing. A few good downpours may have scattered the mob (or at least driven away the looky-loos), but the rain also would have made it harder for them to see approaching attackers. Storm clouds gathered overhead, but the rain never came.

The armed Black guard knew they were making a dangerous choice, one that could lead to them being prosecuted for carrying weapons. They also risked being slaughtered by the segregationists for "being uppity." They all knew of people killed for less. Just a few years back, two Black Florida teachers—Harry T. Moore and his wife, Harriette—were murdered by the Klan because Harry had registered voters and challenged wage discrimination and investigated lynchings. And just a year earlier, four white men in Mississippi had gunned down Lamar Smith, a Black farmer and voting rights activist, on the county courthouse lawn in front of dozens of witnesses. None of the white men were indicted.

But just as their children were asserting their rights by going to school, Herbert Allen and Robert Cain Sr. and Eugene Weaver and Allen McSwain and the rest of the men who'd taken up arms were demanding equality. This was about their manhood. For generations, the white people around them had denigrated them and treated them like children, not men. White folks didn't even use honorifics when they spoke to the adults but felt free to use their first names or overly familiar nicknames. Way these men figured it, though, they had the same responsibilities for their families as the newly deputized white men had. So they would protect their neighborhood when white leaders like Buford Lewallen refused to do so. Though they were glad none of the rioters had challenged the Hill's ad hoc defense.

The men froze as yet another carload of white rioters barreled through, heading toward the square. Well, none had challenged them so far.

—

As dusk drew nearer, the segregationist crowd around the square continued to swell, but everyone remained oddly polite, apologizing when they accidentally bumped into each other or into one of the many journalists covering the story. Some white teens even posed for the cameras, mugging and laughing and cutting up. There were men and boys, of course, but there were also many white women, the ones whose purity was supposedly being defended, along with children and even babies. Entire families had come to town like it was any other Saturday night. But this night, they weren't in Clinton to grab a Coke at Hoskins before catching *The Fastest Gun Alive* at the Ritz. Everyone who had ventured into town was there for the rally. And now they were ready for the racist show to start.

From his perch inside the courthouse, Buford watched the auxiliary police officers poke and prod at the crowd, trying to keep everyone swirling and circulating, hoping they could keep trouble at bay if folks couldn't congregate. As more arrived, however, movement became harder. From where Buford sat, he couldn't tell who was deputized and who was a segregationist, but the people seemed to know who stood against them. They began to jostle and jeer at the deputies.

Auxiliary policeman Harold McAlduff asked one woman to move and then winked at her to show he was being friendly. "Don't look," she said. "Don't wink at me, you SOB."

"Why can't I stop here?" another crowd member asked one of the policemen. "It's my courthouse."

Seems "like we don't have a constitution anymore," another man complained.

The mood was souring.

Then at 6:37, a fifty-five-year-old farm laborer named Lee Moneymaker stopped on Main Street.

Move on, the deputies told him.

No, he said.

The deputies tried again.

No, he repeated. And then he refused again. So they arrested him.

A few minutes later, an Oak Ridge machinist was arrested for similar obstinacy. Next, the auxiliary officers picked up another man from Oak Ridge, a technician in applied nuclear physics. He was charged with resisting arrest as well. When she heard this, his wife was distraught. They had only come to Clinton to shop, she insisted. Neither of them cared what happened in Clinton High. This wrongful arrest would cost her husband his very good federal job!

As the crowd saw their comrades dragged away to jail, they turned on the volunteer deputies. First came the cursing. Soon people were acting out. Some slashed tires, perhaps hoping to damage cars belonging to the Home Guard. Others busted out the windows of passing cars, maybe just because it was fun. A few more were arrested for disturbing the peace.

Grabbing a nearby telephone, Buford dialed his friend Governor Frank Clement. "You better get out here with your highway patrolmen," Buford said. "We're going to have a riot." Frank wasn't convinced, so Buford held the phone out the window, letting the governor hear the shouts from below. At 6:45 that night, the governor agreed to send help. The crowd members "better be prepared to go to bed or go to jail," the governor said.

"We're taking over the whole damn county," a highway patrolman told a reporter. But the officer was driving one of the nineteen cars stationed at the Governor's Mansion in Nashville, several hours from Clinton. He wouldn't make it in time to save Leo Grant and his men. Lucky for the auxiliary police, other highway patrol officers were a couple hours closer.

—

Buford could see the spectators converged on one side of the courthouse, cheering and shouting. Their numbers were up to a thousand, perhaps two thousand, maybe more. There'd be no more circulating. It was time for the deputies to organize. Leo Grant called for his men. The thirty auxiliary police formed a line around the courthouse, standing at attention, their rifles braced across their chests. Then in lockstep, the men advanced on one of the largest clots of people. "Come on," the crowd taunted in response. For a few minutes, the crowd and the officers stared at each other. Then the front line of white supremacists started to shout: "Where are our rights?" and "Nigger lovers!" and "We're taxpayers!" and "Let's get the nigger lovers!" and "Let's get their guns and kill them!"

Leo Grant knew his men might have the rioters outgunned (maybe), but they were so severely outnumbered that the weapons hardly mattered. In an actual uprising, the auxiliary police could be slaughtered by the mob on the square. Though dusk had barely fallen, it was time for applying his last resort.

Leo fiddled. Then he fumbled. Then he pitched a canister into the center of the crowd. It was the first of the squad's five tear gas grenades. He heard a hiss as he tossed it. There was a breath of silence as those nearest the fallen orb looked at it in confusion. Then the grenade exploded with a bang and a riffle of vinegary acidic smoke billowed through the mob. Those nearest the cloud pulled back but didn't retreat. Maybe they didn't know what it was. Hard to conceive of, but civilians might be that naïve.

"Tear gas!" Leo shouted.

The pain wasn't immediate. Then the protestors breathed in, sucking the cloud's toxic crystals into their nasal passages and mouths. The aerosolized compounds targeted sensitive mucus membranes. The residue clung to the crowd's eyes and their tear ducts. It entered their lungs. Twenty seconds later, their eyes streamed with tears, snot poured from their noses, and their airways spasmed as their bodies tried to expel the irritant. They hacked and clutched at their chests, pushing away from the gaseous substance. They waited for the cloud to dissipate. When the poison cleared, they surged forward.

Leo reached into his arsenal. Another fumble, another hiss, another bang, another flash, another cloud, another retreat, another pause, another surge.

The pattern repeated. Fumble. Toss. Hiss. Bang. Flash. Cloud. Retreat. Surge.

Repeat.

Fumble. Toss. Hiss. Bang. Flash. Cloud. Retreat. Surge.

Now everyone knew the steps to this dance. Who would lose their footing first?

A final time. Fumble. Toss. Hiss. Bang. Flash. Cloud. Retreat.

And then that was it. The deputies were out of canisters. They were out of options. The next surge would have to be met with guns.

But as the last canister landed in the crowd, its hiss and bang couldn't be heard, drowned out by the sirens of thirty-nine Tennessee Highway Patrol cars. The squadron surrounded the square, ringing the rioters and Home Guard alike as one hundred officers clambered out. Last to unfold himself from his vehicle was Highway Patrol Commissioner Greg O'Rear. Almost seven feet tall, he slung a sawed-off double-barrel shotgun over his shoulder as he stood. "Boys," he said, "it's all over." At his appearance, the milling and surging and threatening ceased, but only a few crowd members were ready to go home. The square stayed packed, and the patrolmen stayed in place. It was 8:10 p.m.

But not a single highway patrolman had turned to go check on the families who lived on the Hill.

—

Two representatives of the Tennessee Federation for Constitutional Government slunk into town shortly behind the highway patrol, carrying a loudspeaker and microphone. Leo Grant, who'd had about enough of the protestors' antics, warned one of the men they'd be arrested if they provoked any violence. The man patted Leo on the shoulder. "We're going to have a peaceable, nonviolent meeting," he said.

Yet again, the rally began with a prayer led by the Reverend Alonzo Bullock. Then came the speakers. One man, a Nashville attorney, told the crowd that desegregating schools placed communities in an impossible position. The only solution was for the people to take the money the state collected to support public schools and use it to open private, segregated schools. "It's just as if the federal law said you can't drive down the right side of the street and the state law said you can't drive down the left side of the street," he explained. "What would you do in that case? Why, you would take over the streets and make them private streets." Other speakers advocated sacking the Anderson County Board of Education and impeaching the governor. But, the leaders warned the crowd, they were not advocating violence. "I am glad to meet you people and you all look like peaceful people to me," one speaker said.

Someone shouted back, "We can get rough if we have to!"

"Bouncing cars and throwing tomatoes are childish acts," another said. "You all know that." Violence only agitated the state authorities and made the white residents of Clinton look like savages, an appellation they preferred to use against other races of people. "That's playing right into the hands of our enemies. Let's leave the race riots to Chicago and Detroit."

With the highway patrol watching the rally, the white auxiliary police deputies drifted away home, anxious to tell how they had saved the town.

Up on the Hill, the Black families listened and watched and waited and worried and prayed. They knew no one official would be coming to protect them. But over in Oak Ridge, sixteen cars were loaded down with pistols, revolvers, rifles, and shotguns along with enough ammunition to defend the Hill for up to six hours of active battle, according to the calculations of the veterans among them. The Knoxville backup was prepared as well.

NINE

Invasion

G ail Ann Epps was flustered. She must've shifted on the hard wooden pew of Mt. Sinai Baptist Church and smoothed her hands over her skirt. She was usually so calm, so peaceable, but this Sunday, she must've struggled to sing along to the hymns Mrs. Allen played, to follow the sermon the Reverend O. W. Willis delivered, to nod appropriately as he prayed over her and the other students in the congregation. Best she could tell, all around her, everyone else was having the same trouble concentrating. Unsurprising after the week they'd withstood. And soon as the service was over, she wouldn't get to rush to the front steps, the Epps sisters and the Allen sisters playing their very silly game guessing which fist had the marble. Not this morning. This morning, she and Jo Ann would be trapped inside, all the older folks grabbing at them, anxious to say, "We worry about you girls," and "Aren't we all so grateful for your bravery."

Maybe Gail Ann planned her afternoon, looking for a bit of fun before classes started up again. She must have hoped her boyfriend, a Navy sailor stationed in Knoxville, would come for supper. Or perhaps she'd climb the Hill to visit with Jo Ann. Yes, and then the girls would sing and sing, the way they loved to do. She bet they'd make time for their favorite hits, all featuring a tight harmony between two female voices, of course: one part for Gail Ann and another for Jo Ann. Maybe they'd start with "Tonight You Belong to Me" (the new Patience and Prudence cover, not the old-timey version made when her grandmother was her age). Then they might twang their way through Eddy Arnold's "Anytime." Or maybe they'd laugh along to Patti Page plaintively asking about that doggie in the window. And they'd do the barks, of course.

But Gail Ann couldn't settle. Nothing seemed right.

Then she felt a distant shudder through the floorboards of the Mt. Sinai sanctuary, a vibration from somewhere deep down in the earth, like when a coal miner set off a charge in a cave connected to the limestone bedrock upon which she sat. The sensation grew stronger. Everyone in the congregation tensed. Soon the rumble became sound. Was it familiar? Maybe? Yes! That was it. It was the grumbling of large engines!

Some in the congregation ran to the church's windows. As Gail Ann stood, she heard the folks already at the windows gasp, kids and adults alike leaning over the sash to get a better view. Gail Ann joined them and could hardly believe what she was seeing. Tanks were pulling into Clinton. Beside her, Gail Ann heard her sister giggle. "Look! Look!" the younger girl shouted.

Gail Ann couldn't think of what to say. Was this help, finally? Real help? For them too? Or would these tanks also be just for the white people downtown?

Next in the convoy were three armored personnel carriers followed by a line of jeeps carrying khaki-suited, helmeted soldiers who braced automatic rifles in their arms. In the back of one jeep, a man was standing, hanging on to a mounted machine gun. He'd looped its ammunition belts over its barrel. Downtown, the handful of people on the streets stared silently at the parade passing by. The vehicles just kept coming.

The soldiers—645 Tennessee National Guardsmen and their officers— hailed from some two hundred miles west, over around Nashville. They'd brought trucks and ambulances to Clinton. They carried with them their own bathing facilities and a complete communication network so patrols could stay in contact with the command center. On Monday, a helicopter would arrive as well.

Governor Frank Clement had summoned them for "Operation Law and Order" just after supper the night before. The Guardsmen canceled their Labor Day plans—homework for their high school calculus classes (Guardsmen could be as young as seventeen), fishing trips with their buddies and hunting trips with their kids, and honey-do lists they'd promised to complete for their wives. One man was supposed to lay the foundation for a new house he hoped to build. Another left a girlfriend in tears when he ducked out on a date she'd been looking forward to. They'd assembled late Saturday night in Crossville, a little town about two-thirds of the way to Clinton, and then been shipped off to the infamous Brushy Mountain State Penitentiary, constructed in 1896 in a mountain hollow just the other side of Oliver Springs to house the convicts working the state's coal mines. Folks around Tennessee knew Brushy was the end of the line, the place judges sent prisoners who were past saving. The Guardsmen went there for a nice, hot breakfast.

After circling through downtown, the National Guardsmen parked their vehicles behind the Memorial Recreation Center, which put them between the courthouse and the high school. Adjutant General Joe Henry made the center his headquarters and first-aid station. He set up satellite administrative offices in the Clinton High band room.

—

The arrival of the Guard in Clinton stopped churches around town mid-service, a relief for some of the white preachers who hadn't really known what to say to their congregations. Perhaps the boldest statement made in a white church in Anderson County that day was a prayer offered up by a layperson in Clinton's white St. Mark's United Methodist Church. "Show us the need to live peacefully together, all men of all races," he'd begged of God.

Over at the white First Baptist Church, the largest congregation in town, the Reverend Paul Turner tried to call his people toward a kinder white supremacy. "It is important to be a Christian first and a segregationist second, not a segregationist first and a Christian second," he told worshipers. Perhaps as he said that, he looked at Willard Till, the founding head of the Anderson County White Citizens' Council and a church leader. "I cannot see how a conscientious Christian can be part of mob violence."

After the service, Paul asked Willard and his wife to come meet with him sometime that week. They needed to talk. A few days later, the three gathered in Paul's church office.

Drop the segregationist activity, Paul begged the couple.

The Tills withdrew their membership from First Baptist instead.

Paul shouldn't have been surprised by the hatred he had seen in Clinton that past week. He'd grown up in a small rural community outside

Memphis, raised on racial inequality and the Baptist Church. Paul (who'd had the call and started preaching before he'd left high school) had come to Clinton straight from seminary. Six feet tall with dark hair, blue eyes, a square chin, and a remarkable charisma, he'd commanded attention. That coupled with his sermons—his were the sort of messages that caused a pew warmer to think about their faith—made him an influential member of the town. Between his arrival in 1948 and the summer of 1956, his church had grown from fewer than nine hundred members to almost fourteen hundred, many pilfered from smaller churches around the county. And he led local campaigns against bootlegging and juvenile delinquency.

Now as he watched his flock attack other Christians, he ruminated on the lessons he'd learned from Olin T. Binkley, his professor at Southern Baptist Theological Seminary who supported integration and the social gospel. Under Olin's guidance, Paul had read about Christian interracial experiments like Koinonia Farm, an integrated community in Georgia where several of Olin's students lived and worked after graduation. Paul had questioned whether racial inequality was as biblically mandated as he thought. He'd wondered what Jesus would say to the American South and its white Christians. It had been an interesting intellectual and spiritual exercise.

When he arrived in Clinton, he tried to implement Olin's ideas without abandoning segregationism. Paul befriended the Reverend O. W. Willis and the two men traded pulpits once a year. Occasionally each also sent his choir to the other's church and they co-hosted missionary group meetings. And when the Black congregation had dedicated their newly constructed $40,000 building a couple years earlier, Paul brought members of his white congregation to the celebration. None of those were revolutionary gestures, but they were steps, right?

Olin Binkley, however, was done with Paul's dithering. He needed his former pupil to take a stand for Jesus and justice. Olin, now the academic dean of Southeastern Baptist Theological Seminary, had too many start-of-term duties to visit Clinton himself, so he sent an emissary, Yale-educated Methodist minister Dr. Roy C. DeLamotte. Roy understood the risks Paul took if he spoke up. A couple years earlier, Roy had lost his pulpit in Jackson, Mississippi, because he'd objected to racial segregation in the Mississippi Methodist Conference. He'd then bounced about Tennessee before settling in Augusta, Georgia, where he and his wife taught at historically Black Paine College.

Roy arrived in Clinton that Sunday in time for Paul's sermon. He heard Paul's mincing, placating appeal for decency before the National Guardsmen's arrival interrupted the final hymn. After the service, Roy privately confronted the younger man.

You are failing to live up to your ministerial vows, Roy told him. Refusing to lead your people into godliness and charity.

Paul replied that he believed his decision to work for peace rather than for a social cause was the godly choice.

Roy disagreed.

—

At noon, about the time the National Guardsmen were unloading their packs, Frank Clement took to the airways to justify his intervention in Clinton. He reassured his audience that he did not support integration. This was about respect for social order. If the rioters "can take over Tennessee because of one issue, they can take it over others," he warned. "It may be your home next."

But what if he had just provoked a more violent response? He invited Nashville's religious leaders to the capitol and asked them to pray for the safety of the National Guard.

The troops spent their Sunday afternoon setting up housing. The largest encampment was at the Anderson County fairgrounds a mile out of town. Another forty men erected quarters on the tennis courts behind the recreation center so they could keep an eye on their machinery. A third contingent bivouacked on the Clinton Dragons' football field, sleeping on the yard lines where the team had won glory just two nights before. Once all the pup tents were erected, the chaplain offered a vesper as a substitute for the services the men'd missed that morning.

By afternoon, downtown bristled with rifles, a show of force meant to overwhelm any would-be troublemakers. The general centered them around the courthouse, doubling the troops up by sending one man to stand on the curb of each street corner and another beside the stone fence just on the other side of the sidewalk. A handful more troops stood at attention in the middle of each block. And patrols of twenty-five men plus a command-ing officer circled past the high school at regular intervals. Joe Henry also announced new regulations to guarantee the peace. No one would park near the courthouse. No public addresses or "outdoor speaking." And start-ing at 5:00 each night, he declared, his men would be manning roadblocks around the city. Those who didn't have to pass through Clinton would be sent on a detour. Those with business in the city would be steered away from the square. No civilians would be on the square after dark.

Some in town questioned whether Joe Henry had the authority to impose martial law like that, dictating that everyone in town abide by his whims. Joe pooh-poohed such quibbling. He was both a soldier and a law-yer. Fact was, he'd been a lawyer first, earning his license to practice in 1940. He'd barely hung out his shingle down in Pulaski, Tennessee, when he'd felt a patriotic conviction. He'd been taught to value justice and freedom, raised to believe it was his duty to defend those ideals wherever they were threatened. He'd enlisted in 1941, joining up even before Pearl Harbor. When the USA entered the war, he'd shipped off to Italy as a private, ready to do his part destroying fascism. He'd ended the war as a major. Back in Tennessee, he'd returned to his office, and he'd supported Frank Clement's political bids. In 1953, Frank had rewarded that loyalty by making him ad-jutant general. In 1956, he'd been promoted to major general. He'd added that second star to all his uniforms and his vehicles. Now he was here in Clinton, ready to again do his part in defeating fascism and hate, this time at home. Not that he was an integrationist, of course. Still, under his watch the National Guard would defend everyone in the city, regardless of their race. Time to teach those so-and-sos terrorizing the people of Clinton a lesson or two about what a real white American looked like.

—

Gail Ann and her little sister were sitting quietly in their home that after-noon when they again felt the rumble of a heavy engine. Gail Ann followed her sister to their upstairs bedroom for a better look. Below them, they saw a jeep full of troops trundle by, men with rifles in one hand clinging to the side of the vehicle with their other arm, trying not to get tumbled into a Clinton ditch. Up on the Hill, a jeep (the same one?) came through, also overspilling with armed white men. Then a tank navigated the neighborhood's narrow, winding streets. The adults on the Hill watched the passing troops from their front porches, but the children—kids who'd spent the past week hiding in Mt. Sinai's basement, praying their neighbors wouldn't kill them—ran into the gardens and onto the driveways to cheer. For the first time, the Hill was one of the best-protected areas in Anderson County. A little while later, Adjutant General Joe Henry himself arrived, in full uniform. He even wore his polished pot helmet with its two shiny stars and metal "H-E-N-R-Y" soldered on the brim. He went door to door, visiting with the twelve Black students. He seated himself in their living rooms, making promises of protection and safety. He asked the Black men to trust him and put away their guns.

A white stringer for the International News Service trailed behind the general, asking the folks living on the Hill how they felt. Several refused to speak with him. If they said what they really thought, they might lose their jobs, they said.

Josephine Allen scolded the reporter. "It's the Sabbath," Josephine said, "and I've been to church to pray and seek consolation. I found my consolation there and don't want to talk to anyone today."

But Bobby's mother, Beatrice, did agree to talk. "All we're asking for is an education," she said. Her son deserved the high school diploma she had not been able to earn.

Then the jeep and the tank and the general left the Hill. As their defenders drove away, some wondered what this would mean for other Black people in the county. If the mobs couldn't terrorize the Hill, where would they go next? At least the men in Clinton lived close enough that they could put together a guard. Would the others be so prepared?

—

That evening, about 150 protestors stuffed themselves into tiny Blowing Springs Grammar School, three miles north of Clinton. Another forty or fifty milled around outside. Hearing about the gathering, *Life* magazine's Richard Stolley and Robert W. Kelley went to get a look. They were met by angry white men who chased them back to their cars, hurling rocks and shouting, "Nigger lovers!" and "We'll break your damn cameras if you try to take any pictures!" The reporters retreated. A little while later, another group of newsmen approached. This time, the segregationists had set up a roadblock to keep journalists away. Two men guarded it, throwing rocks at the cars. But the virulent segregationists hadn't surrendered Clinton yet. Just after dark, they made their way back to the square. Within an hour, the crowd numbered well over a thousand, maybe fifteen hundred, maybe two thousand, perhaps as many as three thousand, depending on who you asked. Despite Joe Henry's warnings, the National Guard did not stop them.

A little after eight that evening, nineteen-year-old sailor James Chandler walked onto the square in his naval uniform. He knew about the trouble that had happened over the past week, of course. That was why he was here, really. After all the hullabaloo, he'd needed to check on his girlfriend, Gail Ann—just needed to see her face and make sure she was doing all right. When he'd heard the National Guard had come and General Henry had made new rules for the town, he had assumed he'd be safe to visit. Now he saw that was a serious miscalculation. When his bus arrived from Knoxville at 4:00, the only white men he'd seen had been the National Guard troops. Now the white people on the edge of the crowd noticed him and began to shout. His uniform infuriated them. Someone threw a glass soda bottle, shattering it right at James's feet. He felt an urge to run, but wouldn't that make the mob even angrier? Give them the scent of his blood? He forced himself to keep the cadence of his steps steady.

He felt the white people falling in behind him. How many were following? He would not turn around and look.

"Let's get him!" some shouted, and "He's ours!"

James wouldn't make it to the bus station; he felt the certainty in his guts. Maybe he'd have had a shot if he'd come in civies, but a Black man in uniform? In the past decade, white mobs all over the country—in Texas, Alabama, Michigan, California, New York—had assaulted and even murdered Black soldiers for the crime of wearing their uniforms. James tried not to think about the many ways other Black men had died when they'd miscalculated white people's racist fury.

And then there was a trooper beside him, a rifle in his hands. Just one white man against the many, but that was better than facing the mob alone. In the distance, the Guardsman's partner was roaring off in their jeep, calling for backup. The lone National Guardsman shuffled James into a gas station and stood guard outside. The white rabble was a little more hesitant to attack a white boy-soldier, so he kept the jeering mob at bay just long enough for a convoy of five jeeps stuffed with his fellow Guardsmen to extricate them both. No bus for James that night. The soldiers drove him back to Knoxville.

As James left town, Joe Henry sent three hundred Guardsmen—about half his force—to the square to end the insurgency. True to his word, Joe sent his men in fully armed. Before they left, he told them to load live cartridges into their rifles and affix their bayonets. He couldn't have the protestors threatening men in uniform, not even when the uniform was being worn by a Black man. And he also couldn't have the people of Clinton so openly defying his new orders. When the troops reached the square, they arranged themselves in two long lines to face off against the crowd. The sight of three hundred armed men, the lights of the Ritz Theater glinting off their lacquered steel pot helmets, was enough for some. The older ones and the more careful ones, they began to disperse. Others, though, were riled up by these young white men set to drive them out of their own town square. They yelled insults and spat epithets. They shouted out fake commands, trying to rattle the more inexperienced Guardsmen, the troopers freshly turned seventeen and not yet graduated from high school. Well-trained, the soldiers stood still. Kids threw firecrackers at them. The troops stayed in position. So then the town's teenage boys formed their own line and advanced on the Guardsmen. They pressed forward, leaning against the soldiers' bayonets, daring the men to either retreat or respond. Still, Joe Henry's men held their line. By midnight, the bulk of the crowd had had enough, but the teenage protestors stayed on the square, jeering and dancing and taunting the Guardsmen until about 1:00 a.m.

And behind the soldiers' backs, another contingent of white supremacists had skirted the patrols and ducked onto the Clinton High School campus. There they'd erected a large cross on the sidewalk. Then they'd set it alight. The flames went out before the firemen arrived.

—

Over in Oliver Springs, someone in town—no one was quite sure who'd said it first, but it sure seemed believable enough to spread—some unnamed source, had heard from a reliable authority that Black teenagers were planning to desegregate the Oliver Springs High School over the coming week. Didn't matter that the number was at most a handful,* any integration was cause for a fight. And wouldn't you know, that was the school run by the father of Clinton High's principal. Why, he was likely to open the school doors!

And so on Sunday night, one hundred white residents gathered in downtown Oliver Springs, a small district where most everything needed in entertainment, food, or shopping happened within three city blocks. On this night, though, all the usual business was suspended while the white people handled this much more important issue. This wouldn't happen in their town, they pledged. If anyone tried to make them go the way of Clinton, blood would run in the streets.

Joe Henry wanted to send a few jeeps over to Oliver Springs to check up on things, but with the problems in Clinton, he didn't have many men to spare. He didn't want to splinter his troops into units too small to defend themselves. He had reason to be wary. Some ninety miles southwest of Clinton, two members of a different National Guard unit were driving toward Chattanooga that evening for a routine drill when five white men stopped their car and forced the soldiers onto the roadside.

"Are you on your way to Clinton?" one of the civilians asked the soldiers.

"No," the Guardsman replied. "We're on our way to drill."

"Would you go to Clinton if they ordered you to?"

"Yes," he replied.

At that, the man drew his knife and attacked, cutting one of the soldiers viciously about the face. The other he slashed in the leg, a wound so deep it took thirty-two stitches to close.

---

* Out of the 1,163 people living in Oliver Springs in 1960, only 62 were Black.

TEN

How to Dodge a Lynch Mob

Labor Day morning, the white members of Magnet Knitting Mills' American Federation of Hosiery Workers woke up early, downed their coffees, and hustled their kids through their morning routines. They were off for their annual holiday picnic. This day marked ten years since the mill had unionized, so it should've been more special than usual, a celebration of a hard-won victory against the bosses, but as the workers drove out of town they were forced to yield and even pull off the road for tanks rumbling along the streets. They passed a barricaded checkpoint staffed by armed guards directing holidayers and rubberneckers alike away from Clinton. Already the line of cars stretched miles down the highway. Could they get back into their town? And would the soldiers believe they were residents and not outsiders? When union members arrived at the park, far away from all the foofaraw at last, a pall still loomed over the day. As the kids climbed trees and skipped rope, the adults gossiped. Who'd gone downtown? What had they seen? Wait, was anybody here part of that there Home Guard that had thrown grenades at the protestors? And hadn't the last week shown how different some folks felt about the troubles that had come to Clinton! Hopefully by next Labor Day life in Clinton would be back to normal. Maybe. How that'd happen, though, well, wasn't that anybody's guess? This thing sure would be damn hard for anyone to forget.

—

Adjutant General Joe Henry woke up Labor Day morning ready to win the battle for Clinton's streets. After a short meeting with the mayor and the Board of Aldermen, he called a press conference. As of that moment, he announced to the twenty-two assembled reporters, he'd be enforcing his rules. No more milling about on the courthouse lawn.

The reporters jumped in, shouting questions over each other. What was going to happen tomorrow? Would the National Guard be at the school? Would they allow picket lines? Would they arrest any and all protestors?

Well, now, Joe Henry replied, the Guard would be over there at the school on Tuesday morning, and they'd be keeping an eye on things.

Would the Guard escort the Black students?

No, no, there'd be no formal escort, but the Guard would be on hand. They were there to protect every resident's life and property.

But what if a picket line formed?

A picket line? On that, the general would just have to wait and see. He didn't think a small picket line would be a violation, but of course anything that got too large or out of hand would be a different situation.

What would make a picket line too large?

It couldn't impede anyone entering the school.

What about the Guardsmen who'd been downtown last night? Where were they now?

Well, the men were sleepy after the excitement of the weekend, but by evening they'd be ready for action. And they weren't there to bother the townspeople, only there to keep the peace.

Is this martial law? one reporter eventually asked.

Not at all, the general replied.

Joe Henry's decrees appeared to do their job. On Labor Day, Clinton was quiet for the first time in over a week. It might not have felt like peace, what with the turreted tanks trundling by. No, the day wasn't peaceful, but even this tense quiet was a relief. As evening neared, however, the National Guardsmen prepared for potential upsurgences. When they saw neighbors hailing each other downtown, the soldiers stepped up and asked that the townspeople keep it moving, in a polite and friendly way, of course, with plenty of "sirs" and "ma'ams" and "pleases." Most civilians obeyed and went home. A few ducked into Hoskins Drug Store, which had a record-setting day of business selling Cokes and chocolate milkshakes and hamburgers to the curious.

Other businesses in town, though, were suffering because of the chaos. An owner of another café who also ran two gas stations was about to list two of his businesses for sale. "No tourist in his right mind would stop here after all the hell that's been raised," he told a reporter for the *Baltimore Afro-American*. "If I can get my money out, I'm leaving." A novelty store owner said he hadn't earned enough in the past week to even cover his light bill, and a taxi driver said he hadn't had a single fare since the trouble started.

But maybe all that was about to get better since, true to Joe Henry's word, no one but the Guard stepped foot on the courthouse lawn. Well, just after dusk a group of about fifty folks tried to gather, but the soldiers quickly dispersed them. The protestors left without making a fuss.

The journalists sat in their makeshift headquarters in the front of the Southern Bell Telephone Office, waiting for action. The photographers had managed to grab some pictures of the tanks rumbling around this small mountain town, but the writers were going to need a story to keep their editors happy. They would give it a day, or maybe two, before they headed off in search of the next headline.

By 10:00 that night, many folks in Clinton felt safe enough to go to bed. But they were awakened an hour later by the sound of a convoy of armed vehicles speeding out of town, pushing their overburdened engines as fast as the machines could go. Clinton might have been quiet, but Oliver Springs had exploded. Rumor was, someone had even been shot! Joe Henry ordered his men to "lock and load," driving into town with their weapons armed with live cartridges. Eighty men and a tank should be enough, he calculated.

The members of the Southern War Correspondents Association grabbed their notebooks and their cameras and hurried to join the caravans heading east on SR61. Though they left after the deployed Guardsmen, the journalists managed to beat the soldiers to Oliver Springs, passing the tank and the jeeps in their faster civilian automobiles.

Seven miles outside town, SR61 took a sharp right, veering through a mountain pass. Though the soldiers were supposed to have spent their free time catching up on sleep, the man driving the tank hadn't yet recovered from the hours he'd missed over the weekend. He was drifting off when he reached the turn. He veered into the Mountain View Service Station, ran straight over one of the pumps, hit one of the business's lights, and took off part of its sign. He then plunged the tank down a small embankment and drove across a neighbor's lawn before he made it back onto the highway. Debris from the tank and bits of the gas pump and glass from the light were strewn across the service station's parking lot and the neighbor's grass. The driver never stopped. He left it to the neighbor to call the gas station's owner and let him know. The businessman wasn't quite sure what he was going to do about the repairs. He owned the building, but the gas pump was on lease from the petrol company. Could he get money from the state for damages incurred in the line of duty?

—

D. J. Brittain Sr.—principal of Oliver Springs High School and father of Clinton High's principal—thought the rumor about Oliver Springs High's pending desegregation was a new plot to hurt his son, a plan by the White Citizens' Council to divide the Brittain family, alienating father from son by pointing out one man had desegregated his school while the other had stood firm. However it had started, that gossip had festered and spread. Two hundred and fifty or perhaps five hundred white people had gathered in front of the theater down by the railroad tracks to listen to speakers shout about their Southern heritage. Police officers from Oliver Springs called the sheriffs of Roane and Anderson Counties for help. When the mob outgrew the combined forces' efforts to contain it, they reached out to the local highway patrol. Next had come the call to Joe Henry.

When the first squad of Guardsmen arrived in town, the troopers lined up on one side of Main Street, again facing off against jeering white civilians across a town's thoroughfare. The photojournalists jumped into the gap between the two groups to document the standoff. The sight of these men snip-snapping away outraged many of the protestors. The mob attacked two reporters from the *Tennessean*. The journalists only escaped because the soldiers extricated them and took them back to Clinton in protective custody. Bob Kelley of *Life* magazine was taking photographs from on top of one of the National Guard jeeps when five men came toward him carrying shotguns. He jumped to the ground ready to flee. Instead, he broke his leg. Rather than helping him, the men smashed his camera, an

$800 loss. Terror-stricken, other photographers stashed their cameras in their cars or under bushes. Then the mob turned on the soldiers. A highway patrolman radioed back to Clinton, telling General Henry to send more backup. "They're as mad at the Guard down here as much as they are at the Negroes," he warned. Joe gathered up a few more men and set off for Oliver Springs to oversee the situation himself.

That's when William Capshaw, L. T. Spraggins, and two friends returned to Oliver Springs from a weekend-long squirrel-hunting expedition. When they'd left a few days earlier, they'd assumed that they would be fine if they avoided downtown Clinton. In fact, the mountains might be about the safest place for young Black men while the white folks marched and rioted in the county seat. They hadn't heard the rumor about Oliver Springs' own school desegregation, and no one had a way to warn them. Now they found themselves in the middle of the white mob. They sped out of Oliver Springs as the crowd hurled rocks at the vehicle. After dropping off their friends, L. T. and William faced a choice. Would they drive miles out of their way on a detour back home to Oak Ridge or would they attempt to again cross through downtown? They'd made it the first time, right? Surely, they'd be OK a second time.

L. T. started back down Main Street. One white man on the perimeter of the crowd began beating on his car. Others joined. They shook the automobile, rocking it on its axles, lifting the wheels all the way off the ground and then letting the vehicle fall back onto the pavement. L. T. inched his way through the rioters and pulled away from the mob. Then he got out of his car and shouted back toward the segregationists. "What are you doing?" he asked.

"Better get out of here!" one man warned him. Others called him a series of hateful and predictable names.

L. T. hopped back in his car and sped away, but three autos stuffed with white people followed. SR61 between Oliver Springs and Oak Ridge was a winding, twisting path notoriously popular with drag racers, who frequently crashed while speeding around its corners. In other words, it was the sort of route where enraged white men could force a Black driver into a fatal wreck and have it ruled an accident. Maybe that's why L. T. swung his car off 61 just east of Oliver Springs. Safer to try to lose his trackers on a dark country road. The white men turned too. He was close to a friend's home. Maybe he and William would find shelter there. He pulled into the driveway and the two men ran for the porch, hoping to get inside before they were seen. They weren't fast enough. One of the white men pulled his vehicle across the friend's driveway. The white passengers surrounded L. T.'s car and began to vandalize it. L. T. started down the porch steps to try to stop them. Someone shot at him. He fired back with his squirrel-hunting rifle, shooting without aiming. He just wanted to buy himself enough time to run into the weeds and hide. One of his pellets struck sixty-year-old Jack Payne in the arm.

Or that's what L. T. told the *Oak Ridger*. William gave the *Clinton Courier-News* a different account. He said he had been the one to grab his shotgun and that L. T. had been holding a pistol. L. T. fired at the ground to scare the men away, but William shot toward the advancing posse. One of his shotgun pellets had struck the retired coal miner in the right biceps.

Perhaps the men were trying to protect each other by both claiming credit or maybe, in the confusion, they genuinely did not know whose gun had shot Jack Payne.

No matter who shot the rifle, a white man had been injured. This could mean death. Both William and L. T. got back in the car, somehow outmaneuvering the blockade of people after them. The pair sped away. The white mob chased them, their numbers swelling as word spread, perhaps reaching six hundred strong. The Roane County sheriff and the local highway patrol joined in. At one point, the sheriff and a patrolman thought they'd spotted the men's car hidden in an Oliver Springs alleyway, but when they followed the car its passengers reportedly fired upon the lawmen before squealing away. The sheriff gave chase, following the vehicle back into the Anderson County countryside. When the car finally stopped, he cautiously approached the automobile, wary lest the men shoot again, but William and L. T. had disappeared, losing themselves in the woods. The white mob descended and surrounded the grove, trying to hem the two Black men in. They carried shotguns, pistols, and clubs. But the National Guard had regrouped, its ranks filled out with additional men and the general himself. Joe Henry tried to reason with the crowd, begging them to go home. The Black men would face prosecution, he promised; they could entrust justice to him. A few gave in and headed out. Most stayed where they were.

"Can we have our hands on that nigger just one time?" one of the crowd asked Joe.

Those who wouldn't listen would have to respect force. The general told his soldiers to break up the would-be lynching party. The Guardsmen plunged into the melee, forcing them back to their cars and then herding them toward their homes. Fifteen armed white men resisted, so troopers took the group into custody and shipped them to the Clinton jail, holding them without bond on charges of breaching the peace. Every one of the men arrested was a local. One was forty-six. The rest were between seventeen and thirty-one years of age.

Though the white rioters had been dispersed, they weren't finished. Earlier that night, the folks in the tiny Black section of Oliver Springs had been jolted awake (if they'd managed to fall asleep) by a blast of dynamite. Then another. And another. And then a fourth. And a fifth. No property damage was done; that wasn't the point. The bombers meant to terrorize, and they accomplished their mission. These were the first bombings of the campaign to take back Clinton High.

Another contingent of white men marched over to Harlan Sisson's house and fired up a six-foot cross wrapped in rags and soaked in kerosene. Harlan, a white man who owned the general store in Oliver Springs, had nothing to do with the events in Clinton, but his brother was a member of the Anderson County school board. The cross was a message for the family.

Still, the *Clinton Courier-News* did manage to find one bright spot in the weekend's events. Thanks to the looky-loos and the holiday travelers and the roadblocks, cars had often gone no more than ten miles an hour as they traversed Anderson County. For the first Labor Day in recent memory, there hadn't been a single traffic death.

ELEVEN

Learning the Rules

At 7:30 on Tuesday morning, the day after Labor Day, a car pulled away from a small frame house in Oliver Springs. The Black man at the wheel probably tried to look relaxed, his wife perhaps fidgeting as the sun edged its way over Walden Ridge. Nothing to see here. Nope. Just their usual commute, him shuttling her to her job in Oak Ridge before heading to his own workplace. But every move must've felt a little too stilted, a bit too practiced. This commute was not normal. This morning, they had L. T. Spraggins hidden in their car. Was he crouched in the back seat? Shut in the trunk? Wherever they'd stuffed him, he was their refugee. They were smuggling him out of Oliver Springs and back into Oak Ridge.

During the night, L. T. had separated from William Capshaw. He'd waited in the woods until he saw a light flicker on at his friend's home. And for the first time in hours, L. T.'s luck held. No one saw him creep onto their back porch and tap lightly on the door. No one glimpsed him slide into their car. Now no one paid the vehicle a never mind as it puttered out of Oliver Springs. But in a small county, L. T. knew he'd be recognized. His luck was temporary. He turned himself in to the Oak Ridge police at 9:59 a.m. William Capshaw had snuck back into Oak Ridge too. Hoping to escape, he'd boarded one of the morning buses to Knoxville. When the bus stopped in downtown Clinton, however, he was seen. Two Anderson County deputies arrested him there a few minutes before 10:00. Both men were charged with felonious assault and attempted murder.

Sheriff Glad Woodward had his men, but that meant he was now responsible for keeping them alive long enough to stand trial. Could he guarantee their safety? Kidnapping and lynching Black men held in custody was a long-standing and ongoing vigilante tradition in the South. Just nineteen years earlier, the sheriff of Tipton County, Tennessee, had been forced off the road by six armed, masked white men. One of them shouted, "To hell with the law!" as they seized Albert Gooden, a Black man accused of shooting a white policeman. They hung Albert from a bridge, shot him more than thirty times, cut him down, and left his body partly submerged in the creek. Five years later, a seventeen-year-old inmate at Tennessee's reformatory facility for Black teenage boys was kidnapped from custody by eight to ten white men who took him to the home of the school superintendent and shot him to death on the front lawn for allegedly assaulting the superintendent's wife and killing his daughter. The school's white bookkeeper said the mob had wanted to hang the boy on school grounds, but the assistant superintendent convinced them to take him to the site of the crime. After killing him, his attackers left his body where it lay. The other incarcerated teens were then paraded past his corpse.

And in the fall of '56, Jesse Woods—a Black Floridian accused of saying, "Hey, honey," or maybe, "Hey, baby," to a white teacher—was arrested for insulting her. When his family came to pay his fifty-dollar bond, they noticed white men skulking about, so they left Jesse in jail for his protection. A few hours later, the only officer in the building went to gas up his patrol car, leaving the jail unguarded. When he returned, Jesse was gone. Inside his cell were signs of a struggle: an overturned bunk and walls splattered with blood. A few days later, investigators found Jesse's blood-soaked cotton plaid shirt and black felt hat about three and a half blocks from the jail. Many assumed Jesse was dead, but somehow after a severe flogging with a leather strap he escaped and made his way to friends who spirited him over state lines into Alabama. There he hid out with a Black pastor and recovered from his injuries.

Glad Woodward didn't want the Black students at Clinton High, but neither did he want William Capshaw and L. T. Spraggins dead, especially not on his watch. Just in case the lynch mobs came for his prisoners, the sheriff drove them to the Knoxville jail, locking them up in the same building (though not the same cell) as John Kasper, who was still awaiting his bond hearing. While there, they, too, became subjects for *Life* photographer Howard Sochurek's growing collection of portraits from Clinton, standing in their shirtsleeves, unsmiling by the facility's barred walls and reinforced windows.

—

That Tuesday morning, twenty-four-year-old Woody Joe Duncan had awoken on the wrong side of the bars for the first time in his life. Born in Oliver Springs to circuit court clerk Woody O. Duncan and his wife, Nola, Woody Joe was the youngest of ten boys and two girls. After graduating from Clinton High, he'd entered the family business: the military. All nine of his brothers and both brothers-in-law had served before him. Two of them—twins—had been at Pearl Harbor on December 7, 1941. Three others were wounded in combat during World War II. Their commitment was so notable even President Franklin D. Roosevelt had lauded the family's allegiance to their country. All that to say, the family's patriotism wasn't at 100 percent, Woody Joe's Air Force recruiter told a Knoxville paper when he enlisted. It was 110 percent. Woody Joe was so fervent that he'd convinced three friends to enlist with him. And he did the family proud: he became a decorated war hero for his time in Korea.

After being discharged, Woody Joe had bounced around jobs. He ran to be a district squire, which was like being a county magistrate, but he lost. Next, he was a police officer, first in Oliver Springs and then in Clinton. After he resigned those positions, he went to work in his brother Kyle's trucking business. But even out of public service, Woody Joe knew he was the same as he'd always been, a true patriot and an excellent citizen. Now he thought back over the preceding night. Those very qualities had landed him in jail. How was that justice?

The first dynamite blast in Oliver Springs had exploded while he was on a drive-in movie date with his girlfriend. Always a gentleman, he'd seen her home before investigating. Concerned by the size of the crowd, he went up to some of the highway patrol officers to see if they needed help. Way he figured it, once a law enforcement officer, always a law enforcement officer. They told him to get his gun. They told him to help keep the peace. And that was what he'd been doing, hunting down those two attempted murderers. So why was he now locked up with his brother Ivan and thirteen other white men from Oliver Springs? He'd just been ensuring the two Black men got the justice they had coming.

—

While Woody Joe stewed over his fate, U.S. Marshal Frank Quarles trudged toward Clinton High School, maybe feeling a few of his fifty-eight years after the excitement of the past week. Raised the other side of Knoxville, he'd been a lawman for much of his working life, first as a sheriff's deputy and then as a sheriff and now as a U.S. Marshal. He'd also served as a floterial Republican representative to the state senate during World War II. In all those years of public service, had he ever thought he'd see this day, when he—a good white Southerner—would tell a schoolful of white kids how to treat the Black students studying at desks alongside them? Some 150 white teenagers met him at the west side doors. Already accustomed to the demands of the national press, one of them crouched down so the newsman behind him could see Frank standing bareheaded above the kids, reading the court injunction aloud to them.

As the marshal finished, the Black teenagers pulled up, chauffeured safely there in their parents' cars. Only nine of them had come to school that morning. Some said the other three were home because their parents had decided desegregation wasn't worth it. Not true, Assistant Principal Juanita Moser discovered. One girl was sick with an asthma attack, and two boys hadn't yet returned from their Labor Day vacation. As the nine walked through the school doors, a few of the white boys called out jeers and obscenities at them in defiance of Frank Quarles.

Only 266 white students followed them inside. A full two-thirds of the white teenagers enrolled at Clinton High had stayed home that day. Principal D. J. Brittain Jr. thought most of the students were afraid. He'd heard about the phone calls and the other threats white parents had received. He knew how bad his own harassment had been. Because of that, he would not be turning anyone over to the truancy officer. Not yet. But he warned that they would fall behind. Classes were continuing.

The teachers tried to forge ahead as though everything was normal. The tension, however, disrupted learning. In one class that day, Jo Ann chose the desk nearest the door. She sat with her chin in her hand, listening to the teacher's lecture while perhaps also planning how she would escape if necessary. Bobby sat next to her, his arms crossed. The only other student in the room was a white girl who sat two rows over and four desks up. She angled her feet toward the windows and leaned as far away from the Black students as she could.

At least the sounds outside the school had changed. Instead of the shouts of the protestors, students now heard the rhythmic ticking of tank plates on pavement filtering through the open windows as the M-41s paraded past the school. Maybe they still startled at a raised voice, but on this day it was just instructions shouted by the soldiers who popped out of the turrets' hatches, watching for pedestrians and stray kids on bikes. The teens might've relaxed in the sudden silence when the tanks parked a block away from them, forming an impenetrable cordon between the school and the courthouse. Then they'd have heard the troops crawl through the hatches to lounge on top of the armored vehicles, laughing and smoking. Maybe they even listened in when the white townspeople stopped to chat with the soldiers, asking questions about the weapons or reminiscing about their own time in service or heckling the men for protecting the Black teens or flirting with the cute guys decked out in khaki.

Just after lunch, the National Guard headquarters received a tip: there was a bomb on Clinton High's campus. Without evacuating the students and teachers, a contingent of troops searched the building. They found nothing. Classes continued. When the school day ended, the Black students walked through the front doors of the school rather than sneaking through a side exit. Anna Theresser Caswell was relieved. She'd even managed to get some actual schoolwork done! Now she balanced on her crutches and waited for the school bus from Green McAdoo to pick her up on its way out of town, standing under the watchful eye of a team of National Guardsmen who had stationed their tank on the corner. The men would be there every afternoon they were in town, sent by Joe Henry to make sure she had no trouble.

That same Tuesday morning, students in Oak Ridge started their school year, a week behind the kids in Clinton. Just like the year before, the Oak Ridge schools were integrated. There was no racist trouble reported.

Students in Oliver Springs High School also came back to class. No Black students attempted to transfer in, but just so everyone was clear, Principal D. J. Brittain Sr. announced he would not be accepting any students trying to desegregate the school. If they wanted an integrated education, they could do what the students in Clinton did and sue the county for it. Seven Black students in Knoxville did attempt to enroll in white schools. They were turned away.

—

Midafternoon, Kyle and another Duncan brother begged Adjutant General Joe Henry for Woody Joe and Ivan's release.

No, Joe said.

Would the general at least set a bond for them?

Absolutely not, he replied. He would be holding those men, and he would hold them without bond, until peace was restored.

What if the older brothers promised to keep the troublemakers busy in the trucking firm? Kyle asked.

Joe Henry still didn't relent.

This didn't sit well back in Oliver Springs. A few hours later, about two hundred and fifty or maybe five hundred or perhaps six hundred white folks gathered downtown to protest. The crowd began to get riled when a carload of Black travelers tried to sneak through on SR61. Some catcalled the visitors. A few kicked at the vehicle as it sped away. The mood turned. If the crowd couldn't get their fifteen white men out of jail, then they wanted to get their hands on "those Negroes" who had started it all. Imagine shooting a white man and thinking you could get away with it. Time to "spring" them from jail. But William Capshaw and L. T. Spraggins were a safe distance away thanks to Glad Woodward's prescience.

Oliver Springs' night police chief worried that the situation would get out of control and others would be attacked in their stead. Forty-eight National Guardsmen were already in Oliver Springs, just in case, but as he looked at the crowd, that seemed insufficient to him. He called for more. Joe Henry responded by sending two truckloads of men and two jeeps with mounted machine guns. The locals booed the soldiers as they arrived at about 9:00 that night.

As the extra troopers pulled up, *Life* photographer Don Cravens made a dangerous error. He had wormed his way deep into the crowd, using the chaos and confusion and darkness to shoot pictures from amid the masses, presumably increasing his ISO enough he didn't need to use a flash. Then one of the locals saw him checking an exposure reading. They had a journalist in their midst! A couple dozen men took off after Don, yelling death threats. Other photographers stationed on the edge of the crowd snapped their own images of the scene, provoking more mayhem.

Joe Henry was fed up. Go home! he told the crowd. Then he looked at the journalists behind him. The next person to take a picture would be going to jail, where he could sit alongside all the other folks arrested for disturbing the peace in Anderson County.

By 10:30 that night, everyone—protestors and troops and journalists included—had disappeared from the streets. Woody Joe and the others still sat in jail, but no one else from Oliver Springs had joined them.

Over in Oak Ridge, however, the Black community had heard the mob from Oliver Springs would be coming their way. Seventy-five or perhaps one hundred gathered to protect themselves from the attack that never materialized. Most folks scattered when the police arrived, but five Black men stood their ground. They were arrested and charged with threatening a breach of the peace. They were taken to jail in Clinton.

That night, two Black students were hung in effigy at Knoxville's all-white Fulton High. The people who strung up the ten-foot-tall stuffed rag dolls hung signs from their necks: "This is Fulton's first nigger, and the last. Amen." And "This is Fulton's first nigger. Who's next?"

—

Wednesday morning, 324 students—including all 12 of the Black teens—showed up at Clinton High School. Again, the white students gathered in front of the school. When the Black pupils arrived just in time for the opening bell, they had to walk single file through their white peers, but for the first time since opening day no one shouted any racial slurs at them. All they could hear were a few muttering, "Here they come."

A journalist with one of the national wire services asked Principal D. J. Brittain Jr. his goal for the school year. "I must be fair to all," he replied.

D. J. turned away from the files piled on his desk and away from the journalist across from him. He stared through his window toward downtown, where he could see both the jail and the courthouse. The morning light threw the bruising circles sleeplessness had carved below his eyes into deep relief. "I have been in Anderson County just about all my adult life," he said softly in his deep voice. "I know many of the people" fighting for segregation, fighting me, D. J. continued. He'd been predestined to be an educator, though once he'd hoped to be anything but a teacher. It was his fate. "My father, D. J. Brittain, has been principal of Oliver Springs High School for thirty years," he said. And there was his uncle the superintendent, his mother the teacher, his wife who also taught. "I had always thought that schoolwork was the last thing in the world I wanted to do, but as I grew older, I saw that it was the thing I knew most about." And he knew he'd been a good principal. Look at his accomplishments: two consecutive conference football titles, rising enrollment, growing numbers of graduates, new accreditations, better facilities. All seemed at risk now, however, his plans for Clinton High sacrificed for other people's dreams. D. J. watched the townspeople going about their business, trying to ignore the National Guardsmen staked out around the square. "I am abiding by the laws of the land," D. J. concluded. "I cannot do anything but abide by the law."

—

At the recreation center/National Guard headquarters across the street, Adjutant General Joe Henry also met with the press that morning to reiterate his guidelines. No one was to step foot on Clinton High's campus except for students, teachers, administrators, and parents, he announced. And yes, that meant journalists were to stay away. He'd had enough of this "carnival atmosphere" the newsmen encouraged with their pictures and their interviews and their antics.

Had he heard that some of the Oliver Springs ruffians had announced he had until 7:00 p.m. to free the fifteen white men arrested there or else? a journalist asked him.

They were welcome to try, he replied. What he didn't say was he'd already arrested the man delivering that ultimatum, charging him with attempted breach of the peace.

The journalists didn't have to go to Clinton High to get that day's story. Around about noon, the National Guardsmen lined up Woody Joe Duncan and the rest of the Oliver Springs prisoners. Wynona McSwain had neither the space at the jail nor the supplies needed to feed them all lunch, so a local restaurant had prepared cafeteria-style trays for the men. The troopers marched the guys across the street and then made them crouch in a rain-soaked parking lot where they ate off trays balanced on their knees or set on the ground. Soldiers guarded the perimeter, most propping bayonetted rifles on their hip bones. One man slung his rifle across his back so he could smoke a cigarette. Then they marched the men back to the jail. As they reentered the prison, the policeman counting up the flatware discovered he was missing a spoon. No one needed a shiv in the back. As the Guardsmen frisked the prisoners, *Tennessean* photojournalist Jack Corn bent low to snap images of the search. One of the men, a nineteen-year-old kid, lunged at Jack, trapping the photographer between a spindly shrub and the brick wall of the jail, knocking Jack about the head and face. A blow to the left side of Jack's face broke the skin across his cheekbones. Seeing the blood he'd drawn, the prisoner pulled his fist back for another go. One of the sentries coldcocked Jack's attacker with his rifle butt.

As a Guard dragged the prisoner up, he turned toward Jack. "I'm getting tired of having my picture taken and put in the papers like a dog," he said.

Wanna press charges? one of the Guardsmen asked Jack Corn.

No, Jack replied. "I guess this is what you would loosely call an occupational hazard." He paused so the stringer from the AP could photograph his busted cheekbone and the trail of blood flowing down his angular face and dripping onto his starched white collar. "You guys want my press agent to make a statement?" he joked to his colleagues. Then he picked up his camera and got back to work. Some of his coworkers at the *Tennessean*, appalled at how one of their own had been treated, would write about this event repeatedly over the coming weeks. Most other magazines and newspapers ignored the abuse the reporters were taking. The journalists were never supposed to be the story.

—

At 8:00 p.m., an hour after the deadline imposed by the Oliver Springs contingent, Joe Henry released his fifteen white prisoners. (No civilian would be giving him an ultimatum.) Before the inmates stepped out of the door, the Guard's executive officer spoke to the gathered reporters. "We are not going to protect them from you," he warned, "and we are not going to protect you from them." The prisoners walked through the assembled journalists peacefully, but three of their relatives attacked a cameraman from NBC and a photographer from Telenews. The armed National Guardsmen stood by and watched. Later, the Guard's press officer told the upset newsmen they were overreacting. "We were about to move in," he claimed. "We wouldn't have let it get out of hand." The men from Oliver Springs climbed into two cars brought over by the Duncan brothers. A reporter from the *Knoxville Journal* followed the cars back to the town where a crowd of about two hundred people had gathered to celebrate their return. For a while, the writer hid in the crowd, but when he stepped into a service station to buy a soft drink someone recognized him. Men surrounded him. One carried a blackjack, or a leather billy club. They "escorted" him through the crowd and back to his vehicle, all while smashing their fists into his jaw and the back of his neck. When they let him go, he sought out hospital treatment to seal his wounds.

At 10:00 that night, Joe Henry released the man who had threatened mob violence if the National Guard did not make his 7:00 p.m. deadline. Then he sent home two hundred Guardsmen (or about a third of his contingent). Some needed to get back to jobs or families, but most were high school football players wanting to play in their Friday night games.

TWELVE

Vining Out

And then Anderson County settled down. Or gave up. Or seemed to. Or maybe folks had just changed what their measure of too much disturbance was. The segregationist meetings and rallies certainly continued, but they no longer felt like riots, now that the white folks in Clinton knew what a real riot felt like. So, yes, most white people agreed, things were better. After a few days of that good-enough peace, the Guardsmen left in Clinton reported they were bored, and not all of them were standing guard when they were at a post. What could you expect of a seventeen-year-old sent to monitor a street corner for hours at a time? Some took breaks at Hoskins Drug Store, drinking milkshakes and flirting with the local girls. Others snuck off to see movies.

As the news of the city's respite spread, folks outside Clinton questioned how bad the situation had really been. Who'd ever heard of a serious civil uprising shut down in a couple days? Maybe Governor Frank Clement had overreacted, they said. Or maybe Clinton officials had exaggerated their situation and the governor was too quick to believe them. Yes, that seemed right: the Anderson County sheriff was weak, the mayor was a ninny, and the governor was their pigeon.

Angry at the suggestion he'd been suckered, on Thursday, September 6, Frank Clement wrote a scolding letter to Glad Woodward, the sheriff sworn into office during the rioting, and sent it by special courier. Glad received it at six that evening. Within an hour, he had assembled county leaders. The National Guard was in town at the governor's orders, so Frank's displeasure meant their protection would end soon. The mayor and Board of Aldermen authorized the city to hire six more police officers, doubling their force, but when faced with thousands of rioters, twelve men was hardly better than six. The sheriff reactivated eighty-nine former law enforcement officials, calling anyone who'd ever been a sheriff's deputy or police officer or member of the military police to report to his office before 6:00 p.m. on Sunday to be deputized. Ironically, one of the men who received this notice would've been Woody Joe Duncan.

While Glad Woodward was scrambling to assemble his deputy force, the members of the Southern War Correspondents Association received an unexpected notice. Woody Joe Duncan, his brother Kyle, and three other men arrested in Oliver Springs wanted to meet with the press. The journalists tentatively agreed. Twenty-four newsmen met the contingent in the makeshift press room in the telephone offices, facing off across the desks. John Popham of the *New York Times* moderated.

The real problem, Woody Joe explained, was that the men in Oliver Springs had been double-crossed by the police. The officers had encouraged them to arm themselves because the Black fugitives had guns. And then they'd let the Guardsmen arrest the locals for carrying guns. The fifteen men who'd volunteered to help instead were locked up where they were put in overcrowded cells, fed bad food, and never told the charges against them. As Woody Joe talked, the newsmen started to empathize with him. Maybe they had misunderstood the events of that night? Sure was hard to meet this kind-faced, well-spoken, hardworking white veteran and remember the cry of, "Can we have our hands on that nigger just one time?" And of course Woody Joe and the others were angry at Jack Corn and Don Cravens. Those reporters hadn't tried to understand local white grievances! Well, time someone heard them out.

The men from Oliver Springs talked with the journalists until after midnight. As Woody Joe left, he shook hands with one of the *Life* photographers who'd been roughed up in Oliver Springs.

—

On Friday, 419 students showed up for classes at Clinton High and Principal D. J. Brittain Jr. announced during his press conference that soon he'd turn the missing students over to the truancy officer. Everyone knew it was safe to return. Time to buckle down to the business of the year.

Since the situation had improved, Joe Henry had sent home all but two hundred of his men. "In view of your doubts as to your ability to prosecute the affairs of your office with a sufficient degree of diligence to preserve the peace and tranquility within your jurisdiction, I am temporarily leaving a detachment of National Guardsmen in Clinton," the governor telegrammed Glad Woodward. But Glad's timeline would be short.* It was the local sheriff's job to maintain order, the governor reiterated.

By the weekend, the Southern War Correspondents began to leave town, reassigned to hotter stories—a new altitude record for an unmanned aircraft, a train crash in New Mexico, other potential racist uprisings as the five other schools ordered to desegregate began classes—but many thought the violence would resurge in Clinton. They'd seen such superficial calm in other strife-torn communities. "See you when the Guard leaves town," the newsmen said to each other.

Saturday night, some two hundred Knoxvillians attended a Klan rally held in a field near the city's airport. The hooded Klansmen burned three twenty-five-foot crosses while one of their leaders lambasted the court decision desegregating Clinton High and Judge Bob Taylor, who had decreed it. Then the night riders went on home to their suppers. Looked much like the many other Klan rallies that had been held in the area over the past few years, some of the segregationists in Clinton must've said, and just like all the others, it accomplished nothing. Sure, a couple hundred gowned and masked Kluxers intoning racist hymns by the flickering light of a burning cross was a glorious and hateful pageant, but what had the klavern done lately? The fancy dress and fire might be fun, but Anderson County's white residents needed themselves a new organization, one with

---

* Privately, the governor also composed a longer note that was not sent Glad Woodward's way. "May I respectfully state first of all that I have been most disheartened at your pessimistic and defeatist attitude," Frank's unsent letter began. "I am sure you are a fine man and that your intentions are good. I am equally assured that if the Number One law enforcement officer of a county—the Sheriff—does not show courage, determination, and fortitude that the illegal forces of lawlessness and mob violence will take over and good citizens will have no rallying point." The governor urged the sheriff to buck up and prepare for whatever might be coming his way. "The life of an officer is hard," the governor concluded, "and one who undertakes it must be prepared to pay the price."

a bit more grit and fight in it. Maybe they'd find it in the White Citizens' Council. Not that they dropped their memberships in the Klan or the Tennessee Federation for Constitutional Government. Way they saw it, the more dissent the better.

Willard Till's Anderson County White Citizens' Council met for the first time on that same Saturday. They gathered on a farm outside the city limits, believing that by meeting on private property they didn't violate the prohibition against assembly. Two uninvited guests showed up. First, the sheriff came to remind them that the federal injunction barred them from interfering at the school or gathering in public. (That's why we're meeting here, the organizers retorted.) The second to crash the event was John Kasper, bailed out of jail that afternoon by Clyde Cook and Mary Nell Currier's husband, Charles, both of whom had taken out liens against their homes so they could pay his $10,000 bond. John demanded that they put their club under the umbrella of his Seaboard White Citizens' Council, merging with his own organization, the White Citizens' Council of Anderson County.

I believe we need to be separate, Willard replied. After all, folks in Anderson County knew what happened when they let outsiders get involved. Strangers always promised to do good things, but then they protected their own agendas, ignoring what the locals wanted. Frankly, John Kasper seemed even less trustworthy than the Manhattan Project people had been. The attendees voted unanimously to keep their club.

After expelling Glad and John, Willard and the others began discussing how their White Citizens' Council would unseat the Black teens from the school. They started by stating that the obvious foundation of all their actions was their faith. They were "set up on prayer or Christianity." To keep that central for all members, they agreed to pattern meetings on Evangelical worship services. They would always open with prayer, usually led by the Reverend Alonzo Bullock. Then they'd sing hymns, each member bringing their own songbook. Only then would they begin their business. Segregation was created by God, these white supremacists believed. God himself had created the races, giving each different purposes and roles. The white race had the hardest and most demanding job of all: policing the racial hierarchy and ensuring everyone lived within the limits

God had inscribed into their minds and onto their bodies. Godly white people, therefore, had to enforce segregation. Any who didn't abandoned the lesser races to their sinful natures.

Other Christians called this racist take on the church heresy. "It is difficult to view these utterances with anything but a feeling of melancholy and disgust," wrote an editorialist for Kentucky's Black *Tri-State Defender.* Imagine a preacher "lending his 'holy' voice to the gospel of confusion and hate at the very moment when more and more cries are being raised in massive protest against the evil of racial segregation." Black Christians around the South relied on their faith for comfort, and they read within the Bible a promise of a better future to come. But Christians dedicated to racial justice couldn't trust progress would happen no matter what. "Enlightened metropolitan public opinion may smother this dangerous movement," the writer warned. "But it will not do so by complacency nor by ignoring the destructive power of any itinerant Caesar bent on changing the course of history."

—

On the Monday of the third week of school, 529 students showed up for class, and Principal D. J. Brittain Jr. asked the county truancy officer to chase down the 257 missing pupils. A few Guardsmen were at the rec center doing paperwork, but the marching band was out practicing on the football field, no trace left of the pup tents lined up there a few days before.

At dusk that evening, Wynona McSwain sat in her rocking chair on the front porch of her large, rambling house, the home she and Allen had expanded over the years to fit her twelve children and six grandchildren. As she rocked, she looked over Clinton's downtown and wept. Soon as Allen got home from his job over in Oak Ridge, the McSwains would pile into his car to leave town. Everyone knew about Wynona's sixteen-year fight for her children's education, how she and her family had originated the lawsuit. Home was not a safe place for them to be, not even with the Guard around. They'd be sleeping somewhere else, same as they had every other night since school started. Somewhere secret. Somewhere so safe, even most folks on the Hill wouldn't know where they went.

But for other families both Black and white, a bit of normalcy had returned. Kids rushed through their homework and their dinner and their chores. They had a deadline. At seven o'clock, all those lucky enough to have a television clicked over to Knoxville's WBIR Channel 10, the local ABC affiliate. Those who didn't own a set popped in on a friend with one. The teenagers in Clinton—along with 60 million other viewers, or almost 83 percent of all television watchers that night—wanted to see Elvis Presley's debut on *The Ed Sullivan Show*.

And then the twenty-one-year-old singer strutted onto the screen, collar popped, his used Martin D-28 guitar hung from his neck, a guitar he'd struggled to afford a scant year earlier. Now he'd added a tooled leather cover to it, and the studio lights glinted off the embossed lilies. The girls in the live studio audience screamed. Girls across Clinton squealed. More than a few of their mothers sighed. Elvis smiled, glanced offstage, looked down as though a bit embarrassed by the attention he wasn't yet accustomed to receiving. Then he cleared his throat. "Wow," he said, wiping his forehead. "This is probably the greatest honor that I've ever had in my life." He launched into "Don't Be Cruel." Ed was still running a family show, so the cameras stayed pinned on Elvis's face, avoiding his gyrating pelvis, but Elvis's snarl and shoulder pops accented his sensuality.

The next morning, Clinton's officials discovered the last members of the National Guard had slipped away overnight. "We can now handle any situation by ourselves," Glad Woodward claimed. "And we don't anticipate further trouble." A few more parents agreed with him; 590 students were in Clinton High School and 36 had officially withdrawn. But not everyone was so confident.

"I feel sure we will have violence," the Reverend O. W. Willis told a reporter for the *Baltimore Afro-American*.

"When the Guard leaves, maybe each man had better have a gun," D. J. Brittain Jr. was overheard saying.

—

On Wednesday, September 12, 1956, Herbert Allen watched as his daughter Jo Ann headed off to school. He was astounded by the confident, poised young woman she was becoming. No wonder all those out-of-town journalists had wanted to interview her.

For Herbert, the conflict of the past couple weeks boiled down to one simple question: either Black Americans were citizens of the United States, or they were not. He'd spent his whole life hearing he was, but he'd never been treated that way. He thought it was about time to settle the issue once and for all. And that was why he kept sending Jo Ann back down Freedman's Hill to Clinton High.

Way Herbert saw it, white people's currish behavior toward him, toward his daughter, toward the eleven other students, toward the residents of the Hill, well, all that ugly hatefulness wasn't really about the Black people at all. It was an infection— No, it was an infestation in the white people's souls, an invasive weed planted inside them when they were infants. As he thought about this, was he perhaps looking at a kudzu patch,* the vine the Civilian Conservation Corps had said would protect the Southeast from erosion? Racism was supposed to remind white folks of who they were and who they belonged with. But the vine and the malignity both grew and spread, one across the landscape and the other across souls, choking out all life wherever they took root. Sometimes he'd seen white folks who tried to prune their noxious, hateful weeds, a painful process that was only a temporary fix. Prejudice spawned a thousand feeder roots that popped back to life. What would it take to exhume all the taproots and runners and tubers and seedpods keeping hate alive in white people's hearts? Was anyone brave enough to dig down to where their bones and their ghosts lay? And who would do that over and over again for the rest of their lives? So maybe Herbert understood why they hesitated to undertake that process. But until they did, his Jo Ann would never be safe.

---

* Herbert Allen talks about racism being a plant that takes seed in white people's hearts when they are young and ends up deeply (and deleteriously) rooted. I've expanded that into the kudzu analogy in a not-very-subtle homage to Alice Walker, who wrote in *In Search of Our Mothers' Gardens*, "but in Mississippi (as in the rest of America) racism is like that local creeping kudzu vine that swallows whole forests and abandoned houses; if you don't keep pulling up the roots it will grow back faster than you can destroy it." And Herbert certainly would have known about kudzu, and he likely would have battled it.

Herbert figured the white law-and-order crowd had stopped whatever little pruning they were doing when they heard John Kasper was touring the racist organizations connected to Asa Carter. (It was time for an "anything goes" policy, John told an audience one night. "The wild grass will grow over their dead bodies.") Reports of his violent words filtered back to Clinton through the newspapers and through phone calls from white Alabamans looking for information, every bit as skeptical of the Yankee as the people of Clinton were. But the white townspeople had moved on to other, better news, acting like this crisis was over. They'd been really proud when Sheriff Glad Woodward had captured his first still and arrested his first moonshiner. He'd posed for the *Clinton Courier-News* next to the fifty-gallon copper tank, hands tucked in his belt loops and his chest thrust forward.

But still Herbert fretted. How long would peace last without the Guard in town? He wasn't concerned for his own life so much, but what of his wife and children? What would he do if Josephine was bushwhacked by a Citizens' Council member some night? Or what if one of those Black Jackets attacked Jo Ann while she was in class? That was why he'd joined the committee of men patrolling the Hill. That's why he was still keeping watch.

Sometimes, though, he thought maybe he and Josephine had made the right choice, sending Jo Ann to Clinton High. Like when Jo Ann and Carole Peters, the girl who'd nominated Jo Ann as homeroom vice president, were invited to Washington, D.C., by the creator and moderator of *The College Press Conference*, part of ABC's Sunday afternoon news lineup. She arranged for the two girls to interview United States Attorney General Herbert Brownell. Appearing alongside the high schoolers would be Allard K. Lowenstein, a Jewish graduate student at the University of North Carolina who was already a political activist and would become a U.S. congressman and representative to the UN Human Rights Commission. Both Carole and Jo Ann proposed questions for the attorney general to answer, but all of Jo Ann's questions, ones she pieced together through long conversations with her family, were vetoed. She suspected they were too pointed. So she asked him easier questions like whether the president would make a speech about civil rights while on the campaign trail that fall. Even on that one, the attorney general fudged. "I don't know," he replied.

The girls seemed to have so much in common, Jo Ann thought, even though Carole and her mom went to a white hotel while Jo Ann was whisked away to the Black YWCA, where she stayed on her own, almost like a real grown-up instead of a girl newly turned fifteen. Maybe her friendship with Carole meant her time at Clinton High was about to turn around. Maybe she would get to have the high school experience she'd dreamed of. Maybe her goodness and her abilities would show the White Citizens' Council members and all the other white people they needed to give in and accept the inevitable: the Black students were in Clinton High to stay.

Other Black students were also having some wins at the high school, even if those successes didn't lead to national television appearances. One Thursday in September, first-year history teacher Sue Byerly called Bobby Cain to the front of the classroom. She asked him to recite the Declaration of Independence from memory. He stood straight and proud. " 'We hold these truths to be self-evident, that all men are created equal,' " he said to his white classmates. " 'That they are endowed by their Creator with certain unalienable rights, that among these are life, liberty, and the pursuit of happiness. That, to secure these rights, governments are instituted among men.' " He made it to the end of the document without a stutter or a stammer or a misplaced word. This—his public reclamation of the American dream—was his first real academic achievement at Clinton High School. And it was one all the students' parents could feel swelled up over.

But talking to Bobby's parents, Herbert knew the strain of the preceding weeks had already changed their son. "He reminded me of the men I had interviewed when I served as a Marine combat correspondent in World War II," reporter George McMillan noted after he spoke with the boy that same week. "As we talked, drops of sweat gathered on his forehead and began to run down his cheek [and] he pressed his palms together nervously." George thought Bobby had blocked some of his memories because when he tried to answer questions his words would trail away and he would seem to get lost in his thoughts. "It is impossible for men who have really 'had it' to talk about their experience until their memories have had an interval in which to reject the intolerable," George explained to his readers. He suggested that the violence of the past few weeks had given the teen combat fatigue,* or what we'd today term post-traumatic stress disorder.

Bobby'd always been patient and kind with his siblings, but lately he'd been snapping at them, sometimes without provocation. His mother thought about lecturing him, but how could she add any more stress to his days? Surely, it was enough that he awoke, dressed, and walked down the Hill to school.

—

Classrooms at Clinton High were almost 80 percent full by the second week of September. "It is just like we've always been going to school with them," one white senior girl told a local reporter. "We don't bother them, and they don't bother us."

"They're here, we might as well make the best of it," another said.

But not all the white students who had returned to school were as resigned toward the Black students' presence as those two claimed to be. Some of them were there because they understood that while their parents could get by without a high school diploma, their generation faced different requirements, especially if they wanted to work in Oak Ridge or some other job outside the mines and the textile mills. These students were only playing at peace. "This thing is not over," segregationist student Jimmy Ray McGill told a reporter. "I have talked with a lot of parents and students. They are not satisfied with this thing as it is."

And though the segregationists were no longer holding open meetings in the streets, they were still gathering. Every week, there were more

---

* As an adult, Bobby Cain agreed with McMillan's comparison. He told me that when he reads about the problems faced by soldiers who fought in Iraq or Afghanistan he recognizes himself. "I probably needed some of that [help the Veterans Administration offers to returning soldiers]," he told me as he recounted the ways his time at Clinton High continues to affect him today.

speakers, more rallies, more organizational conclaves, more cross burnings. Several times over that fall, the segregationists interrupted school board meetings. At one of these, Willard Till—accompanied by Chris Foust and William Brakebill and a few other leaders from the new Anderson County White Citizens' Council—began his list of demands by saying, "Is it out of order to ask is there anyone here who wants niggers to go to Clinton High School?" The school board members had shifted a bit uncomfortably at the public use of the slur, but yes, they had all been looking for ways to take back Clinton High. They were law-abiding men, however. They'd tried appeals and petitions and requests for time. They needed a new legal (or at least a legal-enough) remedy. After three hours of debate, the school board agreed that unfortunately the ideas set forth by the White Citizens' Council were neither practical nor legal. The board members sympathized with the demands. No, they didn't just sympathize; through their actions, the board members proved they agreed with the Citizens' Council cause, at least in principle. But the board members weren't going to jail to protest Clinton High's desegregation. They would sacrifice their convictions if it kept them on the right side of the law.

And some white business leaders reported that they'd had visits from members of the White Citizens' Council, been threatened, been told that if they didn't join the council they'd face a boycott. And some had heard rumors that the Anderson County White Citizens' Council was getting political aspirations, that they had plans for the mayoral election that December. Did they even have their own slate of candidates? And then John Kasper, out on bail while his lawyer appealed his federal conviction for contempt of court, came back to town. A grand jury indicted him on local charges of sedition and inciting a riot.

—

In late September, local Democratic Party leaders hosted a rally. Some fifteen hundred or maybe two thousand people attended it. One of them was Sheriff Glad Woodward, a lifelong Democrat. And who did he see but John Kasper and a handful of other men—or maybe twenty-five or perhaps fifty—standing next to some Confederate-flag-bedecked cars carrying segregationist signs?

"I'm the sheriff of Anderson County," Glad announced. "You're under arrest."

"On what charges?" John asked.

"Sedition," Glad said.

"What's sedition?" John asked.

Instead of replying, the sheriff grabbed John by the arm and walked him toward the patrol car Glad'd parked a few blocks away. When the pair passed one of Oak Ridge's police officers, Glad asked him for help. The cop grabbed John's other arm. When they reached the patrol car, though, Glad let go of John's arm to open the back door. John jerked free of the Oak Ridge officer and ran away, shouting, "Show me a warrant!" over his shoulder. The sheriff and the officer gave chase. Seeing the ruckus, the Oak Ridge police chief joined them, and then an off-duty constable. Soon the fugitive, who wasn't running terribly hard, was leading the lawmen on a mocking, merry chase that would've made a good comic cartoon short at the Ritz's Saturday matinee. Hoping to end things, the constable cut around some of the cars. He dived to tackle John, but the man was only five feet four inches, not nearly large enough to take down the six-foot seditionist. He went through John's legs. John pinned him and began whaling on him, punching him some dozen times before Glad was able to pull John off.

Surely, this sort of behavior would make people reconsider John Kasper, the sheriff thought. It was one thing to attack Black kids desegregating a school; it was another to assault an officer. But when Glad shoved his prisoner into his car to transport John to jail, four of John's female supporters stuffed themselves into the front seat and refused to get out. By the time the sheriff and his passengers arrived in Clinton, a crowd of about a hundred people had already gathered outside the jail, threatening to storm the building and free John. The sheriff called up twenty members of his auxiliary unit to guard the prison.

Just shy of midnight, two local men paid John Kasper's $2,000 bond. He was arraigned the next morning and his trial date set for November 5. Encouraged by the show of support, John again urged the local movement to make him their head. The segregationists would protest his arrest, but they weren't about to hand their association over to him. They would not be merging with John Kasper's rival group, the White Citizens' Council of Anderson County. Willard Till retained control.

—

On Wednesday, September 26, at 10:15 p.m., the first bomb exploded in Clinton, set off in a ditch near the homes of Ronald Hayden, Minnie Ann Dickie, and Alvah Jay McSwain. It shattered one of the Haydens' windows, rattled china cabinets across town, and showered debris on roofs around the Hill, but it did little real damage. The bombers had used blasting powder, an explosive designed for softer materials like coal, rather than dynamite, which was about one thousand times more powerful. Police guessed that the attackers had filled two beer cans with the powder and wrapped the canisters in newspapers before hurling them from the window of a passing vehicle. This was good news, authorities said. Everyone familiar with mining knew powder bombs were designed to scare, not harm. No one should worry until dynamite was used.

Then dynamite was found outside the home of the Reverend O. W. Willis, one of the parents who brought the original desegregation suit against the county. Dynamite, now, well, dynamite could maim or kill. But since it hadn't exploded, it was just a threat. After all, miners knew what they were doing. Had they meant it to blow up, it would've.

Still, Herbert Allen was through with crouching in the dark. He wasn't going to wait, wasn't going to give those people any more chances to hunt his wife or his children. He picked up his gun, the same .38-caliber revolver he'd been carrying while patrolling the Hill for the past month—the same weapon the police and the sheriff and the National Guard knew he'd been packing—and stood in front of his house, ready to shoot anyone who came for his family. Glad arrested Herbert for carrying arms. The sheriff was fine knowing Black men had armed themselves and then hidden. He could even use that threat to control the rioters. But he couldn't allow Black men to stand up openly and defiantly, armed and ready to fight.

Josephine phoned up her employer Mrs. Crenshaw, who contacted her husband, the president of the Magnet Knitting Mills, who called in a favor. He arranged for Herbert to be released under a $250 bond. But that didn't save Herbert from the charges. His indictment was one of the last the grand jury handed down that month. Two other defendants named in indictments that morning were L. T. Spraggins and William Capshaw, both of whom were charged with felonious assault.

No one was ever arrested for throwing the exploding beer cans or leaving the dynamite. Glad Woodward implied the blame lay partly with the men patrolling the Hill. They gave such conflicting reports of vehicles used by the attackers, he said, that he had no clear leads to go on.

THIRTEEN

Small-Town Games

On Saturday, October 13, 125 cars packed with hooded Kluxers—led by a vehicle rigged up with a lit electric cross on the back of it—paraded through downtown Clinton, circling the square and stirring up a ruckus. Then the caravan pulled up to a vacant lot south of the city where the police were on hand to direct traffic. While four crosses burned, the crowd, which was somewhere between one hundred and fifty and four hundred strong, listened to the anonymous hooded speakers shout about "the nine devils on the Supreme Court." Despite the injunction officially banning events like this, no one broke up the meeting or threatened to arrest the organizers. One week later, the Tennessee States Rights Party kicked off five days of segregation. Willard Till was the organizer and master of ceremonies for the local events. The first one was held at Claxton Elementary School, one of the feeder schools for Clinton High. That was followed up with a Saturday night rally in the Clinton High School auditorium. Principal D. J. Brittain Jr. told the local journalists still following events in Clinton High that Willard had promised the purpose of the meeting was peaceable.

Still, the white townspeople thought they'd survived their crisis. They refocused on the newest stage of an old conflict. Every two years, the people voted whether to be a dry or wet county. Most years, about 49 percent voted wet and 51 percent voted dry, but when the wets were organized and the drys were apathetic, the liquor vote passed. This year, the wets predicted, Oak Ridge residents—that hotbed of worldly outsiders—would outnumber the Southern Baptist, Primitive Baptist, Church of Christ, Pentecostal, and Holiness congregants who campaigned against the demon alcohol. The drys were led by the Committee of One Hundred.

The Reverend Paul Turner took charge. "We won't let any liquor petition go unchallenged," Paul promised a reporter for the *Oak Ridger*. "We shall seek to enlighten the county on the evils of legal liquor and seek to enlist the people who believe that way."

The 1956 presidential campaign was also drawing to a close. Incumbent Republican president Dwight D. Eisenhower was facing a rematch against his opponent from four years earlier, former governor of Illinois Adlai Stevenson. All the pollsters said Eisenhower would win. Then he interrupted the Suez Canal Crisis and bypassed a shadow war with the Soviets. Egyptian president Gamal Abdel Nasser had nationalized the Suez Canal, meaning Egypt was now profiting off the trade transversing the waterway instead of the British and French shareholders who had owned the canal previously. On October 22, the United Kingdom, France, and Israel met to plan an invasion of Egypt, hoping to recapture control of the canal and unseat Nasser. Before they could carry out their plans, however, a new international crisis began. On October 23, Hungarian college students took to the streets to protest their pro-Soviet government. Three days later, troops from the USSR invaded the nation to squash the rebellion. Pictures from Hungary dominated the front pages of American newspapers, the images of the mutilated cadavers of dead anti-Communists reprinted above the fold. Refugees from Hungary fled toward Western Europe as the Soviets recaptured the nation and reimposed Communist rule.

Despite the growing Cold War conflict, three days after the Soviets entered Hungary, Israel invaded Egypt, backed up by British and French fighter pilots. As the soldiers advanced, reports filtered out that they were killing local civilians and Palestinian refugees as well as armed fighters. For once, the United States and the USSR agreed: the invasion of Egypt had to stop, and they could come together on that, sidestepping the crisis in Hungary. President Dwight D. Eisenhower pressured the Western countries to withdraw, and the UN General Assembly demanded an immediate cease-fire as well. Eisenhower got all the credit for ending the affair. Americans loved their reluctant but decisive general who tried to avoid conflict but would intervene before the world went from the Cold War into a hot one.

As attention drifted away from the battle for Clinton High School, Willard Till and his allies used the break to plan their next steps. They had to manage their public image, especially with outsiders. Too many people dismissed them as ignorant hillbillies. "Whenever embittered whites are quoted, any grammatical lapse in their speech is mercilessly recorded verbatim—including such phrases as 'them niggers,' 'we seen,' 'ain't gonna,' etc.," William Brakebill explained to a local newspaper editor. And then the segregationists never simply said anything; instead, they would "'snarl,' 'yell,' 'scream,' 'snap,' and howl.'" He contrasted that with how the media handled the Black students and their families: "The little Negro pupils, when quoted, invariably speak perfect English. Aside from Clinton's unrest, these children also are newsworthy because they seem incapable of those grammatical imperfections common to their race. Indeed," they spoke so perfectly "that these colored children should be teaching English instead of studying it."

Well, fact was, Jo Ann Allen probably *could* have been teaching English. Her mother had coached her speech since she was a toddler. No slang, Josephine had told her. No "ain'ts" or "nopes" or "It's like wow." And never, absolutely never, use words as crass as "cool cats" or "daddy-o." Furthermore, pronounce "pen" and "pin" differently, and remember that it's "get," not "git." Whenever Jo Ann slipped up and let a "sure thing" or an "okay" slide by, she knew her mom's next question would be: "Don't you know how to speak the King's English?"

Sure, the perfect diction and careful syntax earned Jo Ann and her little sister some razzing from their peers at Green McAdoo. Who did the Allen girls think they were, the other students would mock, Mrs. Crenshaw? But their mother believed she was thinking ahead. Her kids were going to get the very best education she could manage, but even if they graduated from Harvard, other folks—mostly white folks—would question the Allen children's credentials and abilities, whether they were really good enough for reporters from *Life* magazine, whether someone else should've appeared alongside the attorney general. So yes, Josephine did teach Jo Ann to speak like the richest of the rich white people, but even so, the racists around Josephine couldn't appreciate her daughter's brilliance. Meanwhile, so many of the white people reveled in devaluing education.

Or, as one mother of a stay-away sixteen-year-old boy said, "Before I'd raise my children up with a Negro, I'd raise them up dumb, like I am."

The segregationists, however, weren't ready for that bit of truth. They decided the key to controlling the stories written about them was having their own newspaper. They launched the *East Tennessee Reporter*, led and mostly written by editor Leo Ely. From Appalachian Kentucky, Leo dropped out of high school his freshman year, worked a bit, and then joined the Navy at eighteen, a scant few months before World War II broke out. By the end of the conflict, he had won two Purple Hearts and two Bronze Stars for his actions overseas. Leo promised the new paper would fight the town's leaders, folks like Buford Lewallen and his wife, Celdon, those " 'go-alongers,' " who let white people's "freedom . . . be snatched away." He dismissed Robert Taylor as one of the judicial " 'mouth-shutters' who by the thump of a gavel and issuance of a decree can silence the people's opposition." He disparaged "civil officials with itchy 'trigger fingers,' " such as the men who joined the auxiliary police. He also pledged that his coverage would reveal false friends like John Kasper and other "wolves in sheep clothing" who came to Clinton promising support but whose actions undermined the movement. (By the way, was John turning a profit at this thing? Had anyone looked at where the membership dues went?)

Yes, there sure were a lot of people Leo's paper would fight, but his special targets were the Lewallens. This was Leo's chance for revenge. Eight years earlier, Buford had represented Leo's ex-wife in their divorce case, alleging Leo had beaten her. Then one night during the custody hearings for their four kids, Leo and his brother pulled up alongside a car parked on the shoulder of SR61 some miles outside Oak Ridge. Leo recognized his soon-to-be-ex-wife's profile. She was in that car with a man! That man was Buford. Buford claimed he'd been driving her home after a meeting. Leo, though, knew what handsome lawyers and pretty clients did in parked cars after dark. He and his brother attacked, but Buford managed to escape. The Elys chased him, forcing the car off the road. This time, the brothers came to the car with guns drawn. The almost-ex Mrs. Leo ran for help, but Buford, who still needed a cane to walk, had no hope of fleeing. The two men pummeled him with their guns and a flashlight. Buford tried to protect himself with a knife, so when police arrived they arrested all three.

The brothers were charged with felonious assault with attempt to commit murder as well as highway robbery (they must've picked up a bit of memorabilia from the car). Buford was charged with drunk driving and felonious assault with a knife. The brothers went to jail, but Buford went to the hospital for his injuries, which included "a kick in the groin." Then the authorities withdrew all the warrants and dropped the case, presumably with the agreement of the parties involved.

—

On Wednesday, October 24, Celdon Lewallen came home to find a mob of robed men on her front lawn preparing to burn a cross. She escorted her daughter, Dancy, past them and into the house and then grabbed the derringer her husband, Buford, had given her. What she didn't know was that Buford had never loaded her derringer. He thought a weaponized Celdon was a greater danger to herself than to others.

Celdon should've expected something like this to happen sooner or later. After all, it wasn't the first time a cross had been burned in her front yard. One had been torched there in May 1949. Near it, the arsonists left a note on tablet paper: "You'll try to find out who we are, but you can't. Your motives are selfish. You had better get out of town.—Knights of the Ku Klux Klan." Buford said it was because he'd been trying to oust the sheriff, the man he'd accused of spreading vice around the county.

This time, though, Celdon had been the one to provoke them. She'd done her level best to control her wannabe activists, shutting them up whenever they tried to agitate in her classroom. When that didn't work, she'd taken them head-on, knowing she could talk circles around any of them. When she'd walked in for several mornings in a row to "Mrs. Lewallen's a nigger lover" scrawled on her blackboard, she'd cornered the young white boys—a group of known troublemakers—she thought were the most likely culprits.

"What do you think you'll be doing until graduation?" she asked them.

"We'll be right here in this school," they replied.

"Not in my room, you won't," she said. She told those kids that whenever they misbehaved she would put a zero in her grade book by their name, didn't matter whether they did their work or not. And they better not think they could escape her by enlisting or taking a job in Oak Ridge.

"I'm going to write on your permanent record that you were not fit for service with any branch of the government," she threatened. "Do we understand each other?"

"You can't do that!" they told her.

"You can't do what you're doing either, but you're doing it," she retorted. They should think of this as an object lesson: "This is discrimination. It's the best example you'll find of it."

But still, there was this one little fiery son of a bitch who kept running his mouth. Well, one day she called him to the front of her classroom.

"Just get up here and talk about what all this is doing for you," she said to him. Then she interrupted him. "I think you're dumb," she said. "I'm white, but it didn't cost me twenty dollars to prove I'm white," presumably a reference to the dues people paid to join the White Citizens' Council. "That's all you're buying is something to say you're white." But maybe that was the secret. Maybe he wasn't really white. Was he worried that somebody somewhere had muddled up his racial lines? "Well, you look white to me," she said, shrugging.

So now her students had gotten their daddies involved. She could see where her crybabies had gotten it from. Anyone who dressed in a robe and only went out after dark was lacking in intestinal fortitude. As she stepped onto the front porch to confront the men, those hooded cowards who couldn't even show their faces, she heard her daughter's voice from within the house. "Mother," Dancy reminded her, "you don't know how to shoot a gun." Celdon figured that made her even more dangerous to the poltroons outside. She might even hit one of them without meaning to. Oops.

Startled by her reappearance, the crowd shifted but said nothing. "What the hell do you think you're doing in my front yard?" Celdon demanded. She walked toward the men. "You can either get out, or I'll call the police. I'll go back in and get a shotgun, and I don't shoot very well." The men grumbled a few profanities at her and then left. As they drove away, Celdon made note of the license-plate number of one of the cars, and she reported it to the police.

Expelled from the Lewallens', the cross burners headed to the home of Eleanor and Sidney Davis. Like Buford, Sidney had been one of the assistant district attorneys who fought the original desegregation lawsuit but was now a law-and-order acolyte, and Eleanor was another English teacher at the high school. She hadn't wanted desegregation, but now that it had happened, she was trying to be fair to all her students. The Davises had also had a cross burned in their front yard the same time as the Lewallens had, presumably for the same campaign against the sheriff.

On that Wednesday night, Sidney was at a city council meeting and Eleanor was at a rehearsal for a school play she was directing, so their three boys were alone, studying in the den of their home, an isolated spot on the road to Oak Ridge. When the men arrived, the oldest, a freshman at Clinton High, fetched his bow and arrow, preparing to shoot anyone who came near the house. The hooded men set fire to an eight-foot cross in the front yard. None of the neighbors called to check on the boys, though surely someone must have seen the flames even across the Davises' forested couple acres. Or maybe the neighbors were distracted, eating their dinners or watching television or checking kids' homework. The boys would handle their own defense. While the oldest guarded the front door, one of the other boys called the fire department. The firemen said they wouldn't help because the Davises lived outside the city limits. The child then called the police department. They also refused to come. The boy then called the manager of the telephone company. When he also said no, the kid said it was a real tall cross, that the flames were reaching toward the telephone wires, that it might melt the wires and disconnect service for everyone down the line. Concerned about his company's property, the manager sent some men. The hooded delegation dispersed, and the flames were extinguished finally. The next day, the three Davis boys carried the remnants of the cross, a slapdash contraption of two-by-fours wrapped in old bedding, into the backyard to hide it from the neighbors just in case the people next door hadn't seen the conflagration.

That night, Glad Woodward's officers picked up John B. Long, house painter and suspected Klansman who owned the car Celdon had called in. The district attorney decided Celdon's notations were enough to hold John on charges related to what happened at her house, but only circumstantial evidence linked him to the cross burned on the Davises' lawn. He was charged with night-riding, an old-timey reference to vigilante acts carried out by masked white men who committed terrorism at night. The sentence carried a fine of between $50 and $100 accompanied by six to twelve months in the county jail. The following morning, he was bound over to the grand jury under a $750 bond.

—

Buford and Sidney wanted to exact their own revenge. The two men knew the local klavern met in the feed room of a general store owned by a former city council member. When the attorneys confronted the store's manager, the man claimed to have nothing to do with the Klan. He gave them access to the room because they paid for it. After some pressure from the attorneys, the manager agreed to let Buford and Sidney wire the room, just to see what they could learn. On the night the Kluxers met, the two sat in the apartment next door, listening in and recording all that happened from the members' arrival through their sacred rituals to the drinking time afterward when the men laughed at how they'd "scared the hell" out of the lawyers' wives. Since the recording was obtained under less-than-legal means, the attorneys couldn't present it in court, but they could use it to threaten the men who'd attended the meeting. One by one, Buford went to them and said, "Sit down. I want to play you something."

The militant segregationists struck back. In mid-November, Buford was driving through Oliver Springs when he noticed his car was low on gas. He pulled into one of the service stations in town. James Duncan, one of Woody Joe's brothers, and a group of other men gathered around his car. They started yelling at him about desegregation, calling him the usual names. Then they attacked, breaking his nose. Buford pulled out his automatic pistol and threatened to shoot the next man who got near him. Well, that was attempted murder. Soon Buford had a warrant out for his arrest, sworn by James Duncan. The attorney turned himself in. Officers from the Tennessee Highway Patrol carted him over to the Roane County Jail, their cars followed by a caravan of about twenty folks from Oliver Springs. Buford was released under a $2,000 bond. He had waived his right to a preliminary hearing because the crowd outside the jail had already started to grow. He wanted to get out of town as quickly as possible. Eventually the charges were dropped. But it felt like the racist activists were escalating their fight, making it ever more dangerous to be a white law-and-order leader.

FOURTEEN

Ramping Up

Like the proverbial cat with more lives than wisdom, John Kasper came back to Clinton in early November. On November 3, he crashed a meeting Willard Till and his Anderson County White Citizens' Council held inside Clinton High. When John attempted to take the microphone, the local segregationists banned him from all future events the group might plan. The Anderson County klavern also sent word he should stay away. But as much as the local movement wanted to disown John Kasper, they could not yet abandon him. He was about to go on trial in Clinton, a local trial for sedition and inciting to riot, one that was separate from the federal trial that had already found him guilty of violating Robert Taylor's injunction. If he was found guilty of these actions, too, the verdict would leave all the other protestors vulnerable to a similar fate in the Clinton court system. And so on the morning his trial began, a small group picketed, carrying signs proclaiming: "No Rigged Jury" and "We Demand a Fair Trial for Kasper." Inside, the members of the local Citizens' Council and the States Rights Party used their testimonies to show how unimportant John Kasper was to them. The charge of inciting to riot was especially useful. John could only be guilty of that if he had sway over them, and they were so sick of hearing that he was their leader! They were not the patsies of this Ivy League fop, thank you. They took the witness stand in John's defense. They sat on that wooden chair and, under oath, told the world this truth: Clinton High was their fight, and John Kasper could go get bent.

The trial dragged on for almost three weeks, largely because of all the witnesses called. The district attorney's case relied on ten people, mostly law-and-order types who talked about the violent rhetoric they'd heard John use. The DA also besmirched John's reputation by highlighting his relationship to Ezra Pound and his history of having friends—and even girlfriends—who were Black.

As though that would hurt the local Citizens' Council members! Willard Till and the others muttered. Why didn't folks understand that they didn't care who John dated? They wanted nothing to do with him.

After the state rested, the defense brought fifty-eight witnesses. Almost all of them testified that John truly believed in segregation and he had never actually advocated violence. They said that any violence that happened was the fault of the law-and-order auxiliary police. They also testified to how widespread and established the segregationist resistance was before John Kasper had shown up a handful of days before Clinton High opened. They described how it had thrived after he left. Based on the defense's witnesses, the all-male, all-white jury deliberated for forty-five minutes before declaring John Kasper was not guilty on November 20. Cheers erupted in the courtroom.

"Things sure are going to be different around here now!" one white man yelled over the tumult.

John Kasper, dapper in a gray suit, white shirt, and dark tie, was immediately surrounded by well-wishers. A young white girl of perhaps nine or ten clung to his left hand. Her bob was shiny and straight, but her front fringe had curled rebelliously in the heat of the courtroom. An older white woman pressed his right hand in congratulations. A high-school-aged white girl chewed her thumbnail while she waited her turn to say her piece. Middle-aged white men stood in a ring, watching the melee and perhaps hoping John Kasper would finally move on. He had to have understood the underlying message in their testimony, even if others had not, right?

—

While John Kasper's trial had dragged on, the Black families on the Hill faced increasing violence. First the threatening phone calls started back up, often coming in late at night.

Don't send your kids back to Clinton High School, the anonymous callers warned. The white students "would whip . . . [them] real good."

Next came rocks thrown at windows. So the men went back out guarding the Hill, if they had ever relaxed their vigils. They were the ones who noted an uptick in the number of suspicious cars passing through, their drivers slowing down, surveying the neighborhood, looking for vulnerabilities.

Then after midnight on Tuesday, November 13—the same day that the United States Supreme Court declared segregated public transportation illegal, ending the year-long Montgomery Bus Boycott—Steve Williams called Clinton's chief of police. A car had driven past his home just about 12:45 that morning. Someone, presumably the passenger, had fired two shots at the Williams home where his nephews/wards Alfred Williams and Maurice Soles were sleeping. The police chief sent a couple officers. But, he told Steve Williams, don't expect any arrests to be made. Steve hadn't given him many clues to go on, after all.

Another night around that time, Gail Ann Epps and her sister were in their rooms upstairs when Gail Ann heard a noise. It wasn't a banging. More like a scraping, like someone was trying to break into the house. She tried to remind herself that she was safe. Her uncles were posted in their living room with shotguns, and her dad was outside, also armed and guarding the house. But guns wouldn't stop dynamite.

Turn on the back lights, her grandma instructed her mom. Maybe they'll scurry away.

So Gail Ann's mom flipped on the spotlights installed on the back of the house. They heard a car start up somewhere in the woods nearby. As it drove away, Gail Ann's aunt Mattie Bell ran to the bathroom to throw up, vomiting away the fear that had gripped her guts.

The next morning, one white man who seemed to know what had happened the night before pointed at Gail Ann as she walked into the school building and said, "Don't you know they came back here again this morning?"

Had he been the man trying to break through her back door? she wondered.

It's so bad, Bobby Cain's mother told a friendly white woman, some nights her family was so frightened they would all "sleep together and hold on to each other."

—

Next, the violence came into the school. Some of the white girls at Clinton High—the same ones who'd stood sneering and whispering at the Black students on the first day of classes—started wearing a new racist accessory, pinning small buttons reading "Keep Our White Schools White" to their cardigans. Suddenly there seemed to be an unlimited supply of the badges, the girls handing them to any white student who wanted one. Believing peer pressure explained the button wearing, Eleanor Davis banned the pins inside her classroom. She thought most white students looked relieved to take them off as they walked through her door. Other teachers claimed adults had bribed the students. Hadn't folks heard about that one boy who'd admitted he'd been offered fifty dollars to assault a Black student? But the buttons were more than a racist accessory forced on children by their parents. The segregationist students, especially the segregationist girls, were finding their voices.

After school one day, seventeen-year-old junior Betty Lou Miller was hanging out with some friends, listening to the radio, when the announcer started interviewing Principal D. J. Brittain Jr. Everything was going swimmingly, the principal said. The kids were no trouble. They were all getting along. The earlier issues had been caused by adults manipulated by that meddling John Kasper. The local segregationists were just dupes, nothing but pawns.

Betty Lou and the others were irate! Who was that principal to say that the teenagers didn't want this and didn't want that? The girls knew exactly what they wanted. They wanted segregation. It was what was moral and right. The fight for it was godly and brave. They were protecting their Black neighbors from disobeying God's law, guarding their own purity, and waging a patriotic battle to save their nation from God's judgment. If they failed, much as God had thrown the Israelites out of the Promised Land for failing to obey the laws given to Moses, America would cease to be, probably transformed into an atheist Soviet client state by the Communists using civil rights as a cover for their nefarious plans.

The girls had watched their parents apply for a charter to make the Anderson County White Citizens' Council legal and official, so the girls launched their own organization, the Tennessee White Youth. After receiving their charter on Wednesday, November 14, they wrote a press release announcing their presence. They also asked the White Citizens' Council in Washington, D.C., to send them membership cards. While they waited for these to arrive, they passed around a petition among their friends, taking the names of anyone who wanted to join. The group quickly grew by word of mouth, so the young women set up a temporary office and called their first meeting.

It was time to register their club. The following Monday, Betty Lou Miller, Carolyn Hutton, and Shirley Way went to the Southland Cafeteria armed with their charter and a list of thirty-seven charter members. Located just off the square, the Southland was a favorite eating spot for the White Citizens' Council's leaders, so the girls were certain they could find some adult—Willard Till or Lawrence Brantley or William Brakebill or Clyde Cook or Mary Nell Currier or Clifford Carter or Alonzo Bullock; anyone would do—to drive the teens to see a notary public. Clyde Cook was there. He squired them to pick up three more of their friends and then took them to see a local farmwife who could notarize their document. After that, the passel (which had added the Reverend Alonzo Bullock to their number) went to the Anderson County registrar of deeds. Alonzo gave his son Earl the money to pay the requisite filing fee so the kids could complete the process themselves. Two of the founders of the organization—Betty Lou Miller and Carolyn Hutton, both decked out in matching white turtleneck sweaters emblazoned with Confederate flags—handed the notarized paper and the payment over to the registrar.

And for the first time, these girls, these country girls and girls from the lower-class families who hitherto had little social standing within the school, ran an influential club on campus. They suddenly rose in the social hierarchy, and it was a new position they'd created for themselves. The Tennessee White Youth also gave the girls a way to participate in the conflict without joining in the overtly violent tactics used by the boys.

Over fifty teenagers came to the first meeting of the Tennessee White Youth the next Sunday. They met at the Embassy Club, a social spot on the outskirts of Clinton where the local White Citizens' Council occasionally had their meetings and where the county sheriff made regular liquor raids. The girls asked Alonzo Bullock to open the meeting with a prayer. Then the club's officers passed out membership cards. "I _____, a white citizen, believe in the separation of the races as ordained by the CREATOR," the cards proclaimed. I "uphold racial segregation, am loyal to the United States of America, its Constitution, and believe in the divinity of Jesus Christ." Though some of the students needed their parents to drive them to the meeting, the gathering was youth led, the adults waiting outside until the Tennessee White Youth's business was completed. Within a week, the group's official membership was up to 107 teens.

—

With their curly hair and bobby socks, the teen girls who led the club knew they were a potent symbol for the white adults around them. The fear of miscegenation was one of the most effective tactics white supremacist agitators had, so the girls played up their roles as sexualized innocents. They told Leo Ely, editor of the *East Tennessee Reporter*, about the "inappropriate" interactions they had witnessed between Black and white students. Soon—white adults had no idea how soon—someone's white daughter would marry a Black man.

The girls also wanted to learn about the electoral process, though it would be several years before most of them could vote. They canvassed for the municipal elections scheduled for December 4. Especially important, they knew, was the mayoral race. W. E. Lewallen wasn't running for reelection, which meant the segregationists might have a real shot at taking his office. The Anderson County White Citizens' Council had endorsed a slate of candidates. The girls passed out literature and encouraged segregationists to vote their consciences.

And inside the school, the white students began openly harassing the Black students again. First came what Principal D. J. Brittain Jr. called "little incidents." A white student poured ink into Alvah Jay and Ronald's lockers, ruining the books stored inside. Someone else put new locks on, making the Black pupils late to class. Bobby Cain and Alfred Williams changed their locks for combination locks that would be harder to pick, so some of the white youths slapped KKK stickers on the doors. Or white kids smashed eggs between the pages of the Black teens' books. Or they stole Gail Ann and Minnie Ann's English books, broke the spines, and left the pages out in the rain. Or they muttered racial slurs and threats at their

Black peers, saying, "Go home, you black bitch." And someone painted: "Coon, Go Home" in a bathroom. And they put thumbtacks on the Black students' seats. That's kinda stupid, Jo Ann Allen thought as she brushed her chair clear, as though she wasn't going to check her seat.

They also targeted any white student who was kind to a Black teenager. A few white teens had been letting the Black students know they weren't on their own. Football players would ask Bobby Cain how he was doing. Another white kid always chose one of the Black boys first when it came time to pick teams for gym class. The individual moments weren't dramatic, just a few seconds of shared humanity. They added up, however. Now those minor but reassuring interactions slowed and then ceased.

As allies drifted away, the hostile students began openly attacking the Black teens. Bobby Cain and Maurice Soles were in the same gym class. When they showered after exercising, someone would flush the commodes, causing bursts of scalding water to pour out of the showerheads. White troublemakers tossed nails in the faces of the Black kids or brandished knives and ice picks at them as they walked to class. Alfred Williams slid into his desk for English class and felt an unexpected roughness to the wood. His fingers traced the letters carved into its top: " 'Get out of School Alfred Williams,' signed, 'John Kasper, nigger hater.' " Gail Ann Epps and Jo Ann Allen both had long hair that they wore in ponytails. White students would walk behind them, grab their ponytails, and yank the girls' hair straight down, snapping their chins toward the ceiling. Or sometimes the girls' schoolmates walked on the girls' heels until blood flowed into their shoes. The football team attempted to patrol the halls of the school, but they couldn't be everywhere at all times. Anna Theresser Caswell was particularly vulnerable, as she spent most of the year on crutches. Now white teenagers who were much taller and stronger than she was knocked into her or hit her on the head. She soon startled when anyone approached her from behind.

One white boy twisted a piece of twine into a noose and, looking straight at one of the Black students, stuck his finger into it, mimicking a lynching. Business teacher Margaret Anderson overheard another white teen say, "If you come back to school, I'll cut your guts out." One day after school, a white student accosted Bobby Cain. The youth reached into his pocket where he presumably had stashed his knife, looked at Bobby, and said, "I hope you got yours because I've got mine." Another day in study hall someone threw a snake around Maurice Soles's neck. He assumed it was a play snake and so did not react until he felt it move. That night, he begged his uncle to let him stay home. "Oh, you're going back to school tomorrow," Steve Williams replied. "Just watch who's behind you from now on."

Gail Ann Epps was walking along the school's second-floor hallway, a corridor lined with open, unsealed windows that looked down into the auditorium, when she felt someone grab her and begin to push her through an open window. She struggled to get away, but her attacker was much larger than she was. Looking down at the auditorium seats more than a story below, she thought about how her body would be broken on the chairs if she didn't escape. She elbowed her attacker hard in the stomach. When he released her, she ran out of the school but never reported the incident. Who knew what would happen if she said anything? Would anyone believe her? Being a tattletale would only make the abuse worse. Besides, even if she wanted to turn to her teachers for help, she seldom knew who had hurt her. Before most attacks, a whole group of white students gathered around. Who could say who did what?

Still, some of the white teachers tried to help. One teacher stopped Bobby Cain in the hall and apologized to him, saying "We're sorry you have to go through this." Margaret Anderson caught some white kids harassing Regina Turner during a study hall. That night, she called Regina at home to hear about what had occurred. The next day, Margaret publicly reprimanded the white teens. When Celdon Lewallen saw a group of white students gang up on one of the smaller Black pupils, she grabbed her thermos and charged into the fray. She yelled, "Get the hell out of my way!" before cracking her thermos over the head of one of the attackers and rescuing their victim.

And so the Tennessee White Youth turned on the school's faculty. Whispers restarted that Principal D. J. Brittain Jr. was actually a Jew. That was why he was so diminutive. It also explained why he had sold out real white Americans. Someone hired a private detective to watch him, searching for evidence to discredit him. The harassing phone calls got to be so troublesome that he and his wife changed their number multiple times. The phone kept on ringing. Hate mail also poured in, sometimes filling a mailbag a day. And then there was that teacher, Eleanor Davis. She was the one who had let Jo Ann Allen be elected an officer of her homeroom, you remember? Well, just look at Eleanor's black hair and dark eyes and full lips. Wasn't it obvious that she had African blood running through her veins? No wonder she and her husband were preaching law and order. People vandalized teachers' cars, turning on the lights to run down the batteries, ripping off the door handles, and jamming the gearshifts. Sometime in the night of Monday, November 26, vandals smashed the plate glass window in front of Lewallen-Miller Store.

"I have been teaching here for eight years, and I have taken more abuse in the past three months than I have in my whole career," one teacher told civil rights researcher Anna Holden.

—

On Tuesday, November 27, a group of white students was waiting for the Black kids as they walked to school. The white teens pelted their Black peers with eggs. After giving the white assailants "a strong talking-to," D. J. let them go back to class. Later that morning, white boys surrounded two of the Black girls in the school's library. The girls told D. J. that the white boys had threatened them and "used abusive language."

Robert Thacker and William Latham went to see their principal that day. "We're tired of being molested," they told D. J. "What would you do?" they asked.

"Do what you think is best for you," D. J. replied.

Robert Thacker and William Latham left the school and told their families they would not be returning. Their education at Clinton High had ended.

—

That night, nine of the ten remaining Black students met to confer and plan. (Anna Theresser Caswell had stayed home as she was ill.) They decided to take a day off, a wise decision, because the next morning protestors took back the streets around the school. Still, local newspaper reporters seemed surprised that none of the Black pupils returned. They called Jo Ann Allen. "We may be back tomorrow," she told them.

The next day, though, there were yet more people outside Clinton High. The Black families announced their children would boycott the high school until the town provided them with the protection needed to ensure their safety. If he wanted to do so, Judge Robert Taylor could choose to say this placed the school, Principal D. J. Brittain Jr., and the Anderson County school board in contempt of the federal court order. Some white folks around Clinton started worrying about what that would mean. Who knew what that judge would do next? Use this as an excuse to take control of the school? The district? Was this how he'd make them desegregate the state?

When he heard about the Black students' decision, D. J. asked the police to provide increased patrols around the school and told the student body that "any further acts against the Negro students would result in the expulsion of whoever committed the acts." But when the chief and his officers tried to break up the crowd gathered in front of the school that day by forcing people to move their cars out of the road, the segregationists taunted them, saying, "Why don't you go ahead and write me up?" The police—all dozen or so of them—gave up.

The following day, a Thursday morning, Bobby Cain and four others tried to go to school, but a truck sporting a White Citizens' Council sticker and filled with white men blocked their route off the Hill. The students turned back. When the editor of the *Clinton Courier-News* investigated their continued absence, he reported that the men were able to set up their roadblock because there were no police officers patrolling the school. He asked the chief of police where the officers were. The chief replied that he had sent his officers to "a meeting somewhere." If the Black teens had made it past the roadblock, they still might not have gotten into the building. One hundred members of the Tennessee White Youth had gathered on the schoolyard.

After the first bell rang that day, the superintendent and a few of the school board members came to see D. J. Brittain Jr. at the high school. This was the first time the board had discussed desegregation with the principal.

"Well, it's about time," D. J. said when he saw the men. "Now, how are you going to help me?"

"Just let things go," one of the board members told him. "They'll drive the Black children out of school."

Aghast, D. J. asked that they give him that order in writing.

"Oh no, we will not put this in writing," his visitor replied. "We're just giving you good advice."

D. J. refused to take the advice. And so the board undermined him. Whenever white students appealed their punishments, the board overturned the principal's rulings. In response, D. J. announced that he would finish the school year, but that was it. He'd be leaving Clinton High. "Right now, I am the only person between these Negro pupils and those people," D. J. told the *Southern School News*. "I am going to do my duty as I see it, at least for this year." But he couldn't take it any longer than that.

On Friday, the Black students stayed away again, but they also turned down a new offer by the school board to transfer them back to Austin High. "We want to continue in Clinton High," one girl told a reporter for the *Oak Ridger*. "That's where we belong."

FIFTEEN

Who, Then?

O n Sunday night, the Allens' telephone jangled. Knowing Josephine, whichever of the Allens answered the phone would have followed proper etiquette. They would've raced to pluck the handset out of its cradle before its third ring. "Hello," they would have said. Or perhaps, "Good evening." And then, "This is the Allen residence. May I ask who is calling?" or something similar. Or they would have before desegregation began. Perhaps the family had learned to be more cautious than etiquette allowed. Whoever answered the phone, they must've been surprised to hear the slower West Tennessee accent of the Reverend Paul Turner on the other end of the line. He was calling with a proposal, Paul said when he had one of the adult Allens—most likely Herbert—on the phone. He was worried that the Black students hadn't yet returned to school. They'd fought so hard for their right to be in the classrooms (and yes, there were strategic as well as practical reasons for their boycott over the past week), but Paul thought the gambit was going to backfire. The school board had shown little interest in supporting the Black students so far, and Judge Robert Taylor seemed hesitant to involve himself further in the conflict. If they stayed away too long, Paul warned, they might not be able to return. His proposal was this: he would walk them to school himself.

Why in the world would he make such an offer? the Allens asked.

"As long as they have a desire to go to the school, it is their moral right to come unheckled and unhindered," the white preacher replied.

Well, he certainly had given them something to consider, the Allens said. They'd confer with the other parents. A quick poll, however, decided it. The families appreciated what the preacher was offering, but they would stick with their plans. They wanted their demands met. They wanted protection for their children. They wanted the Tennessee White Youth shut down, at least inside the school. They wanted Willard Till's Anderson County White Citizens' Council and John Kasper's rival organization, the White Citizens' Council of Anderson County, kept off the streets and out of their neighborhood. They wanted official acknowledgment from the school board that their kids had a right to be in Clinton High School. They wanted more than any one man could provide, even the pastor of the largest white church in town.

The parents had reason to think they might get what they wanted. Just a few nights back, some school board members and the police chief had come visiting. The white men had offered to pay for the Black students' tuition and transportation if the teens transferred back to Knoxville's segregated Austin High School. While the families were debating how best to reject the idea without alienating such powerful white men, attorneys Sidney Davis, Buford Lewallen, and Eugene Joyce reached out. They wanted the students to stay at Clinton High. The students' bravery and stick-to-itiveness was making the town into an example for the entire South, the attorneys said.

Paul Turner told the Allens that he understood, but he asked them to call him back if they ever changed their minds. He needed to help however he could. That was the godly thing to do.

—

Paul had been wrestling with the question of racism and the gospel ever since Labor Day weekend when his seminary professor Olin Binkley had sent him Roy DeLamotte, another white pastor, who, unlike Paul, was a committed integrationist. After Roy had left, he continued his conversation with Paul through letters. His purpose was not "to win an argument (I hope!) or to get in the last word," Roy explained, but "to exhort a brother clergyman not to let a priceless chance slip past to make a witness for the kingdom." Roy reminded Paul that he was responsible for the souls of his congregants. In this time of upheaval, his flock was "fearful, confused, victims of rumors and gossips and lies and slanders and threats." Paul's message of law-and-order segregationism was not the "clear Scriptural word [the people needed] to steer by in this terrifying situation."

Roy chastised Paul for saying obedience to the law "was in line with what was American and Christian." That was drivel, Roy continued, because "surely with the exception of a few lunatics . . . no sane Christian is against law and order." Paul should use his pulpit to fight "the cancer of race pride" and the "violence, hatred, fear, suspicion" gripping his town. "If we are called of God at all," Roy concluded, "if all men ARE brothers, if Christ died for the lowliest members of society, then let us not put [the] whole church and our own professions ahead of the Kingdom!"

Even some white church members had scolded Paul Turner for not taking a bolder stand. One woman wrote to tell him that though she and her husband "bear no ill will or hard feelings toward you or the First Baptist Church of Clinton," they were transferring their membership. She reminded Paul of the many times he'd used his pulpit to stand against alcohol sales in the county. "You did not seem to mind stepping on church members' toes then," she reflected. "In fact, you quite frankly said many times you did not want that kind of church members anyway." That was why "we cannot understand your failure to take a stand now against what we consider so much greater evil—hatred and ill will," she explained. "If the church cannot lead the way on social problems, I fear for our county and country."

Paul still had refused to advocate for racial equality, partly because he didn't believe in it and partly because he didn't want to "be seen as 'a crusader.'" Besides, at that point in the fall, the Black children were in the school and the rioters were out of the town square. What, really, was there for him to do?

Then the two factions of the White Citizens' Council formed, the Tennessee White Youth got themselves organized, the protestors reappeared around the school, the Black teenagers launched a boycott, and Paul Turner found himself out of excuses.

Before reaching out to the Allens, Paul tried to find white support for his actions. He organized a meeting with sixteen other local white pastors to discuss the situation over at the school. They were all staunchly law-and-order segregationists, but they were troubled by the violence those kids were facing just for wanting to learn. That seemed the greater wrong. No, they wouldn't be making any grand gestures, but they'd talk to their flocks about what it meant to be good Christians.

Paul knew he was called to do more. He had talked enough. It was time for him to prove his faith through his deeds.

—

On that November Sunday morning just a few hours before he called the Allens, Paul Turner had stood on the stage at First Baptist Church and announced he believed the Black children had a right to attend Clinton High School. For his sermon that day, he chose the Parable of the Good Samaritan from the Gospel of Luke. In it, a highwayman attacked a Jewish traveler. Beaten and robbed, the traveler lay abandoned in a ditch. First a priest and then a ruler passed the man. Both looked the man over and concluded he had died. Since they had spiritual duties they couldn't perform if they touched a corpse, they hurried on their way. Then a Samaritan came. Though descended from common ancestors, the Jews and the Samaritans had been enemies for centuries. Nevertheless, when the Samaritan saw the traveler lying there "he had compassion, and went to him and bound up his wounds . . . set him on his own beast and brought him to an inn." The next morning, the Samaritan had to continue his journey, but he gave the innkeeper a large sum of money, asking that he care for the man until the Samaritan returned.

This parable was about three types of Christians, Paul told his people, but only two of the types could be seen in Clinton in 1956. The members of the White Citizens' Councils and the Tennessee White Youth were like the robbers, who said, "What's yours is mine. I'll take it if I can." The town's white law-and-order Christians were acting like the priest and the ruler who said, "What's mine is mine. I'll keep it." The godly response is to say with the Samaritan, "What is mine is yours. Take it if you need it."

"Our Christian religion is not one of philosophy but one of action," Paul concluded. Local, state, and national leaders had failed to properly plan for and facilitate integration, so Clinton's white Christians needed to shoulder responsibility and give every child in the town the best education possible regardless of skin color.

Most congregants left that day without saying much to their preacher, but one man pulled Paul aside. Leo Burnett was the production-planning supervisor at the Magnet Knitting Mills in Clinton. Beatrice Cain, Bobby Cain's mother, had been his family's housekeeper for years. Now that the situation was heating up again, Leo had read in the paper that the boy was taking an ever more public role in the conflict, walking at the front of the group and fielding interview requests from journalists both locally and around the nation. What would happen to Bobby if the kid put too large a target on himself? Whatever Paul had planned, Leo wanted to help him with it. Would that be satisfactory? Leo asked.

It would, Paul replied.

And so Paul reached out to the Allens. He must have been surprised when they turned him down. But though the Allens had rejected Paul Turner's offer of help, Paul, Leo Burnett, and two other white men climbed the Hill on Monday morning and again offered to walk the students to school. The students again declined.

As the four men walked back downtown, they were met by a small group of segregationists led by the Reverend Alonzo Bullock. Alonzo told the other preacher and his friends that "if they did not 'get that bunch of "niggers"' out of there, someone was going to get killed."

—

Monday morning, the Black families learned that rather than planning for the Black students' safety, six of the seven board members had met up at the school board offices near the courthouse, gathering before the first class bell rang, to draft a letter to the U.S. Justice Department abdicating responsibility for events at Clinton High. When the men finished drafting their statement, they invited Principal D. J. Brittain Jr. and the superintendent of schools into the room. The board chairman read the letter aloud. In short, the school board declared, what's happening at Clinton High isn't our problem. If Robert Taylor wants the school desegregated, let him enforce his ruling. They sent the letter to Attorney General Herbert Brownell by airmail, special delivery. When Horace Wells asked them about the letter, one of the board members simply told him, "Mister, we're on a spot, really on a spot."

Later that morning, the superintendent phoned the Knoxville City school board to ask whether he could transfer the Black students back to Austin High. The Knoxville superintendent agreed to raise the question at the next board meeting in a week's time. But the transfer would have to be voluntary on the part of the teens, the Knoxville superintendent clarified. He wasn't interested in breaking federal law.

Oh yes, on a voluntary basis, of course, the Clinton superintendent replied.

That night, the Allens called Paul Turner back. They were ready to accept his offer, if it was still good.

It was, he assured them.

—

Tuesday morning, the girls in the Tennessee White Youth must've woken up certain they'd won back their school. The Black students had missed almost a week of classes, putting them further and further behind. And now it was election day. Their base was energized on the key issues: states' rights and segregation. What did those law-and-order whites really have going for them? A commitment to civic harmony over moral convictions? No wonder they were only nominally interested in their candidates. At the school that morning, segregationist supporters—mostly friends and family—filled the schoolyard, stretched across the street, and curled around the corner. Clinton's police attempted to direct traffic through the racist throng, but the streets near the school had turned into a parking lot.

Did the girls notice two white men walking around the crowd and up the Hill? There was Paul Turner, who tugged on his dark fedora, shielding his face from the morning mountain fog. Next to him, Leo Burnett adjusted his thick leather gloves against the chill. A couple of the adult segregationists were at the foot of the Hill, keeping watch in case the Black students descended.

"Preacher," Clyde Cook, a prominent local segregationist who'd helped the Tennessee White Youth finalize their charter, yelled at Paul Turner, "what business have you got up here?"

"Sir, I do not care to discuss the matter with you," Paul answered.

"If a lot of these 'Negro lovers' would keep their noses out of it," said the Reverend Alonzo Bullock, "things would be all right." (Well, they said something like that. When Paul Turner retold the story for a federal court, he clarified that their real words were "commingled with profanity as well as vulgarity.")

Paul hailed a passing policeman and told him the men were hassling him. The officer said there was nothing he could do about it. What were a few words? And what had the pastor expected? Clyde resumed his heckling. "You can't get away with this," he warned. "You know you can't. We won't let you."

Clyde and Alonzo stopped at the railroad tracks that bisected the Hill. Paul and Leo continued on, eventually crossing onto the Green McAdoo schoolyard where attorney and First Baptist Church deacon Sidney Davis waited with six Black teenagers. The students and their escorts paused to pray; then they started the walk to school, forming up in a tactical formation.

Maurice Soles, the youngest and the smallest, took the lead, a position usually held by Bobby Cain. He looked over the passing fields, watching for an ambush. Regina Turner and Jo Ann Allen and Alvah McSwain stayed in the center of their phalanx, the most protected position. Sidney Davis and Leo Burnett walked in the street, putting their bodies between the students and anyone who might come at them. Bobby Cain and Alfred Williams joined Paul Turner at the back of the group, men keeping an eye on their tiny flock.

Clyde Cook and Alonzo Bullock joined up with them at the railroad tracks, still yelling insults. The school would not be integrated again, Alonzo warned Sidney. Anyone who tried to aid the Black students "would have trouble."

Sidney called out to the police. This time, the cop joined their entourage.

What do you mean by that? the officer asked.

"You will see," Alonzo replied.

More protestors joined the group. Mary Nell Currier accosted the officer.

Don't target me, he warned her.

I'll do as I please, she answered.

He took her to police headquarters, but he was told he could not keep her there. Who would believe a woman hit a police officer?

The students and their escorts reached the edge of the schoolyard where the sidewalk sloped below the embankment. Paul Turner drew nearer to Jo Ann Allen, chanting, "Don't be afraid. Don't be afraid." And as she had every other day, she kept her back straight and head high. Her enemies wouldn't get to know her fear. Rocks and eggs whizzed by. Still the girl looked down the sidewalk, refusing to turn even when the missiles were whistling close. The protestors pressed in, forcing the students and their escorts to walk single file. Their eyes looked a bit touched, Sidney Davis thought, a little too fierce for sane, rational thinking.

Members of the Tennessee White Youth leaned out the school's windows to yell threats. If you bring the Black students in here, you "better get ready to escort them all day long!" one of them yelled at Paul.

"Nigger lover!" others shouted. And "Negro-loving preacher!"

A substitute teacher stood in an upstairs classroom, watching the melee below. She recognized some of her friends among that "most menacing mob of people." How could folks she knew speak—shout—those filthy, jeering words?

But a knot of white teens met the group at the door, welcoming the Black students back to school and offering to walk with them to their classes. Their job done, Sidney and Leo left, but Paul spoke briefly with Principal D. J. Brittain Jr. Then the white pastor, too, walked out of the school door. One of the television journalists followed him, a member of the Southern War Correspondents Association who'd come back to town, sensing Clinton's story was getting interesting again.

—

The segregationists taunted Paul. You "ought to be ashamed," one of them said, "working to get the Negroes in school." They followed him as he headed to his church. At a nearby intersection, the chief of police was directing traffic.

Would you write down the names of these people who are threatening me? Paul asked him.

The chief urged the hecklers to break it up, but Paul's angry cortege kept pace. Outside the police station, Paul saw four more men waiting for him. Clyde Cook stood at the front, just a yard or so away. When Paul tried to pass, Clyde jumped on the preacher and punched him in the neck. Paul threw him off. Clyde wasn't much of a challenge, some half a foot shorter and Lord knows how many pounds lighter than Paul.

Then: "Watch out!" Paul heard someone yell. "That man has his hand in his pocket!"

Did someone have a knife? A gun? Paul's distraction gave the scrum the break they needed to catch him. They pushed Paul up against a building, pinning him against a plate glass window. The window bent under the pressure. Dipped. Began to cave.

"Nothing much I could do but do what I could," Paul decided. Before the glass behind his back splintered, he struck against his attackers, grabbing Clyde by the neck and throwing him to the sidewalk. The preacher would've easily won in a fair fight, but Clyde was not fighting alone. Looking at the pack of segregationists closing in, Paul knew every one of them. There was William Brakebill, who ran a gas station. And local handyman Clifford Carter. And tiny Zella Lou Nelson, accompanied by her new husband and his brother. And even Alonzo Bullock, another man of the cloth.

Now the preacher lost track of the action. Was it Clyde's head that rammed into a parked car? Paul sure hoped it wasn't his own. The crowd of segregationists pulled Paul off Clyde, and this time he was certain it was his head that bounced against the rear door of a late-model DeSoto Coronado.

"Kill the —— —— Negro lover!" someone yelled.

Forget journalistic objectivity, CBS news reporter Bob Allison decided. They would murder the preacher. He shoved at the segregationists closest to him, but he couldn't get through the swinging fists. A nearby businessman, the man who owned the plate glass window Paul had been pushed up against, opened the door and called for the minister to run to his office for safety. Paul could not make it. The businessman's secretary ran up and saw the pastor, her pastor, his face covered in blood. Seemed he was bleeding from his mouth, his nose, even his eyes.

"What are they doing to Brother Turner!" she screamed. She turned to another bystander, a man who looked hefty enough to help. Please, please help Brother Turner, she begged.

The man refused.

Well, she'd save her pastor herself. She ran to the fray and pulled on the arms of the men who were holding him.

Stop! she cried. Don't hit him again!

The men ignored her. But one of the women—possibly Mary Nell Currier—turned on her, scratching at her face and striking her about the head.

Eventually, two police officers arrived, sent either from the police station or from their patrol around the school, Paul would never be sure which. They corralled the pastor's many assailants, clearing space so Paul could assess his injuries. When he stood, he saw his blood smeared across the Coronado. A thick stripe swept over the door seal where his hand must have scrabbled and flailed. Smudges pressed into the trunk and the wheel well and the molding and the rear door and the back window from where his bloodied face had collided and slid. Splattered droplets darkened the conquistador medallion affixed to the hard top. Pools stained the sidewalk and curb.

The officers arrested Clyde Cook for the assault and took him to the Clinton City Jail, where he was charged with disturbing the peace and placed under a fifty-dollar bond. That afternoon, some members of the White Citizens' Council paid his bail and gave each of the officers a Ku Klux Klan sticker.

—

Unaware of the pastoral beating outside the school, Principal D. J. Brittain Jr. was meeting with a school board member when he heard a commotion. "Hold on, we've got more trouble," the principal said. He ran to investigate. He found students and teachers clustered around his wife, Clarice. She told him two white teenage boys had invaded the school. One was stay-away student James Dale Patmore. Another white teenage boy—one of the law-and-order students—had seen them wandering the halls. He knew they didn't belong. What are you doing here? the kid demanded.

I'm here to "get" one of the Black students, Jimmy replied. Take me to one of them.

No, the boy said.

The teens scuffled, and the noise of their shouts and blows brought Clarice Brittain into the hall. The two dropout teens had run off, but Jimmy shoved her as he fled. When D. J. heard that story, his mind was set. It was no longer safe in the building. The school board member told him to do whatever he thought best. D. J. didn't want to turn the students loose, easy targets for the mob outside, so he asked police officers to escort the Black teenagers back up the Hill to safety. He then summoned the buses and announced, "We are going to close the school today, close it tomorrow, and close it until it is safe for children to attend."

That did not sit well with the law-and-order pupils, teachers, and parents. The Student Council met that afternoon to denounce the violence. Student Council president and football team captain Jerry Shattuck took control of the meeting. It was time for all this harassment to end, he told his classmates. The troublemakers had already messed up his senior year. He wasn't about to let them ruin his future. The Student Council passed a resolution, all forty members voting unanimously to ask the Anderson County school board to immediately reopen Clinton High School, to comply "with the Federal Court order to provide an education for all the citizens of Anderson County who desire it," and to keep Principal D. J. Brittain Jr. and all other faculty "in their present capacity."

The faculty council met next. They, too, issued a statement denouncing the "minority group" that "has tried to prevent us from carrying out our professional obligations." In particular, the teachers continued, they wanted the dissolution of the Tennessee White Youth. "The activities of this small group in our school have been of a vicious nature," the teachers explained. "This minority movement is depriving more than seven hundred children, some of whom are our own children, from receiving the education to which they are entitled." They closed by urging all "conscientious parents . . . and all interested residents of this county to investigate the current activities of this minority group which is bringing about a breakdown of respect among the young people for law and order, contributing to delinquency, and an overthrow of authority which results in mob rule." What was happening "affects the whole future of their children and our democratic way of life."

—

When Federal Judge Robert Taylor heard what had happened, he was irate. Then on Tuesday afternoon, a delegation of Clinton's officials and leaders, including the Reverend Paul Turner, whose nose and eyes were swelling, came to see him. Clearly the situation was beyond the control of local authorities. Robert sent Federal Marshal Frank Quarles and his deputies, the law enforcement arm of the federal courts, to Clinton to investigate the situation.

Paul Turner's beating had also appalled most of the law-and-order white residents in town. They'd felt rather humdrum about the election, but they were electrified now. They flooded the polls. "Tuesday was a black day in Clinton, and tears were shed as word of the brutal and unprovoked attack upon the beloved Paul Turner spread," Horace Wells wrote. "Many felt a personal responsibility, a personal failure to do something—but no one knew just what he might have done—except to get out and vote." One man rushed back from Pittsburgh, sliding into town in time to cast his ballot. A coed returned home from college. Lines at the polling places stretched out of the buildings and down the streets outside.

When the votes were tallied, the White Citizens' Council candidates had lost in a landslide, their mayoral nominee receiving only 353 of 1,697 votes cast. (Two years earlier, only 708 people total had voted in the election that made W. E. Lewallen mayor of Clinton.) The new mayor was a fifty-seven-year-old white judge who believed in segregation but supported law and order above his personal racial convictions. Yes, when the school first desegregated, he'd offered up a thousand dollars of his own money to help pay to transport the Black students back to Austin High. But the law was the law, he said. Besides, what happened in the school was none of the mayor's business. He would leave educational policy to the school board and the principal to figure out.

The results were so overwhelming that by late that evening the outcome of the election was clear even though not all the ballots had been counted. Principal D. J. Brittain Jr. was relieved by the news. "I'm going to bed now and get a good night's sleep," he told a reporter for the *Oak Ridger*.

Paul Turner and his wife, Jane, felt similarly. "We would have all had to leave town" if the White Citizens' Council ticket had won, she wrote her family.

—

While some of the white community celebrated the election results, the Black community braced for the segregationists' retaliation. That very night someone threw four or five lit sticks of dynamite out of the window of a moving car, tossing them toward the Country Club, a tavern in the Black section of Oliver Springs. The blast blew a hole in the ground about eighteen inches deep. The explosion knocked down the three-year-old daughter of the white tavern owner and jarred their television set off its stand. A spent casing fell next to the playpen where his twin infant sons were sleeping. They, thankfully, were unharmed. George Harris, the Black manager of the tavern, was reading in his basement apartment when the detonation occurred. Rocks and dirt shook loose from the floor joists and rained down upon him.

Then the Klan rode through the Hill.

Herbert, Josephine, and Jo Ann Allen had spent all afternoon discussing the events of the day. Seemed to them, the segregationists had no limits. After all, "If people will beat up a man of God, what *won't* they do?" and "If boys will set upon the home ec teacher, who *won't* they strike?" The answers to their questions terrified them. That led them to one final, critical inquiry: Why was Jo Ann responsible for changing the world? And then the Klan came back. Herbert again picked up his gun. He walked out his front door, down his porch steps, through the yard, and to the gravel along the edge of the road. There he stood ramrod straight and watched the caravan pass. His wife and children stayed inside the house, praying and weeping. One armed Black man versus the entire local klavern? Mercy. They could shoot him where he was and no one would do anything about it. When the Kluxers had gone on, the police arrested Herbert for the second time.

Josephine Allen was finished with the Clinton High experiment. Were her husband and her daughter racing to see who could incite the racists the most? She had to act before one of them died. As soon as Herbert was released, she decided, they would join her brother's family in Los Angeles. Maybe there she'd even go to night school and pick up typing. Secretarial work sure would be an upgrade from domestic labor. The Allens left so quickly that they abandoned most of their furniture, books, and toys, only bringing what fit into Herbert's Buick. Things, though, they could replace after finding work. Jo Ann was saddest about leaving Minnie Hopper, her grandmother and the seamstress who'd stitched up all her beautiful clothes back in the summer when everyone felt such hope.

Herbert Allen wasn't thrilled to have moved. "Jo Ann and I are both stubborn," he explained. Still, it felt necessary. "I don't believe there will be an opportunity for my children in Tennessee because no matter how much education they get here, there's no place for them to use it." Maybe the situation in Clinton would improve, but "sometimes you have a big fire and a rain comes along and puts it out and you hope it's all over," he told a reporter for the *Chicago Defender*. "Then when it's dry, a little smoke comes out and whoosh, up goes the blaze again." In Clinton, he still smelled the racist smoke hanging low in the air.

Publicly, Jo Ann said she was relieved to be in Los Angeles. "I'll be glad when . . . I can get back to school—a peaceful school!" she told a reporter. "Just think, I won't have to worry about anything except getting good grades." Privately, however, she resented being forced to abandon her friends in the middle of the year, in the middle of their fight. She also felt even more alone than she had before. Who could understand what she'd endured except for Gail Ann and the other Black students who'd braved Clinton High with her? Her transition to her new high school was not an easy one. "When I first started going there," she later recalled, "it was like being in a foreign country. It was so different from what I knew. It was much larger, and I had Black teachers, white teachers, Asian teachers, Hispanic teachers. Wow. I didn't quite know what to do with that."

After having spent the last semester trying to be invisible lest she attract unwanted attention, she struggled to make eye contact with or say hello to her fellow students, which made it hard for her to make friends. She was so used to being on guard that she no longer knew how to interact with people of her own age. It took her more than a year before she could relax.

SIXTEEN

Tick. Tick. Tick.

The day after the attack, as a man from the telephone company hosed Paul Turner's blood off the sidewalk, Federal Marshal Frank Quarles, two of his men, and a cadre of local officers climbed into the town's patrol cars, armed with warrants for fifteen local white adults and Jimmy Patmore. The charges included planning "a campaign of intimidation against school officials," "joining a White Citizens' Council aimed at preventing the effectiveness of integration," "threats of violence," "picketing and congregating near the school building," "instigating acts of violence by white students," and "acts of assault and battery against Negro students on their way from school or against white persons accompanying Negro students." The three marshals and their police escorts drove away from the jail with their emergency lights flashing and sirens blaring. Five carloads of reporters and photographers chased after them, winking their own headlights and honking their horns.

The attack on the Reverend Paul Turner had drawn America's attention back to Clinton, and reporters had rushed back to town to satisfy their audience's curiosity. Jane described the chaos that soon overtook the house. "The phone rang as fast as you could hang it up yesterday—many calls from all over [the] U.S.— People we never heard of," she wrote to her parents. Harold Stassen, the former governor of Minnesota and aide to President Eisenhower, telegrammed Paul "as a fellow Baptist and fellow American" to celebrate Paul's "courageous, forthright, and righteous action." Bernice Cofer of the Baptist Home Mission Board thanked him for having "defended the rights of human souls. . . . History has forced you to be a 'first.' Thank God it is for his children." An English nun wrote that she had blessed a candle for him.

Other communities around the nation who were about to undergo de-segregation themselves had anxiously watched Clinton. Black families in Little Rock had been paying particularly close attention. They knew their own battle would start the following fall, and they wanted to prepare for the opposition they might face. After the attack, several of them wrote, praising Paul for his "courage and Christian convictions."

"We are proud that a Baptist minister has been one of the first to take a dangerous stand . . . for loyalty to Christ and to our country," wrote the parents of one of the teens who would become part of the Little Rock Nine. "Whenever Christians begin to take their responsibilities seriously, [the result] is one of danger and suffering. The call of Christ is not to 'flowery beds of ease' but to 'blood and sweat and tears.' 'In this world ye shall have persecution.' May you know, too, that he 'has overcome the world.'"

And in southeastern Alabama, John Lewis, a sixteen-year-old Black kid, monitored the news from Clinton. Seeing what happened to other Black teenagers just like him helped solidify his interest in civil rights. He would go on to be one of the leaders in the Nashville sit-in movement, a founder and chairman of the Student Nonviolent Coordinating Committee, an organizer of the 1963 March on Washington, a leader of the first Selma to Montgomery March, and a United States congressional representative.

—

The officers' first arrest attempt "resembled more closely a scene from a 'Keystone Kop' movie than a legitimate law enforcement effort," a local newspaper editor wrote. The officers and their journalistic entourage stopped at William Brakebill's grocery store/filling station. The attendant said William was away from the shop, but the law enforcement officials searched the building and property to be sure, hampered by the members of the press who trailed along behind them, generally getting in the way. The hullabaloo drew the attention of other folks in the vicinity who lined up around the parking lot to laugh at the scene. Marshal Quarles ordered everyone back to the police station to regroup. "You're hindering the cause," Frank told the newsmen; then he told them to wait at the jail.

The journalists protested. Eventually the marshal relented and let one car of photographers follow him.

They found William. Next, they picked up Alonzo Bullock. Then came South Clinton grocer and car dealer Lawrence Brantley, allegedly head of the local klavern. His wife and daughter followed him to the jail in their shiny new Cadillac. Willard Till came in handcuffs. He'd greeted the officers with an automatic pistol. Union Carbide fireman Clyde Cook was arrested while at work at the Oak Ridge Y-12 plant. Also arrested that day were house painter Clifford Carter; carpenter's helper J. C. Cooley; bus driver Mary Nell Currier; Magnet Mills knitter, school bus driver, and former deputy sheriff Chris Foust; house painter and carpenter John B. Long (the same man arrested for night-riding at the Lewallens' house); unemployed Cleo Nelson, who'd quit his carpentry job to be a full-time segregationist; nineteen-year-old Zella Nelson and her husband, Henson, a clerk at a Kroger grocery store; sixteen-year-old Jimmy Patmore; Knoxville Utility Board employee Thomas Sanders; and house painter Raymond Wood.

During the trial and after, both the prosecutors and the press said these people were part of Appalachia's undereducated and underemployed white working class. And a few of them were. Most of them, however, were comfortably middle class. They were entrepreneurs and business owners and former police officers. They were professionals and church leaders. Some had served with distinction in the Armed Forces. They had education and influence. They were not the dispossessed hillbillies and mountaineers other people insisted they were. They had plenty to lose.

The belief that only working-class whites fought racial progress was a myth. The story of working-class white violence and ignorance served (and continues to serve) an important purpose for those who wanted to believe they did not share society's racism. If violence and hate was a product of poverty, middle-class white people could congratulate themselves on being hardworking, upstanding citizens who didn't have prejudice. They'd used their own bootstraps, an attitude that ignored how race and class had stiffened those supports. If prejudice stemmed from a lack of education or intelligence, other white people could assume they did not share those ideas. Instead, they could enjoy their superior minds while denigrating the terrible decisions that had left these other white people so misinformed.

Yes, this story of lack and stupidity was an essential tool for the many white people in Clinton and across America who did not want to see how closely their own beliefs aligned with the sixteen headed off to jail.

Of those arrested, everyone except for Lawrence Brantley was a member of the White Citizens' Council. Though only four had kids at the high school (and unsurprisingly, all of those children were founding members of the Tennessee White Youth), most had ties to the institution. In addition to the two who drove school buses, Zella Lou Nelson had recently graduated from Clinton High, and she had twin sisters who had signed the charter for the Tennessee White Youth.

As news of the arrests spread, families and friends and curious bystanders gathered around the jail. Some warned the arrests would restart the riots. Others discussed breaking the defendants out. As the afternoon wore on, a few of those gathered outside set up mourning as though they were at their loved one's wake. "Lord, have mercy on my baby!" Zella Nelson's mother cried out. "Lord, have mercy on Clinton!" (Zella's mother was also Mary Nell Currier's oldest sister, and Mary Nell had lived with Zella's family when the girl was a toddler.)

Journalists and cameramen ringed the onlookers, their camera flashes and whirring film reels adding to the chaos. Paul Turner arrived amid this ballyhoo to identify his attackers. That accomplished, the fifteen adults were taken to Knoxville for their arraignment. Sheriff Glad Woodward added one more man to the transport cars, a moonshiner named Doyle Justice he'd been wanting to apprehend for a while now. "As long as the marshals were here, I figured they might as well take Justice along with them," Glad said. As the marshal's cars pulled away, Zella Nelson's family again shouted out above the fray. "Don't worry, honey, I'll take care of your baby!" one of them called to her.

In Knoxville, the Clinton defendants were deposited in a jail cell in the marshal's office. They had a battalion of volunteer defense attorneys from around the South, including the attorneys general of Georgia, Louisiana, and Texas, and Mississippi governor Ross Barnett. Asa Carter nominated himself to raise the money to pay the fees and other costs associated with the defense. Before the prisoners would agree to meet with their lawyers, however, they paused for prayer, again led by Alonzo Bullock. Their resounding "Amen" at the end of it could be heard up and down the court corridor. Within a few days, the lawyers had charges dismissed against J. C. Cooley on technicalities. The rest were released under bond, the cost of which ranged from $1,000 for Zella Nelson to $12,000 each for Willard Till and Clyde Cook. During the arraignment hearing, Judge Robert Taylor had ordered the marshals to arrest one more man. Joseph Diehl, a Knox County man who had sometimes let John Kasper use his farm for meetings, was passing out "'inflammatory' literature" in the courtroom's lobby. "When good Christian people are arrested like they were in Clinton, we have a Hungarian situation here at home," Joseph had written. He handed one of the papers to the U.S. district attorney, who passed it to the judge. "It would be most difficult to think of any more disrespectful language than that which compares the arrest of people in Clinton . . . with the Russian oppression in Hungary," Bob Taylor retorted.

But like Joseph, many local white residents believed the government was overstepping. Fifty-eight families in Anderson County even unplugged their telephones and asked the Southern Bell Telephone office to come rip out their lines, claiming the FBI had tapped their phones. Eventually, the FBI would concede that yes, after Paul's beating they had sent ninety-two agents to Clinton to investigate the violence, and yes, they did tap a number of telephones, monitoring them from the local office. "That's untrue!" the telephone manager said. But folks were sure they'd heard that telltale click of a G-man listening in.

—

That next Sunday, Paul returned to his pulpit, black eye and all, standing before 650 congregants and a bank of television cameras. Among them was influential television journalist Edward R. Murrow, who'd told Paul he'd "been waiting for a church to take this stance." Paul had agreed to help his *See It Now* program create a documentary on Clinton. Now the *See It Now* team captured Paul announcing, "There is no color line at the cross of Jesus." But then he clarified that statement. Jesus was not a racial radical. "Right now, here in Clinton, we're not against integration, we're not against segregation," Paul explained, "but we are positively against disintegration of our body politic and community.

"Either we assert ourselves in the spirit of the Christian ideal," he continued, "or life and government and business and economics and peace and community integrity and joy and Christian usefulness are all on a toboggan, sliding backwards."

Not everyone in Paul's life was pleased with this stand, even though it fell far short of demanding total racial equality. "Dear Paul," his father wrote. "What have you done?" His parents' church in Jackson, Tennessee, had considered calling Paul to be its head pastor, but now that was an impossibility. A few members of Clinton's First Baptist Church had already left because of Paul's actions. The following summer, an anonymous writer told Paul that his church was "not happy. . . . You Are Done. Get Smart Go—Go—Go—Go—Go—Not. Wanted."

Paul also worried about his safety as well as the safety of his wife, Jane, and their two young children, both adopted, the older of whom was still a toddler. Death threats came in among the hate mail and harassing phone calls. "Once I knew a minister by the name of Peck that fell in a well and broke his neck," one Knoxville businessman wrote. "It served him right. He should have stayed at home, took care of his members, and let the school business alone." The church deacons sent a guard to patrol the Turners' yard, and Paul began sleeping with a pistol and a shotgun.

Even those who had sided with Paul Turner were vulnerable. When a pastor in Knoxville announced he would preach a sermon supporting Paul, some White Citizens' Council members drove a black hearse to his door and asked where the dead body was, a threat similar to hanging the man in effigy. They also tried to discredit the Knoxville pastor by having bootleggers place liquor by his front door and take pictures.

But Paul stuck it out.

—

After taking the weekend to regroup, D. J. reopened Clinton High School on Monday, December 10. Eight of the Black teenagers returned, as did 585 white pupils. Before sending students to their homerooms, the administrators and faculty directed everyone to the auditorium where the Anderson County attorney general stood at the podium. He read aloud the federal injunction prohibiting anyone from interfering with the Black students at Clinton High School. He told the white kids they could believe whatever they liked, but this was how they "must act as . . . a student in this school:" any "uncalled-for provocation will be dealt with swiftly and harshly," he warned. This included "gathering outside the school, messing up lockers, filthy language, pouring ink on books, and anonymous letters to teachers." It also meant they should stop wearing their segregationist paraphernalia. Anyone who disobeyed his instructions would be expelled. Or maybe school officials would call in the FBI to investigate, and the student might end up like Jimmy Patmore—sitting in a federal court facing federal charges. Most of the white students took that threat seriously and the campus settled into détente.

On Friday, December 14, eight of the Black teenagers left Clinton as soon as school was dismissed, shuttled to the Highlander Folk School for a weekend away. Highlander had begun in 1932 as a labor rights organization and adult education facility. During the early 1950s, however, it shifted toward civil rights. In 1955, Rosa Parks trained there, learning about nonviolent protest in preparation for her part in the Montgomery Bus Boycott. Over the summer, the school had hired Black educator and activist Septima Clark as its workshop director. After Paul Turner's beating, she'd visited Clinton and invited the Black teens to come "for a weekend of fun and relaxation." They could sleep soundly for a few nights, knowing they were safe. This was also a chance for them to connect to the larger civil rights movement, to see they weren't fighting alone. To that end, she also invited activists and high schoolers from Nashville and Chattanooga, along with Rosa Parks and her mother.

On Friday night, the kids and their new friends watched movies. Saturday morning, they hiked the grounds and went searching for a Christmas tree. The staff made sure to choose a route Anna Theresser could navigate despite her disability. After lunch, they trimmed the tree together, hopefully belting out their favorite carols. Dinner was a wiener roast followed by a few hours bopping around the jukebox. At 8:30, the staff surprised them with a Christmas party. During the party, Rosa Parks took a few minutes to explain nonviolent resistance to the students; then they opened presents. When Septima had visited Clinton, she'd reported some of the Clinton teens needed new clothes. When they heard that, the younger staff had organized a gift exchange for them. "The Negro high school students are, as all teenagers are, but even more than most, in a highly competitive situation, and should not be handicapped by a lack of suitable clothing," one of the weekend's organizers explained.

While the students had played and laughed and relaxed, their parents met with Septima. Could the staff come to the Hill and host a workshop on nonviolent resistance? the parents asked. Maybe some of the white folks would even participate. The staff was skeptical. They'd tried to convince some of the white high schoolers to join their Black peers for the weekend, but no one had agreed to come. That was the other reason they had brought kids from Nashville.

—

No one expected this latest cease-fire to last. And they were right. Friday morning—the same Friday the kids went to Highlander—a gaggle of white elementary students on their way to school had found a package in a ditch. The kids told a neighboring farmer, who sent them on to class and stood guard over the explosives until police arrived. When officers opened the container, inside was 103 sticks of dynamite, five caps, and a roll of fuse. It was nothing, officers declared, just dynamite fallen from a passing truck. And there was a lot of dynamite in Anderson County, some of it smuggled home illegally after a day on the job, some of it bootlegged from a nearby coal bank, and some of it purchased from the local hardware store. The lawmen investigated no further. No one reported the dynamite missing.

A week later, at 2:30 on the morning of December 22, three sticks of dynamite placed on a cross girder of the Clinch River Bridge exploded, shattering the beam and tearing apart its riveted joints.

Another device blew up at 3:30 on Christmas morning. Clinton's sleepless residents heard a subsequent explosion an hour and a half later, but no one could find the bomb site.

A fourth detonated in nearby Andersonville at 2:00 that afternoon. That one had been set in front of the Andersonville Baptist Church near the parsonage. It did little damage. No one knew why that spot was targeted.

Three days later, John Kasper's meeting site was destroyed. John had rented the small concrete block building a half mile south of Clinton for fifty dollars. He only came to Clinton a few days a month, but when he was there he used the downstairs as a base for his struggling branch of the White Citizens' Council—usually only a handful showed up at meetings—and he lived upstairs. The dynamite was situated to obliterate the structure. The blast occurred at 9:33 in the evening, less than fifteen minutes after a White Citizens' Council meeting ended. The only reason John was not injured was that he'd left for Knoxville immediately after dismissing the confab, a fact that his attackers may not have known. John Kasper discovered the bombing the next morning when he came back from Knoxville and found Sheriff Glad Woodward investigating. He would not use the place for meetings any longer, John told Glad, a rather obvious concession given the state of the building.

John Kasper appeared to get the message. After the explosion, he seldom returned to Clinton. But he didn't have many other places to go at that point. His bookstore in Washington, D.C., was set to close at the first of the year. The landlord was replacing it with a camera shop, a neighboring storekeeper told a reporter. Then the neighbor started laughing so hard that the reporter couldn't get any more information out of him.

John tried to keep his influence over the Knox County White Citizens' Council, but when he attended a council meeting on January 25, gathering with about one hundred local segregationists at a Baptist church, one of the attendees singled him out, asking John why he had come to Tennessee to "carpetbag." The local klavern, part of the Knights of the Ku Klux Klan that did not recognize Asa Carter's group as legitimate Klansmen, was also skeptical about John's motives. They reached out to their national leadership for support in driving out John Kasper and his allies. Their Imperial Wizard came to Clinton in late March to investigate. He alleged that John and Asa were co-opting the segregationist movement "to mislead and swindle people out of their money." They sure hadn't advanced the cause! All the outsiders had done was create divisions and dissension. It would be okay, the man said. "We rid the South of carpetbaggers once," the Wizard said. "We can and will do it again if necessary."

Just after New Year's, someone tried to blow up the railroad tracks on the Hill. They'd buried three sticks of dynamite under the crossties and set it off. The blast didn't damage the rails, but it did create a hole beneath them. Since the explosion happened just a few minutes before the next train reached Clinton, no one warned the engineer. The train drove right over the crater, but it didn't crash.

Then at 11:30 p.m. on Tuesday, January 15, someone threw a couple sticks of dynamite at the police chief's house. No damage was done, but some of the chief's neighbors thought they heard a second blast some ten or fifteen minutes later. Sheriff Glad Woodward went over to the Brushy Mountain State Penitentiary the next morning and brought back bloodhounds, hoping to track down the bombers plaguing the city. No one asked how he thought the dogs would be able to track a car.

Local, state, and federal investigators pursued all these incidents, but they never arrested anyone for the crimes. No one seemed to doubt which group set the dynamite, though. The segregationists might not be shouting on street corners anymore, but they weren't resigned.

SEVENTEEN

Alfred Williams

Alfred Williams didn't fit in at Clinton High, and he knew it. Who would be comfortable as one of just nine Black kids in a school of almost seven hundred students? Even if he'd had white skin, though, most folks wouldn't have thought he belonged there. He'd turned twenty-one on December 6. Being the only full-grown man studying alongside a bunch of punk kids, well, some days it was hard to remember why he was there. And it was hard to thrive with so much animosity pulling him down. He'd heard some of the journalists and the like talking about how he and the others were making history. He didn't know about that. All he was trying to do was follow the law of the land, obey his uncle, and earn his diploma.

He was smart enough to attend high school; he'd never doubted that. Trouble was, his education had been catch-as-catch-can. He'd been born in 1935, the oldest of three boys in a working-class family down in Anniston, Alabama,* a little town sixty-some-odd miles east of Birmingham and Asa Carter's birthplace. Alfred's father died shortly after his brother Eddie's birth, and his grandmother, Mary Williams Royston, had moved in with the family to provide childcare. Alfred's mother worked at a dry cleaner,

---

* Segregation structured life in Anniston even more severely than it did in Clinton. The community's most famous moment would come in 1961 when a mob of local white citizens would firebomb a bus full of college-aged Freedom Riders who were protesting the ongoing segregation of public transportation despite Supreme Court rulings in favor of integration. When the riders started trying to escape the burning vehicle, the waiting mob brutally beat them. Eventually, the state highway patrol showed up, which probably saved some of the riders from being lynched.

and Mary was a cook in white people's homes. With both their incomes, the two women probably made a reasonably stable, comfortable life for Alfred and his three brothers—by now his mother had given birth to his half brother, Maurice—but then Alfred's mother died in 1947. Twelve-year-old Alfred may have heard talk about being the "man of the house," but he didn't have much chance to step into that role. The Williams family split the boys up. Mary kept his youngest brothers, Maurice and Eddie, with her. She sent Alfred and his brother Charlie to Anderson County to live with her brother, Alfred's great-uncle Steve Williams. But *great-uncle* was an unwieldy nomenclature for a relative this close to the boys. Pretty soon, he was simply their uncle Steve.

Most of the men in the Williams/Royston family worked in the ironworks in Anniston, but Steve learned how to do automobile maintenance and repair. Sometime early in Oak Ridge's founding, Steve had moved to Anderson County, settling on the Hill in Clinton near the Cains and the Allens. He joined Mt. Sinai Baptist Church and he was made a head deacon. He married a local girl, though they didn't have any children of their own. He'd stayed out of both World War II and Korea because the auto repair business was an essential service in the Atomic City. When his great-nephews came to live with him, Steve was a middle-aged, childless man who'd escaped poverty and made something of himself. He wanted the boys to have even better opportunities. He enrolled Alfred and Charlie in Green McAdoo Grammar School. After they finished eighth grade, they started commuting to Vine Junior High School in Knoxville. When Alfred began at Austin, though, his grades slipped. Maybe that was why Steve had sent the brothers back to Anniston to live with Mary. Then had come the desegregation ruling. Mary brought all four boys to Clinton. But it was only Alfred and Maurice down at the school, two easy targets for the racist bullies.

And now Alfred had failed all his classes the first semester, every last one. What could they expect? How was he supposed to concentrate at that school, what with people yelling out terrible things and throwing rocks and punching on him? How could he study or rest at night when there were Klan parades and drive-by shootings and exploding dynamite? He knew Bobby and some of the others managed decent grades despite the chaos during the day and the danger stalking them at night. Alfred didn't see how. Took all his energy to attend to himself and Maurice. And Maurice, well, seemed like he got jumped just about every day he was there. Alfred felt even worse about his situation when he heard about life over at desegregated Oak Ridge High. Their basketball team had played at Clinton High in the district quarterfinal game. A minute and a half in, a Black senior entered the game, becoming the first Black player to play in a white high school basketball tournament. He scored nine points and Oak Ridge won. What would life have been if he lived over in that city?

Alfred had intended to do better during the spring semester. Surely, the hallways would quiet down after the Christmas break, now that the fifteen segregationists were jailed and the Tennessee White Youth had been called out as the hoodlums and troublemakers they were. Little had changed in the new year, however. The White Youth members were still provoking Alfred and Bobby. Forget a more peaceful semester. Alfred thought it was all about to escalate.

—

Late at night on Wednesday, January 9, two effigies were hung on the grounds of Clinton High School. One swung from a light fixture on the east entrance to the school. The other one was left on the ground beside a tree with a card pinned to it: "Keep our white schools white." The teenagers who created the dummies also smashed four windows in the band room and busted out a large six-by-eight-foot glass window in the main building. After that, they went to Clinton Grammar School, where they broke two windows in the new auditorium/cafeteria. Alfred and Bobby understood the meaning of those effigies far too well: two murdered, desecrated dummies for two endangered Black seniors. So much harassment when the only thing Alfred Williams wanted to do was go to school and finally earn his diploma.

The police investigating the incident discovered two different groups of white youths had sewn and stuffed the effigies. Because the teens were minors, the local newspaper did not give their names, but it did describe them. Four girls created and hung the effigy from the light pole. One of these girls attended Lake City High School, one attended Clinton Grammar School, and the other two were Clinton High dropouts. Two were officers in the Tennessee White Youth. Nine boys—all notorious juvenile delinquents—had hung the other effigy. They originally placed it on the playground at South Clinton Grammar School, but they'd moved it to Clinton High. Three of the boys were Clinton High School students, two others attended different local schools, and the rest were dropouts.

The police let the girls go, but they took the boys in. When they arrested the teens, two of the boys were driving a stolen truck full of goods taken during earlier robberies over the previous few months. The police suspected the group had also vandalized local schools, stolen guns, and snatched hubcaps. They learned the boys also had wanted to break windows at the *Clinton Courier-News* building, but when they got to the newspaper they saw a light on in the upstairs office and lost their nerve. The judge sentenced four of the white boys to a year at the State Agricultural and Industrial School in Nashville, but he paroled them to the care of their parents. Their freedom was contingent on attending school, having good conduct, and obeying their parents' curfews.

One of the remaining five boys was James Dale Patmore, out on bail for his role in the December violence. After Jimmy's birth near Oxford, Mississippi, his father had disappeared (whether by death or abandonment isn't clear). Within a few years, his mother, Ruby, had found a new husband, and the two of them had moved north to work in Oak Ridge. Jimmy's stepfather had taken him in, but Jimmy had never settled into his mother's second family. By middle school, he was a known troublemaker. Now the judge decided it was time to get the kid off the city's streets. He sentenced him to two years at the industrial school in a neighborhood of Nashville known as Jordonia, which was also the school's nickname.

Two months later, Jimmy and three other East Tennessee inmates attacked a night guard. Jimmy had somehow gotten his hands on a two-by-four that was studded with nails. He swung, hitting the guard in the head. The other boys then attacked with pilfered scrub brushes and their fists. When they'd finished, the man was unconscious and blood flowed from his mouth, ears, neck, and hands. Another attendant heard the commotion and summoned help, who grabbed the assailants and called emergency services. The supervisor was transported to Baptist Hospital.

The damage done to him was extensive. One of his head wounds required thirty stitches.

Jimmy told a reporter that the attack was an escape plan. After getting out, he'd thought he'd hide in New York City until the search for him was called off.

Why had he done it? the reporter asked. Had he been mistreated?

No, Jordonia had been fine.

Then why had he done it?

"I always have an urge to get out," Jimmy Patmore replied. "Yeah, I guess I'm sorry I hit the supervisor." Jimmy paused and considered this. "I guess I am."

In punishment, the superintendent of the school transferred the sixteen-year-old Jimmy to the adult federal penitentiary nearby. Jimmy said he found that comforting.* "At least I know when I get out," he said. "At the pen, I won't have that urge to break out."

But that was in the months to come. Back in Clinton, the police chief was amazed by how much trouble the teens had caused. "It is difficult for me to conceive of youngsters, fourteen and fifteen years old, staying away from home all through the day—not in school—and hanging out in joints through the night," he said. "What are their parents doing? Why can't they give some attention and supervision to these children?"

A lawyer connected to the defense team hired to help the fifteen segregationists retorted that the teens' actions had nothing to do with their parents. The youths had acted because of their own convictions. "It looks like the kids are making the school boil again," he crowed. "Some of the die-hard integrationists want to blame it on outside interference. They

---

* Jimmy Patmore was released from the adult penitentiary on February 16, 1959. In 1961, he was returned to the state prison for fraud. In December of that year, he beat up another guard. In 1963, he was part of a hunger strike to protest the treatment inmates received in solitary confinement. A few years later, he was released again. Then in 1973, a man by the same name and of a similar age was incarcerated in Illinois. That James Patmore participated in another hunger strike in protest of treatment. When the hunger strike went on for too long, that James Patmore cut his Achilles tendon so he would be able to spend time in the hospital eating food he liked.

don't want to admit that they just can't indoctrinate those kids to accepting the situation."

—

On Thursday, January 31, Alfred Williams stayed behind at the school, hoping to catch up on some work. He'd fallen so far behind. He couldn't keep going this way and have any hope of graduating. When he was finally ready to leave, he walked toward his locker, assuming he was the only Black student left in the building. He passed a white student, the fifteen-year-old paper boy who delivered the *Clinton Courier-News* to subscribers on the Hill every morning.

"There he goes," the paper boy said.

"Here I go," Alfred replied. "What of it?"

Then he looked down the intersecting hallway and saw Maurice. A group of white teens, about ten of them, had surrounded his brother and were taunting him, pushing him, jabbing at him. Well, didn't that just figure, them jumping on his little brother when they thought no one was around to save the kid? Alfred couldn't let that stand. As he neared the group, he heard someone say, "We're going to kill him." Right, Alfred thought, this was why he and Bobby had practiced. He flipped open his penknife as he pulled it from his pocket and charged into the clustered white kids. If they are going to fight my brother, they're going to have to kill me too, he decided.

Dan Ward—a white fifteen-year-old who appeared to be one of the ringleaders—heard Alfred mumbling something as he shoved his way toward Maurice. "What did you say?" Dan demanded. Alfred grabbed Dan and shoved him into a locker. Or maybe he punched him. Or maybe both. Alfred noticed Dan kept his hands in his pockets, so he assumed Dan must have a knife also. He brandished his weapon in Dan's face and yelled, "Do you want to fight him now? You've been picking on him when I'm not around!"

"Get him!" Dan yelled to his friend Jimmy Ray McGill, a seventeen-year-old senior and a football player.

"I know who you are and I'm gonna cut your —— out," Jimmy claimed Alfred said. But even with his knife, Alfred was unlikely to win the fight.

As he scrambled and scrabbled, Alfred noticed the paper boy standing with the rest of the white students attacking him and his brother. So the kid hadn't been there in the hallway by accident. He'd been a lookout. Alfred knew that kid. He knew all of them. Some of them had played summertime games of pickup baseball with him. Others had liked the same fishing spots. How could they be doing this? He knew he'd always been a hothead, but he was so worn-out after the past semester packed with brouhaha. He was just trying to go to school. Why was that so hard?

If you come up on the Hill again, I'll "cut your guts out," Alfred said to the paper boy.

"He waved that knife around," Jimmy Ray explained to Leo Ely, editor of the *East Tennessee Reporter*. He "threatened to cut us to pieces if we came to school tomorrow."

The white students had been preparing the newspaper's readers for this moment. On January 10, one white student reported to Leo that Alfred had pulled a knife on him.

And that wasn't the first time! another chimed in. Both Alfred and Bobby had threatened him with knives before. And at school, no adult did anything about it.

That's true, a third white teen said. Bobby walks down the hall elbowing every white student he passes—even the girls!—trying to pick a fight.

"Something happens at the school every day," yet another boy said, "but nothing is reported about it."

On this day, the white students must've assumed they had Alfred and Maurice cornered, but Regina Turner and Gail Ann Epps had also stayed behind. They did not carry knives, but they did have umbrellas. When they heard the yelling, the girls joined the fray, walloping on the white students with their rain gear.

Eventually teachers broke up the fight and released all the students except for Alfred and Maurice. They were worried Alfred's knife wasn't the penknife he claimed it was. The white boys had talked about how he had flipped it open. It must be a switchblade, the white teens had told their teachers, and those types of knives were illegal. Yes, it was an illegal knife with a blade that was five—no, it was six inches long—and it had a yellow handle.

The teachers quickly figured out that the knife Alfred carried was just a run-of-the-mill pocketknife, the same as kids across the mountains had with them at all times. They returned it to him and sent the brothers home. But, they told Alfred, he should report to the office tomorrow instead of to homeroom.

Dan Ward and Jimmy Ray McGill knew this was their shot to get Alfred out of the school. They couldn't trust D. J. Brittain Jr. to do it, however. Their principal was far too lax with the Black students. Knowing him, D. J. might let Alfred off with nothing but a warning! To ensure that couldn't happen, the two white boys reported the altercation to the police. After hearing their account—an illegal knife—the police chief got in an unmarked car and drove toward the Hill. Alfred and Maurice were walking home. He stopped the brothers and he searched them for weapons, even looking in their shoes. The only weapon on either boy was Alfred's one-and-a-half-inch pocketknife. The officer then asked Alfred what had happened. Perhaps to keep his brother out of trouble, Alfred did not mention the attack on Maurice. He said Dan Ward had left a thumbtack on his seat earlier in the day. When he saw Dan standing in the hall, Alfred said, he confronted the white teen about it. Dan then called him a dirty name and said, "What if I did?"

That's when I hit Dan, Alfred told the chief. He "was very sorry about it."

This wasn't a case for the police, the chief decided. An inch-and-a-half knife? If those Tennessee White Youths were scared off by a tiny, blunt blade like that, well, they needed to toughen up. No charges would be filed against the Black students. School administrators would have to handle the situation.

Determined to have Alfred arrested, the parents of Dan and Jimmy Ray went to the police station to try to obtain their own indictment against Alfred. Their petition was denied. At that point, Dan Ward's parents pulled him out of school. "I would rather have him home than in that mess up there," his father told Leo Ely. Dan didn't stay out of school long. His father's company quickly transferred him to a segregated town in Middle Tennessee. Dan started classes there.

Alfred Williams didn't have any way to avoid his fate. The next morning, Assistant Principal Juanita Moser (presumably with the permission of

Principal D. J. Brittain Jr.) suspended him indefinitely for carrying a knife on school grounds. Furthermore, school administrators thought Alfred's "age and apparent inability to keep up with his classmates [meant that] he should enroll in a vocational school or obtain employment," the official notice sent to Mary Royston explained. His suspension would become a permanent expulsion unless his family appealed the case to the school board. They had ten days to file.

Mary wasn't angry with Alfred. "Alf stood as much as he could take," she told a reporter for the *Pittsburgh Courier*, a Black newspaper, "then he just lost his temper." But was the case worth appealing? That was a hard question to answer. Much as he needed the diploma, maybe her grandson was better off out of that building. Alfred wasn't sure either. Maybe if he let the white people kick him out, he'd be the scapegoat who made the situation better for everyone else. After a few days, however, the Williams family changed their mind. They needed to expose the daily struggles faced by the Black students, and if Alfred faced punishment for the incident, then Dan Ward, Jimmy Ray McGill, and the rest of the white attackers should too. Both Steve and his wife, Lucille, wrote letters, asking the school board to reconsider Alfred's suspension.

—

The white supremacist campaign intensified during the weeks between the attack on the brothers and Alfred's hearing. The same night as the fight, someone threw dynamite at Horace Wells's home. They didn't throw hard enough, however, so it exploded on the next-door neighbor's property. No damage was done. The next day at about 3:30 in the afternoon, a passerby found a brown paper sack placed about twenty feet away from the Anderson County Courthouse. Inside, the bomber had wrapped an American flag (or maybe it was a Confederate one) around unexploded TNT. Whoever left the parcel had lit the fuse, but a passing rainstorm had extinguished it before it could detonate and destroy the municipal building.

Over the next week, white merchants downtown found hand-printed golden-colored postcard-sized stickers affixed to their windows. Similar ones were left on the courthouse and around the high school. Some said:

"The Clinton High underground is watching you" and "Keep Our Schools White." Some had "illogical and untrue statements which intended to slander officials and others." All those targeted by the messages were white, and all of them had been part of the official push for law and order.

And then at about 10:15 on Valentine's Day night, the men guarding the Hill watched as a white man dressed in khaki-colored clothes stopped his car about fifty feet from the Chicken Shack, the neighborhood's restaurant and nightclub. They observed as he crossed to the passenger side, knelt along the running board, and fiddled around with something, his body blocking their view. Then he got back in his car and drove away. Had anyone seen what he'd done? The men gathered and cautiously approached the spot. "Do you smell gunpowder?" one of them asked. The bomb detonated.

Turned out, the white intruder had pulled out a suitcase stuffed with upward of ten sticks of dynamite, placed it on top of a four-inch-thick concrete-and-steel drain, lit the fuse, and driven away.

People around Clinton were startled awake by the explosion. The blast threw pieces of the reinforced culvert across the neighborhood. The dynamite also destroyed two cars and shredded a steel drum, which pierced the walls of nearby homes, some of the shrapnel passing all the way through the outer facades and lodging in interior walls. One eight-inch piece knocked off a table leg and tore a hole in a woman's skirt. The Chicken Shack was obliterated. Ethel Gallaher, the Shack's owner, was thrown across the room by the blast. Her eleven-month-old daughter was cut by flying debris. The house next door was also demolished. A woman in a house across the street was injured when the boards of her ceiling fell on her. Green McAdoo's windows were shattered. Twenty-five other houses had damage—some a quarter of a mile away—ranging from broken pictures and knocked-over clocks and fragmented mirrors to splintered windows and crumbled walls and collapsed ceilings. One of the houses to suffer the worst damage was that of Steve Williams, where Alfred and Maurice lived.

"Is this happening in America?" one resident asked Horace Wells.

"Somebody will be killed the next blast we have," predicted an Anderson County constable.

That night, the men of the Hill demanded identification from every white person who tried to drive through their neighborhood. Neither the sheriff nor the police stopped them.

—

Exactly one week later, the Anderson County school board met for a special session. All the board members were there along with the superintendent of schools, the county attorney, the local head of the Tennessee Federation for Constitutional Government, Principal D. J. Brittain Jr., and Assistant Principal Juanita Moser. Alfred brought along his aunt and uncle, Lucille and Steve Williams. Regina Turner and Maurice Soles came as his witnesses. Before proceedings began, the board announced that the point of the hearing was not to ask how the last six months of racial conflict had contributed to the incident but "to determine the facts of the suspension and whether or not the Williams boy was guilty of breaking school rules." No one but Alfred was in trouble, according to them.

Assistant Principal Juanita Moser, who had suspended Alfred, was first. She testified she based her decision on four factors: he had assaulted another student and threatened him with a knife; he was not passing classes at Clinton High School; his grades at his previous school were poor; and he was too old to be a high school student. When Principal D. J. Brittain Jr. spoke, he agreed with Juanita, adding that Alfred had missed many days of school, skipping history class eighteen times and math class thirty-two times. That was too many absences for the senior to say he was prioritizing his education. Keeping him in Clinton High School prevented him from moving forward with his life. Alfred should learn a trade, D. J. concluded.

By the time Alfred's witnesses took the stand, they knew what the outcome of the hearing would be. Before he gave his statement, Steve Williams asked the board if he could pray, perhaps hoping the men could hear in a prayer what they could not hear in a testimony. "Father, I ask for your protection," he pled. "Father, we know we have no power but to depend on you. Help this school board. Go with them who hate us and despise us," a telling pairing of intercessions. "Go with my boy," he said next. "Go with this school, bless the principal, and help him." After closing his prayer, he told the board that his nephew deserved a chance to "receive [the] educational advantage which he did not get."

Finally, Alfred spoke. Yes, he'd struck Dan Ward, but he insisted Dan had a knife also and would have used it on Maurice if Alfred had not intervened. "These boys had been picking on my brother all day," Alfred explained. All day? Make that all year. He insisted the pocketknife Police Chief Francis Moore had confiscated was the one he had pulled on Dan and Jimmy. He didn't own a switchblade.

The school board members asked Alfred about the other reasons he'd been suspended. Did he think he had the ability to finish his coursework?

"I shot a whole lot of classes," Alfred admitted, "but I don't think I ought to have been failed in history."

Given everything that had happened, though, did he even want to return to school?

"I couldn't learn anything there," he said. "Somebody's all the time picking at me."

"What do you want to do?" one of the board members asked.

"I've been going to school for twenty-one years to get a piece of paper," Alfred replied. "If I've got to stick my neck out and be ridiculed every time I go to class and run the risk of getting killed, I don't want to go."

At that point, the school board polled all three of the Williamses. The only acceptable answer was a yes or a no. Did they want Alfred to go back to Clinton High School?

"We would rather he didn't," Steve and Lucille replied, "but he can make up his own mind."

"No," Alfred said.

His suspension became an expulsion.

EIGHTEEN

A War of Nerves

Bobby Cain was alone. On his own. The only senior among the dwindling brigade of Black students.

Worse yet for him, the Tennessee White Youth had won their first major victory. Sure, other Black students had dropped out or transferred, but Alfred Williams's suspension was the first time Principal D. J. Brittain Jr. had kicked one of them out. Now the white students knew it was possible. Time to recommit to their tactics, harassing Bobby and the others in the hallways, threatening them whenever the teachers looked away, and reminding the Black students they weren't safe anywhere, not even on the Hill. Eventually Bobby would crack, D. J. would cave, and they would win. Because if that didn't happen and Bobby graduated, they would have lost Clinton High forever. Thus began what D. J. called "a war of nerves."

On the Wednesday of Valentine's week—after Alfred had been suspended but before the hearing that expelled him—Jimmy Ray McGill and white freshman Eddy Denny got into a verbal altercation with Bobby Cain. No one knew what had set the boys off, but that morning all the students had been called into a special assembly to watch Edward R. Murrow's two-reel *See It Now* special, "Clinton and the Law," a presentation that fell on the side of law and order. Maybe that was the catalyst. Whatever the reason, D. J. ushered all the boys into his office and ordered them not to fight. None of the three boys gave him that promise. The next morning, Eddy and Bobby exchanged more words in the hallway. The teachers broke them up. When he heard about it, Jimmy Ray went out to the shop in the vocational building where one of his friends was assembling a knife. Jimmy put the knife up his sleeve and started into the school with it. Then he changed his mind and returned the knife to the shop. Someone told on him, however, earning all three boys another trip to the principal's office.

He thought it was a real nice knife, Jimmy Ray insisted. He wasn't gonna do anything with it. He just wanted to show it off.

That afternoon, D. J. issued an ultimatum: "If there is any more trouble, I'll hold both sides equally responsible," the principal said. "I'll expel both parties until I can ferret out the facts."

D. J. wanted to know who was coordinating the white teens' actions. He knew they wouldn't do all this on their own without someone—some dastardly adult—egging them on. Last semester he'd thought it was John Kasper, but these days John was seldom in town. (Funny how a well-timed bombing could move a man along.) If he wasn't the Tennessee White Youth's Pied Piper, who was? D. J. and the other white leaders next thought it might be Clyde Cook, recently elected white man of the year by the local Anderson County White Citizens' Council, but he didn't have much to do with the students. Now a new man had stepped into the position: John Ballard Gates.

—

John Gates came from Appalachian Virginia, born near the border with Kentucky. He'd been a good kid, active in a local version of the Boy Scouts and playing on a Little League baseball team, though he'd had one serious run-in with the law when he and four other guys had snuck into Tennessee to steal gasoline from cars. But that'd happened back in 1938 at the height of the Great Depression, a time when lots of people made bad choices while trying to make ends meet. No one would hold it against him.

John had enlisted in the Army in October 1940 and was stationed at Pearl Harbor at the time of the Japanese attack. His experiences there shook him physically and emotionally. He soon received a medical discharge because of the stomach ulcers he'd developed in the aftermath of the assault. Then he was diagnosed with a heart condition, and he suffered from "frequent blind spells." He may also have had an addiction to alcohol, but he gave up drinking entirely about 1950. After his discharge, he moved to California and then up to Oregon before returning to Appalachia and marrying a woman named Ann.

When the young couple arrived in Clinton along about 1948, John Gates first ran a taxicab business and then established the Southland Cafeteria. He and his wife opened Ann's Café a few years later at the corner of Main Street and Market. There they added entertainment, inviting customers to "dine and dance to the music of 'The Roving Tennesseans' EVERY SATURDAY NIGHT." The event lasted from 8:30 until the last diner/dancer went home. John and Ann had been using their restaurants to host White Citizens' Council meetings since before the organization officially existed. During the first few weeks of school, Clyde Cook and William Brakebill and Clifford Carter and Willard Till and Mary Nell Currier and Alonzo Bullock and Lawrence Brantley would all gather around the Gateses' tables. There they'd spread out papers and discuss the latest news, or sometimes they'd bring in a typewriter to compose broadsheets or pen letters to politicians and editors, pleading the case for segregation. On January 11, about 180 members of the Anderson and Roane County White Citizens' Councils had packed themselves into Ann's Café to talk about integration and pass a joint resolution demanding Clinton city officials ban fluoride in the water.

John had also befriended the members of the Tennessee White Youth. The girls had stopped in his Southland Cafeteria when they first received their charter, looking for a couple adults who could help them get it notarized. They'd started sharing their stories with him, telling him about all the ways they were being mistreated by the Black students. "These kids have come to me—as if I was their daddy—and told me things which were happening up at that school which would make your blood boil," he told Leo Ely, editor of the *East Tennessee Reporter*:

They'd tell me about the Negro boys threatening them with knives—sounded like some of them were big enough to row a boat with—and using this foul language around the white girls, and just being obnoxious in general. I would many times ask them why they didn't just go tell on them. After a while they'd just laugh at me. They would tell me that was one good way to really get in trouble. They said the principal and teachers would try to make them (the white students) feel like fools, said they would tell them they shouldn't bother the Negroes—that they were good kids and just trying to get an education. Boy, let me tell you . . . these white kids—especially the girls—are the ones who are getting the education, but in the wrong way. It's all from the gutter.

And those girls, well, weren't they the future hope of the white race? While white men might carry on affairs across the color lines, white women were supposed to keep the race pure. White girls who told those sorts of stories could get Black boys killed. And the girls chatting with John Gates knew that lynching wasn't a dark moment in the Southern past. Just over a year earlier, fourteen-year-old Emmett Till had been kidnapped, tortured, and murdered for supposedly flirting with a white woman. His momma had hosted an open-casket funeral, and she'd allowed journalists to photograph his mutilated body. The white girls might not have seen the images (they were not widely disseminated through white papers), but they would've known about the event.

And according to some rumors around town, if anyone were going to organize a lynching party, it would be John Gates. The best-informed gossips said he'd already been behind some of the violence down at the school, paying nine white boys up to fifty dollars each to pick a fight with Bobby Cain and Alfred Williams. Maybe he'd been behind Alfred's expulsion, some folks speculated. Maybe it'd been a paid set-up job.

Yes, now that the law-and-order folks got to talking about it, they could see it all so clearly. The white teenagers weren't the source of the problems. They were John Gates's pawns.

When D. J. Brittain Jr. and the others told Federal Judge Robert Taylor about John's suspected involvement with the high schoolers and the ongoing Citizens' Council meetings happening at his restaurants, the judge added an amended attachment writ to his earlier arrest warrants, ordering the federal marshals to arrest John Gates too. For good measure, he tacked John Kasper's name on, certain he was guilty even though he'd missed Paul Turner's beating and its aftermath because he had been sitting in a jail in Fairfax, Virginia, unable to pay a $39.25 speeding ticket. But he was always up to no good.

At 3:30 in the afternoon on Monday, February 25, two federal marshals walked into the Southland Cafeteria and asked John Gates if they could speak with him privately.

Sure thing, John replied, showing them into the kitchen.

Once out of the customers' eyes, the marshals served John with the amended order for attachment. He went with them peacefully, so they didn't handcuff him. When they got to the jail, the marshals didn't put him in a cell. They waited with him, staying over three hours past the end of their shifts, hoping someone would come pay his bail, which was set at $5,000. Eventually, the owner of another café in Clinton brought the funds. As he left the city jail, John told the local newspapers that he was innocent, then added, "You know, I could almost understand them arresting me for some of the things I've thought."

Well, John said, he needed to clarify. He had told a few of the boys who hung around the Southland Cafeteria that he'd fight anyone who threatened him, especially if the other guy pulled a knife. "What red-blooded American couldn't say the same thing?" As for letting the Citizens' Councils meet in his restaurants, he was a businessman! He'd take any paying group that showed up, provided they were white, of course.

Though the marshals had tried to make John's experience as quick and as dignified as possible, the stress and shame of being arrested was too much for John Gates. He quit eating and sleeping. Instead, most nights he would get out of bed and sit in a corner. He also stopped speaking to friends and customers alike. He didn't seem to even see other people when they came up to talk to him, Ann noted. No acknowledgment. It was like he didn't notice them at all. Worried her husband's stomach ulcers had flared up again, she put him on a diet of goat's milk and raw eggs. He did not improve.

Then a week after John Gates's arrest, the Reverend Paul Turner talked about him during his sermon. Paul told his congregation to avoid the Southland Cafeteria. Even though John was a teetotaler, Paul implied that the business dealt in bootleg liquor. The Southland was "a nuisance," the preacher said. "It should be closed up" and "John should be run out of town."

That night, John Gates sat alone, murmuring to himself, "I wonder why Brother Turner would say a thing like that," and, "I wonder what they're going to think of next."

As John deteriorated, Ann decided she needed help caring for him. On Saturday night, she finally called their family doctor and he phoned in a prescription for a sleep aid. John took a dose but did not go to bed. A few hours later, John called the chief of police and asked him to come to the Southland Cafeteria. When the chief arrived, John told the man to turn on his siren and summon all the people to the city square so he could make a speech. The chief urged John to go home and get some rest. The chief then returned to the police station. John stayed at the cafeteria with a few close friends who tried to calm him. At about 4:00 a.m., John slipped out of the back of the restaurant. Fifteen minutes later, someone who lived near Clinton High School called the police and reported, "A drunk is raising Cain up here."

The chief of police grabbed a deputy and sped toward the school. From several blocks away, they heard John Gates yelling, his voice carrying through the early morning air as though he had a loudspeaker. By the time they reached the scene, John had smashed out several windows at Clinton High School with a Norris Creamery milk case.

The chief called out, "Here, John, stop that right now!"

I have "the devil chasing me around," John replied, throwing the milk crate at the officers, plus he was suffering from all the "financial troubles, lawyers, and books." Besides, "Paul Turner had a church full of people who also fill the street," John said. Why couldn't he draw a crowd, too, a congregation eager to hear his truths? "It is just not to be," he said. "We missed the schedule."

What did he mean by that? the two officers wondered. Was this about an unsuccessful bombing attempt? Maybe one they didn't even know about?

While the cops looked for a bomb, John kept talking. It "won't work, men," he said. "There's no power on earth that'll make it work." Then he circled back to Paul Turner. Wouldn't the police call Paul to the school? I've "something to say to him."

The lawmen could see lights flicking on in all the houses around the school as John's disturbed shouting roused the neighbors. Soon John might have the street full of people he wanted, but they wouldn't be eager to hear what he had to say, not at that hour. The officers tried to grab John. He pulled out a knife, saying, "Don't you come close to me or I'll hurt you."

Then he turned the knife toward his chest and cried out, "I gave my blood once for these people—I'll do it again!"

Hand over the knife, the chief said. "You're just going to get into trouble."

"I'm already in trouble," John replied. "Just call Brother Turner down here so I can talk to him."

Three more officers arrived. The cops decided to encircle John Gates and try to get his knife. Seeing their movement, John yelled, "What does the Supreme Court know about the stand we've got to take here?" Then he placed the knife on his left wrist and continued, "Yes, I'll take my stand right here on these schoolhouse steps. I gave my blood once. . . . I'll do it again." With that, he slashed his wrist. Blood dripped down on the steps. Then he pointed the knife at his chest and cried out, "I'll stick it in this old heart of mine!" He began hacking at his chest, though the knife was too dull to do more than tear his shirt before his attention drifted. Distracted from his failed attempt to further mutilate himself, he asked, "Why won't Judge Taylor do to the NAACP what he's done to us here in Clinton?"

Suddenly John Gates snapped his head back and forth and blinked rapidly as though waking up from a powerful bad dream, a disturbing hallucination. Noticing the knife in his hand, he folded it closed and tucked it in his pocket. He turned to the chief of police and said, "Well, I guess I've gotten myself into something. What am I doing here?" He would later tell a friend, "I dreamed I was breaking up a big fight. When I woke up, it looked like I had just got in one." The chief asked John for the knife, and the man quietly handed it over. The officers took John to the county jail, but rather than putting him in a cell, they gave him a cup of coffee and called a doctor to treat his self-inflicted wounds. Ann arrived a few minutes later. "I'm sorry, honey," John said. "I don't know. I've messed everything up now, I guess." After the doctor's visit, John drank his coffee, holding the cup gingerly and replacing the lid after each sip. He continued to ramble, repeating some of what he said at the school, though this time more quietly. He also continued to apologize to his wife. "I guess that old 'booger' Judge Taylor'll throw me under the jail now, won't he?" Then, "Why didn't you call Brother Turner down here?" And "I had something to say to him. I don't see how he could have been scared to come down here. He was brave enough to escort those Negroes down to school."

When John Gates seemed settled enough, the police placed him in a cell. John took off his belt, wrapped it around his neck, and attempted to hang himself. The police released John under a $250 bond. Ann took him straight to Knoxville's Eastern State Hospital for treatment.

What the authorities didn't know but Ann did was that John Gates came from a family with a history of mental illness. His sister Octavia, who was living in Clinton, had once been incarcerated in Kentucky's Eastern State Hospital for the Insane, as it was known at the time, and just five months before, his father had died in an incident the family insisted was the accidental discharge of a gun. One night in mid-August, John's stepmother said, her husband was pulling out a dresser drawer, looking for matches. The bottom of the drawer fell out and his .22-caliber automatic pistol fell on the floor, where it fired, sending a bullet up through the man's body and into his heart.

In Knoxville, the doctors diagnosed John Gates with schizophrenia. Within a month, he was dead, his body found by caregivers who'd come to get him ready for electroconvulsive therapy. His widow believed the injuries found on his body at his time of death (burned spots on his forehead and charring inside his mouth that went about an eighth of an inch deep) indicated that he died following a botched treatment session, although this was never proven. He was buried in the National Cemetery in Knoxville.

After John Gates's death, the student-led campaign against Bobby Cain and the other Black teenagers continued unabated. He hadn't been the source of upheaval at the school after all.

—

One day, Bobby was sitting in the library near three white boys; among them was Robbie Moser, Assistant Principal Juanita Moser's son. One of the boys—not Robbie but one of his comrades—said something insulting to Bobby. Robbie pretended he didn't hear. When Juanita Moser learned of the exchange, she told her son to apologize to Bobby for not standing up for him, but Bobby was so on edge that when Robbie came up to him in the hallway Bobby thought the white boy was trying to start something. A teacher intervened before they turned to fisticuffs, and the two worked out their misunderstanding.

Then one morning in late March, Bobby crossed paths with John Harber, the school's janitor. The older man blocked Bobby from entering the toilets.

You shouldn't be allowed to use the restroom that the white men use, John Harber told the boy.

Bobby shoved the white man out of his way and continued on to class. That might have been the end, but somebody told John's son, senior Roy Lee Harber, who was home sick that morning. He came to school to confront Bobby.

What did you say to my father? Roy Lee asked. He told the *East Tennessee Reporter* he thought he should probably have been insulted by Cain's response, but he was not sure. "I never can understand his talk—he just babbles a lot of stuff," Roy Lee sneered.

Then Bobby reached into his pocket for his knife. A teacher stepped in and took both students to D. J.'s office. Because no physical contact had occurred, the principal talked to the boys and then released them. "We have a lot of spontaneous combustion around here," D. J. told the *Reporter*. "It's spring."

The campaign against the Hill also continued. Another dynamite attempt happened in mid-March. The charge failed to fire, but, as Horace Wells wrote, "the murderous intent was there just the same." The bombers had left the weapon outside Alvah Jay McSwain's home. The bomb was a concrete-sealing-compound can filled with thirty sticks of dynamite removed from their paper wrappings, crumbled into smaller pieces, and then packed tightly inside. The detonator and four-foot fuse were attached through a hole in the side. Just after midnight, a white man's car had stalled in front of the McSwains' home. The Black men guarding the Hill intercepted him and pushed his car toward downtown. The police surmised the man had probably set the bomb but had not had time to light the fuse before the Black men came.

Alvah Jay McSwain dropped out of Clinton High School on May 3, just fourteen days before the school year ended. After almost twenty years of fighting, Wynona and Allen McSwain were through with Anderson County. They wanted better for their family, better than bombs and harassment and isolation. The couple had heard how the Allens enjoyed life in California. And in January 1957, their daughter Una—just a few years older than Alvah Jay—had relocated there with her husband, who was stationed at a base near Barstow. Out in California, Alvah Jay enrolled in high school and finished her freshman year. She never returned to live in Clinton, though her parents would come back to Tennessee over the next few years to speak at events at the Highlander Folk School, appearing alongside guests including Dr. Martin Luther King Jr., to share their experiences desegregating Clinton High.

—

John Kasper was finally arrested on Friday, March 22, when he came for John Gates's funeral. The fugitive missed the service, but he went to the cemetery to pay his respects. John Kasper was arraigned the next day and released on a $7,500 bond some unnamed friends had raised. He left town again.

But still things did not quiet down at the high school. Three more altercations happened on Tuesday, April 9. During a class change, someone hit a white student named Doyle Cardwell from behind. Doyle fell. When he got up, he saw Bobby standing nearby, laughing at the white kid sprawled on the ground. Doyle accused Bobby of pushing him. Bobby denied it. Doyle insisted it must have him. Bobby denied it again. At that point, Maurice Soles joined Bobby, so a group of white students gathered around them prepared for a fight. Before things could escalate further, a teacher grabbed Bobby and Doyle and sent both of them to the principal's office. The white students who witnessed the altercation insisted Bobby had attacked Doyle, but D. J. noticed that all Bobby's accusers were known segregationists and so dismissed their testimony. Instead, he threatened to send the boys to see the juvenile court judge. Later that afternoon, someone flipped a cigarette onto Bobby Cain and ten white students jumped Maurice. By midsemester, a few of the white parents decided they should pull their sons from the school before they were expelled. Other teenagers simply dropped out. But most remained.

While the white boys used their fists, the white girls used their words. They told white adults "that Negro boys sometimes jostled white girls in the hallways" and they "muttered lewd words at them." Or the Black boys asked white girls out on dates, inviting the girls "to a 'rock and roll' dance in Knoxville where they wouldn't get back until 'three o'clock in the morning.'" And didn't everyone know rock-and-roll concerts were code for sex? One Black classmate was so insistent, a white girl said, she had decided her only option was to just "keep away from him."

By the spring, only a handful of white students acknowledged the Black students and even fewer stood up for them. On the best days, the Black teens went about the school surrounded by people who looked through them. All their grades fell. Business and typing teacher Margaret Anderson, the Black students' de facto guidance counselor, worried what this experience was doing to her charges. What were the long-term implications for children who survived this much hate and tension?

Raised in Glasgow, Kentucky, she and her husband, Raymond—a music teacher and band director—relocated to Clinton immediately after World War II. She first worked at Norris High, another secondary school in the county, until the late 1940s, when she resigned to give birth to her first child. In 1952, Raymond Anderson accepted an appointment as the band director at Clinton High School. When Margaret returned to teaching, she also took a position at the school. Margaret believed in D. J. Brittain Jr.'s vision for Clinton High, that it could be a place where white Appalachian children could earn the sort of education that would make them competitive for jobs beyond the mountains. To that end, she'd encouraged her students to talk to her about issues they faced outside the classroom. When D. J. had asked her to do the same thing for the new Black students, Margaret, like many white people, had never before questioned the inequality segregation created. She had assumed everyone in the South accepted the hierarchy. Her students had shown her otherwise. Now she was committed to ensuring her Black students achieved the future and the opportunities they were fighting for.

That spring, Margaret called one of the older girls, possibly Gail Ann, in to talk about college. The girl was failing a class because she had simply stopped turning in assignments. "I could have passed that course, only I was so upset," the girl said. "You know how it was." When Margaret wrote about this exchange a few years later, she noted that the girl had gone on to excel in a much more challenging version of the course in university. But as Alfred had pointed out, who could learn when there was nowhere safe to study?

At the end of the first year, Margaret asked Regina Turner if she would discuss her struggles that year so that Margaret could prepare to help the incoming Black students. At the end of their conversation, Margaret asked Regina if she would do it all over again. The girl paused and thought for a long moment. Then, "I don't know," she said.

"Do you think what you've gone through is really worth it?" Margaret pressed the teen.

"I don't know," Regina said again. "I've thought about it a lot." The girl fell silent. Margaret noticed that she seemed to age, like she was thinking over all the terrible events of the preceding two semesters. She closed her eyes, appearing to be in pain. "The only thing I know is maybe it will be easier for someone else." Regina opened her eyes again. They were full of tears.

NINETEEN

A Desegregated School

Bobby Cain would never know whose hand had done it. Was it one of the other eighty-eight graduating seniors? An underclassman? A football player who'd joined the honor guard to patrol the ceremony? Even one of the teachers? Or a parent? Or someone else who snuck into the cafeteria? Bobby only knew one thing for sure—the hand that flicked off the light switch was fish-belly white.

Disoriented, Bobby didn't understand what was happening. How silly was that, after the year he'd just survived? But here he was, still in his graduation robes, fresh from walking across the stage and shaking Principal D. J. Brittain Jr.'s hand and receiving his diploma. The event had felt so peaceful, so normal. Plus, he'd done it. He'd graduated. For a few minutes, he had assumed the Tennessee White Youth and their Citizens' Council allies would let him have this day. Then the lights cut out.

In the darkness, Bobby heard another kid, the white teenager standing right beside him, yelp. He remembered the group of white boys who'd walked toward him just before the electricity flickered off. And like that, he knew, it was an ambush. Of course it was. The whole posse had come for him, ruining even this day. Why didn't they have the decency to fight him one at a time? Instead, here he was, trapped in the dark cafeteria, unable to see who they were or where the attack was coming from. More fools them. They might've lined Bobby up, but they'd missed. Bobby felt a flicker of pity for the kid standing next to him who'd taken his hit.

Then the lights came back on, and Bobby started swinging. He wanted to hit somebody, anybody. Enough was enough.

The lights died again. It didn't take a rocket scientist to figure out what to do. Bobby hit the floor, hands still fisted. He felt the scars on his fingers, the thin pink lines that were souvenirs of the previous fall when he and Alfred had dueled to see who could draw their pocketknives fastest. Bobby had weathered this year—the insults and threats and riots and bombings and knives and sticks and loogies and punches and isolation—all so he would reach this day. He thought they'd at least give him this.

It was three years to the day since the United States Supreme Court had handed down their decision in *Brown v. Board*, and on this day Bobby, a Black boy, had earned his diploma. That 8 ½-by-11 piece of parchment certified that Robert Lynn Cain Jr. had satisfied the requirements as prescribed by the Anderson County Board of Education and was therefore an alum of Clinton High School. Even if they killed him tonight, he'd done it. He'd graduated. Clinton High School had been desegregated.

So why was he lying on the cafeteria floor?

The lights turned on again, and Bobby saw his father standing in the door of the cafeteria, brow wrinkled like he was trying to figure out what was going on. "Let's go," Bobby said. His father didn't move. "I'm ready to go."

Outside the cafeteria, the dark had drawn off the mugginess of the day. This year, summer had come early to the Tennessee mountains. The heat had still lingered when the Clinton High band played the eighty-nine graduates to their seats. The teenagers sat there in tightly packed rows, stuffed into their nicest church duds and wrapped in black robes. The heat from their bodies pressed wrinkles into their good attire, ruining pictures for parents who hadn't snapped enough photos ahead of time. Good thing Bobby and his folks had already taken all the pictures they wanted: a few candids before the ceremony, a moment of laughter with his little sister Hattie.

The administration had crafted a program that was both snappy and thorough, balancing the official speakers with entertainment to wake the audience back up. The night moved quickly: invocation, salutatory address, solo performance, valedictory address, trio singing, official graduation address, citizenship awards, diplomas, and then everyone out.

Last-minute changes had threatened to derail the ceremony. Six days earlier, the valedictorian, student council president, and football captain Jerry Shattuck—and about the closest thing to an ally Bobby'd had—had been speeding across the infamous bit of road between Oak Ridge and Clinton where the Black Jacket gang ran their drag races. Maybe it was just a moment of carelessness or distraction, but he hit John French's car while going around a sharp curve. John, a college student at the University of Tennessee, was Betty Lou Miller's fiancé. Both drivers had broken legs. Jerry was unable to attend graduation or give his valedictory speech.

The state troopers investigating the accident concluded that both young men had been speeding, but they placed the blame on Jerry. John sued, alleging that Jerry's driving constituted "gross and wanton negligence." When John won the case, he insinuated to a reporter for the *Clinton Courier-News* that Jerry had been intoxicated. Jerry, a freshman at Yale by then, was appalled. "I received the *Courier-News* today, and as usual, I enjoyed reading all the news from my hometown," he wrote to the paper. However, "I feel that what little prestige I did have in Clinton has been greatly reduced." Jerry had been speeding, he admitted, but he had not been drunk. "The plaintiff failed to bring one witness forward to testify 'that young Shattuck was driving under the influence of intoxicants.'"

But Jerry was a responsible kid. He wasn't going to let this moment of carelessness mess up the night for the other seniors. He wrote his speech and sent it to a friend to read. The ceremony rolled along without him.

Principal D. J. Brittain Jr. and the other event planners had worried that the segregationist protestors would cause a scene. Exactly one week before the graduation ceremony, the Ku Klux Klan had sponsored a motorcade through Clinton, including "a tour" of Freedman's Hill. They'd invited all interested white people to join them, meeting up at 7:30 that night at a livestock auction barn just outside the city limits. The planners of the parade let "the first car to show up with a lit cross on its hood" take the lead. Organizers had expected between three and five thousand people to attend. Anyone was welcome, even journalists . . . well, the planners hedged, almost anyone. John Kasper and his cronies were not invited. Klansmen were encouraged to wear their robes and hoods but no masks. The only interruption to the parade came when a Black man from Lake City stalled his brand-new car in the middle of the road through the Hill, forcing the caravan to grind to a halt in front of the bombed-out Chicken Shack. While the Klansmen pushed the vehicle out of the way, the men of the Hill stood silently, holding large sticks in their hands, armed and clearly ready to fight. Since they had clubs instead of guns, the sheriff didn't arrest them.

The cavalcade ended in a field in South Clinton where the Klansmen burned three crosses. Two of the flaming symbols were twenty feet high. The third was thirty feet high. All three could be seen from US 25W. The public was invited to stay, though only Klansmen could enter the inner circle of the gathering. About twenty-five hundred people observed the three-hour ceremony, a smaller number than the organizers had hoped but still a terrifying flashback to Labor Day weekend for many.

Of course, John Kasper couldn't stand being barred from the event and showed up during the keynote address, given by a Nashville pastor. The pastor asked John to leave, so John went across the street into a neighboring driveway and began trying to drum up his own competing soapbox. The Klansmen shooed him away.

But amazingly, none of the white supremacists disrupted the graduation ceremony. In preparation for that night, D. J. Brittain Jr. had approached some of the young men who had fought against Bobby during the preceding year to try to convince them to remain peaceful during the celebration. "Well, I'll tell you, Mr. Brittain," one of them replied. "You know how I fought this thing. . . . [But] after all that boy's [been] through, we'll do everything we can to help things go smoothly." By that night, D. J. thought, most of the white students and their parents felt similarly.

There were also no journalists present. The three national television networks had wanted to film Bobby walking across the stage, the only one of the Black kids who entered a newly desegregated school the previous fall to make it to graduation, but Principal D. J. Brittain Jr. said no. While the graduating football players guarded Bobby, the underclassmen on the team were stationed at the doors to the gymnasium to search everyone who entered, confiscating cameras from anyone unrelated to a graduate. He'd had about enough of the circus the reporters always drummed up. Only one tried to disobey D. J.'s order: Leo Ely, the cameraman/writer/editor of the pro-segregationist *East Tennessee Reporter*. When the football players stopped him from entering, he fought back. The police evicted him. After the ceremony, Leo had followed the seniors to the cafeteria where they were disrobing and returning their graduation vestments. There he'd tried to sneak pictures of Bobby through the open windows. Some of the students yelled at him. A few flipped him off. Juanita Moser turned away.

The graduates raised the window and dumped a jug of water on Leo's head, drowning his camera. Bobby's honor guard then chased him through the parking lot. Leo demanded that the principal punish them, but D. J. just replied, "School is out. If you want to do something about it, then go ahead."

Now that Bobby thought about it, though, the chase through the parking lot had left him unprotected when the blackout happened. How planned had his attack been? Was it an opportunity or an orchestrated maneuver? Regardless, it was behind him now. Bobby was out. His nightmare was over.

Bobby and his family walked toward the elementary school's parking lot where they'd left their sedan. A figure hurried away as they approached. Too many things had been exploded over the last nine months for this not to cause alarm. The Cains knew that white people in Clinton owned dynamite and liked dynamite. They especially liked to use it against their Black neighbors. Bobby's father sent his family to the other side of the parking lot. He unlocked the sedan's door, sat down in the driver's seat, depressed the brake, and turned the key. The engine coughed to a start. No explosion.

Bobby Cain, however, was done. He kept it together just long enough to get home, just long enough for his father to drive them over the train tracks, past Asbury Methodist, around Green McAdoo Grammar, and into their driveway. The teen jumped from the still-moving car, marched to his father's closet, and grabbed his dad's shotgun. The gun had always been a defensive weapon, but Bobby was ready for some offense. He was going to shoot anybody who came over the Hill who wasn't Black. This wasn't how his family wanted his graduation day to end. They wrestled the shotgun away from him and then tried to calm him down. Don't ruin everything now, they urged him, you have too many places to go now that you've survived Clinton High.

Bobby Cain spent little of that summer in Tennessee. For him, the months between Clinton High School and college were packed with invitations and accolades. Adam Clayton Powell booked him at Abyssinian Baptist Church, one of the largest Black churches in Harlem. The Reverend Gardner C. Taylor—who would be awarded a Presidential Medal of Freedom for founding the Progressive National Baptist Convention, a key Northern civil rights organization—invited Bobby to speak at Concord Baptist Church, one of the oldest Black churches in Brooklyn. Over the summer, he was also featured at a rally hosted by the youth division of the NAACP. There he stood on the stage alongside baseball player Jackie Robinson, singer Dinah Washington, and Birmingham pastor Fred Shuttlesworth, cofounder of the Southern Christian Leadership Conference, while one thousand people cheered them on. In his address, Bobby told the crowd the only way the world would change would be if young people made terrible personal sacrifices.

Bobby also gave interviews. The most revealing ones were with writers from the *Pittsburgh Courier*, a Black newspaper with a national readership that had started a scholarship fund for the teen. Hearing all he'd gone through, Black folks from Oklahoma City to Charleston to Seattle to Houston mailed checks to the paper in Bobby's honor, giving whatever they could, whether that was twenty cents or fifty dollars. Marie Cato of Marrero, Louisiana, only had a dollar to donate to the fund. "The amount is very small," she admitted, "but I hope every Negro will send you one dollar, and I pray God that you will make it." People around the nation wanted him to be able to succeed, to have his dream of attending historically Black Tennessee Agricultural and Industrial State College, known today as Tennessee State University. The Cains needed the help. Even a state school was beyond their means by the end of 1957. "I'm a carpenter and a good one," his father told the *Courier*'s writer. "But when Robert went into that school, it became harder and harder for me to get steady work." His mother told the paper she hated that they needed to ask for help like this. She "wants no favors," the writer explained. "But willingness to work is one thing . . . [ellipses theirs] and finding work is another." The *Courier*'s readers pulled through. Between the money they sent, a $250 scholarship from the Black branch of the Elks, and a work-study grant, Bobby was able to start college that September. He studied social work at Tennessee A&I and graduated debt-free.

—

In mid-July, the segregationists arrested the preceding December finally went to court. Despite the rift between John Kasper and the other defendants, Judge Robert Taylor refused to separate their trials. The number of defendants had decreased, however. During the previous spring, prosecutors had dropped charges against three of them because of a lack of evidence. Since Jimmy Patmore was already serving time in the adult penitentiary in Nashville, Bob canceled his charges as well. He also dropped the charges against Zella Nelson, as she was pregnant. When Bob granted the accused the right to a jury trial, the defense lawyers predicted that the twelve white people chosen to serve would acquit their clients with little trouble. What white Southern jury had ever incarcerated other white Southerners for maintaining racial order?

At the trial, spectators sat intermingled, Black observers next to white ones. The attorneys squabbled. Federal prosecutors argued the defendants knew Bob had barred any interference with Clinton High's desegregation and had willfully "conspired . . . to violate the injunction." The penalty was up to six months in jail and a $1,000 fine. And beating Paul Turner was an obvious and violent violation of multiple laws. The crowd of defense lawyers, which still included political leaders from around the South, decided on a multipronged and convoluted defense. First, they argued, the defendants had exercised their constitutionally protected freedom of speech by protesting. Second, the federal court did not have the jurisdiction to enforce integration (nor could they say who had that jurisdiction). Third, federal marshals had failed to properly serve the defendants with Bob's rulings. Marshal Frank Quarles needed to have read it out to the crowd instead of allowing John Kasper to take it, read it, and interpret it.

The phalanx of defense attorneys created chaos. The team had named Grover McLeod of Birmingham their "Chief Objector," but often his compatriots were out of their seats shouting before he had a chance to respond. His voice was "like a sparrow in a boiler factory," one Knoxville reporter noted. "Sometimes they see errors before I do," Grover told the journalist. "And that's jolly good."

Soon the jurors embraced the informality. The women took off their hats, and one of the men nodded at a reporter near the jury box. Another dozed off during testimony, and a reporter heard the snoozing juror's neighbor mutter, "I'll be doing the same thing in a minute." Everyone drifted off, even the U.S. district attorney, when the secretary of the *East Tennessee Reporter* and the White Citizens' Council of Tennessee read the names of everyone who had joined the council, a recitation that took her forty-five minutes. But the attorney hadn't been as oblivious as he seemed. As soon as she finished, he leapt to his feet. She'd said Alonzo Bullock's name twice, he pointed out. He joined twice, she replied.

Soon the witnesses were getting a little salty. Some began poking fun at the lawyers and their questions. One of the defense attorneys wanted to prove that Sidney Davis had thrown the tear gas during the Labor Day riots. "No," Sidney replied, grinning. "I didn't know how to pull the pin. I was in the Navy." By the end of his seventy-five-minute testimony, the defense attorney was red-faced and sweating. Sidney laughed as he left the witness stand. When a severe thunderstorm swept through on Wednesday, July 17, hail ricocheted off the windows and thunder drowned out the witness. "God is watching all these proceedings," John Kasper, the same man who'd been kicked out of Sunday school for calling everyone there a hypocrite, told the reporters nearest him, "and this storm is a manifestation of it."

Outside the courtroom, spectators swirled and chatted, trading gossip and looking for inside scoops. Witnesses waiting to be called entertained themselves best they knew how. Two women in sleeveless dresses messed around with Dr. I.Q., a handheld, four-sided version of Chinese checkers. A county deputy played canasta with a white boy from Clinton High. Betty Lou Miller French and four of the girls who helped found the Tennessee White Youth studied fashion magazines. W. T. Dabney, a brickmason and Klansman testifying for the government, counted how many of his fellow Kluxers were there. One Thursday morning, he claimed twenty-seven attended the trial. One day, Lawrence Brantley and Raymond Wood scooped up a CBS television cameraman and hauled him to U.S. Marshal Frank Quarles's office.

He took our picture without our permission, the defendants said. He should destroy his film.

The cameraman apologized and promised not to name them. The Clintonians let him keep the shots.

But journalists remained a target throughout the trial, even on the witness stand. The judge scolded one of the defense attorneys when he accused a *Life* photographer of having "smeared" the defendants. You have "no interest in humanity," the lawyer told the cameraman. A few days later, Defense Attorney Robert Dobbs said the reporters were no better than roaches. And so the reporters covering the trial formed a new branch of the Southern War Correspondents Association, the Objective Order of Migrant Cockroaches. They gave Robert Dobbs a book about cockroaches, and to the U.S. District Attorney, who was always polite to them, they gave a cut of his favorite chewing tobacco. The reporters didn't forget about Judge Robert Taylor either. They gave him a white rose and a red rose and a thank-you note, a nod to when his father and his uncle had run against each other for governor, a race nicknamed the War of the Roses.

Testimony wrapped up after nine days. Throughout the trial, not a single attorney or witness had mentioned the terror faced by the families on the Hill. No one had included the Black students and their experiences. The testimony instead had focused solely on Paul Turner and other white law-and-order types.

On July 23 after only two hours of discussion and only one ballot, the jury returned its verdict. William Brakebill, Lawrence Brantley, Alonzo Bullock, Clyde Cook, Mary Nell Currier, John Kasper, and Willard Till were all found guilty. The other four were acquitted. Judge Robert Taylor sentenced Kasper to six months in a federal penitentiary, in addition to the twelve months he had already received for his actions in Clinton. Robert placed the remaining five individuals on probation, during which time some unnamed federal officer would monitor them, making sure they made no more trouble down at the school. At the verdict, pandemonium erupted. Clyde Cook's young daughters "broke into hysterical sobs and ran from the courtroom, fleeing down the halls," a local reporter observed. Willard's wife "slumped forward, hands covering face, in despair."

"We've gotten a rotten deal," Willard muttered through clenched teeth. Mary Nell Currier wiped away tears with a green handkerchief, surrounded by her family, who tried to comfort her. The state head of the Tennessee Federation for Constitutional Government denounced the decision. "The jury, in spite of defense arguments, forgot the basic reason for a jury system," he said. "The jury stand sat [as] a bulwark between potential judicial tyranny and the people. . . . The jury sitting in judgment of the Clinton Ten will go down in history as a tragic failure." Meanwhile, civil rights advocates were thrilled. No one expected a white Southern jury to convict white defendants in a civil rights case.

Up on the Hill, most of the parents and relatives of the Black students gathered at Steve Williams's house to celebrate. "Lord, I sure am glad," Mary Royston told a reporter for the *Pittsburgh Courier*. "I guess we won't have any trouble—maybe—next month when school opens." Bobby Cain's family didn't go to the Williamses' because his mother was recovering from surgery. July 23 happened to be her birthday. What a wonderful birthday present the verdict was! "Thank God," Beatrice Cain said.

"Amen," her husband agreed.

Paul Turner was also pleased. "I think the verdict is the right one, of course," he told a reporter for the *Knoxville Journal*. "I hope now that all the bitterness and hard feelings will be forgotten as rapidly as possible so that we can all go about our business as neighbors."

National politics also appeared to be swinging behind the Black students. Despite South Carolina senator Strom Thurmond's record-setting twenty-four-hour-and-eighteen-minute filibuster, the Civil Rights Act of 1957 was set to be passed. It would be signed into law on September 9, the first piece of civil rights legislation to make it through the Senate since 1875. The act was supposed to protect Black voting rights by letting federal prosecutors obtain injunctions against anyone who kept legal voters from registering. It also created a federal Civil Rights Commission charged with investigating discriminatory behaviors and recommending solutions. Opponents, however, quickly found ways to limit its impact.

After the trial, some of the White Citizens' Council members tried to keep their protests going, sending white parents unsigned postcards asking: "Are you going to keep your children out of school until you know whether the school will be black or white?" As far as the administrators could tell, however, no white child planned to boycott their education.

The Black students also faced pressure to avoid the school. Shortly before registration was supposed to begin, Clinton's new mayor visited the Black families and again offered to provide the students with tuition to attend segregated Austin High School in Knoxville, along with a private bus driven by a Black driver to ferry them to and from their classes. The families turned him down.

—

On September 3, 1957, nearly seventeen-year-old senior Gail Ann Epps led five Black teenagers—three of whom were freshmen—into Clinton High School. One of the boys in the group hadn't been to school in two or three years, he told a journalist lingering outside. And no, he would not share his name. Another Black freshman girl walked into the building a few minutes later. Then Anna Theresser Caswell and Henrietta Thomas, a sophomore newly relocated from Detroit, were dropped off by the school bus for Black kids that headed from their neighborhood to Green McAdoo Grammar.

Only one protestor stood, watching the Black children enter the building, the Reverend Alonzo Bullock. He hustled away soon after the bell rang. One lone police car guarded the empty streets. The quiet wasn't an accident. The new principal of the school, Principal William Dudley, or W. D., Human had cleared the grounds, shooing loitering white students into the school and then marching them to their classrooms. He barred all journalists from the campus. Then he went inside, leaving one white male teacher to guard the entrance until the Black students were all safely dispersed to their homerooms. At the end of the first day, 801 students had registered for school, the same number as were supposed to be in classes at Clinton High the previous year. The next day, 5 more registered, a new record.

Down in Little Rock, on the other hand, segregationists who'd watched the events in Clinton were planning for their own uprising when their schools opened the following day. Arkansas governor Orval Faubus had begun his career as a racial moderate, but attacks from the right had driven him deeper into white supremacy. He had no interest in following in Frank Clement's footsteps, tarnishing his legacy and limiting his future prospects. Oh yes, he, too, would be calling out the National Guard and sending them to a newly integrated high school. The Arkansas National Guard would not be guarding Black teenagers under Orval's watch, however. He would line the troopers up against them.

Principal W. D. Human had taken over D. J.'s job and purchased D. J.'s home when he'd moved to Clinton from neighboring Morgan County, where he'd been a popular teacher and then the county's school superintendent. When he'd lost the race to keep his seat in August 1956, he'd enrolled to get a doctorate in education, but he was eager to get back into the classroom. Despite having some similar academic aims and now the same address as D. J., though, the new principal was a very different educator than D. J. had been. W. D. had served overseas during World War II as a United States Army captain, and he carried his experiences leading young recruits through battle with him into the halls of Clinton High. His approach to the students was to be strict, regimented, and fair. He planned to "rule with an iron hand," he warned them. There'd be no allowances for the Black students, nor would he take guff from white troublemakers. In fact, he dared them to raise a ruckus in his hallways. Where D. J. had made his number unlisted to try to escape the harassing phone calls, W. D. made his public. And, he bragged, he'd not received a single "unpleasant" phone call. Students and teachers would never love him with the same loyalty and passion as they had loved D. J., but W. D. wasn't the sort of man to be concerned about that. Respect would do him just fine. After all, D. J.'s fans hadn't given him much respite from the pressures of the previous year. Between the first day of school and Christmas 1956, he had lost 50 pounds, going from 165 pounds to 115. His enemies had gloated over that. "Glad to see you're in bad health," one man had written. "I just hope it's fatal."

The Black students in Clinton must have worried that W. D. wouldn't protect them in the same way D. J. had tried—but so often failed—to do. Sure, the new principal promised to treat everyone equally, but the teens knew when white adults said that it usually meant the adults would look the other way when bad things occurred. W. D., however, followed through. One day, Gail Ann and her little sister were waiting for a bus downtown when some of the white high school boys got in their way, blocking the entrance to keep the girls from boarding. Gail's sister grabbed her umbrella and started poking the boys with it. W. D., who happened to be waiting for the same bus, intervened, snatching up the boys by the arms. He shoved them onto the bus, saying, "If you are going to get on the bus, get on the bus."

But the principal wasn't around all the time. White kids still shoved the Black children when teachers weren't looking. Or stepped on their heels. Or whispered dirty names. And still the Black children were barred from all extracurricular activities.

More serious violence also remained a threat. In late September, Tom Powell, a local white man, called Sheriff Glad Woodward's office. He'd been down along the Clinch River (presumably on a fishing expedition), and right about where the US 25W bridge sat he'd found himself something interesting. Glad needed to have a look. Sure enough, there on the riverbank right where Tom had said they should go, Glad and his deputies found a potato sack shoved under some bushes. The logo on the front had once advertised CALIFORNIA POTATOES in bold, colorful letters, but now the image was smudged and soiled from a couple weeks out in the elements. Glad opened the bag. Inside were 154 sticks of dynamite,* each just a little bit larger than one of Winston Churchill's overstuffed cigars. Twelve days later, a teenager named Avon Nolan, imprisoned on charges of larceny, told officers they'd only found half the dynamite. Sheriff's Deputy Frank Butler went back to the riverbank. There it was, another potato sack stuffed with another 156 sticks of dynamite concealed under vines about fifty feet from where the first sack had been.

The lawmen needed to find whoever had put the explosives out there. Not only was it a terrifying amount of TNT—one investigator estimated the three-hundred-some-odd sticks were enough to destroy about half of the downtown district—but the decision to leave them out in the elements had potentially destabilized them. Wet dynamite could detonate, and moisture and temperature changes could make nitroglycerine explode spontaneously. Glad Woodward went back to Avon Nolan and demanded he start singing out everything. Avon obliged.

It all started, the boy explained, when Edward Cline came to see him. Edward, a forty-four-year-old sometimes-mechanic, had given generations of sheriffs trouble. He was in and out of work, and his search for employment made him a nomad. He'd drive cows to market for a Knoxville farmer and then go to Kentucky to work in the mines and then visit Illinois for a factory job and then head down to Florida when rumors of another position reached him. When he was between gigs, he had a penchant for stealing automobiles and getting caught while doing so. At one point in 1949,

---

* In 1963, racist bombers would use nineteen sticks of dynamite to destroy Birmingham's 16th Street Baptist Church, killing four Black girls. Over 150 sticks would've been enough to obliterate Clinton High and all the surrounding homes.

he was on parole from federal prison for transporting a stolen car across a state line when he was arrested for stealing cars in Morgan and Anderson Counties. He then escaped from jail and stole another car. When police picked him back up, he was with two more stolen vehicles. Somehow, however, he kept getting turned free. Now he had a new way to make money, he told Avon. He'd share some of it if Avon would be his accomplice.

The two decided they needed a third, so Avon contacted twenty-year-old Clifford Lowe of Foley Hill, a friend who had worked with Avon on at least one previous larceny job. Clifford agreed to join the bombing squad. Edward offered the two younger men $250 each for their assistance. Not that the sometimes-employed Edward had that sort of money. Oh no, all three men would be paid by an unidentified Nashvillian. He'd handed Edward a thousand dollars total; Edward would keep half the money for himself.

The three guys picked up two cases of dynamite from a secret stash some unnamed purveyor had left for them. They stored the explosives in Edward's house. Over the next three days, they debated how best to destroy Clinton High, settling eventually on putting the dynamite into the coal bin of the high school and exploding it at about two in the morning when no one would be in the building.

Then I got cold feet, Avon said. He was a coal miner's son who knew the damage a single stick of dynamite could do. Over 300 sticks? "Someone would get killed."

The three men carted the dynamite to the riverbank to hide it until they could figure out what to do with it. A few days later, a red-and-green car pulled up to Edward Cline's house. Then one of the occupants—Edward never saw their face—pulled out a pistol and started shooting. Edward dropped and scrambled for safety. Another shot. And another. The shooter fired seven times before peeling away. As soon as the bullets stopped flying and Edward knew he was unharmed, he packed his car up and headed to Peoria, Illinois, somewhere he assumed he'd be safe. Responsibility for the TNT now fell to Clifford and Avon. Then Tom Powell found the dynamite before they could get rid of it, and now Avon was sitting in jail.

Glad must've wondered whether to trust Avon Nolan's testimony. The nineteen-year-old had never been an upstanding citizen. He and Clifford were already charged with the earlier robbery attempt, which hadn't even gone to trial yet! And Avon didn't come from the best family either. Just a few months back, the whole lot of them had been evicted from their home. These days, Avon's father was off working in a coal mine up in the New River area, one of the rougher parts of the county, while his mother, brothers, and sisters were leaning on the generosity of the state. Of course, Nolan himself had been out of the house long before the eviction happened. By sixteen, he'd been living on his own, making his way on the wages he got for selling concessions at the Ritz Theater. Glad Woodward probably didn't hold much more hope for Clifford Lowe's future. Sure, the man was newly married and newly employed as a furniture salesman, but he had never seen the inside of a classroom. Absolutely illiterate! What sort of future could either of those two have had? Glad must've wondered.

Well, lucky for Glad Woodward, just a year earlier the state legislature had given him a new law, drafted and passed for exactly this sort of situation. It would let him lock these jokers up for a good long time. It was now a felony in Tennessee to possess or transport dynamite, dynamite caps, fuse, detonators, or wiring with the intention of destroying property or causing loss of life. Avon and his alleged accomplices were the first ever to be charged under the new law, which carried a sentence of two to ten years. They were also charged with conspiracy to damage or destroy Clinton High School, another three to ten years if convicted. Local Trial Justice Leon Elkins set Avon and Clifford's bond at $4,000 each, a sum neither of their families could pay. The second week of December, officers in Joliet, Illinois, called Glad up with good news. They had captured Edward Cline. On January 1, three detectives and one sheriff drove over from Nashville to question Cline. They'd had a school bombing as part of their school integration conflict the preceding fall and they hoped he could help them identify some suspects. Edward gave them a description of the man who'd approached him, but he didn't help narrow their pool down much. He was a tall, black-haired man, Edward said.

On February 11, the case went to trial. It took the judge and lawyers about two hours to find their jury: twelve local white fathers. Then the lawyers got busy. First, Buford Lewallen, Avon Nolan's court-appointed defense attorney, had the charges against Avon dropped. If his client wasn't set free, Buford told the court, he wouldn't testify. And if he didn't testify, the prosecution didn't have much of a case. Next, Sheriff Glad Woodward took the stand. He explained how he and his men had found the dynamite and where they'd picked up their prisoners. Then was a former coworker of Edward Cline's who, like Edward, moved frequently looking for work. This spring the man was down in Florida, but back in the fall he'd been employed by a Kentucky coal mine. Twice, Edward came to see him, asking the man to steal ten dynamite caps from his employer. The man refused. Avon Nolan then stepped to the stand, the only one who could tie his former codefendants to the dynamite and then explain how the men planned to use the dynamite to destroy the school. He said everything the prosecutors hoped he would. Then Clifford Lowe spoke. He had never been part of any dynamiting plan, he told the jury. He had never gone anywhere with Edward and Avon, though yes, he knew them. And yes, he'd made a few trips to Nashville and Illinois with Edward. But no, he wasn't part of any bombing conspiracy! In fact, he was a newlywed, and he'd spent every single night with his wife. Then came the final witness, Edward's ex-roommate. And he told the jury how he'd seen Edward, Avon, and Clifford leave the house together one night that past September, though he'd never seen any dynamite.

Testimonies and closing statements wrapped up about five that day, and the jury began their deliberations. At 6:43 they asked for a dinner break. Then they returned to their task. At 11:18 p.m., the twelve men returned. The jury foreman, an engineer at Oak Ridge, read the verdict. Edward Cline was guilty of conspiracy, they decided, and they recommended he serve ten years in prison. They acquitted Clifford Lowe.

—

Despite the ongoing turmoil and danger, Gail Ann Epps survived her senior year at Clinton High. In May 1958, she donned her own graduation robe and she marched across the stage, becoming the first Black girl to graduate from a desegregated high school in Tennessee. Gail Ann would be the last of the twelve Black students to graduate from Clinton High.

TWENTY

Boom

At 4:30 in the morning on Sunday, October 5, dynamite destroyed Clinton High School. The bombers set three separate charges at strategic spots in the hallways, exploding them approximately three minutes apart. The first, left outside the boys' restroom, blew out a brick-and-tile wall fourteen inches thick and left a four-foot hole in the concrete slab floor. The second, located by the cafeteria, obliterated three classrooms, collapsing their walls and crumping away the floors. The third threw a wall of lockers into the courtyard, along with the nine-inch-thick brick edifice that supported them. Sixteen of the building's twenty classrooms were demolished, and all were damaged. Investigators estimated the bombs contained one hundred sticks of dynamite in total. Only the gymnasium and band room—separate from the main structure—were left standing.

Just a few hours earlier, the campus had been bustling with students. The Clinton band had spent the weekend in Bristol competing with other schools around the region, and they'd come home flush from their performance. The teenage musicians and their parents had milled about in the high school's parking lot, congratulating each other. They'd departed just shy of midnight. In the predawn hours, thankfully, the campus was deserted.

First on the scene were Cliff Roberts and his son, a 1958 Clinton High graduate. The Roberts family lived less than a block away, and Cliff had been thrown from bed by the first bomb. The family'd gathered together and listened to the next two explosions rumble through the building. After waiting for a few minutes to be sure a fourth charge wouldn't be ignited, father and son had rushed over to the school to save as much of the building as they could. Inside, they saw sparks shooting out of an electrical outlet on one of the few walls left standing. Cliff's son managed to find a fire extinguisher among the debris and smothered the flames before they could spread. A few minutes later, two girls ran up to Cliff, crying. They were members of the band who'd stashed their instruments at the school after their weekend trip. Now, the girls hoped to find and salvage them.

Nationally syndicated columnist Drew Pearson visited the site the next day and described the scene. On the floor of one classroom "among ripped books and shattered plaster," he saw a note. "I love you Aleeda," was all it said. Though the attackers decimated the campus, "they did not erase the lesson of 'English III Literature assignment for November.'" The students were to have spent their weekend reading William Cullen Bryant, James Fenimore Cooper, Oliver Wendell Holmes, Henry Wadsworth Longfellow, James Russell Lowell, and John Greenleaf Whittier. "Poking through that debris, you couldn't help but wonder what Whittier or Longfellow or Lowell would have written about the hate and vengeance wreaked upon children," he wrote. "Longfellow and Holmes, Bryant and Whittier would have stirred up the Nation against such vengeance."

Anna Theresser Caswell, now a junior and the only one of the original twelve Black students still enrolled at Clinton High, spent that Sunday listening anxiously to the radio, trying to learn whether she would be able to return to school or if the segregationists finally had won. The announcement went out that Sunday night, twelve hours after the bombing: the school would reopen the next morning. Classes would meet on the front lawn until a new building could be procured. When Theresser arrived the next day, she overheard someone say, "Well, here come those damn niggers again." As classes started, however, the white and Black students settled back into the tense, silent truce normal at Clinton High.

While the teachers and students adapted to their new open-air classrooms, thankful that October was usually mild and sunny, Principal W. D. Human, Margaret Anderson (recently promoted to assistant principal), and a cadre of white parents scrambled to prepare a new, semipermanent home for the student body. The town of Oak Ridge offered them Linden Elementary School, a Black institution closed when the Oak Ridge system desegregated three years previously. Grateful for the space, some of the volunteers sorted through the Clinton High rubble for any useable desks or books. Others converged on Linden to scrub it clean, haul off the child-sized desks, and replace them with appropriate equipment.

None of the white adults organizing the new school arrangements suggested resegregating the student body—at least not publicly. Most were simply resigned to the situation. For a few of them, however, the events of the past few years had changed them from reluctant participants in desegregation into committed integrationists. Margaret Anderson didn't want her town to be misconstrued by journalists parachuting in to cover the bombing, so she wrote an article for the *New York Times*. In 1956, she'd been one of the many white people who pledged to follow the law. Now she wrote: "Integration will work. It is already working in many places. It will continue to work because it is just and right and long overdue." Setbacks—even the violent destruction of a school—should not "stop integration, for that would be to go backward." Still, she believed too much of the fight had fallen on her students. "Today's children are having to pay such a high price emotionally, socially, and academically," she told her readers. "Are we taking every precaution to guard the safety of these children from enemies we do not know, or cannot identify?" The rubble around her was her answer.

By Thursday morning, the substitute building was ready. When the buses pulled up to the front of the new Clinton High, the Oak Ridge High School marching band stood waiting, playing Clinton's school song. "For the first time in history (probably) students were delighted to have their books," the school's newspaper reported. "By Friday, every nook and corner having been inspected, school became school again. Perhaps time will erase the initial feeling of loss, the feeling of physical sickness that one or several persons could have so much hate and venom."

Though the parents, teachers, and volunteers had refitted the elementary school with larger desks, they were unable to replace everything. High school boys bent double, trying to see themselves in bathroom mirrors hung for a typical seven-year-old. The toilets were also child-sized, a challenge for adolescent bodies to use comfortably. The water fountains became a joke.

While the students and teachers adjusted to their new facilities, Principal W. D. Human and the school board went to Washington, D.C., to ask for federal aid in rebuilding the school. When they arrived, President Eisenhower said he was too busy to see them. They learned that he was playing bridge with friends. He'd shuffled them off on representatives from the Department of Education who said the best the federal government could do was offer $20,000 toward the county's maintenance expenses, an amount that hardly offset the $750,000 the rebuilt school ended up costing. The Clinton representatives were furious. "When we were forced to integrate . . . the government gave us no protection," one of the men complained. "They said the protection of the school and the children was a local problem. Now when our schoolhouse is blown up, again Washington says this is your problem." Another school board member explained that they had already spent close to $4 million in the last ten years to rebuild other schools in the county to keep pace with the influx of outsiders coming for the federal projects. And the county had condemned three elementary school buildings. And they needed a new junior high. How were they also to fund a new high school? they asked.

The federal investigation into the bombing was also doomed to failure. When the FBI arrived in Clinton the day after the explosion, the agents discovered the local officers had allowed journalists, politicians, school administrators, and others to tour the scene, contaminating it. The investigators found pieces of the bombs, but they found no sites of probable entry, no fingerprints, nor any other evidence. Witnesses who lived nearby recalled seeing a car speeding away immediately after the first blast, but they could not recall the make or model. They were not even sure of the color and could only say it was a dark hue.

The local police so badly bungled the investigation that some concluded the officers were colluding to protect the perpetrators. For Robert Cain Sr., Bobby Cain's father, the damning evidence was that the police did not immediately go to Clinton High School to investigate. When he heard the first blast, he rushed to his front porch. Despite the darkness, he could tell something had happened down at Clinton High. He could also see a police car parked by Asbury Methodist even though the officers seldom patrolled the Hill. The car wasn't moving. It stayed put until after the second blast went off.

The investigation lasted for three and a half years. In the end, the federal agents determined there was insufficient evidence to indict anyone for the crime, though they suspected the explosion in Clinton was related to other attacks, including the bombing of the Hebrew Benevolent Congregation Temple in Atlanta. Asa Carter's branch of the Klan had established an office in downtown Clinton just one block from the school, and there were ongoing associations between Clinton's segregationists and the National States Rights Party. Members from both of those groups would be accused of being associated with eighty-four other bombings, which destroyed synagogues, churches, and schools across the South including Birmingham's 16th Street Baptist Church.

The failure of the authorities to arrest anyone meant the attacks continued. Over the next two months, two homes owned by Black Clintonians were both destroyed by arson. As 1958 turned to 1959, the agents failed to find many new leads, but they continued to find bombs. One rural family who owned a farm about five miles from Clinton called the sheriff to report that while clearing an unused corner of their land they had uncovered a quart glass fruit jar that had been packed with dynamite. Holes were drilled in the top of it, and two fuses were attached. The local police eventually turned it over to the FBI, but by then it had been handled by most of the Clinton officers and so had no useable fingerprints left on it.

Investigators also visited Edward Cline, jailed six months earlier for trying to bomb Clinton High School. He knew nothing. And he hoped they would reopen his own case. How could he have been convicted of conspiracy when he was the only defendant found guilty? That conundrum was not the investigators' concern. They left him in prison. So he composed a thirty-page handwritten writ of habeas corpus to Federal Judge Robert L. Taylor, arguing that the conspiracy charge was invalid. He also alleged Avon Nolan had given him an affidavit saying he'd lied to escape other criminal charges. The judge turned him down. For one thing, Bob said, Edward hadn't exhausted all his remedies in the state courts, so the federal bench couldn't pick his case up. For another, his convoluted document was so hard to understand—so many misspellings and grammatical inventions—that he couldn't follow the prisoner's contentions.

A month later, the state pardons and paroles board agreed to hear Edward Cline's arguments. It may have been a mercy hearing, as Edward had developed tuberculosis and was living in the prison's hospital. Even before his arrest and illness, he'd been a thin man, the sort of thin where every bone in his face and every ligament in his neck looked like it might cut through the fragile coating of skin. Illness must have made him look emaciated. Again, Edward alleged his innocence. The parole board chairman told the convict that they were not interested in retrying the case. The board was only there to decide whether to parole him, a question complicated by Edward's two previous federal convictions. The parole board denied Edward Cline's petition. He tried again the next year. They turned him down again. He would go before them five more times before finally serving out his sentence.

—

When the bomb went off that October, many Americans had forgotten about Clinton High School, distracted by events in Little Rock and Nashville and other larger cities around the South. The bombing reminded them, and many wanted to help the Appalachian town, especially when they heard the federal government was refusing to pay to rebuild the school.

Drew Pearson decided Clinton High would be a pet project. Throughout his career, he'd used his muckraking style of journalism to take on human rights and justice issues: reconstructing a Serbian town after World War I, trucking supplies to post–World War II France, and helping unseat the rabble-rousing anti-Communist senator Joseph McCarthy. But for Drew, Clinton superseded these previous efforts. "I've thought sometimes that I would like to have written on my tombstone," he wrote toward the end of his life, "that I was the rebuilder of the Clinton, Tenn., High School." He used his column to rally his readers and fundraise for the new facility. He asked each high schooler in America to donate a nickel, or the price of one bottle of Coke. Each foregone Coke would buy the people of Clinton a brick for their high school, a "friendship brick," to combat the hate they'd experienced.

Evangelist Billy Graham joined the effort. On December 14, 1958, he conducted a one-day revival in Clinton. His sermon that day was the first time he spoke to a community that had recently experienced racial violence, and it was the first time he directly connected his work as a Christian evangelist to his support for the growing civil rights movement. Billy Graham was a social conservative on many issues, but he believed in racial equality and integration. He insisted on preaching before an integrated audience, a position he took no matter where he preached in the South or across the globe. When the local segregationists heard of his stand, they threatened his life. The evangelist replied that their threats proved he was doing the right thing.

Billy Graham began his day in Clinton by having breakfast with some of the local civic and religious leaders (though not Paul Turner, who had left a few months earlier, accepting a call from a larger Baptist church in Nashville). Then Billy walked into Clinton High School's gymnasium, the building that survived the bomb and the site of his address. The location meant that Billy, his attendants, and all his audience would walk through the high school and see the destruction for themselves. Three thousand people came to hear him speak. Or maybe it was five thousand. Whatever the number, the crowd exceeded the gymnasium's seating capacity, so the moderators ran a phone line to Clinton's First Baptist Church's sanctuary to provide overflow seating.

The meeting opened with columnist Drew Pearson presenting the school board superintendent with a check for $27,000—or more than five hundred thousand foregone Cokes—the first installment toward a new Clinton High, and one that already exceeded the federal government's donation. Then Billy took the podium.

"If God is a God of love, why does not God stop all the war and the suffering and the hatred in the world?" the evangelist asked. "Wasn't Christ called on that first Christmas 'the Prince of Peace'? Wasn't he announced as 'the Prince of Peace'? All right, if he's the Prince of Peace, why doesn't he bring peace? Has Christ failed? Has Christianity failed? Has the church failed? What's wrong?"

He continued, "God is a holy God and a righteous God, and the Bible tells us that God cannot stand for evil to be in his sight. . . . But the Bible tells us something else. The Bible tells us that God is a God of love."

Because God is loving, God needed other beings to love. That is why God created humans and made them in God's image. "Now when I look at you, I don't see God's image," Billy said, "because when I look at you, I don't see you. I only see the house you live in. Your body." That superficial awareness of others as bodies instead of souls was the source of racism, Billy said. Then he issued an altar call, inviting his listeners to come forward and receive the forgiveness God offered for the times they had been hateful toward others, a forgiveness that would enable them to turn around and forgive the neighbors who had hurt them.

Over the coming months, contributions to rebuild the school continued to pour in from around the nation. The Franklin Institute squadron of the civil air patrol in Philadelphia contributed their weekly dues. Builders' unions volunteered their labor. "People may have mixed opinions about integration," the president of the Building Trades Council wrote Drew Pearson, "but none of them have mixed feelings about using bombs to retard school children. We want to help."

On August 29, 1960, almost nine hundred students—ten of whom were Black—started classes at the rebuilt Clinton High School, a brick International Style building constructed on the site where their old school had been. The new building had banks of long, narrow windows so the institution would be full of light and warmth. The classrooms were spacious. The library restocked. Principal W. D. Human used the reconstruction to institute other improvements as well. He appointed Margaret Anderson as the school's first official guidance counselor. He expanded the teaching staff. The new science laboratories had the latest equipment, and the architects added a language lab that had thirty-six separate booths with microphones and tape recorders so students could practice their listening and speaking skills. A plaque on the wall of the building dedicated it to "Drew Pearson and world-wide friends for time, materials, funds, and labor." Above the dedication was an embossed image of two hands clasped in friendship.

But the move back to Clinton High School did not mark the end of racial problems within the school. Over the next ten years, the administrators relaxed a few of the rules about racial separation, but Black students weren't permitted to join the school's intramural sports teams until 1963. They could attend dances, but they had to stay on the opposite side of the gymnasium. They couldn't share cafeteria tables with white students. And the hallways remained a dangerous place. The shoving and the threats continued. Their echoes could be heard even into the twenty-first century.

—

D. J. Brittain Jr. thrived in New York University's graduate school. Over the winter break of 1956–57, one of D. J.'s former professors had come to visit. The man had told D. J. there was an opening for him to do doctoral studies at NYU if he wanted to continue his education. "That would be a godsend," D. J. had replied. The Brittains had moved to New York in August '57. Somewhat to D. J.'s surprise, he was a celebrity at NYU. After graduation, he worked at New York University for two more years and then was appointed superintendent of schools in Rutherford, New Jersey. His wife went back to teaching home economics.

D. J. likely hoped moving across the country and to the other side of the Mason–Dixon Line meant he'd never face the same troubles as had happened in Clinton, but racism is a national, not a regional, sin. In the late 1960s, he became the superintendent of New Jersey's Ewing Township schools. During a 1969 Martin Luther King Day play at the high school, a fight broke out between the minority and white students. D. J. closed the school to stop the spread of violence. "I had learned some things from Clinton," he explained. This time around, "I sat down with my board of education, and I said, 'Now you're going to be with me on this or you're not.'" Unlike Clinton, the board came to his support, and D. J. reorganized the system to make each local school racially balanced. He adjusted the curriculum to include more Black history, increased the number of Black-authored books in the schools' libraries, and increased the guidance support offered to minority students. His district became noted as having the best practices in the state.

But D. J. could not forget the hate that had ended his time at Clinton High. Before the 1956–57 school year, he was a kind, quiet, religious man. After that year, he was bitter and cynical. He began drinking heavily and questioned his faith. After his retirement from the New Jersey school system, he and his wife moved back to Clinton. For a time, he seemed to enjoy being in his hometown, but when his wife died of cancer in January 1988 he was left rootless and disconnected. That February, he shot himself. The only thing he asked of his family was that they destroy all his papers and records related to desegregating Clinton High School.

Others who had participated in the struggle over desegregation were also traumatized by their experiences in Clinton that year. Those who fight to broaden the American dream of liberty, equality, and justice to include all of us often pay a significant personal price.

Paul Turner had remained at Clinton's First Baptist Church until 1958, muddling through the aftermath of his decision to walk the students to school. After Nashville weathered its own desegregation crisis, one of its largest congregations called Paul to help them navigate their divisions. Paul stayed there until he left the ministry entirely in 1967, beginning a doctoral degree in theology. He wanted to write about his experiences in Clinton, drawing from the hate mail he received to explore the "poisonous and mentally unhealthy sentiments" of his attackers. The "authors [thought] that they had sound 'religious' grounds for taking their 'venomous' stances," he explained in his proposal. "One letter was signed 'God.' " They believed "they were doing the Lord's work in their 'mouthings,' criticisms, and threats." His advisors told him to find a less controversial topic. After graduation, he joined Golden Gate Baptist Theological Seminary in San Francisco as a professor of ministry and the director of professional training.

On December 18, 1980, the Reverend Paul Turner picked up his handgun, went into the living room of his home north of San Francisco, and shot himself. His wife, Jane, found his body. He was fifty-seven years old. His family and friends insisted the root to his depression lay in what happened nearly twenty-five years earlier. Paul Turner had been one of Clinton's favored sons before desegregation. But the hate that surrounded him when he did what he believed to be right overwhelmed him. After Clinton, Paul was plagued by depression. Eventually it became too much.

"The Paul Turner in Clinton was a true Christian minister," a friend wrote in an obituary. But after, "his spirit was broken. The fire that had carried him through Clinton was just a candle glow. . . . Gone was the trust in God to protect him in doing what was right even when it was hard and dangerous." Paul struggled through this doubt and pain alone. "Paul

Turner had no pastor. Paul Turner had no one to whom he could turn and completely open his fears and needs," the man concluded. "I hurt in the loss of this man. I hurt for his family. I hurt for all the servants of God who must face their problems and fears alone."

Many of the original twelve Black students also struggled after leaving Clinton High as they tried to make sense of what happened to them during their time there. Going to Clinton High School had cost them their adolescence. While in school, Anna Theresser Caswell had been too concerned with day-to-day survival to resent missing out on the high school social whirl. Later, though, she heard friends talking fondly about the ball games and school dances they had attended. I was "cheated out of everything," she told me. "I just got cheated out of everything a young person is supposed to do."

As one reporter had noticed when he interviewed Bobby Cain, many of them exhibited symptoms of what we would now call post-traumatic stress disorder. They'd seen their neighbors turn on them in violence. They'd watched as people they trusted looked away while they were attacked. They'd been beaten and bombed and harassed and shunned. They'd lived with the fear—and then the reality—of what could happen to them and their families when they demanded their rights. They'd lost their sense of home and their sense of safety. And afterward, they'd had to make peace with the society that had betrayed them.

"I really did not know that people could be so mean and hateful," Minnie Ann Dickie Jones said.

"The thing that I think now affected me the most was not the physical danger, because you get to the point that you had just about as soon die," Regina Turner Smith said. "It was the realization of how much people could hate us. I never realized before that people could hate us as they do."

TWENTY-ONE

Silence, Spreading

May 17, 2007, was the fiftieth anniversary of Bobby Cain's graduation from Clinton High. At two that afternoon, he and eight of Clinton High's first twelve Black students reunited in the parking lot of the renovated Green McAdoo Cultural Center. More than four hundred dignitaries and townspeople gathered around them to commemorate the event. Tennessee governor Phil Bredesen—who had personally donated $300,000 to the new museum installed in the school—stood at the head of the parking lot and addressed the crowd. Behind him, a zigzagging ramp climbed to the top of Freedman's Hill, tracing its way up a large concrete wall. A quote from one of Paul Turner's sermons ran along the top of the wall: ". . . but we are positively and definitely against the disintegration of our community and our body politic that we cherish above all things, realizing that where anarchy prevails, none of us have anything of any value and none of us have any freedoms anymore." Above the governor, a black plastic tarp hid a recently installed monument. When the sheets fell away, they revealed twelve bronze statues, life-size sculptures of the Black teenagers. Poised above the audience, they stood looking down the Hill as though they were about to begin the long walk to school.

"I never thought this would happen," Bobby told a reporter for the *Oak Ridger.*

Jo Ann Allen Boyce agreed. "I'm blown away," she said. "I'm overwhelmed. I'm humbled."

Bobby Cain and Gail Ann Epps had been the only ones of the original Black students to graduate from Clinton High. By the end of the first year, Jo Ann Allen, Minnie Ann Dickie, Alvah Jay McSwain, Robert Latham, and Robert Thacker had left and Alfred Williams had been expelled.

The next year, Regina Turner's family moved to Florida so she could study in peace. After she graduated, she earned a degree from Knoxville Business College and then went to work in Oak Ridge at Modine Manufacturing.

Robert Thacker's family took him back up to Michigan, where he graduated from the integrated Mount Clemens High School. After that, he served two years in the Army and then went to work at Ford. He eventually opened his own asphalt trucking business.

Maurice Soles enlisted in the Army and was wounded in Vietnam. After his discharge, he moved out to Arizona, where he earned his GED. Later in life, he returned to Clinton. He and his brother Eddie Soles went into the concrete business.

Anna Theresser Caswell finished her education through Austin High's night school program. She stayed in Anderson County, working in Oak Ridge, first in the K-25 plant and then for Martin Marietta Energy Systems Inc.

Ronald Hayden, who had dreamed of being a lawyer, developed a brain tumor. The surgery to remove it robbed him of his sight, so he transferred to a state-sponsored school for the blind. When he was twenty-three, he died at his home in Clinton of a cerebral hemorrhage, presumably a complication of his treatments.

Gail Ann followed Bobby to Tennessee A&I. After graduation, she came back to the mountains. There she married, raised her children, and worked as a substitute teacher at Green McAdoo.

Jo Ann Allen and Minnie Ann Dickie settled in Los Angeles and finished school there. Jo Ann attended Los Angeles City Junior College and Nursing School. She worked for forty years as a nurse, much of that time as a pediatric nurse. She sang semiprofessionally in her free time. Though Jo Ann occasionally returned to Clinton for family reunions, she never wanted to live in Tennessee full-time. Minnie Ann eventually did, however, marrying a pastor in Knoxville.

In May 1957, Alvah Jay McSwain and her family joined the Allens and the Dickies in California. She enrolled in John C. Fremont High, but her grandmother fell ill before Alvah graduated. Because both her parents had to work, she quit school to care for her grandmother, but Alvah Jay was determined to finish her education. She started taking night classes and convinced her mother, Wynona, to join her. "In June 1963, my mother and I graduated from John C. Fremont High School together," she reported proudly. "That was one of the happiest days of my life." After graduation, Alvah Jay, who once told a reporter she was attending Clinton High because her dream was to go to a good college and become a nurse, found a job as a truck driver, first driving a ten-wheeler dump truck and then working as a medical driver until her retirement in 1995. She did not return to Clinton for almost fifty years.

Bobby Cain could not stay in Clinton after all the hate he had experienced. He moved to Nashville, though he went back to Clinton periodically to visit his younger siblings and other family members.

—

Many of the students who desegregated the school stopped talking about their experiences there soon after they left its halls. They did not want their bitterness to infect others. Anna Theresser Caswell eventually had three sons and countless foster children. She knew her kids would go to Clinton High School, where they'd sit in classes alongside the relatives of the people who had tormented, betrayed, and ignored her. "Sometimes kids want to take up for you," she said. "I didn't want them to have chips on their shoulders. I just didn't want that, so I never told them." The first time she ever discussed that part of her life with the younger generation of her family was when the *Knoxville News-Sentinel* did a story on her experiences. She told one of her nephews he should read the story online. He called her back, upset. "I didn't know any of this!" he said. She told him she could not talk about that year with him until she knew the racial situation was "a lot better." She paused, then clarified, "They are not all right, but things are better."

Silence was also self-protection. The students who survived Clinton High felt a deep anger at the way they'd been treated. Bobby Cain worried that his resentment might overwhelm him when he enlisted in the integrated United States Army. "I realized my hostility was not going to get me anywhere," he explained. "I tried to forget everything that I carried at Clinton. I tried putting it in my subconscious mind."

The only reason Bobby's children knew about his past was because his wife, who came from another Tennessee community, had watched news coverage of the events at Clinton High and told their children about his part in the civil rights movement. The kids then told their children. One day, Bobby's grandson invited him to come see his school play, telling his grandfather he'd been given an important role in the production. The boy came out dressed as Bobby had been in one of the photographs from *Life* magazine. He then talked about his grandfather's important part in the fight for equality. "I tell you, that was the most— That was very touching," Bobby told me. "The most gratifying thing that's happened to me, for him to come out and do that. And for him to have learned that . . ." His voice trailed away.

Mostly, though, the friends and families of the Black students accepted their silence. In a larger town, the silence might not have been necessary. Each faction could have retreated into their own community, choosing separate furniture stores, different churches, defined neighborhoods. In Clinton, this wasn't possible. Everywhere folks went—the Ritz Theater, Hoskins Drug Store, Clinton High football games, William Brakebill's grocery store—they bumped into people who had been standing on the other side of the picket lines. Since they could not avoid each other, the community members stopped talking about those years. Individuals of different races and classes lived parallel lives, looking away from the deep social divides Clinton High School's desegregation had uncovered and the lingering anger that existed decades after the violence ended.

Even the school's bombing went unsolved, though locals had plenty of theories about who'd done it. During the time I spent in Clinton, most individuals I spoke with claimed to know who the bomber was, though no one was willing to give me his name and I received varying descriptions of his appearance. Some claimed he had a scar on one cheek. Others said that was his brother. But they all agreed that he was still living and still an integral part of Clinton's civic life. The FBI said it had no leads.

Meanwhile, the national news moved on as the Southern War Correspondents headed to Nashville and to Little Rock and to Charlotte and to Prince Edward County and to New Orleans and to Birmingham and then to places beyond the South like Boston and Chicago. Soon few outsiders remembered the rural Appalachian town that captured everyone's attention for a few years; they forgot to ask Clinton High's Black students to talk about their desegregation experience. And the twelve Black students' refusal to speak meant that no one reminded the American public of what had happened in Anderson County. The silence became cyclical.

Then in 2001, Asbury Methodist, one of the two churches on the Hill, called a new minister named Alan Jones. Alan was an archetypal Renaissance man: Methodist priest, human resources director at Knoxville's McGhee Tyson Airport, and gifted artist who painted under the name Theophilus. When Alan took the pulpit in Clinton, he went to visit Asbury's retired pastor the Reverend C. L. Willis, who'd been there in 1956.

The Reverend Willis told the younger man there was a piece of Clinton's history he needed to know if he was going to successfully minister on Freedman's Hill. Everyone in his church was somehow related to the twelve teens who desegregated Clinton High. Alan, who'd never heard the story before, asked his congregation to tell him more. They tried to answer his questions, revisiting memories the students had spent four and a half decades ignoring. Bobby Cain discovered he had so effectively blocked that part of his past that he could not answer even the most basic questions. He turned to a scrapbook one of his younger sisters had assembled. As he read the clippings and poems Hattie had glued into its pages, the memories came flooding back.

Alan wanted to celebrate the students who had changed American history, but as a pastor of a struggling church with fewer than fifteen congregants most Sundays, he had limited resources and little influence. He brought out his paints and created a commemorative mural for the church, hanging it where an altarpiece traditionally would go. At the center of the picture is a depiction of the students walking down the Hill accompanied by Paul Turner, Sidney Davis, and Leo Burnett. Behind them hangs Jesus on a cross with a dove descending upon him. Rays of heavenly light shine down upon the teenagers and their escorts. Two Black seraphim stand guard.

Because of how much the painting meant to his congregants, Alan Jones pressed on. On May 16, 2004, he organized a reenactment of the march from the Hill to Clinton High led by Bobby Cain and Maurice Soles. About two hundred people attended. First Baptist Church, once Paul Turner's home pulpit, agreed to host the final convocation of that day. Gail Ann Epps Upton had never been inside First Baptist. "We always called it the big dogs' church, siddity uppity uppity people," she said. She walked through the doors and into a sanctuary full of white folks. Some of them were crying. She thought the tears meant things had changed, but one of the pastors pulled Alan aside to ask him why he had interfered. Not everyone in Clinton was anxious to rehash the story of desegregation.

Then the city announced it would raze Green McAdoo. Residents from the Hill went to a city council meeting to request that the school instead be transformed into a community center. The idea quickly evolved into the Green McAdoo Cultural Organization and then the Green McAdoo Cultural Center, culminating in the opening of the museum and the installation of the bronze statues of the students walking down the Hill.

The statues on the Hill are a beautiful, moving memorial to the Black teens' youthful determination. But they are also symptomatic of the problem with contemporary commemorations of the civil rights movement. In this idealistic and celebratory version of the past, the twelve are frozen in their teenage years, bravely facing the walk down the Hill, a walk that— we're encouraged to assume—succeeded. The monument fails to note that the fight for integration has yet to be won.

—

Today schools are resegregating. In the mid-1990s, many judges backed away from the desegregation plans they had overseen, plans for combining schools or busing students put in place because of lawsuits like *McSwain v. Anderson County*. These court orders hadn't been panaceas for educational injustice. As Thurgood Marshall once wrote, "Even if all parties approach the court's mandate with the best of conscious intentions, that mandate requires them to confront and overcome their own racism on all levels—a challenge I doubt all of them can meet."

As happened at Clinton High School, Black students carried the weight of these decisions. They were sent into white schools, and the schools they left behind were stripped of the power that had made them centers for Black life and community. Teaching—a profession that gave many college-educated Black adults a way to both enter the middle class and give back to their communities—became an increasingly white field. Almost forty thousand Black teachers and administrators lost their jobs or

were demoted in the wake of the *Brown* decision. Today, only twenty percent of America's teachers are non-white, and only seven percent identify
as Black, though having Black teachers has proven to be critical to Black
students' success. And often historic Black schools—formerly community
centers and sites of neighborhood pride—were deserted. In Clinton, elementary schools did not desegregate until 1965. When they did, Green
McAdoo was closed as a school and reopened as a Head Start facility. Eventually that, too, was shut down. Then the city's maintenance department
took it over for storage. The place that had raised generations of Black children, giving them shelter where they could learn insulated from white hate
and prejudice, was left to rot until the community forced the city to save it.

Nevertheless, four decades after *Brown*, the courts ignored those clear
signs that desegregation had not accomplished its ends. Ruling integration
had been attained, judges gave power and oversight back to local school
boards and administrators, but as Imani Perry wrote in *South to America*,
"If you think, mistakenly, that American racism can be surmounted by integration, by people knowing each other, even by loving each other, the history of the American South must teach otherwise. There is no resolution
to unjust relations without a structural and ethical change." By 2007, 178
schools had been released from their individual court orders. That same
year, the Supreme Court declared race was no longer a valid criterion for
determining school assignments. Resegregation accelerated. School systems
freed from court-ordered desegregation plans dismantled their programs,
often using the language of "neighborhood schools," or the romantic and
nostalgic idea children should attend the school closest to them, one they
could hopefully walk to. But over the years since *Brown*, residential segregation had deepened, spurred on by ongoing inequality in banking practices, prejudices by real estate agents, the historic racial nature of inherited
wealth, and the systematic (and systemic) destruction of historically Black
neighborhoods across many urban centers. According to a nationwide survey conducted at UC Berkeley, 81 percent of America's metropolitan areas
were more segregated in 2019 than 1990. Residential segregation and other
forms of racism sometimes called de facto Jim Crow had replaced the legal
Jim Crow system of the 1950s . . . and spread. The increasing racial divide
meant school systems could justify rising educational inequity.

As a result, school segregation more than doubled between 2001 and 2016, and the number of intensely segregated minority schools (or schools that were at least 90 percent non-white) had tripled since 1988, going from 5.8 percent to 18.2 percent. In 2016, the most segregated states for Black students were New York, Illinois, California, Maryland, and Texas. And America's schools were more segregated than they were in 1968, the year of Martin Luther King Jr.'s assassination.

Pinellas County, Florida, was under court-mandated desegregation for thirty-five years. During that time, the county was one of the most integrated systems in Florida and its students thrived. When federal oversight ended in 2007, the school board reverted to neighborhood-based school assignments. By 2013, five elementary schools in the district were over 80 percent Black, and these same five institutions also received less money per student than any other school, as funding was distributed throughout the district based on the percentage of property taxes a neighborhood paid and the amount of booster/PTA dollars raised. All five were rated as failing. In one of them, only 6 of 160 students passed both their math and reading standardized tests.

Other communities are just now going under court-monitored school desegregation. Cleveland, Mississippi, is about two-thirds Black, but four of the town's eleven schools are 95 percent Black or higher. Black parents call them the track schools, built to contain the students who live on the east side of the abandoned Illinois Central Railroad tracks. Though a group of parents filed a desegregation suit in 1965, a federal decision was not reached until May 2016. And then there's New York City, the most segregated educational system in the nation. For decades now, principals on the Upper West Side have left desks empty rather than admitting students from Harlem and Manhattan Valley.

Was Governor George Wallace's "Segregation today. Segregation tomorrow. Segregation forever" perhaps a prophecy rather than a campaign pledge?

—

From within their classrooms, Clinton's students and teachers stood on the front lines of the conflict. They were the ones who actually desegregated the school, not the judge or the lawyers or the National Guard. At any point, the individuals inside Clinton High could have decided the dream wasn't worth it. Black students could have refused to put themselves in danger. Teachers could have quit or gone on strike. The white student body could have refused to come to school. By going to classes each day, they made history. And they were the ones the rest of us forgot, replacing their story of determination with our own tale of failure, resegregation, and school closure. Despite the white supremacist uprising, students, teachers, administrators, local leaders, and state officials worked together to keep the students—regardless of color—in the school. Their examples can expand our imaginations as we search for new ways to equalize education in twenty-first-century America.

Elsewhere in the South, the law-and-order crowd were able to implement a far more successful form of segregationism, often called the Nashville Way for the city that used civility and an intentionally slowed version of desegregation to minimize the impact *Brown* had on white children. By agreeing to token concessions, Nashville's white leaders at first limited desegregation to a handful of schools. This gave white parents time to make alternative plans for their children. A bevy of white private schools launched during this era. Some white families moved into the surrounding counties where public schools were still segregated. A decade after desegregation, nine out of every ten Black children enrolled in the Nashville/Davidson County school district still attended an all-Black school. The federal courts finally stepped back in and announced they would take control of desegregation. A year later, the number of students enrolled in Nashville's public schools dropped by over 11 percent. The entirety of the loss was among white students. In 1971, a federal judge ordered schools in Nashville/Davidson County to begin busing to reduce segregation. Another 14 percent of students left the school system, cutting white enrollment from seventy-four thousand to fifty thousand students.

But in Clinton, where school administrators were forced more quickly into desegregation, a belief in law and order kept many white people away from the rallies and the riots, preventing them from being radicalized further. And some of the white law-and-order folks—from the football players to Celdon Lewallen to Paul Turner to Margaret Anderson to D. J.

Brittain Jr.—ended up being transformed into valuable advocates for the Black students, even if that advocacy happened somewhat against the white Clintonians' wills.

For me, one of the most challenging parts of the Clinton story is the gap between participants' beliefs and their actions, particularly among the white law-and-order crowd. In our current polarized political situation, we demand perfection of our friends and allies. Our world is bifurcated, and no matter which side of the divide we stand on, whether we consider ourselves progressives or conservatives, anyone who is not always in agreement with us can quickly become an enemy.

When we tell people they do not belong in our movement—that they must go out and find their own resources and do the internal work before they can be of any use to us—we are ignoring the ways actions themselves can invoke internal change. D. J. Brittain Jr. didn't create a Black studies program in New Jersey simply because of what he'd read in graduate school. He started on that path because in 1956 he decided to obey the law rather than follow the racist principles he'd been raised to believe. People of color, of course, should not have to lead wannabe white allies further down the path to being accomplices in what John Lewis called the Good Trouble. That burden needs to be undertaken by white antiracists, and hopefully this book will be part of my contribution to that cause. But when we deny people grace and refuse to allow them to join us as the broken people they are, we risk deepening the divisions that threaten our body politic. And if we shun them when they show they have not yet fully uprooted the racism from their minds and their souls, we far too often lose their aid rather than showing them how to finally eradicate the ugliness they inherited.

In Clinton, Tennessee, a handful of folks on both sides of the color line muddled their way—often imperfectly, especially in the cases of the white townsfolk—toward equality. Bobby Cain, Margaret Anderson, Wynona McSwain, Paul Turner, Jo Ann Allen, D. J. Brittain Jr., Gail Ann Epps, and others are most notable for their very ordinariness. None of them had the makings of heroic leads. But they persevered. The rest of us have yet to measure up to their bravery. We haven't overturned the ways racism and generational wealth and unequal opportunities have shaped our communities. We have accepted (and, many of us, profited from) rising gentrification and the segregation that attends it instead of demanding integrated neighborhoods with affordable housing. We fight for what is to the short-term benefit of our own children instead of fighting for a society in which every child in America thrives.

Addressing the problems facing America and the world today means reconstructing every part of our society. The systems structuring our nation were developed by people who believed in inequality. They gave us judicial practices that entrapped generations of minorities in jail, and they founded educational institutions that limited learning for most students. They set up banking networks that did not lend to certain people in certain neighborhoods and food systems that kept many people from eating a nutrient-rich diet. They plotted out transportation infrastructure that obliterated neighborhoods, walling residents off with roads, and then encouraged real estate regulations that kept cities segregated. They legislated healthcare systems that made a long life too expensive for most to attain. And though the resulting society deepens the divisions among us, reinforcing and perpetuating inequity, too many of us accept it as is. We must demand all those systems change. We must find, nurture, and elect leaders willing to intervene quickly and decisively whenever the vulnerable among us are at risk, and they must be visionaries who can help us imagine a better way. And they need to be the rare sorts of politicians willing to do the unpopular thing that betters the nation, even if it means they risk losing the next election. And when we cannot find them, we must run for office ourselves. We must work together to create the world the students of Clinton High fought to attain.

Before we can do that, however, we must change our history. When we remember the Clinton Twelve, the Little Rock Nine, the students who claimed seats at the Woolworth lunch counters, and the myriad of other young faces around the South as bronzed statues frozen in time, when we celebrate their actions as examples of a triumphant past, we participate in the storytelling that allows America's educators, policy makers, and voting public to pretend that segregation and racism no longer exist.

Jo Ann Allen, Bobby Cain, Anna Theresser Caswell, Minnie Ann Dickie, Gail Ann Epps, Ronald Hayden, William Latham, Alvah Jay McSwain, Maurice Soles, Robert Thacker, Regina Turner, and Alfred Williams deserve better than that. It's time we pick up their fight.

From the Top of Freedman's Hill, July 2009

I sat in a canvas lawn chair, baking in the July sun on Maurice Soles's front deck some five years after my first trip to Clinton. The story I'd heard during my initial assignment to the town had so gripped me that after my research fellowship ended I'd gone to the University of North Carolina at Chapel Hill to pursue a PhD in history and write a dissertation on the high school. Though I'd collected almost fifty voices already, some of the people I most wanted to meet hadn't responded, ignoring my letters and my phone calls. Maurice was one of them.

I decided to forego propriety. I ambushed him at the bottom of his steep driveway, intercepting him on his way to his mailbox. He swore he hadn't ignored me on purpose, that he'd thrown my letters away unread. "I thought they were junk mail," he said. Then he guided me onto his wood porch and motioned for me to take a seat.

Maurice and I had been talking over the part he had played in this history for more than an hour under the unrelenting summer sun. I pressed my right forefinger against my biceps, evaluating the depth of my burn. This was one of the hottest summers on record in Southern Appalachia, and I was a definite Swedish pink. I wanted to ask to come inside, but I was an uninvited guest. Still, I was surprised Maurice had left me on his unshaded porch while he took a phone call. This was becoming part of a trend I recognized. Most folks invited me to their homes for an interview, but Black men did not. They met me at the library or in a city park or in the gymnasium of the Green McAdoo Cultural Center. I watched a school bus pull into the museum's parking lot and thought about this pattern.

And then it struck me, the one very good reason these men would not meet with me inside their homes: they were the same generation as Emmett Till, the Black adolescent tortured and murdered for allegedly whistling at a white woman in Mississippi in 1955. At a niggling memory, I flipped through my notes. Yep, Maurice Soles even shared Till's exact birthday: July 25, 1941.

Through the manufactured home's thin beige walls, I heard Maurice on the phone. He'd already fielded calls about me from a neighbor and then his wife. I assumed this time he was explaining me to the man in the blue pickup who drove by, slowed down, and backed up at the sight of me perched on Maurice's wood-slat front porch deep in the Hill. His friends and family were rallying to protect him. For him, someone who looked like me could mean death. That threat wasn't just in the past. A year earlier, a local white man had burned a cross on his niece's lawn, right in front of the home she shared with her Black boyfriend. As Emmett Till's cousin told a reporter on the fiftieth anniversary of the boy's abduction, "A white woman? Oh no, it's better to play with a rattlesnake."

Maurice Soles finished his phone call and returned outside. I flipped my recorder back on, and he continued his story, the tale of the racist violence and mayhem that had exploded when he became a Clinton High School Dragon. As he spoke, I looked at the landscape around me and tried to envision the men who had defended the Hill that Labor Day weekend, just a scant five days after the teenagers desegregated the school. Maurice's uncle and older brothers had been among them.

I studied Maurice Soles as he talked. He was one of those rare people who really hadn't changed much since his high school days, still thin and angular with one shoulder hitched a hair higher than the other. He reminded me a bit of another child who was also slightly built, with a charming, shy smile.

That boy was in my fourth-grade class. We attended the sort of rural Tennessee school where boys were paddled and girls did write-offs and of course Black boys got more strokes and Black girls were given more sentences to do. It was the 1980s, and we were the most integrated generation of students America had produced. After *Brown v. Board*, civil rights advocates, federal agencies, and the nation's court systems fought to turn their initial gains into true educational equality for all students, altering the racial composition of many of America's schools but—as was true in my elementary school—not always changing much at the classroom level. Only two Black kids were left in my class. Though there was little difference between our grades or our test scores, the other Black students had been shunted into the slower class, a practice known as "second-generation segregation." Poorer children were also far more likely to be moved into the less-academic classroom.

"They told us we were the stupid class," my friend Crystal said when I asked her about it. Then she reminded me of one time when her class outscored mine on a test. The teacher threw out the scores, accusing Crystal's class of cheating. But being in the "faster" class might have meant that this one Black boy was more vulnerable. Our teacher paddled him frequently, and often I wasn't sure what he had done wrong.

I suppose I should say our generation was the most desegregated, not integrated. At the end of fourth grade, the Black boy was held back and the other Black child went down into the other class. I would not be in the same classroom with a Black student again until high school. But my experience, that less-than-equal attempt to put children of different races in the same building, that's the best we've managed to do.

For the students, parents, and activists who fought to open white schools, integration meant more than allowing a few Black children to enroll. They believed students who studied and played together would graduate from school accepting the social, political, and economic equality of the races. Integration is the dream: the full elimination of discrimination based on color. A truly integrated school would be one in which every student has the same opportunity to succeed, has friendships with other students from different racial groups and other economic classes. It would be a place where every child feels safe and welcome. Or, as Clinton High School teacher Margaret Anderson explained in an article for the *New York Times* in 1960, "Desegregation involves the admittance of Negro students into a white school in compliance with the law. Integration involves the conversion of the two groups into a smooth-running system, with a working relationship free of tensions."

When I talk about school integration, I often call it a failure, but what I really mean is that it is an experiment we have yet to try.

ACKNOWLEDGMENTS

This section is usually an annotated list of those who made a project possible, and after almost twenty years of work, my list of people to thank is substantial. I'll get to that in a second. First, I need to tell you a story.

In 2018, I decided to give up on this book. I'd defended my dissertation about five years earlier, and I'd been trying to find an agent for it ever since. Several had asked for my book proposal, but none had decided to represent me. Throughout this process, my family, especially my parents, had encouraged me to keep going. My folks even sacrificed their foyer, taking down a piece of art my mother treasured so I could hang giant corkboards from their walls. I had pinned note cards to these boards, plotting out yet another version of the narrative. And then one more. After developing five different outlines, I was done. I called my mom and told her to throw the cards away because I was moving on. And then in the summer of 2019, I published a story in *Oxford American* about the fight to equalize education in Lake City, a little town near Clinton. Agent Susan Canavan read it and reached out to me, asking about Clinton High's desegregation. I pitched her three other unrelated ideas. She told me she wanted a proposal for the Clinton High book on her desk within two weeks. I panicked. I had deleted all my draft book outlines and told Mom to trash my note cards. Thankfully, instead of dumping the corkboards, my folks had carefully unpinned the cards, keeping them in order, and put them into a metal card box for safekeeping. Those note cards are the skeleton for the book you just read.

Now, time for the acknowledgments: first, I owe a debt to the people of Clinton who shared their memories with me. I cannot imagine confiding in a stranger as so many of my narrators have. Our conversations have changed me. I hope that I have done justice to the trust placed in me.

I am also grateful to the many librarians and archivists who have helped me along the way, especially at the Tennessee State Library and Archives; the University of North Carolina at Chapel Hill; Special Collections at the University of Tennessee, Knoxville; and the Knox County Public Library. Staff at these institutions led me to sources I would have never found on my own.

I am thankful for Dr. Carroll Van West and the Middle Tennessee State University's Center for Historic Preservation for guiding me to this story. Then, when I decided I needed better research skills, my professors at the University of North Carolina helped mold me and stretch my work in the directions it needed to go. Thank you especially to my committee, Drs. W. Fitzhugh Brundage, Laura F. Edwards, Crystal Feimster, William R. Ferris, and James L. Leloudis. And to my advisor, Dr. Jacquelyn Dowd Hall. Throughout her career, she has modeled what it means to transform a banal, celebratory version of the past into the sort of messy, complicated narrative that can lead to actual social change.

John Grammer, April Alvarez, and the instructors and students at the Sewanee School of Letters helped me remember what it meant to be a writer. Officially, I've only taken one class with them, but I've been crashing events down there for almost a decade now, soaking up as much craft as possible. My beta readers Marlayna Maynard, Lauryn Peacock, and Sam Warlick dived into an earlier draft of this narrative, helping me see what was and was not working. And thanks also to Luke Anderson, whose messages of support always arrived at just the right moment.

My agent, Susan Canavan of Waxman Literary Agency, resurrected this book, and I am incredibly grateful to her for seeing who I wanted to be as a writer and a researcher and then encouraging me forward into that. And as for Megan Hogan, my editor at Simon & Schuster, well, words fail me. I thought I understood what good editing meant, but I have never known anyone who could work through my drafts, encouraging me and challenging me and pushing me and reassuring me, in quite the same way. Her knowledge of storytelling is astounding. But she also makes space for humanity within both the narratives she directs and the authors she works with. Together, these two women made *A Most Tolerant Little Town* possible.

Finally, I must again mention my family. Thank you. Readers, may you, too, have a person or two who believe in your calling even when you do not.

NOTES

A NOTE ON LANGUAGE

xi *The word was considered:* United States District Court, *"Bullock,"* December 4, 1956, 28–44, July 15, 1957, 645–54, July 16, 1957, 761–65; Anderson, *The Children of the South,* 18–19; "Witnesses Tell of Violence at Trial of Kasper and 14," *Clinton Courier-News,* July 18, 1957, 1, 6.

PROLOGUE: COMING TO THE CLINCH, SEPTEMBER 2005

1 *of some ten thousand residents:* U.S. Census Bureau, "Clinton City, Tennessee," https://www.census.gov/quickfacts/fact/table/clintoncitytennessee/SBO020217.

1 *the hills crack:* Coskren and Hay, *Field Trip Guides,* 1–23; Department of Energy, "Oak Ridge Reservation Annual Site Report—2013," 1.3.5; Department of Energy, "EA-1042," 3.4.

1 *The first people moved:* Arnow, *Seedtime on the Cumberland;* Fielder, *Archaeological Survey,* 5; National Park Service, "Geology and History of the Cumberland Plateau," 5.

1 *White settlers renamed the peaks:* For instance, of fifty-five slave-owning families living in the county in 1802, thirty-seven reported owning only one enslaved person, likely a lonely existence for the sole Black individual on a farm or in a household. In 1860, fewer than 2 percent of local white residents owned any humans, and of the 110 slave owners in the county, more than one half owned fewer than five individuals. Nevertheless, by 1860, of the 1,068 persons living in the county, 583 were enslaved. In addition, the free Black population, which had been forty-one in 1850, had fallen to eight by the eve of the Civil War. Adamson, "The Lit Stick," 11; Bell, *Circling Windrock Mountain,* 42–43, 46–47; U.S. Census Bureau, "1860 Anderson County Census," digital image, Ancestry.com; U.S. Census Bureau, "1860 Federal Census, Slave Schedule, Anderson County," digital image, Ancestry.com.

2 *After Emancipation, many:* Brittain, "A Case Study," 29; James L. Cain interview; Goodspeed, *History of Tennessee,* 839–40; Hoskins, *Historical Sketches,* 213–14; Seeber, "A History of Anderson County, Tennessee," 71–73; West, "The Civil Rights Movement in Clinton"; Mrs. J. H. Hansard, "Clinton Reader Points Out," *Knoxville Journal,* September 26, 1956, 4; U.S. Census Bureau, "1870 Anderson County Census," digital image, Ancestry.com.

2 *Like most other Black neighborhoods:* Adamson, "The Lit Stick," 6; James L. Cain interview; U.S. Census Bureau, "1920 Anderson County Census," digital image,

Ancestry.com, "1930 Anderson County Census," digital image, Ancestry.com, "1940 Anderson County Census," digital image, Ancestry.com, "1950 Anderson County Census," digital image, Ancestry.com.

2   *Downtown, postbellum prosperity:* "Mines Employment Cut by Half Since 1950," *East Tennessee Reporter,* June 28, 1957, 3; Hoskins, *Anderson County,* 3, 49–51, 57; Seeber, *Good Morning, Professor,* 42–47; Sims, "Magnet Mills," 140–43; Goodspeed, *History of Tennessee,* 839–40.

4   *Clinton's then-mayor, Winfred:* Wimp Shoopman interview.

4   *the feature film was:* "Halting and Fitful Battle for Integration," *Life,* September 17, 1956, 35-37; "Weekend Violence Brings Guards and Peace," *Clinton Courier-News,* September 6, 1956, 3; Holden, Valien, and Valien, *Clinton, Tennessee,* 6–9; "Guard Commander Bans Outdoor Meets," *Oak Ridger,* September 3, 1956, 8.

4   *sat the war memorial where:* Anderson, *The Children of the South,* 15–16; Herd, "Then and Now," 44–45.

5   *I passed the empty lot:* Howard Sochurek, TimeLife_image_113356167, *Life,* September 9, 1956; Howard Sochurek, TimeLife_image_113356181, *Life,* September 9, 1956; Howard Sochurek, TimeLife_image_113356174, *Life,* September 9, 1956; Howard Sochurek, TimeLife_image_113356173, *Life,* September 9, 1956.

5   *Most of the old structure:* Steve Hoskins interview; West, "Description, Green McAdoo School."

8   *She was nervous: "When":* Margaret Anderson interview.

8   *William Faulkner was right:* Faulkner, *Requiem for a Nun,* 85.

ONE: DESCENDING FREEDMAN'S HILL

11   *In the packed schoolyard:* Jo Ann Allen Boyce interview; Regina Turner Smith interview; Howard Sochurek, TimeLife_image_113356039, *Life,* September 1956; Howard Sochurek, TimeLife_image_113356041, *Life,* September 1956.

11   *Yes, on the morning:* Jo Ann Allen Boyce interview.

11   *Jo Ann Allen found the silence:* Ibid.; Robert W. Kelley, TimeLife_image_11332 2134, *Life,* September 1956; Robert W. Kelley, TimeLife_image_113322051, *Life,* September 1956.

12   *As ready as she could be:* Jo Ann Allen Boyce interview; Bobby Cain interview; Regina Turner Smith interview; Gail Ann Epps Upton interview; Boyce and Levy, *This Promise of Change.*

12   *the ten students held hands:* Boyce and Levy, *This Promise of Change,* 67; McMillan, "'The Ordeal.'"

12   *a mere week after:* Brill, "*Brown* in Fayetteville," 337–59; Vervack, "The Hoxie Imbroglio," 17–33.

13   *They'd all heard the rumors:* "Suit Seeks to Bar Negroes From School Here," *Clinton Courier-News,* August 23, 1956, 1, 6; "Most People in Anderson County Do Not Want Mixed Schools," *Clinton Courier-News,* August 23, 1956, 5; "Clinton

High Now Integrated," *Oak Ridger*, August 27, 1956, 1–2; United States District Court, "*Bullock*," July 15, 1957.

13 *any family members who could:* Bobby Cain interview; James L. Cain interview; Alfred Williams interview; "Turner, Wm.," *1955 Clinton City Directory*, 269.

13 *Half-brothers Alfred Williams and Maurice:* Howard Sochurek, TimeLife_image_113356128, *Life*, September 1956; Maurice Soles interview; Alfred Williams interview.

13 *paid scant attention:* Adamson, "The Lit Stick," 4, 80–81; Holden, Valien, and Valien, *Clinton, Tennessee*, 5–6; Roberts, *High School*, 54–58.

14 *they'd made plans to return:* Bobby Cain interview; June Adamson, "The Walk," *Knoxville News-Sentinel*, December 5, 1993, AC1–AC2; Regina Turner Smith interview; Eddie, Maurice, and Charles Soles interview; Alfred Williams interview.

15 *According to local gossip, Mayor:* Jo Ann Allen Boyce interview; Eleanor Davis interview; Jerry Shattuck interview; Regina Turner Smith interview; Williams et al., "Clinton and the Law."

15 *Less than a dozen:* Adamson, "The Lit Stick," 101–2; Brittain, "A Case Study," 107a; "Agitator Fights U.S. Order Here," *Clinton Courier-News*, August 30, 1956, 1, 8; "School Board to 'Follow All Court Orders,'" *Clinton Courier-News*, August 30, 1956, 1, 8; "Students Attend Classes, Go on with Studies Quietly," *Clinton Courier-News*, August 30, 1956, 1, 8; Horace V. Wells, "As We See It," *Clinton Courier-News*, August 30, 1956, 1, 8; "Clinton High Now Integrated," *Oak Ridger*, August 27, 1956, 1–2; Seivers, "Words of Discrimination," 70.

15 *John Carter, a smooth-faced:* "Youth Is Bitten by Rabid Fox," *Clinton Courier-News*, March 1, 1956, 1; "John Carter Wins District 4-H Speaking Contest," March 22, 1956, 1; *Dragon 1956*, 39; "Bitten By Fox," *Knoxville Journal*, March 2, 1956, 22; "Rabid Fox Bites Boy Going to Aid of Dog," *Knoxville News-Sentinel*, March 2, 1956, 2; "Junior, Senior Winners of 4-H District Speaking Tilt Picked," *Knoxville Journal*, March 18, 1956, 25; "Clinton High Squad," *Knoxville Journal*, August 7, 1955, 17.

16 *John should have been starting:* "Student Protesting School Integration," August 27, 1956, Bettman Archive.

16 *the assistant police chief told:* "Clinton High Now Integrated," *Oak Ridger*, August 27, 1956, 1–2.

16 *The low numbers were:* Ibid.; "Defense in Kasper trial Continues," *Clinton Courier-News*, November 15, 1956, 1, 4.

16 *The network of segregationists had mobilized:* Adamson, "The Lit Stick," 100–101; David Ray Smith, "Oak Ridge 85 Finally Get Deserved Recognition for Desegregating Schools," *Knox News*, February 5, 2021, https://www.knoxnews.com/story/opinion/2021/02/05/oak-ridge-85-finally-recognized-desegregating-schools/6589271002/.

17 *Oak Ridge taught a different lesson:* Adamson, "The Lit Stick," 100–101; Tennessee Federation for Constitutional Government, *Tyranny at Oak Ridge*, 4.

17 *The Tills had only been:* United States Patent Office, "2,548,751: Auxiliary Support for Use with Ironing Boards."

18 *A sturdy man—six feet:* "Glenn to Appear in Feature Event," *News and Observer,* February 12, 1935, 8; "Hopes to Revive Pro Boxing Here," *News and Observer,* October 15, 1935, 10; "Franklinton School Sponsors Fight Show," *News and Observer,* October 17, 1935, 10; "Boxers to Arrive in Raleigh Today," *News and Observer,* October 22, 1935, 10; "Boxing Show Tonight at Franklinton High," *News and Observer,* October 23, 1935, 10; "Pro Boxers Meet in Program Here," *News and Observer,* October 25, 1935, 10; "Big Wedding," *News and Observer,* May 12, 1940, 8; "Births," *News and Observer,* October 17, 1946, 6; "Births," *News and Observer,* April 8 1949, 12; "Willard Harold Till," *News and Observer,* December 30, 2001, 14B; North Carolina State Library, "World War II Draft Cards Young Men, 1940–1947," digital image, s.v. "Willard Harold Till," Ancestry.com.

18 *a God-fearing, churchgoing man:* Mrs. Burke Dwayer, "Clinton Mob," *News and Observer,* May 11, 1957, 4.

19 *Racism was an essential ingredient:* Anderson, *The Children of the South,* 7; Hoskins, *Anderson County,* 61–62; Steve Jones interview; Roberts, *High School,* 51–52; Tennessee Federation for Constitutional Government, *Tyranny at Oak Ridge,* 4; Woodward, *Origins of the New South.*

19 *Four hundred and twenty-four:* "Suit Seeks to Bar Negroes from School Here," *Clinton Courier-News,* August 23, 1956, 1, 6; "Most People in Anderson County Do Not Want Mixed Schools, *Clinton Courier-News,* August 23, 1956, 5; "Clinton High Now Integrated," *Oak Ridger,* August 27, 1956, 1–2; United States District Court, *"Bullock,"* July 15, 1957.

20 *It was a pragmatic decision:* Shumate, "The Effect of Social Classes on the Community and Schools of Clinton, Tennessee," 11–75.

20 *picketers had been shouting and booing:* Jo Ann Allen Boyce interview; Homer Copeland interview; "Kasper and Six Convicted; New Trial Possible," *East Tennessee Reporter,* July 26, 1957, 1; "Raymond Woods Hasn't Changed, He Tells Reporter," *East Tennessee Reporter,* July 26, 1957, 1; "Rev. Bullock Refutes 'Smear' News Stories," *East Tennessee Reporter,* July 26, 1957, 1; "Back Glances Show Incidents of Interest," *East Tennessee Reporter,* July 26, 1957, 2, 8; Jerry Hamilton interview.

21 *Alfred Williams recognized many:* Alfred Williams interview.

21 *As they trudged:* Howard Sochurek, TimeLife_image_113356039, *Life,* September 1956.

TWO: WYNONA'S FIGHT

22 *Wynona McSwain fired up:* Wynona McSwain also at times spelled her name as "Winona," and the more traditional spelling may well have been her "legal" name. In September 1956 when she gave an interview to legendary Black journalist Louis E. Lomax, however, she spelled her name with a *y.* In this interview, she laid

out the ways she and her husband had worked, challenging Anderson County's racist segregated educational system until it benefited their children. To honor that work, I'm going to use the name she chose when asked to speak about her life and her struggle.

22 *chores as cook and cleaner:* Smith, "McSwain Sisters Tell the Story That Predated the Clinton 12."

22 *Wynona had treasured:* Ibid.; "Triplets at Clinton," *Knoxville News-Sentinel,* December 23, 1944, 10; U.S. Census Bureau, "1950 United States Federal Census," digital image, s.v. "Allen McSwain," Ancestry.com.

22 *Seven had been lost:* Based on the records, it seems most of the children Wynona lost died early in her marriage and also early in life. Several of them may have even been late-term miscarriages or stillbirths delivered at home by midwives and then buried in a family plot in graves the McSwains would have been able to identify. Unfortunately, the years the family spent in Ohio, working better-paying jobs than were available to Black adults in Clinton before the TVA and Oak Ridge came along, may have increased the children's risk of death. Segregated Black communities in the North were overcrowded with insufficient infrastructure, housing, or governmental supports. In 1920, children of northern Black migrants were 118 percent more likely to die than the children of rural Black Southerners (those in the urban South, in contrast, were 66 percent more likely to die); Eriksson and Niemesh, "Death in the Promised Land," 16. Unfortunately, I am not sure what happened to all of Wynona's lost children. The National Death Registration Act did not take effect until 1933. The reason Harrison has a death certificate is that he died in 1936.

22 *Harrison, who had died:* Acosta et al., "Diphtheria"; Tennessee Death Records, 1908–1958, s.v. "Harrison Everett McSwain," Ancestry.com.

23 *When Wynona was a child:* Acosta et al., "Diphtheria"; "Innoculate Pupils," *Knoxville News-Sentinel,* June 12, 1935, 7.

23 *she had launched her campaign:* Louis E. Lomax, *Baltimore Afro-American,* September 8, 1956, 1, 13; Louis E. Lomax, "School Case Victory of Struggle," *Baltimore Afro-American,* September 8, 1956, 13.

23 *Wynona had truck:* Shirley and James Davenport interview; West, "Description, Green McAdoo School"; "Anderson School Classroom Asked," *Knoxville Journal,* May 20, 1956, 13.

24 *in 1947 the town's:* Hoskins, *Historical Sketches,* 262–63; National Archives and Records Administration, s.v. "Green McAdoo," Ancestry.com. The origin of the moniker "Buffalo Soldiers" is unknown. It may have come about because many of them wore coats made of buffalo hide during the long, cold winters on the plains. Or perhaps it was because the peoples they fought thought their dark curly hair resembled that of the buffalo.

24 *The spot where Green McAdoo:* Butchart, *Schooling the Freed People,* 165.

24 *particular champion for education:* Jo Ann Allen Boyce interview; Daniel, *The Crozier Family History,* 1–7; Dunaway, *Slavery in the American Mountain South,* 227; Tennessee State Library and Archives, "Tennessee State Marriage Index,

1780–2002," digital image, s.v. "Adaline Staples," FamilySearch.com; U.S. Census Bureau, "1900 Anderson County Census," digital image, s.v. "Adaline Crozier," Ancestry.com.

25 *education gave the Croziers:* Sarah Daffin, "Letter from Clinton, Tenn.," *Christian Recorder*, February 1, 1868, page unknown; E. B. Hudson, "Burning of a Church," *Press and Messenger*, March 10, 1869, 5; John Jarnagin, "Meeting of Citizens of Clinton," *Press and Messenger*, March 17, 1869, 7; Presbyterian Church in the U.S.A. Committee on Freedmen, *Fifth Annual Report of the General Assembly's Committee on Freedmen*, 59; Gardner, *Unexpected Places*, 139–52; Butchart, *Schooling the Freed People*, 37, 194, 203, 207.

25 *Segregation wove its way:* Hoffschwelle, "Public Education in Tennessee."

26 *in 1935 when the town:* "School Additions OK'd," *Knoxville News-Sentinel*, April 10, 1955, 27; "Clinton Man Given State Schools Post," *Knoxville News-Sentinel*, June 3, 1955, 19; "City Asks County Add Room to Negro School," *Knoxville News-Sentinel*, May 20, 1956, 13; "Group at Lake City to Have Own School, *Knoxville News-Sentinel*, June 24, 1956, 2; West, "Description, Green McAdoo School," "The Civil Rights Movement in Clinton."

26 *And while the board:* Smith, "McSwain Sisters Tell the Story That Predated the Clinton 12"; United States District Court, "*McSwain*," April 26, 1952.

26 *provided no high school:* Locke, *Let Me Tell You about Coal Creek*, 6–7.

26 *In 1939, a cadre:* United States District Court, "*McSwain*," April 26, 1952; "Suit Asks White Schools to Admit Negro Pupils," *Knoxville Journal*, December 7, 1950, 12; "Negro School Advantages Called Best," *Knoxville Journal*, February 14, 1952, 9; "Negroes Plan New School Petition," *Knoxville Journal*, July 1, 1955, 28.

27 *Wynona had read the Pan-Africanist:* Smith, "McSwain Sisters Tell the Story That Predated the Clinton 12."

27 *the more she'd always:* Ibid.; Louis E. Lomax, *Baltimore Afro-American*, September 8, 1956, 1, 13; Louis E. Lomax, "School Case Victory of Struggle," *Baltimore Afro-American*, September 8, 1956, 13; "Clinton Now Backs Crusading Grandma," *Baltimore Afro-American*, October 2, 1956, 24; Butcher, "Religion, Race, Gender, and Education," 78–79; Rob Neufeld, "Visiting Our Past: The Allen School in Asheville," *Citizen Times*, April 27, 2014, https://www.citizen-times.com/story /life/2014/04/27/visiting-past-allen-school-asheville/8341369/; Thomas Calder, "Asheville Archives: Allen High School's Impact on City Residents and Beyond," *Mountain Express*, February 23, 2020, https://mountainx.com/news/asheville -archives-allen-high-schools-impact-on-city-residents-and-beyond/; Social Security Administration, "Social Security Applications," digital image, s.v. "Ras Tafari McSwain," Ancestry.com; Titus, "Allen High School History."

27 *the McSwains convinced the county:* "Clinton Now Backs Crusading Grandma," *Baltimore Afro-American*, October 2, 1956, 24; "Holmes, John W. (Mary E)," *Nashville, Tennessee, City Directory, 1949*, 435; Stoecker and West, "Pearl High School (Martin Luther King Magnet) Nashville."

28 *three daughters into Allen High:* Louis E. Lomax, *Baltimore Afro-American*,

September 8, 1956, 1, 13; Louis E. Lomax, "School Case Victory of Struggle," *Baltimore Afro-American*, September 8, 1956, 13.

28 *Now why was he:* Ibid.

28 *He wasn't playing:* Ibid.

28 *Alarmed, Wynona:* Ibid.

28 *Where is the check:* Ibid.

28 *we've cut the check:* Ibid.

28 *Why not? she demanded:* Ibid.

28 *We're not so sure:* Ibid.

28 *Wynona knew he meant it:* United States District Court, *"McSwain,"* April 26, 1952, 40–53, 78–89, 92–120.

29 *City Attorney Buford Lewallen:* Brittain, "A Case Study," 60–61; Buford Lewallen interview; Seivers, "Words of Discrimination," 133–34.

29 *After surveying:* "Clinton Now Backs Crusading Grandma," *Baltimore Afro-American*, October 2, 1956, 24; D. J. Brittain Jr. interview; Seivers, "Words of Discrimination," 76–77; United States District Court, *"McSwain,"* 92–98.

29 *The limited Greyhound:* Boyce, Green McAdoo Cultural Center, "About the Center"; Jo Ann Allen Boyce interview; Bobby Cain interview; Anna Theresser Caswell interview.

30 *days when the students couldn't:* Boyce, Green McAdoo Cultural Center, "About the Center"; Jo Ann Allen Boyce interview; Bobby Cain interview; Anna Theresser Caswell interview; Boyce and Levy, *This Promise of Change*, 24.

30 *Besides, a good education:* Mattie Bell Henley interview.

30 *When the principal and the superintendent:* Louis E. Lomax, *Baltimore Afro-American*, September 8, 1956, 1, 13; Louis E. Lomax, "School Case Victory of Struggle," *Baltimore Afro-American*, September 8, 1956, 13.

31 *Now the team of lawyers:* Trezzvant W. Anderson, "Clinton, Tenn. Integration Battleground," *Pittsburgh Courier*, June 22, 1957, 38; Ramsey, *Reading, Writing and Segregation*, 72–73; Smith, "McSwain Sisters Tell the Story That Predated the Clinton 12."

31 *Clinton was a consolidated:* United States District Court, *"McSwain,"* 1952.

32 *number of plaintiffs:* "School Additions OK'd," *Knoxville News-Sentinel*, April 10, 1955, 27; "Clinton Schools Open Aug. 29," *Knoxville Journal*, August 5, 1955, 19.

32 *They placed no time frame:* Ogletree, "All Deliberate Speed."

33 *On June 3, 1954:* Brittain, "A Case Study," 60–61; "Integration in Anderson High Schools Ordered," *Knoxville News-Sentinel*, January 4, 1956, 1, 2; Buford Lewallen interview; Seivers, "Words of Discrimination," 133–34.

33 *About thirty or so Black:* Eddie, Maurice, and Charles Soles interview; McMillan, "The Ordeal," 68–69.

34 *Adaline Crozier's descendants had inherited:* Daniel, *The Crozier Family History*, 1–7; Hays and Stacey, "And Her Name Is Adaline"; "Oak Ridge, Tenn., Embraces the History of 85 Black Students Who Overcame Segregation," NPR, February 23, 2021, https://www.npr.org/2021/02/23/970555503/oak-ridge-tenn-will-teach

-history-of-its-black-students-who-helped-end-segregati; U.S. Census Bureau, "1910 Anderson County Census," digital image, s.v. "Jackson Crozer," Ancestry.com, "1920 Anderson County Census," digital image, s.v. "Jack Crazier," Ancestry.com.

34 *And of course Alvah:* Louis E. Lomax, *Baltimore Afro-American,* September 8, 1956, 1, 13; Louis E. Lomax, "School Case Victory of Struggle," *Baltimore Afro-American,* September 8, 1956, 13; Alex Wilson, "She Has Daughter in the School," *Tri-State Defender,* September 1, 1956 1, 2.

THREE: BEHIND SCHOOL DOORS

35 *Brittain Jr. had known this day:* D. J. Brittain Jr. interview; Celdon Lewallen interview; Seivers, "Words of Discrimination," 76–77; United States Court of Appeals, "*McSwain,*" 92–98.

35 *A slight and bespectacled:* Robert W. Kelley, TimeLife_image_113322146, *Life,* September 1956.

35 *D. J. was destined:* D. J. Brittain Jr. interview; Roberts, *High School,* 49–53; Anderson County, TN, "School Board Minutes," April 17, 1941, and April 29, 1941.

36 *After earning an M.Ed.:* Ibid.; Margaret Anderson interview; Brittain, "A Case Study," 46–47.

36 *D.J also courted:* Ibid.; Adamson, "The Lit Stick," 40–42; Anderson, *The Children of the South,* 7; "Timely Topics Hears Panel Talk on Local Problems," *Clinton Courier-News,* March 1, 1956, 2.

36 *But Anderson County continued to grow:* Ibid. In the early 1960s, University of Tennessee graduate student Janie Chadwick Farmer used Clinton High School student records and yearbooks from the mid- to late 1950s to explore the way class and location divided the school's white students. She found measurable correlations between the students' place in the school and their backgrounds. First, she established that white students who lived in town had significantly higher grade-point averages than their white peers who lived in the rural areas outside Clinton: though less than a third of the Clinton High's students came from within the city, more than half of the top 10 percent of the students were Clintonians. Then she analyzed how white students' family financial situations affected their school activities. For instance, two-thirds of the cheerleaders came from middle-class families, as did all the football homecoming queens, prom queens, Miss CHSs, Future Farmers of America queens, and representatives to Boys and Girls State during that era. The working-class students, on the other hand, made up the majority of members in the Future Farmers of America and the Future Homemakers of America. Chadwick, "A Comparative Study," 23, 26–41.

37 *For now D. J. was setting:* Brittain, "A Case Study," 67; D. J. Brittain Jr. interview; "Clinton High Plans for Integration; 12 Negroes Enrolled," *Clinton Courier-News,* August 9, 1956, 1, 4, 6; Horace V. Wells Jr., "As We See It!" *Clinton Courier-News,* August 9, 1956, 1; "Facts on How Integration Came to Clinton," *Clinton Courier-News,* September 6, 1956, 1; "Weekend Violence Brings Guards and Peace,"

Clinton Courier-News, September 6, 1956, 1; Horace V. Wells Jr., "As We See It!" *Clinton Courier-News*, September 6, 1956, 1; Holden, Papers; Celdon Lewallen interview.

37   *D. J. predicted:* Margaret Anderson interview; Brittain, "A Case Study," 64–72; "Clinton High Plans for Integration; 12 Negroes Enrolled," *Clinton Courier-News*, August 9, 1956, 1, 4, 6; Horace V. Wells Jr., "As We See It!" *Clinton Courier-News*, August 9, 1956, 1; United States Court of Appeals, "*McSwain*," August 30, 1956, 15; P.T.A. Minutes, February 14, 1956.

37   *They all had to make:* "Agitator Fights U.S. Order Here," *Clinton Courier-News*, August 30, 1956, 1, 8; "Shattuck Is Student of the Month at CHS," November 29, 1956, 3:5; Diane Pemberton interview; Seivers, "Words of Discrimination," 135, 174–75, 188; Jerry Shattuck interview.

38   *Every spring, D. J.:* Margaret Anderson interview; Brittain, "A Case Study," 74–76; Buford Lewallen interview.

38   *While Margaret met:* Boyce and Levy, *This Promise of Change*, 52–54; D. J. Brittain Jr. interview; "Clinton High Plans for Integration; 12 Negroes Enrolled," *Clinton Courier-News*, August 9, 1956, 1, 4, 6; Horace V. Wells Jr., "As We See It!" *Clinton Courier-News*, August 9, 1956, 1; "Weekend Violence Brings Guards and Peace," *Clinton Courier-News*, September 6, 1956, 1.

38   *Still, he insisted:* Margaret Anderson interview; Brittain, "A Case Study," 74–76; Buford Lewallen interview.

38   *And now the Black students:* Jo Ann Allen Boyce interview; Bobby Cain interview.

38   *most of the white students followed:* Brittain, "A Case Study," 107a; "Clinton High Now Integrated," *Oak Ridger*, August 27, 1956, 1–2.

39   *Jerry Hamilton:* Jerry Hamilton interview.

39   *the mass of white students flowed:* Robert W. Kelley, TimeLife_image_113322162, *Life*, September 1956; Robert W. Kelley, TimeLife_image_113322172, *Life*, September 1956; Robert W. Kelley, TimeLife_image_113322178, *Life*, September 1956; Robert W. Kelley, TimeLife_image_113322055, *Life*, September 1956.

39   *Bobby Cain folded himself:* Bobby Cain interview.

40   *Robert Thacker leaned against:* Ibid.; Robert W. Kelley, TimeLife_image_113 321940, *Life*, September 1956; Robert W. Kelley, TimeLife_image_113322155, *Life*, September 1956; Robert W. Kelley, TimeLife_image_113322154, *Life*, September 1956.

40   *Jo Ann Allen had landed:* Jo Ann Allen Boyce interview; Davis, *Gifts Given*, 2–3.

40   *Eleanor made a big:* Jo Ann Allen Boyce interview; Eleanor Davis interview; Jerry Shattuck interview; Williams et al., "Clinton and the Law."

40   *"Jo Ann is so pretty":* Williams et al., "Clinton and the Law."

41   *A few periods later:* Jo Ann Allen Boyce interview.

41   *What did she like:* Ibid.

41   *Thankfully, Jo Ann:* Ibid.

41   *All in all, Jo Ann thought:* Ibid.

41   *a promising start:* Louis E. Lomax, *Baltimore Afro-American*, September 8, 1956, 1,

13; Louis E. Lomax, "School Case Victory of Struggle," *Baltimore Afro-American*, September 8, 1956, 13.

41   *Gail Ann Epps was grinning:* Boyce and Levy, *This Promise of Change*, 64; Gail Ann Epps Upton interview; Mattie Bell Henley interview; Moses Newsom, "Mixed Schools 'Old Hat' to One Junior in Clinton," *Chicago Defender*, September 13, 1956, 10.

41   *When a reporter for the* Chicago: Moses Newsom, "Mixed Schools 'Old Hat' to One Junior in Clinton," *Chicago Defender*, September 13, 1956, 10.

41   *Why, they'd probably get:* Ibid.

42   *Robert Thacker was sanguine:* Louis E. Lomax, *Baltimore Afro-American*, September 8, 1956, 1, 13; Louis E. Lomax, "School Case Victory of Struggle," *Baltimore Afro-American*, September 8, 1956, 13; Mississippi Department of Archives & History, "Mississippi Enumeration of Educable Children, 1850–1892; 1908–1957," digital image, s.v. "Thacker, Roosevelt," FamilySearch.com; Alex Wilson, "She Has Daughter in the School," *Tri-State Defender*, September 1, 1956 1, 2.

42   *Another boy asked to join:* Louis E. Lomax, *Baltimore Afro-American*, September 8, 1956, 1, 13; Louis E. Lomax, "School Case Victory of Struggle," *Baltimore Afro-American*, September 8, 1956, 13.

42   *Bobby Cain, however, was not:* McMillan, "The Ordeal," 338; Adamson, "The Lit Stick," 101–2.

42   *teachers were as hopeful:* Adamson, "The Lit Stick," 31, 101–2; Margaret Anderson interview; Anderson, *The Children of the South*, 4; Brittain, "A Case Study," 64–72; "Agitator Fights U.S. Order Here," *Clinton Courier-News*, August 30, 1956, 1, 8; "Federal Judge Bans School Picketing," *Clinton Courier-News*, August 30, 1956, 1, 4; Holden, Valien, and Valien, *Clinton, Tennessee*, 6–9; "Clinton High Now Integrated," *Oak Ridger*, August 27, 1956, 1–2; "750 in Classes at Clinton High," *Oak Ridger*, August 29, 1956, 2; "P.T.A. Minutes," February 14, 1956; Roberts, *High School*, 60.

42   *the first of what would:* Ibid.

43   *Men who cared:* "Agitator Fights U.S. Order Here," *Clinton Courier-News*, August 30, 1956, 1, 8; "Federal Judge Bans School Picketing," *Clinton Courier-News*, August 30, 1956, 1, 4.

43   *That night, Principal:* "750 in Classes at Clinton High," *Oak Ridger*, August 29, 1956, 2.

FOUR: A CARPETBAGGING TROUBLEMAKER

44   *Tuesday morning dawned:* Boyce and Levy, *This Promise of Change*, 185; "Agitator Fights U.S. Order Here," *Clinton Courier-News*, August 30, 1956, 1, 8; "Federal Judge Bans School Picketing," *Clinton Courier-News*, August 30, 1956, 1, 4; "Students Attend Classes, Go on With Studies Quietly," *Clinton Courier-News*, August 30, 1956, 1.

44   *Unlike the day before:* Adamson, "The Lit Stick," 101–2; Anderson, *The Children*

of the South, 10–11, 61–62; "Agitator Fights U.S. Order Here," *Clinton Courier-News*, August 30, 1956, 1, 8; "Federal Judge Bans School Picketing," *Clinton Courier-News*, August 30, 1956, 1, 4; "Man Held on Riot Inciting Turned Loose," *Clinton Courier-News*, August 30, 1956, 8; Holden, Valien, and Valien, *Clinton, Tennessee*, 6–9; McMillan, "The Ordeal," 338; Seivers, "Words of Discrimination," 70—71; "Council Man Freed in Clinton," *Oak Ridger*, August 28, 1956, 1.

44 *They were flooding into:* Adamson, "The Lit Stick," 95–97; "Cover Story"; for more information on John Kasper, see Marsh, *John Kasper and Ezra Pound*.

45 *John had been a troubled:* Adamson, "The Lit Stick," 95–97; "Cover Story"; Poetry Foundation, "Ezra Pound"; Academy of American Poets, "Ezra Pound."

45 *John graduated from Columbia:* Adamson, "The Lit Stick," 95–97; "Cover Story," *Metro Pulse*; John Kasper to Ezra Pound, May 24, 1957, quoted in Adamson, "The Lit Stick," 1.

46 *John struggled to match:* Adamson, "The Lit Stick," 95–97; "Cover Story," *Metro Pulse*; Seivers, "Words of Discrimination," 67.

46 *John's social life:* Adamson, "The Lit Stick," 95–97; "Cover Story," *Metro Pulse*; Seivers, "Words of Discrimination," 67; "Kasper Not Wanted in Arkansas," *Arkansas Democrat*, December 2, 1957; "Kasper Ranked with Subversives," *East Tennessee Reporter*, February 8, 1957, 1, 4; McMillen, "Organized Resistance to School Desegregation in Tennessee," 320; Seivers, "Words of Discrimination," 67.

46 *John's first bookstore:* Ibid.

46 *Over the summer of '56:* Federal Bureau of Investigation, "KASPER, Frederick John—HQ 67-105095," 67, 79, 83.

47 *When John arrived in Clinton:* Louis E. Lomax, *Baltimore Afro-American*, September 8, 1956, 1, 13; Louis E. Lomax, "School Case Victory of Struggle," *Baltimore Afro-American*, September 8, 1956, 13; "Agitator Fights U.S. Order Here," *Clinton Courier-News*, August 30, 1956, 1, 8; "Man Held on Riot Inciting Turned Loose," *Clinton Courier-News*, August 30, 1956, 8; Buford Lewallen interview; Purcell, *Hello, Central*, 132–33; Seivers, "Words of Discrimination," 193–94; "Violet, Joe," *1955 Clinton City Directory*, 270.

47 *Then he started walking:* Louis E. Lomax, *Baltimore Afro-American*, September 8, 1956, 1, 13; Louis E. Lomax, "School Case Victory of Struggle," *Baltimore Afro-American*, September 8, 1956, 13; "Agitator Fights U.S. Order Here," *Clinton Courier-News*, August 30, 1956, 1, 8; "Man Held on Riot Inciting Turned Loose," *Clinton Courier-News*, August 30, 1956, 8; Buford Lewallen interview; Purcell, *Hello, Central*, 132–33; Seivers, "Words of Discrimination," 193–94.

47 *At 1:30 on Sunday:* Louis E. Lomax, *Baltimore Afro-American*, September 8, 1956, 1, 13; Louis E. Lomax, "School Case Victory of Struggle," *Baltimore Afro-American*, September 8, 1956, 13; "Agitator Fights U.S. Order Here," *Clinton Courier-News*, August 30, 1956, 1, 8; "Man Held on Riot Inciting Turned Loose," *Clinton Courier-News*, August 30, 1956, 8; Buford Lewallen interview; Purcell, *Hello, Central*, 132–33; Seivers, "Words of Discrimination," 193–94; "Clinton High Now Integrated," *Oak Ridger*, August 27, 1956 1, 2; Adamson, "The Lit Stick," 101.

48   *about two dozen white men:* "Clinton High Now Integrated," *Oak Ridger,* August 27, 1956, 1, 2; "Council Man Freed in Clinton," *Oak Ridger,* August 28, 1956, 1.

48   *Promptly at 9:00:* "Agitator Fights U.S. Order Here," *Clinton Courier-News,* August 30, 1956, 1, 8; "Man Held on Riot Inciting Turned Loose," *Clinton Courier-News,* August 30, 1956, 8; "Federal Judge Bans School Picketing," *Clinton Courier-News,* August 30, 1956, 1, 4.

48   *John was defended:* "Knoxville Browning [sic] Charges Dismissed," *Daily Bulletin,* November 6, 1945, 1.

49   *John Kasper left the courthouse:* "Agitator Fights U.S. Order Here," *Clinton Courier-News,* August 30, 1956, 1, 8; "Man Held on Riot Inciting Turned Loose," *Clinton Courier-News,* August 30, 1956, 8; "Federal Judge Bans School Picketing," *Clinton Courier-News,* August 30, 1956, 1, 4; "High Court Dismisses Local Case," *Clinton Courier-News,* October 11, 1956, 1; United States Court of Appeals, "McSwain," August 30, 1956, 19–23; Herd, "Then and Now," 41; United States District Court, "Bullock," July 15, 1957, 473–74, "*Kasper*" August 30, 1956, 19–30.

49   *John spoke first: The principal:* "Agitator Fights U.S. Order Here," *Clinton Courier-News,* August 30, 1956, 1, 8; "Man Held on Riot Inciting Turned Loose," *Clinton Courier-News,* August 30, 1956, 8; "Federal Judge Bans School Picketing," *Clinton Courier-News,* August 30, 1956, 1, 4; Jim Loggans, "Some Cheer, Others Boo As Speaker Vilifies School Officials, Others," *Clinton Courier-News,* August 30, 1956, 1, 6.

49   *D. J. repeated:* Ibid.

49   *"Look at this big":* Ibid.

49   *"Present me with":* Ibid.

50   *"If you keep this up":* Ibid.

50   *D. J. pointed at:* Ibid.

50   *"Many of them had children":* Ibid.

50   *Did you?:* Ibid.

50   *Yes, D. J.:* Ibid.

50   *John Kasper stayed with:* Ibid.

50   *"We owe you":* Ibid.

50   *"The food they serve":* Ibid.

50   *He tried to organize:* Ibid.

50   *heard the confrontation:* Ibid.

51   *called the students into:* Ibid.; Seivers, "Words of Discrimination," 70–71.

51   *They sent staffers, stringers:* "More Mob Violence in Desegregation Disputes," *Decatur Daily Review,* September 6, 1956, 1; Charles Flowers, "'War Correspondents' Hold Second Reunion," *Knoxville News-Sentinel,* July 8, 1957, 1; Chester Campbell, "Guardsmen Restore Order; Negro Sailor Rescued," *Nashville Banner,* September 3, 1956, 22; "Phone Offices Made into Press Room for Visitors," *Clinton Courier-News,* September 3, 1956, 3; "Newsmen from Far and Wide Come to Cover Story Here," *Cliton Courier-News,* September 6, 1956, 3; Roberts and Klibanoff, *The Race Beat,* 329.

51   *On Tuesday night, two hundred:* "Agitator Fights U.S. Order Here," *Clinton Courier-News,* August 30, 1956, 1, 8; "Man Held on Riot Inciting Turned Loose," *Clinton Courier-News,* August 30, 1956, 8; "Federal Judge Bans School Picketing," *Clinton Courier-News,* August 30, 1956, 1, 4; Jim Loggans, "Some Cheer, Others Boo As Speaker Vilifies School Officials, Others," *Clinton Courier-News,* August 30, 1956, 1, 6; Holden, Valien, and Valien, *Clinton, Tennessee,* 6–9.

51   *local authorities have no guts:* Agitator Fights U.S. Order Here," *Clinton Courier-News,* August 30, 1956, 1, 8, "Man Held on Riot Inciting Turned Loose," *Clinton Courier-News,* August 30, 1956, 8, Jim Loggans, "Some Cheer, Others Boo As Speaker Vilifies School Officials, Others," *Clinton Courier-News,* August 30, 1956, 1, 6.

52   *If the sheriff or the police:* Ibid.

52   *If they did have any guts:* Ibid.

52   *"the hard-working":* Ibid.

52   *Down with the Communists:* Ibid.

52   *He would be there, he:* Ibid.

52   *until Principal Brittain resigned:* Ibid.

52   *Some folks clapped:* Ibid.

FIVE: THE HARDENING

53   *On that Wednesday morning:* Jo Ann Allen Boyce interview; Bobby Cain interview; Anna Theresser Caswell interview; Agitator Fights U.S. Order Here," *Clinton Courier-News,* August 30, 1956, 1, 8; "Man Held on Riot Inciting Turned Loose," *Clinton Courier-News,* August 30, 1956, 8; "Federal Judge Bans School Picketing," *Clinton Courier-News,* August 30, 1956, 1, 4; Jim Loggans, "Some Cheer, Others Boo As Speaker Vilifies School Officials, Others," *Clinton Courier-News,* August 30, 1956, 1, 6; Homer Copeland interview; Jerry Hamilton interview; Maurice Soles interview; Gail Ann Epps Upton interview; Alfred Williams interview.

53   *caught Jo Ann Allen's:* Jo Ann Allen Boyce interview.

54   *a convoy of ten cars:* Agitator Fights U.S. Order Here," *Clinton Courier-News,* August 30, 1956, 1, 8; "Federal Judge Bans School Picketing," *Clinton Courier-News,* August 30, 1956, 1, 4; "Man Held on Riot Inciting Turned Loose," *Clinton Courier-News,* August 30, 1956, 8; Jim Loggans, "Some Cheer, Others Boo As Speaker Vilifies School Officials, Others," *Clinton Courier-News,* August 30, 1956, 1, 6; Robert W. Kelley, TimeLife_image_113332125, *Life,* September 1956; Robert W. Kelley, TimeLife_image_113332116, *Life,* September 1956; United States District Court, "*Kasper,*" August 30, 1956, 59.

54   *Rastus was an insulting:* For instance, there was a Brer Rastus in the first Uncle Remus book, the Detroit Tigers' mascot was known as Li'l Rastus for a while in the early 1910s, and there were a series of short films starring a character named Rastus, including *Rastus Runs Amuck, Rastus among the Zulus,* and *How Rastus Got His Chicken.* And when white Atlanta-based journalist Frank McGill wrote a

series of columns supporting civil rights, white supremacists nicknamed him Rastus McGill.

54   *protestors now threw:* Jo Ann Allen Boyce interview; Bobby Cain interview; Anna Theresser Caswell interview.

54   *the only protection the Black students:* Agitator Fights U.S. Order Here," *Clinton Courier-News*, August 30, 1956, 1, 8; "Federal Judge Bans School Picketing," *Clinton Courier-News*, August 30, 1956, 1, 4; "Sheriff Gets 64th Still," *Clinton Courier-News*, 4; Jim Loggans, "Some Cheer, Others Boo As Speaker Vilifies School Officials, Others," *Clinton Courier-News*, August 30, 1956, 1, 6.

54   *Without security, rather:* Ibid.

54   *Jo Ann Allen comforted:* Ibid.

55   *these guys had felt:* D. J. Brittain Jr. interview; Bobby Cain interview; Anna Theresser Caswell interview; Agitator Fights U.S. Order Here," *Clinton Courier-News*, August 30, 1956, 1, 8; "Federal Judge Bans School Picketing," *Clinton Courier-News*, August 30, 1956, 1, 4; Horace V. Wells Jr., "As We See It!" *Clinton Courier-News*, September 20, 1956, 1; "Sheriff Gets 64th Still," *Clinton Courier-News*, 4; Jim Loggans, "Some Cheer, Others Boo As Speaker Vilifies School Officials, Others," *Clinton Courier-News*, August 30, 1956, 1, 6; "School Board Resignation Demanded by Group Opposed to Integration," *Clinton Courier-News*, November 29, 1956, 3, 5; Michael J. Klarman, "Why Massive Resistance?" in *Massive Resistance*, ed. Webb, 27; Diane Pemberton interview; Beth Roy, "Goody Two-Shoes and the Hell-Raisers," in *No Middle Ground*, ed. Blee, 107–8; Seivers, "Words of Discrimination," 135, 174–75, 188; Jerry Shattuck interview.

55   *the picketers didn't disperse:* Agitator Fights U.S. Order Here," *Clinton Courier-News*, August 30, 1956, 1, 8; "Federal Judge Bans School Picketing," *Clinton Courier-News*, August 30, 1956, 1, 4; Jim Loggans, "Some Cheer, Others Boo As Speaker Vilifies School Officials, Others," *Clinton Courier-News*, August 30, 1956, 1, 6; "Negroes Continue at Clinton High as Incidents of Violence Reported," *Oak Ridger*, August 30, 1956, 1, 7.

56   *four of the town's attorneys appeared:* Daniel, *Lost Revolutions*, 272; United States Court of Appeals, "*McSwain*," August 30, 1956, 58–63.

56   *D. J. let:* "Sheriff Gets 64th Still," *Clinton Courier-News*, 4; Jim Loggans, "Some Cheer, Others Boo As Speaker Vilifies School Officials, Others," *Clinton Courier-News*, August 30, 1956, 1, 6.

56   *no legal way:* Ibid.; Agitator Fights U.S. Order Here," *Clinton Courier-News*, August 30, 1956, 1, 8; "Federal Judge Bans School Picketing," *Clinton Courier-News*, August 30, 1956, 1, 4; Jim Loggans, "Some Cheer, Others Boo As Speaker Vilifies School Officials, Others," *Clinton Courier-News*, August 30, 1956, 1, 6; "Negroes Continue at Clinton High as Incidents of Violence Reported," *Oak Ridger*, August 30, 1956, 1, 7.

56   *"Let's go in":* United States Court of Appeals, "*McSwain*," August 30, 1956, 61–63.

56   *Yeah, Theo Hankins:* Ibid.; "Hankins, Theo," *1952 Clinton City Directory*, 227; Agitator Fights U.S. Order Here," *Clinton Courier-News*, August 30, 1956, 1, 8;

"Federal Judge Bans School Picketing," *Clinton Courier-News*, August 30, 1956, 1, 4; Jim Loggans, "Some Cheer, Others Boo As Speaker Vilifies School Officials, Others," *Clinton Courier-News*, August 30, 1956, 1, 6; "Negroes Continue at Clinton High as Incidents of Violence Reported," *Oak Ridger*, August 30, 1956, 1, 7.

56 *John Kasper began pontificating:* United States Court of Appeals, "*McSwain*," August 30, 1956, 62–63.

57 "*If the law along*": Ibid., 62–71.

57 "*There are six thousand*": Ibid.

57 "*We are going to get*": Ibid.

57 *Jo Ann and Gail Ann found:* Jo Ann Allen Boyce interview; Boyce and Levy, *This Promise of Change*, 87–89; Anna Theresser Caswell interview; Gail Ann Epps Upton interview.

57 *what Bobby Cain really wanted:* Bobby Cain interview.

57 *He met up with Alfred:* Ibid.; Maurice Soles interview; Alfred Williams interview.

58 *After lunch, the girls:* Bobby Cain interview; Maurice Soles interview; Alfred Williams interview; Brittain, "A Case Study," 107a; Jo Ann Allen Boyce interview; Boyce and Levy, *This Promise of Change*, 87–89; Robert Cain Sr. interview; Anna Theresser Caswell interview; Gail Ann Epps Upton interview; Agitator Fights U.S. Order Here," *Clinton Courier-News*, August 30, 1956, 1, 8; "Federal Judge Bans School Picketing," *Clinton Courier-News*, August 30, 1956, 1, 4; Jim Loggans, "Some Cheer, Others Boo As Speaker Vilifies School Officials, Others," *Clinton Courier-News*, August 30, 1956, 1, 6.

58 *Alfred, Maurice, and Ronald weren't:* Agitator Fights U.S. Order Here," *Clinton Courier-News*, August 30, 1956, 1, 8; "Federal Judge Bans School Picketing," *Clinton Courier-News*, August 30, 1956, 1, 4; Jim Loggans, "Some Cheer, Others Boo As Speaker Vilifies School Officials, Others," *Clinton Courier-News*, August 30, 1956, 1, 6; "Negroes Continue at Clinton High as Incidents of Violence Reported," *Oak Ridger*, August 30, 1956, 1, 7.

58 *been taking a working lunch:* Agitator Fights U.S. Order Here," *Clinton Courier-News*, August 30, 1956, 1, 8; "Federal Judge Bans School Picketing," *Clinton Courier-News*, August 30, 1956, 1, 4; Jim Loggans, "Some Cheer, Others Boo As Speaker Vilifies School Officials, Others," *Clinton Courier-News*, August 30, 1956, 1, 6; "Negroes Continue at Clinton High as Incidents of Violence Reported," *Oak Ridger*, August 30, 1956, 1, 7; United States Court of Appeals, "*McSwain*," August 30, 1956, 27–29.

59 *Anna Theresser Caswell was in study:* Anna Theresser Caswell interview; "Police Guard 2 Schools to Foil Integration Riots," *Evening Star*, August 30, 1956, A-2; "Negroes Continue at Clinton High as Incidents of Violence Reported," *Oak Ridger*, August 30, 1956, 1, 7; Seivers, "Words of Discrimination," 205–6.

59 *As the police drove:* Boyce and Levy, *This Promise of Change*, 88–89.

59 *A friend—an anonymous:* Mattie Bell Henley interview; Herd, "The Desegregation of Clinton High School," 48–50.

59 *Back at school, D. J.:* Agitator Fights U.S. Order Here," *Clinton Courier-News*,

August 30, 1956, 1, 8; "Federal Judge Bans School Picketing," *Clinton Courier-News*, August 30, 1956, 1, 4; Jim Loggans, "Some Cheer, Others Boo As Speaker Vilifies School Officials, Others," *Clinton Courier-News*, August 30, 1956, 1, 6.

60   *"I don't know what"*: Agitator Fights U.S. Order Here," *Clinton Courier-News*, August 30, 1956, 1, 8; "Federal Judge Bans School Picketing," *Clinton Courier-News*, August 30, 1956, 1, 4; Jim Loggans, "Some Cheer, Others Boo As Speaker Vilifies School Officials, Others," *Clinton Courier-News*, August 30, 1956, 1, 6; Wallace Westfeldt, "U.S. Court Acts to Muzzle Segregationist," *Nashville Tennessean*, August 30, 1956, 1, 12.

60   *Unsatisfied with the governor's:* Ibid. Two years later, Tom Carter tried to use some of John Kasper's lines. He'd sued his neighbor, and at the hearing he suspected things weren't going to go his way, so he told the local judge deciding the case, "The people will have to take the law into their own hands, because there is no justice in the courts."

"Before you take things into your own hands," the judge retorted, "go over and pay the clerk fifty dollars for contempt of court." "Remark Costs $50," *Knoxville News-Sentinel*, March 2, 1958, 26; "His Free Speech Not Free in Court of Justice," *Knoxville Journal*, February 28, 1958, 6.

60   *U.S. Marshal Frank Quarles was sent:* United States Court of Appeals, *"McSwain,"* September 1, 1956, 148.

60   *Just about then, Eugene:* Brittain, "A Case Study," 187–88; Bobby Cain interview; Robert Cain Sr. interview; McMillan, "The Ordeal," 68–69.

61   *Bobby also determined:* Robert Cain Sr. interview; McMillan, "The Ordeal," 337–38.

61   *"I had to scuffle":* Robert Cain Sr. interview; McMillan, "The Ordeal," 337–38; Bobby Cain interview.

61   *It's not just about his:* Robert Cain Sr. interview; McMillan, "The Ordeal," 337–38; Bobby Cain interview.

61   *Now it had come:* Brittain, "A Case Study," 187–88; Bobby Cain interview; Robert Cain Sr. interview; McMillan, "The Ordeal," 68–69.

61   *rally started at 7:30:* "Negroes Continue at Clinton High as Incidents of Violence Reported," *Oak Ridger*, August 30, 1956, 1, 7; Wallace Westfeldt, "U.S. Court Acts to Muzzle Segregationist," *Nashville Tennessean*, August 30, 1956, 1, 12.

61   *The meeting opened with:* "Negroes Continue at Clinton High as Incidents of Violence Reported," *Oak Ridger*, August 30, 1956, 1, 7; Wallace Westfeldt, "U.S. Court Acts to Muzzle Segregationist," *Nashville Tennessean*, August 30, 1956, 1, 12; Tennessee Valley Authority, "Family Removal and Population Readjustment Case Files, 1934–1953," digital image, s.v. "Alonzo Bullock," Ancestry.com; U.S. Census Bureau, "1950 United States Federal Census," digital image, s.v. "Alonzo Bullock," Ancestry.com.

62   *The preacher was fighting:* "Bullock, Alonzo," *1952 Clinton City Directory*, 208; ibid., *1955 Clinton City Directory*, 208; Horace V. Wells Jr., "As We See It!" *Clinton Courier-News*, September 6, 1956, 1; "Facts on How Integration Came to

Clinton," *Clinton Courier-News*, September 6, 1956, 1; "Weekend Violence Brings Guards and Peace," *Clinton Courier-News*, September 6, 1956, 1, 3; "These Pictures Show Activity Here During the Weekend," *Clinton Courier-News*, September 6, 1956, 6; "Davis Leading Snyder in Circuit Judge Race," *Knoxville Journal*, August 4, 1950, 4; Tennessee State Library and Archives, "World War II Draft Cards Young Men, 1940–1947," digital image, s.v. "Alonzo Bullock," Ancestry .com; United States Court of Appeals, "*McSwain*," September 1, 1956, 131.

62 *Anderson County white men spoke:* Robert W. Kelley, TimeLife_image_113332132, *Life*, September 1956; Robert W. Kelley, TimeLife_image_113332132, *Life*, September 1956; Robert W. Kelley, TimeLife_image_113332130, *Life*, September 1956; Robert W. Kelley, TimeLife_image_113332131, *Life*, September 1956; Robert W. Kelley, TimeLife_image_113332129, *Life*, September 1956.

63 *With theatrical timing, Frank:* Agitator Fights U.S. Order Here," *Clinton Courier-News*, August 30, 1956, 1, 8; "Federal Judge Bans School Picketing," *Clinton Courier-News*, August 30, 1956, 1, 4; Jim Loggans, "Some Cheer, Others Boo As Speaker Vilifies School Officials, Others," *Clinton Courier-News*, August 30, 1956, 1, 6; "Clinton Quiet, Court to Act," *Oak Ridger*, August 31, 1956, 1, 3; United States Court of Appeals, "*McSwain*," September 1, 1956, 140–65.

63 *"The marshal served a":* Ibid.

63 *I might have to step:* Ibid.

63 *After the rally ended:* United States Court of Appeals, "*McSwain*," September 1, 1956, 179.

63 *placed a mock gravestone:* Ibid., August 30, 1956, 27–29; "Agitator Fights U.S. Order Here," *Clinton Courier-News*, August 30, 1956, 8; "Man Held On Riot Inciting Turned Loose," *Clinton Courier-News*, August 30, 1956, 8; "Mobs Mass in New Tennessee Flareup," *Los Angeles Times*, September 5, 1956, 1, 2; "Negroes Continue at Clinton High as Incidents of Violence Reported," *Oak Ridger*, August 30, 1956, 1, 7.

SIX: JUDGING JUSTICE

64 *Early afternoon sun:* Howard Sochurek, TimeLife_image_959248, *Life*, September 1956; Howard Sochurek, TimeLife_image_959247, *Life*, September 1956; Howard Sochurek, TimeLife_image_959266, *Life*, September 1956.

64 *Howard Sochurek had served:* Jones, "Howard James Sochurek (1924–1994)," *Veritas*; "Photography of Howard Sochurek"; "Howard Sochurek, a Photographer, 69," *New York Times*, April 29, 1994, https://www.nytimes.com/1994/04/29/obituaries/howard-sochurek-a-photographer-69.html?smid=url-share.

64 *Howard didn't need:* Howard Sochurek, TimeLife_image_113358871, *Life*, September 1956; Howard Sochurek, TimeLife_image_113358939, *Life*, September 1956; Howard Sochurek, TimeLife_image_113358938, *Life*, September 1956; Howard Sochurek, TimeLife_image_959260, *Life*, September 1956; Howard Sochurek, TimeLife_image_113358875, *Life*, September 1956; Howard Sochurek,

TimeLife_image_113358937, *Life*, September 1956; Howard Sochurek, TimeLife _image_113358879, *Life*, September 1956; Howard Sochurek, TimeLife_image _113358885, *Life*, September 1956; Howard Sochurek, TimeLife_image_1133 58934, *Life*, September 1956; Howard Sochurek, TimeLife_image_113358880, *Life*, September 1956; Howard Sochurek, TimeLife_image_113358881, *Life*, September 1956; Howard Sochurek, TimeLife_image_113358890, *Life*, September 1956; Howard Sochurek, TimeLife_image_113358935, *Life*, September 1956.

65 *Bob Taylor was an enigma:* Agitator Fights U.S. Order Here," *Clinton Courier-News*, August 30, 1956, 1, 8; "Federal Judge Bans School Picketing," *Clinton Courier-News*, August 30, 1956, 1, 4; Jim Loggans, "Some Cheer, Others Boo As Speaker Vilifies School Officials, Others," *Clinton Courier-News*, August 30, 1956, 1, 6; Robert L. Taylor to J. N. Talbot, December 12, 1956.

65 *John Kasper had joined:* "Negroes Continue at Clinton High as Incidents of Violence Reported," *Oak Ridger*, August 30, 1956, 1, 7.

65 *I've just relocated:* Ibid.

66 *John walked up the block:* Ibid.; United States Court of Appeals, "*McSwain*," September 1, 1956, 102–3.

66 *Some students, perhaps assuming: The Dragon 1957*, 61; "Integration Row Halts as Clinton Is Left Alone," *Knoxville News-Sentinel*, August 31, 1956, 1, 2; "New Racist from Alabama Due Tonight," *Knoxville News-Sentinel*, August 31, 1956, 1, 2; "Negroes Continue at Clinton High as Incidents of Violence Reported," *Oak Ridger*, August 30, 1956, 1, 7.

66 *the Black students still believed:* "Integration Row Halts as Clinton Is Left Alone," *Knoxville News-Sentinel*, August 31, 1956, 1, 2; "New Racist from Alabama Due Tonight," *Knoxville News-Sentinel*, August 31, 1956, 1, 2.

66 *No way, Ronald:* "Integration Row Halts as Clinton Is Left Alone," *Knoxville News-Sentinel*, August 31, 1956, 1, 2; "New Racist from Alabama Due Tonight," *Knoxville News-Sentinel*, August 31, 1956, 1, 2.

66 *Principal D. J. Brittain Jr. called:* "Negroes Continue at Clinton High as Incidents of Violence Reported," *Oak Ridger*, August 30, 1956, 1, 7.

67 *He was ready:* "TENNESSEE: Victory for Little Bob," *Time*, August 6, 1957.

67 *Court Crier James Smith pounded:* "Valets, Bailiffs, or Criers?" *Court Historical Society Newsletter*, September 2017, 1.

67 *"Hear ye!":* Ibid.

67 *but his laryngitis was a problem:* United States Court of Appeals, "*McSwain*," August 30, 1956, 12–19.

68 *"I am sorry, but":* Ibid.

68 *D. J. laid out:* Ibid.

68 *The principal walked:* Ibid., 12–29.

68 *"Did you see":* Ibid.

68 *Over the objections:* Ibid.

68 *"Were you surprised":* Ibid, 29–36.

68 *"This is a question":* Ibid.

69 *"Well, I object":* Ibid.

69 *"Why, of course":* Ibid.

69 *"Three of these":* Ibid.

69 *Benjamin tried again:* Ibid.

69 *The next several witnesses:* "Clinton Quiet, Court to Act," *Oak Ridger,* August 31, 1956, 1, 3; Wallace Westfeldt, "Move Tops Off Another Day of Incidents," *Tennessean,* August 31, 1956, 1, 10; United States Court of Appeals, *"McSwain,"* August 30, 1956, September 1, 1956.

69 *The* Brown *decision:* Ibid.

69 *By then, it was:* Ibid.

69 *"Gentlemen, I believe":* Ibid.

69 *At 4:45:* Ibid.

70 *all was not peaceful:* "Negroes Continue at Clinton High as Incidents of Violence Reported," *Oak Ridger,* August 30, 1956, 1, 7; "Clinton Quiet, Court to Act," *Oak Ridger,* August 31, 1956, 1, 3; Wallace Westfeldt, "Move Tops Off Another Day of Incidents," *Tennessean,* August 31, 1956, 1, 10.

71 *A few minutes after:* "Negroes Continue at Clinton High as Incidents of Violence Reported," *Oak Ridger,* August 30, 1956, 1, 7; "Clinton Quiet, Court to Act," *Oak Ridger,* August 31, 1956, 1, 3; Wallace Westfeldt, "Move Tops Off Another Day of Incidents," *Tennessean,* August 31, 1956, 1, 10; Agitator Fights U.S. Order Here," *Clinton Courier-News,* August 30, 1956, 1, 8; "Federal Judge Bans School Picketing," *Clinton Courier-News,* August 30, 1956, 1, 4; Jim Loggans, "Some Cheer, Others Boo As Speaker Vilifies School Officials, Others," *Clinton Courier-News,* August 30, 1956, 1, 6; "Integration Row Halts as Clinton Is Left Alone," *Knoxville News-Sentinel,* August 31, 1956, 1, 2; "New Racist from Alabama Due Tonight," *Knoxville News-Sentinel,* August 31, 1956, 1, 2; "Carter Good at Arousing His Audience," *Knoxville News-Sentinel,* August 31, 1956, 2.

71 *The Reverend Alonzo Bullock again:* "Integration Row Halts as Clinton Is Left Alone," *Knoxville News-Sentinel,* August 31, 1956, 1, 2; "New Racist from Alabama Due Tonight," *Knoxville News-Sentinel,* August 31, 1956, 1, 2; "Carter Good at Arousing His Audience," *Knoxville News-Sentinel,* August 31, 1956, 2.

71 *"Keep the race white":* Ibid.

71 *Twenty-some speakers:* "Ibid.

SEVEN: VICTORY AND DEFEAT

72 *Friday morning, Jo Ann Allen:* Jo Ann Allen Boyce interview; "Clinton Quiet, Court to Act," *Oak Ridger,* August 31, 1956, 1, 3, 7.

72 *they noted a difference:* Ibid.

72 *over in Mansfield:* Ibid.

73 *only 446:* Horace V. Wells Jr., "As We See It!" *Clinton Courier-News,* September 6, 1956, 1; "Facts on How Integration Came to Clinton," *Clinton Courier-News,*

September 6, 1956, 1; "Weekend Violence Brings Guards and Peace," *Clinton Courier-News*, September 6, 1956, 1, 3; "These Pictures Show Activity Here During the Weekend," September 6, 1956, 6; Holden, Valien, and Valien, *Clinton, Tennessee*, 6–9; "Clinton Quiet, Court to Act," *Oak Ridger*, August 31, 1956, 1, 3, 7.

73   *John Kasper returned to:* United States Court of Appeals, "*McSwain*," September 1, 1956.

73   *Where do you live:* Ibid.

74   "*I reside*": Ibid.

74   *Hadn't the marshals:* Ibid.

74   "*They just said*": Ibid.

74   *Buford tried another:* Ibid.

74   *John didn't even bother:* Ibid., 135–43.

74   *the judge wasted:* Ibid.

74   *Benjamin Simmons asked:* Ibid.

74   "*Well, Mr. Simmons*": Ibid.

74   *Disgruntled and rumbling:* Wallace Westfeldt and Mac Harris, "Dynamitings [sic] in Eaststate [sic] Add to Fury," *Tennessean*, September 4, 1956, 2; "'Trouble City' [sic] USA,' Blames All Disorder on Outsiders," *Tennessean*, September 4, 1956, 2.

75   *In the first quarter:* Joe Millsaps, "Clinton Dragons Sweep Lakers Off Feet for 25–0 Opening Victory," *Clinton Courier-News*, September 6, 1956, 2:4; "Dragons Surge in Last Half to Hand Lakers 25–0 Defeat," *Oak Ridger*, September 3, 1956, 5; Seivers, "Words of Discrimination," 196–98.

75   *By the time the game:* Anderson, *The Children of the South*, 15; Horace V. Wells Jr., "As We See It!" *Clinton Courier-News*, September 6, 1956, 1; "Facts on How Integration Came to Clinton," *Clinton Courier-News*, September 6, 1956, 1; "Weekend Violence Brings Guards and Peace," *Clinton Courier-News*, September 6, 1956, 1, 3; "These Pictures Show Activity Here During the Weekend," September 6, 1956, 6; Holden, Valien, and Valien, *Clinton, Tennessee*, 6–9; Seivers, "Words of Discrimination," 196–98; Wallace Westfeldt, "Kasper Gets 1-Year Term in Contempt," *Tennessean*, September 1, 1956, 1–2.

76   *But word had trickled:* Ibid.

77   *Herbert, the eldest:* Alabama Department of Health, "Deaths and Burials Index, 1881–1974," digital image, s.v. "Nove Allen," Ancestry.com; "Pupils Defy Tormentors," *Baltimore Afro-American*, December 8, 1956, 1, 2; U.S. Census Bureau, "1910 United States Federal Census," digital image, s.v. "Herbert Allen," Ancestry .com; ibid., "1920 United States Federal Census," digital image, s.v. "Herbert Allen," Ancestry.com; ibid., "1930 United States Federal Census," digital image, s.v. "Herbert Allen," Ancestry.com; ibid., "1940 United States Federal Census," digital image, s.v. "Herbert Allen," Ancestry.com; ibid., s.v. "Minnie Dean," Ancestry.com.

77   *when Herbert first came to Clinton:* "1940 United States Federal Census," digital image, s.v. "Herbert Allen," Ancestry.com; Jo Ann Allen Boyce interview;

Tennessee State Library and Archives, "Marriage Records, 1780–2002," digital image, s.v. "Herbert Allen," Ancestry.com.

77 *ended her education sooner:* "Pupils Defy Tormentors," *Baltimore Afro-American,* December 8, 1956, 1, 2; "Allen Family Gets Out," *Baltimore Afro-American,* December 8, 1956, 1, 15; Jo Ann Allen Boyce interview; Boyce and Levy, *This Promise of Change,* 10–11, 35, 186–87; Daniel, *The Crozier Family History,* 1–7; Julia Daniel, "William Julian Hopper, Sr.," *Oliver Springs Historical Society Newsletter,* December 1, 2015, 2; "Nelson Merry College," LostColleges.com; U.S. Census Bureau, "1920 United States Federal Census," digital image, s.v. "Josephine Hopper," Ancestry.com; "1940 United States Federal Census," digital image, s.v. "Herbert Allen," Ancestry.com; Vanlandingham, "Sites of Resistance: History, Memory and Community," 12.

78 *Herbert quit the Crenshaws:* Jo Ann Allen Boyce interview; Boyce and Levy, *This Promise of Change,* 82–83, 113–14; Grace E. Simons, "They Threw Rocks, Eggs, Says Girl, 15," *California Eagle,* December 20, 1956, 4; Joe Collins, "Clinton Ado Blamed on Agitators," *Knoxville Journal,* August 31, 1956, 1, 6; Wallace Westfeldt, "Negroes Insist They Won't Quit Clinton High," *Tennessean,* November 30, 1956, 1, 17.

78 *Freedman's Hill had known they:* Anna Theresser Caswell interview; McMillan, "The Ordeal," 338; Seivers, "Words of Discrimination," 150–51; Eddie, Maurice, and Charles Soles interview; Alfred Williams interview.

79 *Every house, however:* Boyce and Levy, *This Promise of Change,* 15, 88–89; Robert W. Kelley, TimeLife_image_113345526, *Life,* September 1956; Robert W. Kelley, TimeLife_image_113345496, *Life,* September 1956; Howard Sochurek, TimeLife_image_113356098, *Life,* September 1956; Howard Sochurek, TimeLife_image_113355989, *Life,* September 1956; Howard Sochurek, TimeLife_image_113355986, *Life,* September 1956.

79 *"You and your people":* Boyce and Levy, *This Promise of Change,* 89.

79 *And so on that Friday:* Ibid., 7; Louis E. Lomax, "Anxiety in Clinton," *Baltimore Afro-American,* September 11, 1956, 2; Jo Ann Allen Boyce interview; James L. Cain interview; Hill, *Clinton,* 17.

79 *Outside, Herbert:* Louis E. Lomax, "Anxiety in Clinton," *Afro-American,* September 11, 1956, 1–2; Robert Cain Sr. interview.

80 *Robert Cain Sr. saw:* Ibid.

80 *At least step:* Ibid.

80 *Robert walked onto:* Ibid.

80 *Since it wasn't:* Ibid.; Bobby Cain Jr. interview; James L. Cain interview; Howard Sochurek, TimeLife_image_959251, *Life,* September 1956; Howard Sochurek, TimeLife_image_113355983, *Life,* September 1956; Howard Sochurek, Time Life_image_113355987, *Life,* September 1956; Howard Sochurek, TimeLife _image_113358932, *Life,* September 1956; Howard Sochurek, TimeLife_image _113358949, *Life,* September 1956; Howard Sochurek, TimeLife_image_113356146, *Life,* September 1956; Howard Sochurek, TimeLife_image_959264, *Life,* September

1956; Howard Sochurek, TimeLife_image_113356145, *Life*, September 1956; Howard Sochurek, TimeLife_image_113358948, *Life*, September 1956; Howard Sochurek, TimeLife_image_113358933, *Life*, September 1956; Howard Sochurek, TimeLife_image_113355986, *Life*, September 1956; Eugene Weaver interview.

80 *the men listened:* Louis E. Lomax, "Anxiety in Clinton," *Afro-American*, September 11, 1956, 1–2; Robert Cain Sr. interview; Bobby Cain Jr. interview; James L. Cain interview; Smith, "McSwain Sisters Tell the Story That Predated the Clinton 12."

80 *"I moved here from Mississippi":* Ibid.

80 *"We didn't start it":* Ibid.

80 *9 o'clock on Friday:* Anderson, *The Children of the South*, 15; Holden, Valien, and Valien, *Clinton, Tennessee*, 6–9; Wallace Westfeldt, "Kasper Gets 1-Year Term in Contempt," *Tennessean*, September 1, 1956, 1–2.

81 *"I'm Asa":* Anderson, *The Children of the South*, 15; Holden, Valien, and Valien, *Clinton, Tennessee*, 6–9; Wallace Westfeldt, "Kasper Gets 1-Year Term in Contempt," *Tennessean*, September 1, 1956, 1–2.

81 *"Asa! Asa!":* Ibid.

81 *"I'm from Alabama":* Ibid.

81 *Asa was a leader:* Horace V. Wells Jr., "As We See It!" *Clinton Courier-News*, September 6, 1956, 1; "Facts on How Integration Came to Clinton," *Clinton Courier-News*, September 6, 1956, 1; "Weekend Violence Brings Guards and Peace," *Clinton Courier-News*, September 6, 1956, 1, 3; "These Pictures Show Activity Here During the Weekend," September 6, 1956, 6.

81 *During his hour-long:* Ibid.; Anderson, *The Children of the South*, 15; Holden, Valien, and Valien, *Clinton, Tennessee*, 6–9; Wallace Westfeldt, "Kasper Gets 1-Year Term in Contempt," *Tennessean*, September 1, 1956, 1–2.

81 *"He's right!":* Anderson, *The Children of the South*, 15.

81 *"Tell 'em":* Ibid.

81 *some of the emerging:* Ibid., 15–16; Anthony Harrigan, "Here's Till's Side of Mixing Events," *East Tennessee Reporter*, February 15, 1957, 3; Anthony Harrigan, "Brakebill Is Bitter Over His Arrest," *East Tennessee Reporter*, February 15, 1957, 3; Anthony Harrigan, "Nation Not Given All of the Facts," *East Tennessee Reporter*, February 15, 1957, 3; Herd, "Then and Now," 44–45; United States District Court, "*Bullock,*" July 18, 1957, 1107–8, 1097.

82 *devolving the meeting:* Adamson, "The Lit Stick," 106–7; Anderson, *The Children of the South*, 16; "Weekend Violence Brings Guards and Peace," *Clinton Courier-News*, September 6, 1956, 3; Anthony Harrigan, "Here's Till's Side of Mixing Events," *East Tennessee Reporter*, February 15, 1957, 3; Anthony Harrigan, "Brakebill Is Bitter Over His Arrest," *East Tennessee Reporter*, February 15, 1957, 3; Anthony Harrigan, "Nation Not Given All of the Facts," *East Tennessee Reporter*, February 15, 1957, 3; Herd, "Then and Now," 42–45; Holden, Valien, and Valien, *Clinton, Tennessee*, 6–9; Seivers, "Words of Discrimination," 73–74, 156–58, 196–98.

82 *perhaps two hundred strong, splintered:* Ibid.; Wallace Westfeldt, "Kasper Gets

1-Year Term in Contempt," *Tennessean*, September 1, 1956, 1–2. In the fall of 1956, protesting teamsters in Knoxville would set off four explosions, destroying a Bush Brothers truck, the Powell Economy Market, a Newman & Pemberton truck, and a Purity Packing Company's car. "Probers to Spotlight Knox Union Violence," *Knoxville Journal*, December 4, 1957, 2.

82   *a car pulled up full:* Horace V. Wells Jr., "As We See It!" *Clinton Courier-News*, September 6, 1956, 1; "Facts on How Integration Came to Clinton," *Clinton Courier-News*, September 6, 1956, 1; "Weekend Violence Brings Guards and Peace," *Clinton Courier-News*, September 6, 1956, 1, 3; "These Pictures Show Activity Here During the Weekend," September 6, 1956, 8; Holden, Valien, and Valien, *Clinton, Tennessee*, 6–9; "Halting and Fitful Battle for Integration," *Life*, September 17, 1956, 35–37.

83   *Another car of unsuspecting:* Ibid.; Adamson, "The Lit Stick," 106–7; Anderson, *The Children of the South*, 16; Anthony Harrigan, "Here's Till's Side of Mixing Events," *East Tennessee Reporter*, February 15, 1957, 3; Anthony Harrigan, "Brakebill Is Bitter Over His Arrest," *East Tennessee Reporter*, February 15, 1957, 3; Anthony Harrigan, "Nation Not Given All of the Facts," *East Tennessee Reporter*, February 15, 1957, 3; Herd, "Then and Now," 42–45; Seivers, "Words of Discrimination," 73–74, 156–58, 196–98; Wallace Westfeldt, "Kasper Gets 1-Year Term in Contempt," *Tennessean*, September 1, 1956, 1–2.

83   *Two minutes after midnight:* "New Sheriff at Clinton," *Knoxville Journal*, September 1, 1956, 1; Wallace Westfeldt, "Kasper Gets 1-Year Term in Contempt," *Tennessean*, September 1, 1956, 1–2.

83   *After the ceremony, he went:* Adamson, "The Lit Stick," 106–7; Holden, Valien, and Valien, *Clinton, Tennessee*, 6–9; United States Court of Appeals, "*McSwain*," September 6, 1956, 229–31.

83   *Why aren't you intervening:* Wallace Westfeldt, "Kasper Gets 1-Year Term in Contempt," *Tennessean*, September 1, 1956, 1–2.

83   *"What can we do":* Ibid.

83   *an FBI agent assigned:* Anderson, *The Children of the South*, 16; Herd, "Then and Now," 44–45; Seivers, "Words of Discrimination," 153–58.

84   *"We need either":* Adamson, "The Lit Stick," 106–7; Wallace Westfeldt, "Kasper Gets 1-Year Term in Contempt," *Tennessean*, September 1, 1956, 1–2.

84   *Lewallen, tried to reach:* Ibid.; Holden, Valien, and Valien, *Clinton, Tennessee*, 6–9, "First Pleas to State Officials Fruitless," *Knoxville Journal*, September 2, 1956, 1, 4.

84   *a convoy of Ku Klux Klan:* Jo Ann Allen Boyce interview; James L. Cain interview; Seivers, "Words of Discrimination," 148–51; Alfred Williams interview.

84   *Woodward warned off:* Ibid.

EIGHT: THE BEST DEFENSE

85   *The couple had fallen:* Buford Lewallen interview; Celdon Lewallen interview; "Lewallen—Medaris," *Knoxville Journal*, August 17, 1941, 36; "Buford Lewallens

Honored with Party at Clinton," *Knoxville Journal*, August 31, 1941, 24; *Volunteer 1942*, 110.

85   *They had planned:* Buford Lewallen interview; Celdon Lewallen interview; Herman, "A Bad Day at Douglas Army Airfield"; "W.B. Lewallen Is Improving after Crash," *Knoxville Journal*, January 4, 1944, 8; "Mayor's Son Missing on Training Flight," *Knoxville News-Sentinel*, December 31, 1943, 7; "Mayor Goes to Son," *Knoxville News-Sentinel*, January 16, 1944, 6; Tennessee State Library and Archives, "World War II Army Enlistment Records, 1938–1946," digital image, s.v. "William B. Lewallen," Ancestry.com.

86   *forest rangers stumbled:* Buford Lewallen interview; Celdon Lewallen interview; Herman, "A Bad Day at Douglas Army Airfield"; "W.B. Lewallen Is Improving after Crash," *Knoxville Journal*, January 4, 1944, 8; "Mayor's Son Missing on Training Flight," *Knoxville News-Sentinel*, December 31, 1943, 7; "Mayor Goes to Son," *Knoxville News-Sentinel*, January 16, 1944, 6.

86   *Buford returned home:* Adamson, "The Lit Stick," 17; Anderson County, "School Board Minutes," September 27, 1949; Margaret Anderson interview; Darnell, *Tennessee Blue Book, 2007–2008*, 505; "Davis Shays Sheriff Made Bold Appeal on Behalf of 'Boys,'" *Knoxville Journal*, July 23, 1947, 9; "Lewallen Withdraws from Race," *Knoxville Journal*, July 22, 1948, 24; "Suit Seeks Ouster of Anderson County Sheriff," *Knoxville Journal*, April 27, 1949, 3; Celdon Lewallen interview; Tennessee State Library and Archives, "William B. Lewallen," https://tnsos.org/tsla/imagesearch/citation.php?ImageID=2411.

87   *following their racist Pied Piper:* Buford Lewallen interview; Celdon Lewallen interview.

88   *Buford didn't want integration:* Ibid.; Brittain, "A Case Study," 60–61; Seivers, "Words of Discrimination," 133–34.

88   *First thing Saturday morning, W.E.:* "Guard Commander Bans Outdoor Meets," *Oak Ridger*, September 3, 1956, 1, 8; Wallace Westfeldt, "Patrol Sent; Guardsmen Due Today," *Tennessean*, September 2, 1956, 1, 2; David Halberstam, "Call to Clinton Duty Finds State Guardsmen Scattered," *Tennessean*, September 2, 1956, 2; "Volunteers for Police Duty . . . and a Quick Test," *Tennessean*, September 2, 1956, 3; "Clinton's Hour of Need," *Tennessean*, September 2, 1956, 4.

88   *the Guard already had some history:* Bynum, "The Uprising of '34"; "Guide to Declarations of Martial Law in the United States; "Two Mills Here Operating; Few Heed Union Call," *Knoxville News-Sentinel*, September 4, 1934, 1, 6; "Strikers Spurn Peace Moves While Violence Takes 10 Lives," *Knoxville News-Sentinel*, September 6, 1934, 1; "F.D.R. Ready to Go to Scene of Strike Riots in Necessary," *Knoxville Journal*, September 15, 1934, 1, 12; Madison, *Indiana through Tradition and Change*, 250; "Mid-Content Refinery Strike," in Oklahoma Historical Society, *Encyclopedia of Oklahoma History and Culture*.

88   *Maybe the soldiers:* Greene, *Lead Me On*, 205; Seivers, "Words of Discrimination," 153–58; Dr. and Florence Stansberry interview.

88   *This situation is "not sham":* Ibid.

88 *While the state politicians worried:* Adamson, "The Lit Stick," 107–11; Margaret Anderson interview; Holden, Valien, and Valien, *Clinton, Tennessee*, 6–9; "Guard Commander Bans Outdoor Meets," *Oak Ridger*, September 3, 1956, 1, 8; Diane Pemberton interview; Seivers, "Words of Discrimination," 158.

89 *The state sold jailed:* Abby Lee Hood, "Tennessee Professors and Historians Uncover History of Convict Leasing in the State," *Tennessee Lookout*, October 6, 2021.

90 *they'd made no preparations:* Agitator Fights U.S. Order Here," *Clinton Courier-News*, August 30, 1956, 1, 8; "Federal Judge Bans School Picketing," *Clinton Courier-News*, August 30, 1956, 1, 4; Jim Loggans, "Some Cheer, Others Boo As Speaker Vilifies School Officials, Others," *Clinton Courier-News*, August 30, 1956, 1, 6; Horace V. Wells Jr., "As We See It!" *Clinton Courier-News*, September 6, 1956, 1; "Facts on How Integration Came to Clinton," *Clinton Courier-News*, September 6, 1956, 1; "Weekend Violence Brings Guards and Peace," *Clinton Courier-News*, September 6, 1956, 1, 3; "These Pictures Show Activity Here During the Weekend," September 6, 1956, 8.

90 *Buford issued an open call:* Anderson, *The Children of the South*, 16; Brittain, "A Case Study," 153–54; Holden, Valien, and Valien, *Clinton, Tennessee*, 6–9; Harold McAlduff interview; Seivers, "Words of Discrimination," 153–56; Dr. and Florence Stansberry interview; Wallace Westfeldt, "Patrol Sent; Guardsmen Due Today," *Tennessean*, September 2, 1956, 1, 2; "Volunteers for Police Duty . . . and a Quick Test," *Tennessean*, September 2, 1956, 3; "Clinton's Hour of Need," *Tennessean*, September 2, 1956, 4.

90 *"We, the undersigned, do solemnly":* Ralph Griffith, "Arrival of 100 State Troopers Halts Mob at Clinton; Guard Units Expected Today," *Knoxville Journal*, September 2, 1956, 1, 4.

91 *"Hell, it ain't":* "Back to School," *Time*, September 10, 1956. Https://content .time.com/time/subscriber/article/0,33009,808549,00.html.

91 *Some faces in the group:* "Guard Commander Bans Outdoor Meets," *Oak Ridger*, September 3, 1956, 1, 8; Herb Stein, "On Its Face, It Was Angry," *Oak Ridger*, September 5, 1956, 4; Wallace Westfeldt, "Patrol Sent; Guardsmen Due Today," *Tennessean*, September 2, 1956, 1, 2; "Volunteers for Police Duty . . . and a Quick Test," *Tennessean*, September 2, 1956, 3; "Clinton's Hour of Need," *Tennessean*, September 2, 1956, 4.

91 *"They were without humor":* Herb Stein, "On Its Face, It Was Angry," *Oak Ridger*, September 5, 1956, 4.

91 *About fifteen of the deputies:* Adamson, "The Lit Stick," 110–11; "Back to School," *Time*, September 10, 1956. Https://content.time.com/time/subscriber/article/0,3300 9,808549,00.html; Brittain, "A Case Study," 153–54; Holden, Valien, and Valien, *Clinton, Tennessee*, 6–9; Ralph Griffith, "Arrival of 100 State Troopers Halts Mob at Clinton; Guard Units Expected Today," *Knoxville Journal*, September 2, 1956, 1, 4; "Clinton Riots Posed Issue of Rule by Mob Violence," *Knoxville Journal*, September 2, 1956, 1; "Highlights, Sidelights in Strife-Torn Clinton, *Knoxville Journal*, September 2, 1956, 1, 4; "Race Riots Bring on State of Emergency," *Herald*

Journal (Logan, UT), September 2, 1956, 1; Harold McAlduff interview; "Guard Commander Bans Outdoor Meets," *Oak Ridger*, September 3, 1956, 1, 8; Seivers, "Words of Discrimination," 153–55, 198–99; Wallace Westfeldt, "Patrol Sent; Guardsmen Due Today," *Tennessean*, September 2, 1956, 1, 2; "Volunteers for Police Duty . . . and a Quick Test," *Tennessean*, September 2, 1956, 3; "Clinton's Hour of Need," *Tennessean*, September 2, 1956, 4.

91   *Most of his men also had:* Anderson, *The Children of the South*, 16; Holden, Valien, and Valien, *Clinton, Tennessee*, 6–9; Harold McAlduff interview; Herb Stein, "On Its Face, It Was Angry," *Oak Ridger*, September 5, 1956, 4.

92   *Leo Grant gave his men:* Wallace Westfeldt, "Patrol Sent; Guardsmen Due Today," *Tennessean*, September 2, 1956, 1, 2; "Volunteers for Police Duty . . . and a Quick Test," *Tennessean*, September 2, 1956, 3; "Clinton's Hour of Need," *Tennessean*, September 2, 1956, 4; "Back to School," *Time*, September 10, 1956. Https:// content.time.com/time/subscriber/article/0,33009,808549,00.html.

92   *a parade of cars screamed:* Holden, Valien, and Valien, *Clinton, Tennessee*, 6–9; "Guard Commander Bans Outdoor Meets," *Oak Ridger*, September 3, 1956, 1, 8; Seivers, "Words of Discrimination," 73–74; Wells, *The Days before Yesterday*, 85.

93   *two Black Florida teachers:* Watts, "Introduction: Telling White Men's Stories," in *White Masculinity in the Recent South*, 7–11.

93   *everyone remained oddly polite:* "Guard Commander Bans Outdoor Meets," *Oak Ridger*, September 3, 1956, 1, 8; Herb Stein, "On Its Face, It Was Angry," *Oak Ridger*, September 5, 1956, 4.

93   *From his perch inside:* "Guard Commander Bans Outdoor Meets," *Oak Ridger*, September 3, 1956, 1, 8; Herb Stein, "On Its Face, It Was Angry," *Oak Ridger*, September 5, 1956, 4; "Weekend Violence Brings Guards and Peace," *Clinton Courier-News*, September 6, 1956, 3; Holden, Valien, and Valien, *Clinton, Tennessee*, 6–9; Seivers, "Words of Discrimination," 198–99; Wallace Westfeldt, "Patrol Sent; Guardsmen Due Today," *Tennessean*, September 2, 1956, 1, 2; "Volunteers for Police Duty . . . and a Quick Test," *Tennessean*, September 2, 1956, 3; "Clinton's Hour of Need," *Tennessean*, September 2, 1956, 4; United States District Court, "*Bullock*," July 16, 1957, 672–73.

93   *Auxiliary policeman Harold McAlduff:* Harold McAlduff interview.

93   *"Why can't I stop here":* Ibid.; Anderson, *The Children of the South*, 16; Holden, Valien, and Valien, *Clinton, Tennessee*, 6–9; Herb Stein, "On Its Face, It Was Angry," *Oak Ridger*, September 5, 1956, 4; Wallace Westfeldt, "Patrol Sent; Guardsmen Due Today," *Tennessean*, September 2, 1956, 1, 2; "Volunteers for Police Duty . . . and a Quick Test," *Tennessean*, September 2, 1956, 3; "Clinton's Hour of Need," *Tennessean*, September 2, 1956, 4.

93   *Seems "like we don't":* Ibid.

93   *Then at 6:37:* Ibid.

93   *Move on:* Ibid.

93   *No, he said:* Ibid.

93   *The deputies tried:* Ibid.

93 *No, he repeated:* Ibid.

93 *an Oak Ridge machinist was arrested:* Ibid.

93 *they turned on the volunteer:* Ibid.

93 *Buford dialed his friend:* Buford Lewallen to Frank Clement, September 15, 1956, Tennessee Virtual Archive; Seivers, "Words of Discrimination," 75–76, 153–58; Dr. and Florence Stansberry interview; Wallace Westfeldt, "Patrol Sent; Guardsmen Due Today," *Tennessean,* September 2, 1956, 1, 2; David Halberstam, "Call to Clinton Duty Finds State Guardsmen Scattered," *Tennessean,* September 2, 1956, 2; "Volunteers for Police Duty . . . and a Quick Test," *Tennessean,* September 2, 1956, 3; "Clinton's Hour of Need," *Tennessean,* September 2, 1956, 4.

95 *"We're taking over the whole":* Wallace Westfeldt, "Patrol Sent; Guardsmen Due Today," *Tennessean,* September 2, 1956, 1, 2; David Halberstam, "Call to Clinton Duty Finds State Guardsmen Scattered," *Tennessean,* September 2, 1956, 2; "Volunteers for Police Duty . . . and a Quick Test," *Tennessean,* September 2, 1956, 3; "Clinton's Hour of Need," *Tennessean,* September 2, 1956, 4.

95 *Their numbers were up:* "Back to School," *Time,* September 10, 1956. Https:// content.time.com/time/subscriber/article/0,33009,808549,00.html. "Weekend Violence Brings Guard and Peace," *Clinton Courier-News,* September 6, 1956, 3; Holden, Valien, and Valien, *Clinton, Tennessee,* 6–9; Wallace Westfeldt, "Patrol Sent; Guardsmen Due Today," *Tennessean,* September 2, 1956, 1, 2; David Halberstam, "Call to Clinton Duty Finds State Guardsmen Scattered," *Tennessean,* September 2, 1956, 2; "Volunteers for Police Duty . . . and a Quick Test," *Tennessean,* September 2, 1956, 3; "Clinton's Hour of Need," *Tennessean,* September 2, 1956, 4; Seivers, "Words of Discrimination," 198–99; "Guard Commander Bans Outdoor Meets," *Oak Ridger,* September 3, 1956, 8; United States District Court, *"Bullock,"* July 16, 1957, 672–73.

95 *Leo fiddled:* "Weekend Violence Brings Guards and Peace," *Clinton Courier-News,* September 6, 1956, 3; "Guard Commander Bans Outdoor Meets," *Oak Ridger,* September 3, 1956, 8.

95 *"Tear gas!":* Wallace Westfeldt, "Patrol Sent; Guardsmen Due Today," *Tennessean,* September 2, 1956, 1, 2; "Volunteers for Police Duty . . . and a Quick Test," *Tennessean,* September 2, 1956, 3; "Clinton's Hour of Need," *Tennessean,* September 2, 1956, 4; "Halting and Fitful Battle for Integration," *Life,* September 17, 1956, 35-37.

96 *The pain wasn't immediate:* Wallace Westfeldt, "Patrol Sent; Guardsmen Due Today," *Tennessean,* September 2, 1956, 1, 2; "Volunteers for Police Duty . . . and a Quick Test," *Tennessean,* September 2, 1956, 3; "Clinton's Hour of Need," *Tennessean,* September 2, 1956, 4; "Halting and Fitful Battle for Integration," *Life,* September 17, 1956, 35–37; Margaret Anderson interview; Anderson, *The Children of the South,* 16; Holden, Valien, and Valien, *Clinton, Tennessee,* 6–9; "Guard Commander Bans Outdoor Meets," *Oak Ridger,* September 3, 1956, 8; Seivers, "Words of Discrimination," 153–55; Adamson, "The Lit Stick," 110–11; Walker, "This Is What It's Like to Get Tear-gassed"; "What Does Teargas Do to People?," *Aftermath,* https://www.aftermath.com/content/what-does-tear-gas-do-to-people/.

96   *Leo reached into his arsenal:* "Guard Commander Bans Outdoor Meets," *Oak Ridger*, September 3, 1956, 8.

96   *The deputies were out:* Ibid.

96   *as the last canister landed:* Adamson, "The Lit Stick," 111–14; Margaret Anderson interview; Anderson, *The Children of the South*, 16; Brittain, "A Case Study," 153–54; Brown, *Strain of Violence*, 96; Horace V. Wells Jr., "As We See It!" *Clinton Courier-News*, September 6, 1956, 1; "Weekend Violence Brings Guards and Peace," *Clinton Courier-News*, September 6, 1956, 1, 3; "These Pictures Show Activity Here During the Weekend," September 6, 1956, 8; Herd, "Then and Now," 45–46; Harold McAlduff interview; "Guard Commander Bans Outdoor Meets," *Oak Ridger*, September 3, 1956, 8; Roberts, *High School*, 60–61; Sievers, "Words of Discrimination," 76–77; Wallace Westfeldt, "Patrol Sent; Guardsmen Due Today," *Tennessean*, September 2, 1956, 1, 2; "Volunteers for Police Duty . . . and a Quick Test," *Tennessean*, September 2, 1956, 3; "Clinton's Hour of Need," *Tennessean*, September 2, 1956, 4.

96   *not a single highway:* "Guard Commander Bans Outdoor Meets," *Oak Ridger*, September 3, 1956, 8.

97   *Two representatives of the Tennessee:* Ibid.; Wallace Westfeldt, "Patrol Sent; Guardsmen Due Today," *Tennessean*, September 2, 1956, 1, 2; "Volunteers for Police Duty . . . and a Quick Test," *Tennessean*, September 2, 1956, 3; "Clinton's Hour of Need," *Tennessean*, September 2, 1956, 4.

97   *Yet again, the rally began:* Horace V. Wells Jr., "As We See It!" *Clinton Courier-News*, September 6, 1956, 1; "Weekend Violence Brings Guards and Peace," *Clinton Courier-News*, September 6, 1956, 1, 3; "These Pictures Show Activity Here During the Weekend," September 6, 1956, 8; "Kasper and Six Convicted; New Trial Possible," *East Tennessee Reporter*, July 26, 1957, 1; "Raymond Woods Hasn't Changed, He Tells Reporter," *East Tennessee Reporter*, July 26, 1957, 1; "Rev. Bullock Refutes 'Smear' News Stories," *East Tennessee Reporter*, July 26, 1957, 1; "Back Glances Show Incidents of Interest," *East Tennessee Reporter*, July 26, 1957, 2, 8; Wallace Westfeldt, "Patrol Sent; Guardsmen Due Today," *Tennessean*, September 2, 1956, 1, 2; "Volunteers for Police Duty . . . and a Quick Test," *Tennessean*, September 2, 1956, 3; "Clinton's Hour of Need," *Tennessean*, September 2, 1956, 4.

97   *"We can get rough":* Wallace Westfeldt, "Patrol Sent; Guardsmen Due Today," *Tennessean*, September 2, 1956, 1, 2; "Volunteers for Police Duty . . . and a Quick Test," *Tennessean*, September 2, 1956, 3; "Clinton's Hour of Need," *Tennessean*, September 2, 1956, 4.

97   *"Bouncing cars and throwing tomatoes":* "Guard Commander Bans Outdoor Meets," *Oak Ridger*, September 3, 1956, 8.

97   *the white auxiliary police deputies drifted:* Ibid.; Horace V. Wells Jr., "As We See It!" *Clinton Courier-News*, September 6, 1956, 1; "Weekend Violence Brings Guards and Peace," *Clinton Courier-News*, September 6, 1956, 1, 3; "These Pictures Show Activity Here During the Weekend," September 6, 1956, 8.

97 *They knew no one official:* Adamson, "The Lit Stick," 111–14; Margaret Anderson interview; Anderson, *The Children of the South*, 16; Brittain, "A Case Study," 153–54; Brown, *Strain of Violence*, 96; Horace V. Wells Jr., "As We See It!" *Clinton Courier-News*, September 6, 1956, 1; "Weekend Violence Brings Guards and Peace," *Clinton Courier-News*, September 6, 1956, 1, 3; "These Pictures Show Activity Here During the Weekend," September 6, 1956, 8; Herd, "Then and Now," 45–46; "Guard Commander Bans Outdoor Meets," *Oak Ridger*, September 3, 1956, 8; Trezzvant W. Anderson, "Clinton, Tenn.—Integration Battleground," *Pittsburgh Courier*, June 15, 1957, 6; Trezzvant W. Anderson, "Now It Can Be Told," *Pittsburgh Courier*, June 15, 1957, 6; Roberts, *High School*, 60–61; Seivers, "Word of Discrimination," 76–77; Wallace Westfeldt, "Patrol Sent; Guardsmen Due Today," *Tennessean*, September 2, 1956, 1, 2; "Volunteers for Police Duty . . . and a Quick Test," *Tennessean*, September 2, 1956, 3; "Clinton's Hour of Need," *Tennessean*, September 2, 1956, 4.

NINE: INVASION

98 *Gail Ann Epps was flustered:* Jo Ann Allen Boyce interview; Boyce and Levy, *This Promise of Change*, 48; Gail Ann Epps Upton interview.

98 *her boyfriend, a Navy sailor:* Ibid.

99 *she felt a distant shudder:* Seivers, "Words of Discrimination," 199–200; Gail Ann Epps Upton interview.

99 *Some in the congregation ran:* Ibid.

99 *Was this help, finally?:* Ibid.

99 *Next in the convoy:* Ibid.

99 *The soldiers—645 Tennessee:* Horace V. Wells Jr., "As We See It!" *Clinton Courier-News*, September 6, 1956, 1; "Weekend Violence Brings Guards and Peace," *Clinton Courier-News*, September 6, 1956, 1, 3; Holden, Valien, and Valien, *Clinton, Tennessee*, 6–9; Wallace Westfeldt, "Clinton Mob Snarls Again," *Tennessean*, September 3, 1956, 1, 4; Robert W. Kelley, TimeLife_image_113345511, *Life*, September 1956; Robert W. Kelley, TimeLife_image_113345512, *Life*, September 1956; Howard Sochurek, TimeLife_image_113356117, *Life*, September 1956.

99 *Governor Frank Clement had summoned:* Horace V. Wells Jr., "As We See It!" *Clinton Courier-News*, September 6, 1956, 1; "Weekend Violence Brings Guards and Peace," *Clinton Courier-News*, September 6, 1956, 1, 3; Holden, Valien, and Valien, *Clinton, Tennessee*, 6–9; Wallace Westfeldt, "Clinton Mob Snarls Again," *Tennessean*, September 3, 1956, 1, 4; "Guard Commander Bans Outdoor Meets," *Oak Ridger*, September 3, 1956, 1; "Guard Says 'All Is in Hand After Fifth Violent Night," *Oak Ridger*, September 4, 1956, 1; "Guardsmen Pulled from Leisure to Alert," *Oak Ridger*, September 4, 1956, 1, 2; Wallace Westfeldt, "Patrol Sent; Guardsmen Due Today," *Tennessean*, September 2, 1956, 1, 2; David Halberstam, "Call to Clinton Duty Finds State Guardsmen Scattered," *Tennessean*, September 2, 1956, 2; "Clinton's Hour of Need," *Tennessean*, September 2, 1956, 4.

100   *After circling through:* Ibid.

100   *a layperson in Clinton's white:* "Local Ministers Join Prayers," *Oak Ridger*, September 3, 1956, 1.

100   *Paul Turner tried to call:* Ibid.; "'Trouble City' [sic] USA,' Blames All Disorder on Outsiders," *Tennessean*, September 4, 1956, 2.

100   *After the service, Paul:* Charles Flowers, "Court Now a Tourist Attraction," *Knoxville News-Sentinel*, July 18, 1957, 16; "Four More Freed in Clinton Trial," *Knoxville News-Sentinel*, July 18, 1957, 16.

100   *Drop the segregationist activity:* Ibid.

100   *The Tills withdrew:* Ibid.

100   *a small rural community outside:* Tennessee State Library and Archives, "World War II Draft Cards Young Men, 1940–1947," digital image, s.v. "Paul Winston Turner," Ancestry.com; U.S. Census Bureau, "1940 United States Federal Census," digital image, s.v. "Paul Turner," Ancestry.com.

101   *Between his arrival in 1948:* Four hundred and ten of these new members were new converts who were baptized into the fellowship. In addition, under his leadership a higher percentage of members were regular attendees. For instance, average attendance at weekly Sunday school meetings grew from 271 to 617. Accompanying this was an approximately $46,000 increase in annual tithes given at the church. Horace V. Wells Jr., "As We See It!" *Clinton Courier-News*, June 28, 1956, 1, 5.

101   *he led local campaigns:* Horace V. Wells Jr., "As We See It!" *Clinton Courier-News*, June 28, 1956, 5; letter from Robert L. McCan to Frank Clement, December 4, 1956, Lee S. Greene Collection, Knoxville, TN.

101   *lessons he'd learned from Olin:* Adamson, "Two Religious Magazines," 11–12; letter from Koinonia Farm, August 18, 1956, personal files of Steve Jones, Clinton, TN.

101   *When he arrived in Clinton:* Adamson, "Two Religious Magazines," 11–12; Trezzvant W. Anderson, "Clinton, Tenn.—Integration Battleground," *Pittsburgh Courier*, June 15, 1957, 6; Trezzvant W. Anderson, "Now It Can Be Told," *Pittsburgh Courier*, Junve 15, 1957, 6; Paul Turner interview; Orville Willis interview.

101   *Olin Binkley, however:* Roy C. DeLamotte to Paul Turner, September 6, 1956, personal files of Steve Jones, Clinton, TN.

102   *You are failing:* Ibid.

102   *Paul replied that he:* Ibid.

102   *Roy disagreed:* Ibid.

102   *Frank Clement took to the airways:* Brittain, "A Case Study," 50–51; "The Halting and Fitful Battle for Integration," *Life*, September 17, 1956, 34–40.

102   *He invited Nashville's:* Ibid.

102   *The troops spent their Sunday afternoon:* "Weekend Violence Brings Guards and Peace," *Clinton Courier-News*, September 6, 1956, 1, 3; "Guard Commander Bans Outdoor Meets," *Oak Ridger*, September 3, 1956, 1.

102   *downtown bristled with rifles:* "Weekend Violence Brings Guards and Peace," *Clinton Courier-News*, September 6, 1956, 1, 3; "Guard Here Has 600 Men,

100 Vehicles," *Clinton Courier-News*, September 6, 1956, 1; Holden, Valien, and Valien, *Clinton, Tennessee*, 6–9; "This Is Tense Clinton in Greatest Upheaval in Community's History," *Tennessean*, September 4, 1956, 8.

103 *both a soldier and a lawyer:* Kirk Loggins, "Henry—Court's Social Conscience," *Tennessean*, June 10, 1980, 1, 6, 7; "Judiciary Suffers Loss in Justice Henry's Death," *Tennessean*, June 10, 1980, 8.

103 *Gail Ann and her little sister were sitting:* Boyce and Levy, *This Promise of Change*, 117–18; Sievers, "Words of Discrimination," 199–200; Howard Sochurek, Time-Life_image_113345491, *Life*, September 1956; Wallace Westfeldt and Mac Harris, "Dynamitings in Eaststate Add to Fury," *Tennessean*, September 4, 1956, 1, 2; "'Trouble City' [sic] USA,' Blames All Disorder on Outsiders," *Tennessean*, September 4, 1956, 1, 2; Gail Ann Epps Upton interview; "Halting and Fitful Battle for Integration," *Life*, September 17, 1956, 35-37.

104 *A white stringer for:* J. Russell Boner, "Quiet Prevails in Negro Quarter of Clinton, Tennessee," *Daily American*, September 4, 1956, 2.

104 *"It's the Sabbath":* Ibid.

104 *"All we're asking for":* Ibid.

104 *Then the jeep and the tank:* Wallace Westfeldt and Mac Harris, "Dynamitings in Eaststate Add to Fury," *Tennessean*, September 4, 1956, 2; "'Trouble City' [sic] USA,' Blames All Disorder on Outsiders," *Tennessean*, September 4, 1956, 2.

104 *150 protestors stuffed:* "Weekend Violence Brings Guards and Peace," *Clinton Courier-News*, September 6, 1956, 1, 3; "Guard Here Has 600 Men, 100 Vehicles," *Clinton Courier-News*, September 6, 1956, 1; "Trouble Spreads to Oliver Springs Over Rumors; 17 Arrested," *Clinton Courier-News*, September 6, 1956, 1, 6; Holden, Valien, and Valien, *Clinton, Tennessee*, 6–9; "Guard Commander Bans Outdoor Meets," *Oak Ridger*, September 3, 1956, 3; Wallace Westfeldt, "Clinton Mob Snarls Again," *Tennessean*, September 3, 1956, 1, 4.

105 *A little after eight:* Ibid; Anderson County, TN, "Clinton City Recorder Minutes," *Anderson County Records*, vol. 12; Adamson, "The Lit Stick," 113; Sievers, "Words of Discrimination," 201–3; Eugene Weaver interview.

105 *"Let's get him!":* Ibid.

105 *James wouldn't make:* Ibid.

105 *trooper beside him:* Ibid.

106 *Joe Henry sent three hundred:* "Weekend Violence Brings Guards and Peace," *Clinton Courier-News*, September 6, 1956, 3; Holden, Valien, and Valien, *Clinton, Tennessee*, 6–9; "Guard Commander Bans Outdoor Meets," *Oak Ridger*, September 3, 1956, 3.

106 *behind the soldiers' backs:* "Weekend Violence Brings Guards and Peace," *Clinton Courier-News*, September 6, 1956, 3; Holden, Valien, and Valien, *Clinton, Tennessee*, 6–9; "Guard Commander Bans Outdoor Meets," *Oak Ridger*, September 3, 1956, 3.

107 *some unnamed source, had heard:* "Oliver Springs This Morning Crowds Dispersed," *Oak Ridger*, September 4, 1956, 1; "Oliver Springs Last Night An Armed

Mob; 1 Slight Injury," *Oak Ridger*, September 4, 1956, 1; "Clinton Last Night Silent Suspense Peaceful Until—," *Oak Ridger*, September 4, 1956, 1; "Guard Says 'All Is in Hand After Fifth Violent Night," *Oak Ridger*, September 4, 1956, 1.

107   *Some ninety miles southwest:* Wallace Westfeldt and Mac Harris, "Dynamitings in Eaststate Add to Fury," *Tennessean*, September 4, 1956, 2; "'Trouble City' [sic] USA,' Blames All Disorder on Outsiders," *Tennessean*, September 4, 1956, 1, 2; "5 Arrested in Attack on 2 Guardsmen in Dayton," *Oak Ridger*, September 4, 1956, 1, 2.

107   *"Are you on your way":* Ibid.

107   *"No," the Guardsman:* Ibid.

107   *"Would you go":* Ibid.

107   *"Yes," he replied:* Ibid.

107   *the man drew his knife:* Ibid.

107   *Out of the 1,163:* U.S. Government Printing Office, *Census of Population, 1960* 44:1 (1961): 44–62.

TEN: HOW TO DODGE A LYNCH MOB

108   *the white members of Magnet:* Holden, Valien, and Valien, *Clinton, Tennessee*, 6–9; Wallace Westfeldt and Mac Harris, "Dynamitings in Eaststate Add to Fury," *Tennessean*, September 4, 1956, 1, 2; "'Trouble City' [sic] USA,' Blames All Disorder on Outsiders," *Tennessean*, September 4, 1956, 1, 2.

108   *Joe Henry woke up Labor:* Holden, Valien, and Valien, *Clinton, Tennessee*, 6–9; "Weekend Violence Brings Guards and Peace," *Clinton Courier-News*, September 6, 1956, 1, 3; "Guard Commander Bans Outdoor Meets," *Oak Ridger*, September 3, 1956, 1; "Clinton This Morning 9 Negroes in Class," *Oak Ridger*, September 4, 1956, 1, 3.

109   *What was going to happen tomorrow?:* Ibid.

109   *Well, now, Joe Henry:* Ibid.

109   *Would the guard escort:* Ibid.

109   *No, no, there'd be no:* Ibid.

109   *But what if a picket:* Ibid.

109   *A picket line?:* Ibid.

109   *What would make a picket:* Ibid.

109   *It couldn't impede:* Ibid.

109   *What about the Guardsmen:* Ibid.

109   *the men were sleepy:* Holden, Valien, and Valien, *Clinton, Tennessee*, 6–9; "Weekend Violence Brings Guards and Peace," *Clinton Courier-News*, September 6, 1956, 1, 3; "Guard Commander Bans Outdoor Meets," *Oak Ridger*, September 3, 1956, 1; "Clinton This Morning 9 Negroes in Class," *Oak Ridger*, September 4, 1956, 1, 3; "Guardsmen Pulled from Leisure to Alert," *Oak Ridger*, September 4, 1956, 1, 2.

109   *Is this martial:* Ibid.

109   *Not at all:* Ibid.

109   *On Labor Day, Clinton:* "Guard Says 'All Is in Hand' After Fifth Violent Night,"

Oak Ridger, September 4, 1956, 1; "Clinton Last Night Silent Suspense Until—," *Oak Ridger*, September 4, 1956, 1; Wallace Westfeldt and Mac Harris, "Dynamitings in Eaststate Add to Fury," *Tennessean*, September 4, 1956, 2; "'Trouble City' [sic] USA,' Blames All Disorder on Outsiders," *Tennessean*, September 4, 1956, 2.

110   *An owner of another café:* Louis E. Lomax, "Merchants in Clinton Hardest Hit by Disturbance Over Integration," *Baltimore Afro-American*, September 8, 1956, 13.

110   *no one but the Guard:* "Guard Says 'All Is in Hand' After Fifth Violent Night," *Oak Ridger*, September 4, 1956, 1; "Clinton Last Night Silent Suspense Until—," *Oak Ridger*, September 4, 1956, 1; Wallace Westfeldt and Mac Harris, "Dynamitings in Eaststate Add to Fury," *Tennessean*, September 4, 1956, 2; "'Trouble City' [sic] USA,' Blames All Disorder on Outsiders," *Tennessean*, September 4, 1956, 2.

110   *The journalists sat in their makeshift:* "Clinton Last Night Silent Suspense Until—," *Oak Ridger*, September 4, 1956, 1.

110   *many folks in Clinton felt safe:* Ibid.; "These Pictures Show Activity Here During the Weekend," *Clinton Courier-News*, September 6, 1956, 6; "Armed Men Held After Rumors Fly," *Clinton Courier-News*, September 6, 1956, 6; "Oliver Springs Last Night an Armed Mob; 1 Slight Injury," *Oak Ridger*, September 4, 1956, 1, 2; Wallace Westfeldt and Mac Harris, "Dynamitings in Eaststate Add to Fury," *Tennessean*, September 4, 1956, 1, 2; "'Trouble City' [sic] USA,' Blames All Disorder on Outsiders," *Tennessean*, September 4, 1956, 1, 2.

110   *Southern War Correspondents Association grabbed:* "Ibid.

110   *Seven miles:* "Tank Levels Gas Pump," *Oak Ridger*, September 4, 1956, 1, 2.

111   *D. J. Brittain Sr.—principal:* "Trouble Spreads to Oliver Springs Over Rumors; 17 Arrested," *Clinton Courier-News*, September 6, 1956, 1, 6; "These Pictures Show Activity Here During the Weekend," *Clinton Courier-News*, September 6, 1956, 6; "Armed Men Held After Rumors Fly," *Clinton Courier-News*, September 6, 1956, 6; Holden, Valien, and Valien, *Clinton, Tennessee*, 6–9; "Oliver Springs Last Night an Armed Mob; 1 Slight Injury," *Oak Ridger*, September 4, 1956, 1, 2; Wallace Westfeldt and Mac Harris, "Dynamitings in Eaststate Add to Fury," *Tennessean*, September 4, 1956, 2; "'Trouble City' [sic] USA,' Blames All Disorder on Outsiders," *Tennessean*, September 4, 1956, 2.

111   *the first squad of Guardsmen:* "Weekend Violence Brings Guards and Peace," *Clinton Courier-News*, September 6, 1956, 1; "Trouble Spreads to Oliver Springs over Rumors; 17 Arrested," *Clinton Courier News*, Spetember 6, 1956, 1, 6; "These Pictures Show Activity Here During the Weekend," *Clinton Courier-News*, September 6, 1956, 6; Holden, Valien, and Valien, *Clinton, Tennessee*, 6–9; "Adj. Gen. Henry Tells of Oliver Springs Experience," *Oak Ridger*, September 4, 1956, 2, "Oliver Springs Last Night an Armed Mob; 1 Slight Injury," *Oak Ridger*, September 4, 1956, 1, 2; Wallace Westfeldt and Mac Harris, "Dynamitings in Eaststate Add to Fury," *Tennessean*, September 4, 1956, 1, 2; "'Trouble City' [sic] USA,' Blames All Disorder on Outsiders," *Tennessean*, September 4, 1956, 1, 2; "The Press: The Southern Front," Mac Harris, "I Was in the Hands of an Angry Mob, a Shotgun Stopped the Photographer," *Tennessean*, September 5, 1956, 1, 4.

112   *That's when William Capshaw:* "Weekend Violence Brings Guards and Peace," *Clinton Courier-News,* September 6, 1956, 1; "Trouble Spreads to Oliver Springs over Rumors; 17 Arrested," *Clinton Courier-News,* Spetember 6, 1956, 1, 6; "These Pictures Show Activity Here During the Weekend," *Clinton Courier-News,* September 6, 1956, 6; Holden, Valien, and Valien, *Clinton, Tennessee,* 6–9; "Adj. Gen. Henry Tells of Oliver Springs Experience," *Oak Ridger,* September 4, 1956, 2; "Oliver Springs Last Night an Armed Mob; 1 Slight Injury," *Oak Ridger,* September 4, 1956, 1, 2; Wallace Westfeldt and Mac Harris, "Dynamitings in Eaststate Add to Fury," *Tennessean,* September 4, 1956, 1, 2; "'Trouble City' [sic] USA,' Blames All Disorder on Outsiders," *Tennessean,* September 4, 1956, 1, 2; "2 Ridgers Arrested on Highway Patrol Warrants," *Oak Ridger,* September 4, 1956, 1.

112   *L. T. started back down Main:* "Weekend Violence Brings Guards and Peace," *Clinton Courier-News,* September 6, 1956, 1; "Trouble Spreads to Oliver Springs over Rumors; 17 Arrested," *Clinton Courier-News,* September 6, 1956, 1, 6; "Adj. Gen. Henry Tells of Oliver Springs Experience," *Oak Ridger,* September 4, 1956, 2; "Oliver Springs Last Night an Armed Mob; 1 Slight Injury," *Oak Ridger,* September 4, 1956, 1, 2; "2 Ridgers Arrested on Highway Patrol Warrants," *Oak Ridger,* September 4, 1956, 1.

112   *"Better get out":* "Adj. Gen. Henry Tells of Oliver Springs Experience," *Oak Ridger,* September 4, 1956, 2; "Oliver Springs Last Night an Armed Mob; 1 Slight Injury," *Oak Ridger,* September 4, 1956, 1, 2; "2 Ridgers Arrested on Highway Patrol Warrants," *Oak Ridger,* September 4, 1956, 1.

112   *L. T. hopped back in:* "Adj. Gen. Henry Tells of Oliver Springs Experience," *Oak Ridger,* September 4, 1956, 2; "Oliver Springs Last Night an Armed Mob; 1 Slight Injury," *Oak Ridger,* September 4, 1956, 1, 2; "2 Ridgers Arrested on Highway Patrol Warrants," *Oak Ridger,* September 4, 1956, 1; "Weekend Violence Brings Guards and Peace," *Clinton Courier-News,* September 6, 1956, 1; "Trouble Spreads to Oliver Springs over Rumors; 17 Arrested," *Clinton Courier-News,* September 6, 1956, 1, 6; Holden, Valien, and Valien, *Clinton, Tennessee,* 6–9; Wallace Westfeldt and Mac Harris, "Dynamitings [sic] in Eaststate [sic] Add to Fury," *Tennessean,* September 4, 1956, 2; "'Trouble City' [sic] USA,' Blames All Disorder on Outsiders," *Tennessean,* September 4, 1956, 2.

112   *Or that's what L.T.:* "Adj. Gen. Henry Tells of Oliver Springs Experience," *Oak Ridger,* September 4, 1956, 2; "Oliver Springs Last Night an Armed Mob; 1 Slight Injury," *Oak Ridger,* September 4, 1956, 1, 2; "2 Ridgers Arrested on Highway Patrol Warrants," *Oak Ridger,* September 4, 1956, 1.

113   *The pair sped away:* Adamson, "The Lit Stick," 115; Holden, Valien, and Valien, *Clinton, Tennessee,* 6–9; Wallace Westfeldt and Mac Harris, "Dynamitings [sic] in Eaststate [sic] Add to Fury," *Tennessean,* September 4, 1956, 1, 2; "'Trouble City' [sic] USA,' Blames All Disorder on Outsiders," *Tennessean,* September 4, 1956, 1, 2.

114   *"Can we have our hands":* Ibid.

114   *The general told his soldiers:* "Trouble Spreads to Oliver Springs over Rumors; 17 Arrested," *Clinton Courier-News,* September 6, 1956, 6; Holden, Valien, and

Valien, *Clinton, Tennessee*, 6–9; Wallace Westfeldt and Mac Harris, "Dynamitings [sic] in Eaststate [sic] Add to Fury," *Tennessean*, September 4, 1956, 1, 2; "'Trouble City' [sic] USA,' Blames All Disorder on Outsiders," *Tennessean*, September 4, 1956, 1, 2.

114   *Earlier that night, the folks:* "Weekend Violence Brings Guards and Peace," *Clinton Courier-News*, September 6, 1956, 1; "Trouble Spreads to Oliver Springs over Rumors; 17 Arrested," *Clinton Courier-News*, September 6, 1956, 1, 6.

114   *Harlan Sisson's house:* "Ibid.

114   *the* Clinton Courier-News *did manage:* Ibid.; Holden, Valien, and Valien, *Clinton, Tennessee*, 6–9.

ELEVEN: LEARNING THE RULES

115   *7:30 on Tuesday: Oak Ridger*, September 4, 1956, 1; Wallace Westfeldt, "Oliver Springs Mob Fades," *Tennessean*, September 5, 1956, 1, 2.

115   *Kidnapping and lynching:* "Youth is Lynched at a Reformatory," *New York Times*, November 24, 1944, 1, 34; *Sarasota Herald-Tribune*, August 18, 1937, 3.

116   *fall of '56, Jesse Woods:* "Kidnapped Negro Alive," *Tampa Times*, November 3, 1956, 1, 11; C.L. Zip Starnes, "Negro Taken from Jail at Wildwood," *Tampa Tribune*, October 29, 1956, 1, 7; Sam Mase, "Clues in Kidnaping Turn Up," *Tampa Tribune*, October 31, 1956, 1, 15; "FBI Finds Negro Alive in Alabama," *Tampa Tribune*, November 4, 1956, 1, 20; Benett DeLoach, "Sheriff Believes Negro Still Lives," *Tallahassee Democrat*, October 29, 1956, 1, 2.

116   *the sheriff drove them:* "An Armed Mob; 1 Slight Injury," *Oak Ridger*, September 4, 1956 1; "2 Ridgers Arrested on Highway Patrol Warrants," *Oak Ridger*, September 4, 1956, 1; Howard Sochurek, TimeLife_image_113358906, *Life*, September 1956; Howard Sochurek, TimeLife_image_113358904, *Life*, September 1956; Howard Sochurek, TimeLife_image_959242, *Life*, September 1956; Howard Sochurek, TimeLife_image_113358892, *Life*, September 1956; Howard Sochurek, TimeLife_image_113358893, *Life*, September 1956; Howard Sochurek, Time-Life_image_113358908, *Life*, September 1956; Howard Sochurek, TimeLife _image_113358917, *Life*, September 1956; Wallace Westfeldt, "Oliver Springs Mob Fades," *Tennessean*, September 5, 1956, 1, 2.

117   *twenty-four-year-old Woody:* Joe Collins, "Veterans Day Parade for Clinton Mother Could Begin with Sons," *Knoxville Journal*, November 12, 1964, 1; "Clinton Youth 10th in Family to Join Up," *Knoxville News-Sentinel*, January 7, 1951, 2; U.S. Census Bureau, "1940 United States Federal Census," digital image, s.v. "Woodie Joe Duncan," Ancestry.com; "Woody Joe Duncan," Find a Grave, https://www.finda grave.com/memorial/91297467/woody-joe-duncan; "Woody Joe Duncan Was Last of 10 Brothers Who Served in Wartime Military," *Knox News*, June 4, 2012, https://archive.knoxnews.com/news/local/obituary-woody-joe-duncan-was -last-of-10-brothers-who-served-in-wartime-military-ep-360691964-356964371 .html/.

117   *Woody Joe had bounced:* "Files Petition," *Knoxville Journal,* May 27, 1955, 23; "Jett Wins Seat on Anderson County Court," *Knoxville Journal,* June 15, 1955, 18; "Officers Recover Handcuffs but Drunk Escapes," *Knoxville Journal,* September 26, 1955, 14; "Snake Hunt Bares Whisky," *Knoxville Journal,* October 14, 1955, 11; "Nine Face Liquor Counts," *Knoxville Journal,* March 5, 1956, 16.

117   *The first dynamite blast in Oliver:* Dick Smyser, "Olivers Men Came—But for Conference," *Oak Ridger,* September 7, 1956, 8; Wallace Westfeldt, "Oliver Springs Mob Fades," *Tennessean,* September 5, 1956, 1, 2.

118   *U.S. Marshal Frank Quarles trudged:* Brittain, "A Case Study," 150; "Weekend Violence Brings Guards and Peace," *Clinton Courier-News,* September 6, 1956, 1, 3; "9 Negroes in Class," *Clinton Courier-News,* September 6, 1956, 1, 2; "Congressional Record," *Proceedings and Debates of the 85th Congress, First Session,* July 26, 1957, 12814; "$300 Reward Stirs Search," *Knoxville Journal,* September 7, 1930, 1; "Quarles Gets Bounds First," *Knoxville Journal,* September 18, 1934, 3; "Two Injured in Collision," *Knoxville Journal,* September 20, 1935, 14; "Suspect Arrested in Sevier Robbery," *Knoxville Journal,* October 25, 1935, 12; "Woman Will Be Quizzed by U.S. Officials," *Knoxville Journal,* March 6, 1938, 1; "Anderson Quits Race in Dandridge," *Knoxville Journal,* April 19, 1940, 3; "Democrats Get 29 Seats in Senate," *Knoxville Journal,* November 5, 1942, 11; Roberts, *High School,* 61; Wallace Westfeldt, "Oliver Springs Mob Fades," *Tennessean,* September 5, 1956, 1, 2; "On 1st Day Back, Under Guard Rule Now, Clinton High Integrates," *Tennessean,* September 5, 1956, 2.

118   *the Black teenagers pulled up:* "9 Negroes in Class," *Oak Ridger,* September 4, 1; Roberts, *High School,* 61; Wallace Westfeldt, "Oliver Springs Mob Fades," *Tennessean,* September 5, 1956, 1, 2; "On 1st Day Back, Under Guard Rule Now, Clinton High Integrates," *Tennessean,* September 5, 1956, 2; United States District Court, "*McSwain,*" September 6, 1956, 227–28.

118   *266 white students:* "Bulk of Clinton Students Refuse to Attend School," *Bristol Herald,* September 5, 1956, 1, 2, 7; "Full School Opening Brings Racial Unrest in 8 States," *Bristol Herald,* September 6, 1956, 1, 2, 3; "9 Negroes in Class," *Oak Ridger,* September 4, 1; Roberts, *High School,* 61; Wallace Westfeldt, "Oliver Springs Mob Fades," *Tennessean,* September 5, 1956, 1, 2; "On 1st Day Back, Under Guard Rule Now, Clinton High Integrates," *Tennessean,* September 5, 1956, 2; United States District Court, "*McSwain,*" September 6, 1956, 224–26.

118   *teachers tried to forge ahead:* "9 Negroes in Class," *Oak Ridger,* September 4, 1; Roberts, *High School,* 61; Wallace Westfeldt, "Oliver Springs Mob Fades," *Tennessean,* September 5, 1956, 1, 2; "On 1st Day Back, Under Guard Rule Now, Clinton High Integrates," *Tennessean,* September 5, 1956, 2.

119   *students now heard:* "9 Negroes in Class," *Oak Ridger,* September 4, 1; Roberts, *High School,* 61; Wallace Westfeldt, "Oliver Springs Mob Fades," *Tennessean,* September 5, 1956, 1, 2; "On 1st Day Back, Under Guard Rule Now, Clinton High Integrates," *Tennessean,* September 5, 1956, 2; Robert W. Kelley, TimeLife_image_1133 45431, *Life,* September 1956; Robert W. Kelley, TimeLife_image_113345488,

Life, September 1956; Robert W. Kelley, TimeLife_image_113345429, *Life*, September 1956; Robert W. Kelley, TimeLife_image_113345406, *Life*, September 1956; Robert W. Kelley, TimeLife_image_113345586, *Life*, September 1956; Robert W. Kelley, TimeLife_image_113345475, *Life*, September 1956; Howard Sochurek, TimeLife_image_113356065, *Life*, September 1956; "Guardsmen Win Clinton Friends," *Tennessean*, September 6, 1956, 2.

119   *National Guard headquarters received:* Anna Theresser Caswell interview; Seivers, "Words of Discrimination," 201; Wallace Westfeldt, "Oliver Springs Mob Fades," *Tennessean*, September 5, 1956, 1, 2; "On 1st Day Back, Under Guard Rule Now, Clinton High Integrates," *Tennessean*, September 5, 1956, 2; United States District Court, "*McSwain*," September 6, 1956, 224–26.

119   *students in Oak Ridge started:* "Oak Ridge Today Attendance High," *Oak Ridger*, September 4, 1; Wallace Westfeldt, "Oliver Springs Mob Fades," *Tennessean*, September 5, 1956, 1, 2; "On 1st Day Back, Under Guard Rule Now, Clinton High Integrates," *Tennessean*, September 5, 1956, 2.

120   *Midafternoon, Kyle and another:* Wallace Westfeldt, "Oliver Springs Mob Fades," *Tennessean*, September 5, 1956, 1, 2.

120   *Would the general:* Ibid.

120   *Absolutely not, he:* Ibid.

120   *What if the older brothers:* Ibid.

120   *Joe Henry still didn't:* Ibid.

120   *A few hours later, about two hundred and fifty or maybe:* "These Pictures Show Activity Here During the Week-End," *Clinton Courier-News*, September 6, 1956, 6; "Olivers Has Trouble, Too; 17 Are Jailed," *Clinton Courier-News*, September 6, 1956, 6; "Armed Men Held After Rumors Fly," *Clinton Courier-News*, September 6, 1956, 6; "70 More Students at Clinton High Today," *Oak Ridger*, September 5, 1956, 1, 2; Wallace Westfeldt, "Oliver Springs Mob Fades," *Tennessean*, September 5, 1956, 1, 2; "On 1st Day Back, Under Guard Rule Now, Clinton High Integrates," *Tennessean*, September 5, 1956, 2.

120   *night police chief:* "These Pictures Show Activity Here During the Week-End," *Clinton Courier-News*, September 6, 1956, 6; "Olivers Has Trouble, Too; 17 Are Jailed," *Clinton Courier-News*, September 6, 1956, 6; "Armed Men Held After Rumors Fly," *Clinton Courier-News*, September 6, 1956, 6; "70 More Students at Clinton High Today," *Oak Ridger*, September 5, 1956, 1, 2; Wallace Westfeldt, "Oliver Springs Mob Fades," *Tennessean*, September 5, 1956, 1, 2; "On 1st Day Back, Under Guard Rule Now, Clinton High Integrates," *Tennessean*, September 5, 1956, 2.

121   *extra troopers pulled up:* Wallace Westfeldt, "Oliver Springs Mob Fades," *Tennessean*, September 5, 1956, 1, 2.

121   *Go home!:* Ibid., Mac Harris, "I Was in the Hands of an Angry Mob, a Shotgun Stopped the Photographer," *Tennessean*, September 5, 1956, 1, 4.

121   *everyone—protestors and troops:* Wallace Westfeldt, "Oliver Springs Mob Fades," *Tennessean*, September 5, 1956, 1, 2; Mac Harris, "I Was in the Hands of an Angry

Mob, a Shotgun Stopped the Photographer," *Tennessean*, September 5, 1956, 1, 4; "These Pictures Show Activity Here During the Week-End," *Clinton Courier-News*, September 6, 1956, 6; "Olivers Has Trouble, Too; 17 Are Jailed," *Clinton Courier-News*, September 6, 1956, 6; "Armed Men Held After Rumors Fly," *Clinton Courier-News*, September 6, 1956, 6; "70 More Students at Clinton High Today," *Oak Ridger*, September 5, 1956, 1, 2.

121   *Over in Oak Ridge, however:* Ibid; "Ridge Enrolls 100 Negroes in Schools," *Knoxville Journal*, September 5, 1956, 16; "Five Arrested in Scarboro Gathering," *Oak Ridger*, September 5, 1956, 1.

121   *two Black students were hung:* "Hanged in Effigy," *Knoxville Journal*, September 5, 1956, 16.

121   *Wednesday morning, 324 students:* "Weekend Violence Brings Guards and Peace," *Clinton Courier-News*, September 6, 1956, 3; "70 More Students at Clinton High Today," *Oak Ridger*, September 5, 1956, 1, 2.

121   *A journalist with one:* J. Russel Boner, "Principal Cites Aim at Fairness," *Knoxville Journal*, September 6, 1956, 11.

122   *D. J. turned away:* Ibid.

122   *recreation center/National Guard headquarters:* "70 More Students at Clinton High Today," *Oak Ridger*, September 5, 1956, 1, 2.

122   *he had until 7:00:* Ibid.

122   *They were welcome:* Ibid.; Mac Harris, "Men Attack Photographers," *Tennessean*, September 6, 1956, 1; Wallace Westerfeldt, "125 Newsmen Cover Clinton, *Tennessean*, September 6, 1956, 1, 2.

123   National Guardsmen lined up: Howard Sochurek, TimeLife_image_113356108, Life, September 1956; Howard Sochurek, TimeLife_image_113356033, *Life*, September 1956; Howard Sochurek, TimeLife_image_113356036, *Life*, September 1956; Howard Sochurek, TimeLife_image_959253, *Life*, September 1956; Howard Sochurek, TimeLife_image_113356106, *Life*, September 1956; Howard Sochurek, TimeLife_image_113356050, *Life*, September 1956; Howard Sochurek, TimeLife_image_113356047, *Life*, September 1956; Howard Sochurek, TimeLife_image_113356107, *Life*, September 1956; Howard Sochurek, TimeLife_image_113356013, *Life*, September 1956; Howard Sochurek, TimeLife_image_113356035, *Life*, September 1956; Howard Sochurek, TimeLife_image_113356025, *Life*, September 1956; Howard Sochurek, TimeLife_image_113356124, *Life*, September 1956; Howard Sochurek, TimeLife_image_113356034, *Life*, September 1956; Howard Sochurek, TimeLife_image_113356111, *Life*, September 1956; Howard Sochurek, TimeLife_image_959259, *Life*, September 1956; Mac Harris, "Men Attack Photographers," Tennessean, September 6, 1956, 1; Wallace Westerfeldt, "125 Newsmen Cover Clinton, Tennessean, September 6, 1956, 1, 2; "Anger Builds in Rain . . . Sudden Attack . . . Bruise, Jail," Tennessean, September 6, 1956, 2.

123   *the kid turned toward Jack:* Mac Harris, "Men Attack Photographers," *Tennessean*, September 6, 1956, 1; Wallace Westerfeldt, "125 Newsmen Cover Clinton,

Tennessean, September 6, 1956, 1, 2; "Anger Builds in Rain ... Sudden Attack ... Bruise, Jail," *Tennessean*, September 6, 1956, 2.

123 *Wanna press charges?:* Ibid.

123 *"I guess this":* Ibid.

124 *At 8:00 p.m., an hour:* Ibid.; "Weekend Violence Brings Guards and Peace," *Clinton Courier-News*, September 6, 1956, 1; "Trouble Spreads to Oliver Springs Over Rumors; 17 Arrested," *Clinton Courier-News*, September 6, 1956, 1; "Clinton High Total Continues Upward," *Oak Ridger*, September 6, 1956, 1.

124 *At 10:00 that night:* Mac Harris, "Men Attack Photographers," *Tennessean*, September 6, 1956, 1; Wallace Westerfeldt, "125 Newsmen Cover Clinton, *Tennessean*, September 6, 1956, 1, 2; "Anger Builds in Rain ... Sudden Attack ... Bruise, Jail," *Tennessean*, September 6, 1956, 2; "Weekend Violence Brings Guards and Peace," *Clinton Courier-News*, September 6, 1956, 1; "Trouble Spreads to Oliver Springs Over Rumors; 17 Arrested," *Clinton Courier-News*, September 6, 1956, 1; "Clinton High Total Continues Upward," *Oak Ridger*, September 6, 1956, 1.

TWELVE: VINING OUT

125 *the Guardsmen left:* "Guardsmen Win Clinton Friends," *Tennessean*, September 6, 1956, 2; Mac Harris, "Guardsmen at Clinton Find They've Got Time on Their Hands," *Tennessean*, September 7, 1956, 6.

125 *folks outside Clinton questioned:* "Text of Woodward's Declaration of Emergency," *Oak Ridger*, September 10, 1956, 1–2; "Sheriff Summons 150 to Maintain Order," *Oak Ridger*, September 10, 1956, 1-2; "Governor Repeats Reason for Help," *Oak Ridger*, September 10, 1956, 2; Russell Bruce, "Anderson Emergency Called," *Tennessean*, September 9, 1956, 1, 6; Russell Bruce, "Students Return to Clinton High," *Tennessean*, September 11, 1956, 15; "Anderson County Officials Deny Help Pleas Too Early," *Tennessean*, September 11, 1956, 15; Glad Woodward to Frank Clement, September 7, 1956, Lee S. Greene Collection, Knoxville, TN.

125 *on Thursday, September 6, Frank:* Ibid.; Anderson County, "Clinton City Recorder Minutes, Volume 12"; "Clinton Quiet as Guard Withdraws; Attendance Is Up," *Clinton Courier-News*, September 13, 1956, 1, 6; "City Bans Meetings, Speakers," *Clinton Courier-News*, September 13, 1956, 1; Horace V. Wells Jr., "As We See It!" *Clinton Courier-News*, September 13, 1956, 1; Herd, "Then and Now," 47; Holden, Valien, and Valien, *Clinton, Tennessee*, 6–9; "70 More Students at Clinton High Today," *Oak Ridger*, September 5, 1956, 2; "Attendance 419; Expect More Monday," *Oak Ridger*, September 7, 1956, 1, 8; Wallace Westfeldt, "Guard, Officers Blamed in Riot," *Tennessean*, September 7, 1956, 1, 8; "Clinton Passes Tough Measures," *Tennessean*, September 8, 1956, 1.

126 *Woody Joe Duncan, his brother Kyle:* Dick Smyser, "Olivers Men Came—But for Conference," *Oak Ridger*, September 7, 1956, 1, 8; Wallace Westfeldt, "Guard, Officers Blamed in Riot," *Tennessean*, September 7, 1956, 1, 8.

126 *The real problem, Woody Joe:* Ibid.; Adamson, "The Lit Stick," 115; Holden, Valien,

and Valien, *Clinton, Tennessee,* 6–9; Wallace Westfeldt and Mac Harris, "Dynamitings in Eaststate Add to Fury," *Tennessean,* September 4, 1956, 1, 2; "'Trouble City' [sic] USA,' Blames All Disorder on Outsiders," *Tennessean,* September 4, 1956, 1, 2.

126   *talked with the journalists until after:* Ibid.

126   *On Friday, 419 students:* Russell Bruce, "Anderson Emergency Called," *Tennessean,* September 9, 1956, 1, 6; "Sheriff Summons 150 to Maintain Order," *Oak Ridger,* September 10, 1956, 1–2.

126   *Joe Henry had sent home:* Frank Clement to Glad Woodward, September 8, 1956, Lee S. Greene Collection, Knoxville, TN; "Attendance 419; Expect More Monday," *Oak Ridger,* September 7, 1956, 1; "Guardsmen on Way Out of Clinton," *Tennessean,* September 8, 1956, 2; "Clinton Passes Tough Measures," *Tennessean,* 1, 2; Russell Bruce, "Anderson Emergency Called," *Tennessean,* September 9, 1956, 1, 6.

126   *By the weekend, the Southern War:* Louis E. Lomax, "Anxiety in Clinton," *Afro-American,* September 15, 1956, 1–2.

126   *Saturday night, some two hundred Knoxvillians:* "Klan Gathers," *Knoxville Journal,* September 10, 1950, 12-A; "Klan Ceremony," *Knoxville Journal,* May 18, 1951, 4; "Klan Burns Cross Near Maryville," *Knoxville Journal,* February 19, 1956, 1; "Ku Klux Klan Rally Set at Chattanooga," *Knoxville Journal,* February 24, 1956, 3; "KKK to Demonstrate," *Knoxville Journal,* July 13, 1956, 18; "Crosses Fired as Klan Holds Airport Meet," *Knoxville Journal,* September 9, 1956, 20-A; "Curious Crowd Gathers for Klan Initiation," *Knoxville News-Sentinel,* September 10, 1950, A-13; "Crosses Burned at Two Residences," *Knoxville News-Sentinel,* April 2, 1953, 18; "50 Years of Litigation on Segregation Seen," *Knoxville News-Sentitel,* June 5, 1955, C-5; Ed Hill, "Integration Red-Inspired, Klan Speaker Charges," *Knoxville News-Sentinel,* February 19, 1956, A-10.

127   *Privately, the governor:* Frank Clement to Glad Woodward, September 8, 1956; Lee S. Greene Collection; Russell Bruce, "Anderson Emergency Called," *Tennessean,* September 9, 1956, 1, 6.

128   *Willard Till's Anderson County White Citizen's Council:* "Clinton Quiet as Guard Withdraws; Attendance Is Up," *Clinton Courier-News,* September 13, 1956, 1, 6; "City Bans Meetings, Speakers," *Clinton Courier-News,* September 13, 1956, 1; "Attendance 419; Expect More Monday," *Oak Ridger,* September 7, 1956, 8; "Guardsmen on Way Out of Clinton," *Tennessean,* September 8, 1956, 2; "Clinton Passes Tough Measures," *Tennessean,* September 8, 1956, 1, 2.

128   *I believe we need:* Ibid.

128   *After expelling Glad and John:* Dailey, "The Theology of Massive Resistance," in *Massive Resistance,* ed. Webb, 151–53; Ed Hill, "Integration Red-Inspired, Klan Speaker Charges," *Knoxville News-Sentinel,* February 19, 1956, A-10; United States District Court, *"Bullock,"* July 18, 1957, 1096–97, 1112–13. For more information on the Appalachian tradition of sacred singing and how it had evolved

alongside white supremacy during the early twentieth century, see Goff, *Close Harmony*.

129   *"It is difficult to view"*: "Unholy Crusade for Segregation," *Tri-State Defender*, September 8, 1956, 7.

129   *529 students showed up:* Holden, Valien, and Valien, *Clinton, Tennessee*, 6–9; "Sheriff Summons 150 to Maintain Order," *Oak Ridger*, September 10, 1956, 2; "Clinton Attendance up to 590," *Oak Ridger*, September 11, 1956, 1; Russell Bruce, "Students Return to Clinton High," *Tennessean*, September 11, 1956, 15.

129   *At dusk that evening, Wynona:* Louis E. Lomax, *Baltimore Afro-American*, September 8, 1956, 1, 13; Louis E. Lomax, "School Case Victory of Struggle," *Baltimore Afro-American*, September 8, 1956, 13.

130   *At seven o'clock, all those:* Boyce and Levy, *This Promise of Change*, 188–89.

130   *the twenty-one-year-old singer strutted:* "Celebrating Elvis Presley's First Appearance on the Ed Sullivan Show (September 9, 1956)"; Moore, "Elvis' 1955 Martin 9-28."

130   *the last members of the National Guard:* "Clinton Quiet as Guard Withdraws; Attendance Is Up," *Clinton Courier-News*, September 13, 1956, 1, 6; "City Bans Meetings, Speakers," *Clinton Courier-News*, September 13, 1956, 1; Horace V. Wells Jr., "As We See It!" *Clinton Courier-News*, September 13, 1956, 1; Holden, Valien, and Valien, *Clinton, Tennessee*, 6–9; "Clinton Attendance up to 590," *Oak Ridger*, September 11, 1956, 1; "Last Guard Leaves Clinton," *Tennessean*, September 12, 1956, 1, 6.

130   *"I feel sure":* Louis E. Lomax, "Anxiety in Clinton," *Afro-American*, September 15, 1956, 1–2.

130   *"When the Guard leaves":* "Sheriff Summons 150 to Maintain Order," *Oak Ridger*, September 10, 1956, 1–2; Wallace Westfeldt, "Guard, Officers Blamed in Riot," *Tennessean*, September 7, 1956, 8.

130   *September 12, 1956, Herbert Allen:* Grace E. Simons, "They Threw Rocks, Eggs, Says Girl, 15," *California Eagle*, December 20, 1956, 4; Wallace Westfeldt, "Negroes Insist They Won't Quit Clinton High," *Tennessean*, November 30, 1956, 1, 17.

131   *For Herbert, the conflict:* Ibid.; Lowenstein et al., "History and Use of Kudzu in the Southeastern United States"; Walker, *In Search of Our Mothers' Gardens*, 165.

131   *Herbert Allen talks about racism:* Grace E. Simons, "They Threw Rocks, Eggs, Says Girl, 15," *California Eagle*, December 20, 1956, 4; Walker, *In Search of Our Mothers' Gardens*, 165.

132   *Herbert figured the white:* "Sheriff Nabs First Still Since Elected," *Clinton Courier-News*, September 13, 1956, 1; "Clinton High up to 630," *Oak Ridger*, September 12, 1956, 1; "Another Clinton Increase," *Oak Ridger*, September 14, 1956, 1; "Sheriff Captures His First Still," *Oak Ridger*, September 14, 1956, 6; "Woodward's First Still," *Oak Ridger*, September 20, 1956, 1; "Liquor Petitions Out; Nov. 6 Vote Likely," *Oak Ridger*, September 20, 1956, 1; "Clinton Attendance," *Oak Ridger*, September 20, 1956, 1; "Battle Integration Openly—Kasper," *Tennessean*, September 13, 1956, 5; "Clinton High Back to Normal," *Tennessean*, September 13, 1956, 5.

132 *He wasn't concerned:* Grace E. Simons, "They Threw Rocks, Eggs, Says Girl, 15," *California Eagle*, December 20, 1956, 4.

132 *Jo Ann and Carole Peters:* Jo Ann Allen Boyce interview; Boyce and Levy, *This Promise of Change*, 150–54; Anna Theresser Caswell interview; "Two Clinton Girls on TV Program," *Clinton Courier-News*, September 20, 1956, 1; "Brownell on Integration," *Indianapolis Recorder*, October 6, 1956, 9; "TV Today," *Knoxville News-Sentinel*, September 23, 1956, 42; Regina Turner Smith interview; "Clinton Panelists Fly Back Home," *Tennessean*, September 25, 1956, 24.

133 *The girls seemed to have:* Jo Ann Allen Boyce interview; Boyce and Levy, *This Promise of Change*, 147–49.

133 *first-year history teacher:* Don and Sue Byerly interview; Bobby Cain interview.

133 *Herbert knew the strain:* The psychological definition of a traumatic event certainly fits the Twelve's circumstances. "A traumatic event is one in which a person feels utterly helpless in the face of a force that is perceived to be life-threatening," explains trauma scholar Susan J. Brison. "The immediate psychological responses of hypervigilance, heightened startle response, sleep disorders and the more psychological, yet still involuntary, responses of depression, inability to concentrate, lack of interest in activities that used to give life meaning and a sense of a foreshortened future." The most damaging type of trauma is that which is inflicted intentionally by other humans. That experience "not only shatters one's fundamental assumptions about the world and one's safety in it, but also severs the sustaining connection between the self and the rest of humanity"; Brison, "Trauma Narratives and the Remaking of the Self," in *Acts of Memory*, ed. Bal, Crewe, and Spitzer, 40.

133 *"He reminded me of the men":* Bobby Cain interview; McMillan, "The Ordeal," 337.

134 *Bobby'd always been:* Bobby Cain interview; McMillan, "The Ordeal," 337; Robert Cain Sr. interview.

134 *almost 80 percent full:* "Clinton High up to 630," *Oak Ridger*, September 12, 1956, 1; "Clinton High Back to Normal," *Tennessean*, September 13, 1956, 5.

134 *"They're here, we":* Russell Bruce, "Anderson Emergency Called," *Tennessean*, September 9, 1956, 1, 6; Wallace Westfeldt, "Control Eludes Guard at Clinton," *Tennessean*, September 9, 1956, 6; "Students Seem to Realize Clinton Issues Go Deep," *Tennessean*, September 9, 1956, 6.

134 *But not all the white:* Louis E. Lomax, *Baltimore Afro-American*, September 8, 1956, 1, 13; Louis E. Lomax, "School Case Victory of Struggle," *Baltimore Afro-American*, September 8, 1956, 13; Louis E. Lomax, "Clinton, Tenn. Pupils Return to High School," *Baltimore Afro-American*, September 8, 1956, 13; Wallace Westfeldt, "Control Eludes Guard at Clinton," *Tennessean*, September 9, 1956, 6; "Students Seem to Realize Clinton Issues Go Deep," *Tennessean*, September 9, 1956, 6.

134 *Every week, there were more:* "School Board Resignations Demanded by Group Opposed to Integration," *Clinton Courier-News*, September 20, 1956, 1, 6; "Comments on Integration Are Many," *Clinton Courier-News*, September 20, 1956, 6; "Another Clinton Increase," *Oak Ridger*, September 14, 1956, 1, 6; United States

District Court, "*Bullock*," July 10, 1957, 124–28, July 11, 1957, 211–12, July 17, 1957, 1057–59, 1062.

134   *As an adult, Bobby*: Bobby Cain interview.

135   *white business leaders reported*: "School Board Resignations Demanded by Group Opposed to Integration," *Clinton Courier-News*, September 20, 1956, 1, 6; "Comments on Integration Are Many," *Clinton Courier-News*, September 20, 1956, 6; "List of Voters Secured by Citizens Council," *Clinton Courier-News*, September 20, 1956, 3; "Halt Called on Copying Vote List by Citizens Group," *Clinton Courier-News*, September 27, 1956, 2:4; Helen Knox, "Sen. Gore Calls for More Peaceful A-Development; Ignores Hecklers," *Oak Ridger*, September 25, 1956, 1, 2; Jim Ryan, "Criminal Grand Jury Indicts Kasper; Sheriff Nabs Him Here; Trial Nov. 5," *Oak Ridger*, September 25, 1956, 1, 2; "Several Cases Tried in Anderson County Court," *Oak Ridger*, October 4, 1956, 7; "Kasper Arrested as Hecklers Join Democratic Rally," *Tennessean*, September 25, 1956, 1–2.

135   *local Democratic Party leaders hosted*: "Kasper Is Indicted for Activities in Integration Riots," *Clinton Courier-News*, September 27, 1956, 1; Helen Knox, "Sen. Gore Calls for More Peaceful A-Development; Ignores Hecklers," *Oak Ridger*, September 25, 1956, 1, 2; Jim Ryan, "Criminal Grand Jury Indicts Kasper; Sheriff Nabs Him Here; Trial Nov. 5," *Oak Ridger*, September 25, 1956, 1, 2; "Several Cases Tried in Anderson County Court," *Oak Ridger*, October 4, 1956, 7; "Kasper Arrested as Hecklers Join Democratic Rally," *Tennessean*, September 25, 1956, 1–2.

136   *"I'm the sheriff"*: "Kasper Is Indicted for Activities in Integration Riots," *Clinton Courier-News*, September 27, 1956, 1.

136   *"On what charges"*: Ibid.

136   *"Sedition," Glad said*: Ibid.

136   *"What's sedition?"*: Ibid.

136   *the sheriff grabbed John*: Ibid.; Helen Knox, "Sen. Gore Calls for More Peaceful A-Development; Ignores Hecklers," *Oak Ridger*, September 25, 1956, 1, 2; Jim Ryan, "Criminal Grand Jury Indicts Kasper; Sheriff Nabs Him Here; Trial Nov. 5," *Oak Ridger*, September 25, 1956, 1, 2; "Kasper Arrested as Hecklers Join Democratic Rally," *Tennessean*, September 25, 1956, 1–2.

136   *when Glad shoved*: "Kasper Is Indicted for Activities in Integration Riots," *Clinton Courier-News*, September 27, 1956, 1; Helen Knox, "Sen. Gore Calls for More Peaceful A-Development; Ignores Hecklers," *Oak Ridger*, September 25, 1956, 1, 2; Jim Ryan, "Criminal Grand Jury Indicts Kasper; Sheriff Nabs Him Here; Trial Nov. 5," *Oak Ridger*, September 25, 1956, 1, 2; "Kasper Arrested as Hecklers Join Democratic Rally," *Tennessean*, September 25, 1956, 1–2.

136   *Just shy of midnight*: Ibid.; "Kasper Trial Slated Nov. 5," *Tennessean*, September 26, 1956, 2.

137   *Wednesday, September 26, at 10:15*: "Blast in Negro Area Shakes Town," *Clinton Courier-News*, September 27, 1956, 1; Jim Ryan, "Blast Near Clinton Negro Home Showers Dirt; Slight Damage," *Oak Ridger*, September 27, 1956, 1–2; "No Clues

in Clinton Blast," September 28, 1956, 1, 3; "Blast Set Off by Clinton Home," *Tennessean*, September 27, 1956, 1.

137   *Then dynamite was found:* Ibid.; "Anti-Integration Blast Rocks Clinton Negroes," *Cavalier Daily*, September 28, 1956, 1, 4; Horace V. Wells Jr., "As We See It!" *Clinton Courier-News*, October 4, 1956, 1, "Blast Remains a Mystery to Local Officers," *Clinton Courier-News*, October 4, 1956, 1.

137   *Herbert Allen was through:* Ibid.

137   *Josephine phoned:* Boyce and Levy, *This Promise of Change*, 164–65; "Anti-Integration Blast Rocks Clinton Negroes," *Cavalier Daily*, September 28, 1956, 1, 4; "Court Moves Slowly as Term Starts," *Clinton Courier-News*, September 27, 1956, 4; "Blast Remains a Mystery to Local Officers," *Clinton Courier-News*, October 4, 1956, 1; "Blast Near Clinton Negro Home Showers Dirt; Slight Damage," *Oak Ridger*, September 27, 1956, 2; "Several Cases Tried in Anderson County Court," *Oak Ridger*, October 4, 1956, 7.

138   *No one was ever arrested:* "Blast Remains a Mystery to Local Officers," *Clinton Courier-News*, October 4, 1956, 1; "No Clues in Clinton Blast," September 28, 1956, 1, 3.

THIRTEEN: SMALL-TOWN GAMES

139   *Saturday, October 13, 125 cars:* "Speaker for Segregations Meeting Ill," *Clinton Courier-News*, October 25, 1956, 8; "Klansmen Gather in S. Clinton," *Oak Ridger*, October 15, 1956, 1; "States Rights Ralley in Clinton," *Oak Ridger*, October 17, 1956, 1–2; "States Righters Planning Series of Rallies in Area," *Oak Ridger*, October 19, 1956, 1; "Schoolfield Talk in LaFollette; Clinton Rally Off," *Oak Ridger*, October 22, 1956, 1; "States Righters Wind-Up Campaign; Set Schoofield Talk at Clinton," *Oak Ridger*, October 31, 1956, 1–2; "KKK Parades, Burns 4 Crosses in Clinton Rally," *Tennessean*, October 14, 1956, 1; United States District Court, *"Bullock,"* July 17, 1957, 1022–23.

139   *refocused on the newest:* "Sheriff Nabs First Still Since Elected," *Clinton Courier-News*, September 13, 1956, 1; "Committee of 100 works to Prevent Liquor Sale Here," *Clinton Courier-News*, September 20, 1956, 1; "Liquor Referendum Petitions Circulated; May Set Vote Nov. 6," September 27, 1956, 1, 6; Horace V. Wells Jr., "As We See It!" *Clinton Courier-News*, September 27, 1956, 1; Herb Stein, "What's Happening, If Anything, About Liquor? Talk Is Plentiful, Action Slight," *Oak Ridger*, September 13, 1956, 1; "Liquor Petitions Out; Nov. 6 Vote Likely," *Oak Ridger*, September 20, 1956, 1.

140   *Pictures from Hungary:* See, for instance, "Rebels Weaken in Budapest," *Tennessean*, October 28, 1956, 1, or "Hungary Strike Broken; Workers Stage 'Slowdown,'" *Oak Ridger*, November 19, 1956, 1.

141   *Too many people dismissed:* "Brakebill Scoffs at 'Hoodlum' Title Given '15," *East Tennessee Reporter*, July 12, 1957, 1; "Injunction Knoxiledge by '15' Not Yet Proved," *East Tennessee Reporter*, July 12, 1957, 1, 6; "Kasper and Six Convicted; New Trial

Possible," *East Tennessee Reporter*, July 26, 1957, 1; "Raymond Woods Hasn't Changed, He Tells Reporter," *East Tennessee Reporter*, July 26, 1957, 1; "Rev. Bullock Refutes 'Smear' News Stories," *East Tennessee Reporter*, July 26, 1957, 1; "Back Glances Show Incidents of Interest," *East Tennessee Reporter*, July 26, 1957, 2, 8; Ethridge, *Citizens' Council*, January 1957, 4; Webb, "Introduction," *Massive Resistance*, 14.

141 *Jo Ann Allen probably* could: Boyce and Levy, *This Promise of Change*, 33–35.

141 *the perfect diction:* Ibid.; "Brakebill Scoffs at 'Hoodlum' Title Given '15," *East Tennessee Reporter*, July 12, 1957, 1; "Injunction Knoxiledge by '15' Not Yet Proved," *East Tennessee Reporter*, July 12, 1957, 1, 6; "Kasper and Six Convicted; New Trial Possible," *East Tennessee Reporter*, July 26, 1957, 1; "Raymond Woods Hasn't Changed, He Tells Reporter," *East Tennessee Reporter*, July 26, 1957, 1; "Rev. Bullock Refutes 'Smear' News Stories," *East Tennessee Reporter*, July 26, 1957, 1; "Back Glances Show Incidents of Interest," *East Tennessee Reporter*, July 26. 1957, 2, 8; Ethridge, *Citizens' Council*, January 1957, 4; Webb, "Introduction," *Massive Resistance*, 14, "Kasper Trial Resumes; 10 Testify," *Oak Ridger*, November 19, 1956, 1.

142 *the* East Tennessee Reporter, *led:* "States Rights, White Citizens 'Not Same,'" *Clinton Courier-News*, November 8, 1956, 1; "Kasper on Stand in Riot Case," *Clinton Courier-News*, November 8, 1956, 1, 5; "Leo Ely," Find a Grave, https://www.findagrave.com/memorial/92884375/leo-ely; "The Reporter—Resumes Publication," *Tennessee Reporter*, October 18, 1957, 1; "A Few Words, If You Please," *Tennessee Reporter*, October 18, 1957, 2; U.S. Census Bureau, "1930 United States Federal Census," digital image, s.v. "Leo Ely," Ancestry.com, "1940 United States Federal Census," digital image, s.v. "Leo Ely," Ancestry.com.

142 *Eight years earlier, Buford:* "Lewallen Charges Dropped," *Chattanooga Daily Times*, December 1, 1948, 15; "Buford Lewallen, Oak Ridgers, Free Under Bond after Midnight Fight," *Knoxville Journal*, November 10, 1948, 1; Willard Yarbrough, "Lewallen-Ely Court Fight Involves Divorce Litigation," *Knoxville News-Sentinel*, November 25, 1948, 1, 20; "Lewallen-Ely Charges Withdrawn," *Knoxville News-Sentinel*, December 1, 1948, 1.

143 *October 24, Celdon Lewallen:* Celdon Lewallen interview; "Cross Burned, as Another Effort Thwarted, Man Held," *Clinton Courier-News*, October 25, 1956, 1; Seivers, "Words of Discrimination," 151–52, 166–68.

143 *One had been torched:* "2 Crosses in Clinton," *Decatur Daily*, May 13, 1949, 1; "Fiery Crosses Carry Notes for Lawyers," *Knoxville Journal*, May 13, 1949, 17; "Crosses Burned Near 2 Lawyers' Homes," *Knoxville News-Sentinel*, May 13, 1949, 17.

143 *Celdon had been the one:* Celdon Lewallen interview; Seivers, "Words of Discrimination," 167–68.

143 *"What do you think":* Ibid.

143 *"We'll be right here":* Ibid.

143 *"Not in my room":* Ibid.

144 *"You can't do that!":* Ibid.

144 *"You can't do what":* Ibid.

144   *there was this one:* Celdon Lewallen interview; Seivers, "Words of Discrimination," 166.

144   *"Just get up":* Ibid.

144   *So now her students:* Celdon Lewallen interview; "Cross Burned, as Another Effort Thwarted, Man Held," *Clinton Courier-News*, October 25, 1956, 1; Seivers, "Words of Discrimination," 151–52, 167–68.

144   *"What the hell":* Celdon Lewallen interview; "Cross Burned, as Another Effort Thwarted, Man Held," *Clinton Courier-News*, October 25, 1956, 1; Seivers, "Words of Discrimination," 151–52, 167–68.

144   *the cross burners headed:* "Cross Burned, as Another Effort Thwarted, Man Held," *Clinton Courier-News*, October 25, 1956, 1; Eleanor Davis interview; "2 Crosses in Clinton," *Decatur Daily*, May 13, 1949, 1; "Fiery Crosses Carry Notes for Lawyers," *Knoxville Journal*, May 13, 1949, 17; "Crosses Burned Near 2 Lawyers' Homes," *Knoxville News-Sentinel*, May 13, 1949, 17; Seivers, "Words of Discrimination," 169.

145   *Sidney was at a city council:* Ibid.; Davis, *Gifts Given*, 5–7; "Man Bound to Jury on Night-Riding; Say Cross Burned," *Oak Ridger*, October 26, 1956, 1–2.

145   *Glad Woodward's officers picked:* "Man Bound to Jury on Night-Riding; Say Cross Burned," *Oak Ridger*, October 26, 1956, 1–2.

146   *men knew the local klavern:* Buford Lewallen interview.

146   *mid-November, Buford was driving:* "Lewallen Charged by Olivers Man," *Oak Ridger*, November 20, 1956, 1; "Lewallen Waives Hearing in Roane," *Oak Ridger*, November 30, 1956, 6; Henry Trewhitt, "Protection, Hatred—Clinton Offers Both," *Tennessean*, November 25, 1956, 21; "Roane County Man Accuses Lewallen," *Clinton Courier-News*, November 21, 1956, 1.

FOURTEEN: RAMPING UP

147   *On November 3, he crashed:* Anderson County, *Anderson County Circuit Court Criminal Minutes*, vol. 9; "Kasper Trial for Sedition Set Nov. 5," *Clinton Courier-News*, November 1, 1956, 1; "Vote States Rights," *Clinton Courier-News*, November 1, 1956, 5; "Defense in Kasper trial Continues," *Clinton Courier-News*, November 15, 1956, 1, 4; "Kasper's Acquittal Sparks Courtroom Demonstration," *Clinton Courier-News*, November 21, 1956, 1; Horace V. Wells Jr., "Kasper Attacking Segregation Group," *Clinton Courier-News*, February 14, 1957, 1, 4; "Attorneys for 16 Fail to File Briefs," *Clinton Courier-News*, May 16, 1957, 8; Holden, publication unknown, December 5, 1956, pgs. unknown; "Testimony Begins in Kasper Trial," *Oak Ridger*, November 5, 1956, 1, 6; "Eight Testify in Kasper Trial," *Oak Ridger*, November 6, 1956, 1–2; "Kasper Testifies in Own Defense," *Oak Ridger*, November 8, 1956, 1, 12; "Trial May Extend into Saturday," *Oak Ridger*, November 9, 1956, 1, 6; Jim Ryan, "Kasper Trial Resumes Nov. 19," *Oak Ridger*, November 12, 1956, 1, 2; "Kasper and Controversy," *Oak Ridger*, November 12, 1956, 4; "Kasper Trial Resumes; 10 Testify," *Oak Ridger*, November 19, 1956, 1, 2; "Kasper Verdict Possible Today," November 20, 1956, 1, 2; "Acquit Kasper on Anderson County,"

Oak Ridger, November 21, 1956, 1; "Kasper Faces Trial Today," *Tennessean,* November 5, 1956, 15; Bill Rawlins, "Witnesses Call Kasper Inciter," *Tennessean,* November 6, 1956, 1, 4; "Kasper Sedition Trial Will Resume Today," *Tennessean,* November 7, 1956, 18; "Dodged Violence Kasper Testifies," *Tennessean,* November 8, 1956, 1; "Kasper Denies Charges on Stand," *Tennessean,* November 9, 1956, 14; "Witness Admits Rumors Linked Kasper, Negroes," *Tennessean,* November 10, 1956, 1–2; David Halberstam, "Kasper Silent on Negro Ties," *Tennessean,* November 11, 1956, 1, 15; "John Kasper Trial Opens Again Today," *Tennessean,* November 19, 1956, 16; Bill Rawlins, "27 Witnesses Defend Kasper," *Tennessean,* November 20, 1956, 9; Bill Rawlins, "Kasper Freed in 45 Minutes; Court Cheers," *Tennessean,* November 21, 1956, 1, 4.

147   *trial dragged on:* Ibid.

148   *Why didn't folks:* Ibid.

148   *the defense brought fifty-eight:* Ibid.

148   *"Things sure are":* Ibid.

148   *John Kasper, dapper:* Bill Rawlins, "Kasper Freed in 45 Minutes; Court Cheers," *Tennessean,* November 21, 1956, 1, 4.

148   *Don't send your kids:* Brittain, "A Case Study," 108; "Negroes Remain Home; Intimidation Increases at Clinton High School," *Clinton Courier-News,* November 29, 1956, 1; "Clinton High Negroes Stay Away from Classes Today," *Oak Ridger,* November 28, 1956, 1–2; "Negroes out for Second Day; Report Block," *Oak Ridger,* November 29, 1956, 1.

148   *Next came rocks:* Brittain, "A Case Study," 108; "Negroes Remain Home; Intimidation Increases at Clinton High School," *Clinton Courier-News,* November 29, 1956, 1; "Clinton High Negroes Stay Away from Classes Today," *Oak Ridger,* November 28, 1956, 1–2, "Negroes out for Second Day; Report Block," *Oak Ridger,* November 29, 1956, 1; "Court Fanned Racial Hatred, Kasper Says," *Knoxville News-Sentinel,* November 8, 1956, 18; "Two Shots Fired at Students' Home," *Knoxville News-Sentinel,* November 8, 1956, 18; "Probe Continues in Race Incidents," *Oak Ridger,* November 14, 1956, 5.

149   *after midnight on Tuesday, November 13:* "Two Shots Fired at Students' Home," *Knoxville News-Sentinel,* November 8, 1956, 18.

149   *Another night around that time:* Boyce and Levy, *This Promise of Change,* 104–6; Leo Burnett interview; Seivers, "Words of Discrimination," 208–10; Gail Ann Epps Upton interview.

149   *one white man who seemed:* Boyce and Levy, *This Promise of Change,* 104–6; Leo Burnett interview; Seivers, "Words of Discrimination," 208–10; Gail Ann Epps Upton interview.

149   *Had he been:* Gail Ann Epps Upton interview.

149   *It's so bad:* Leo Burnett interview; Seivers, "Words of Discrimination," 208–10.

150   *same ones who'd stood sneering:* Anderson, *The Children of the South,* 92–93; "Negroes Remain Home; Intimidation Increases at Clinton High School," *Clinton Courier-News,* November 29, 1956, 1, 4; Eleanor Davis interview; Sam F. Yette,

"Contempt Charged to Sixteen," *Afro-American*, December 15, 1956, 1, 6; "Clinton Too Much for Allen Family," *Afro-American*, December 15, 1956, 1, 6; United States District Court, "*Bullock*," July 15, 1957, 547–48.

150   *After school one day, seventeen-year-old:* United States District Court, "*Bullock*," July 15, 1957, 551.

150   *Betty Lou and the others:* Ibid.; Anderson, *The Children of the South*, 93–95; Brittain, "A Case Study," 98; Chappell, *A Stone of Hope*; Dailey, "Sex, Segregation and the Sacred after *Brown*," 124–25.

150   *girls launched their own organization:* Brittain, "A Case Study," 96–97; United States District Court, "*Bullock*," July 15, 1957, 498–517, 551, 595–96.

151   *following Monday, Betty Lou:* Brittain, "A Case Study," 96–97; "Witnesses Tell of Violence at Trial of Kasper and 14," *Clinton Courier-News*, July 18, 1957, 1, 6; "Kasper and Six Convicted; New Trial Possible," *East Tennessee Reporter*, July 26, 1957, 1; "Raymond Woods Hasn't Changed, He Tells Reporter," *East Tennessee Reporter*, July 26, 1957, 1; "Rev. Bullock Refutes 'Smear' News Stories," *East Tennessee Reporter*, July 26, 1957, 1; "Back Glances Show Incidents of Interest," *East Tennessee Reporter*, July 26, 1957, 2, 8; Charles Flowers, "Courtroom Packed for 'Windjamming,'" *Knoxville News-Sentinel*, July 22, 1957, 1; "'Keep Way of Life,' Clinton Defense Says," *Knoxville News-Sentinel*, July 22, 1957, 1; "Kasper Trial Resumes Today," *Oak Ridger*, November 19, 1956, 1–2; "White Youth Charter Issued," *Oak Ridger*, November 20, 1956, 2; Bill Rawlins, "27 Witnesses Defend Kasper," *Tennessean*, November 20, 1956, 9; United States District Court, "*Bullock*," July 15, 1957, 499–517, 563–69, 599–600.

151   *these girls, these country girls:* Anderson, *The Children of the South*, 93–95.

151   *Over fifty teenagers:* Ibid.; Brittain, "A Case Study," 97–98; Bill Rawlins, "27 Witnesses Defend Kasper," *Tennessean*, November 20, 1956, 9; United States District Court, "*Bullock*," July 15, 1957, 498–517, 557, 570–72, 592–93, 599–600.

152   *With their curly hair:* For generations, white Americans had used the ideal of pure white Southern womanhood to justify their brutal enforcement of their society's racial boundaries. The events of the 1950s—especially the growing popularity of rock 'n' roll with its Black roots and shrieking white female fans—had already made many of these whites nervous. Despite the efforts on the part of the NAACP to downplay white fears of Black male sexuality by focusing solely on desegregating the nation's classrooms, the burgeoning fight for civil rights in the classroom created a perfect storm. "White adults faced the stark reality that it was their own emboldened daughters who might well initiate the sexual 'mixing' or 'integration' in choosing boys to date or marry," historian Susan K. Cahn explains. The young women in Clinton hardly needed to say anything to remind white adults about this threat. Their sexually mature bodies spoke for them. They lived in adult female bodies, but they were also still children, minors who were the responsibility of and answerable to adults in their community. Cahn, *Sexual Reckonings*, 3–5, 243–44; see also Dailey, "Sex, Segregation and the Sacred after *Brown*"; Burlein, *Lift High the Cross*, 8–9.

152   *They canvassed:* United States District Court, *"Bullock,"* July 15, 1957, 521, 549.
152   *Principal D. J. Brittain Jr. called:* Anderson, *The Children of the South,* 61–62; Jo
Ann Allen Boyce interview; Boyce and Levy, *This Promise of Change,* 192; Bobby
Cain interview; Anna Theresser Caswell interview; McMillan, "The Ordeal,"
338–39; "The Inside Story of What Is Happening in Clinton," *Tri-State Defender,*
December 8, 1956, 1, 9.
152   *targeted any white student:* Anderson, *The Children of the South,* 61–62; Jo Ann
Allen Boyce interview; Bobby Cain interview; Anna Theresser Caswell interview;
"School Board Resignations Demanded by Group Opposed to Integration," *Clinton Courier-News,* September 20, 1956, 1, 6; Klarman, "Why Massive Resistance?"
in *Massive Resistance,* ed. Webb, 27; Seivers, "Words of Discrimination," 214–16;
Henry Trewhitt, "Protection, Hatred—Clinton Offers Both," *Tennessean,* November 25, 1956, 21; Gail Ann Epps Upton interview.
152   *One white boy twisted:* Anderson, *The Children of the South,* 61–62; Bobby Cain
interview; Robert Cain Sr. interview; Seivers, "Words of Discrimination," 214–
17; Eddie, Maurice, and Charles Soles interview.
154   *Gail Ann Epps was walking:* Ibid.; Gail Ann Epps Upton interview.
154   *One teacher stopped Bobby Cain:* Anderson, *The Children of the South,* 57–58;
Boyce and Levy, *This Promise of Change,* 197; Herd, "Then and Now," 48–50;
McMillan, "The Ordeal," 341; Regina Turner Smith interview; Eddie, Maurice,
and Charles Soles interview.
154   *Tennessee White Youth turned:* D. J. Brittain Jr. interview; "Negroes Remain Home;
Intimidation Increases at Clinton High School," *Clinton Courier-News,* November
29, 1956, 1, 4; "Police Hunt Vandals for Window Breaking at Lewallen-Miller's,"
Clinton Courier-News, November 29, 1956, 1; Anonymous (attributed to John
Kasper), *Clinton-Knox County Stars and Bars,* February 8, 1957, 1–3; Davis, *Gifts
Given,* 4; "School Authorities Make Attempt to Censor News," *East Tennessee Reporter,* March 1, 1957, 1; "Federal Court Increases Fear in Clinton, *East Tennessee
Reporter,* March 1, 1957, 1, 6; "Last High School 'Incident' Exaggerated, Brittain Asserts, *East Tennessee Reporter,* March 1, 1957, 1; "Report 2 More Clinton
Incidents," November 27, *Oak Ridger,* 1956, 1–2; United States District Court,
"McSwain," August 30, 1956, 23–36, September 6, 1956, 224–26.
155   *"I have been teaching":* Anderson, *The Children of the South,* 93–95; Sam F. Yette,
"Contempt Charged to Sixteen," *Afro-American,* December 15, 1956, 1, 6; "Clinton Too Much for Allen Family," *Afro-American,* December 15, 1956, 1, 6.
155   *November 27, a group:* Brittain, "A Case Study," 108; Bobby Cain interview; Robert Cain Sr. interview; "Negroes Remain Home; Intimidation Increases at Clinton High School," *Clinton Courier-News,* November 29, 1956, 1; "Report 2 More
Clinton Incidents," November 27, 1956, 1–2; "Clinton High Negroes Stay Away
from Classes Today," *Oak Ridger,* November 28, 1956, 1–2; "Negroes out for Second Day; Report Block," *Oak Ridger,* November 29, 1956, 1.
155   *Robert Thacker and William Latham also:* Ibid.
155   *"Do what you":* "Report 2 More Clinton Incidents," November 27, 1956, 1–2.

155   *Robert Thacker and William Latham left:* Brittain, "A Case Study," 108; Bobby
      Cain interview; Robert Cain Sr. interview; "Negroes Remain Home; Intimida-
      tion Increases at Clinton High School," *Clinton Courier-News*, November 29,
      1956, 1; "Report 2 More Clinton Incidents," November 27, 1956, 1–2; "Clinton
      High Negroes Stay Away from Classes Today," *Oak Ridger*, November 28, 1956,
      1–2; "Negroes out for Second Day; Report Block," *Oak Ridger*, November 29,
      1956, 1.

155   *nine of the ten remaining:* "Clinton High Negroes Stay Away from Classes Today,"
      Oak Ridger, November 28, 1956, 1–2.

156   *yet more people outside:* United States District Court, *"Bullock,"* December 4, 1956,
      13–27; *Tennessean*, November 30, 1956, pgs. unknown, Anna Holden Papers,
      Madison, WI.

156   *D. J. asked the police:* United States District Court, *"Bullock,"* December 4, 1956,
      13–27; *Tennessean*, November 30, 1956, pgs. unknown, Anna Holden Papers,
      Madison, WI.

156   *Thursday morning, Bobby Cain:* Brittain, "A Case Study," 108; Robert Cain Sr.
      interview; "Negroes Remain Home; Intimidation Increases at Clinton High
      School," *Clinton Courier-News*, November 29, 1956, 1, 4; "Clinton High Negroes
      Stay Away from Classes Today," *Oak Ridger*, November 28, 1956, 1–2, November
      29, 1956, 1.

156   *After the first bell:* D. J. Brittain Jr. interview; "Weekend Violence Brings Guards
      and Peace," *Clinton Courier-News*, September 6, 1956, 1; *Tennessean*, November
      30, 1956, pgs. unknown, Anna Holden Papers, Madison, WI; "Negro Students
      Are Still Absent," *Oak Ridger*, November 30, 1956, 1; "Tennessee Reports Segre-
      gation Tide Running Strongly in Month," *Southern School News*, December 1956,
      5, "School Boards and Schoolmen," *Southern School News*, December 1956, 5.

157   *"Well, it's about":* Ibid.

157   *"Just let things":* Ibid.

157   *Aghast, D. J. asked:* Ibid.

157   *"Oh no, we will not":* Ibid.

157   *D. J. refused:* Ibid.

157   *the Black students stayed away:* "Negro Students Are Still Absent," *Oak Ridger*, No-
      vember 30, 1956, 1.

FIFTEEN: WHO, THEN?

158   *the Allens' telephone jangled:* Boyce and Levy, *This Promise of Change*, 211–17;
      Cleveland, "Baptist Pastor," 21; United States District Court, *"Bullock,"* December
      4, 1956, 37–44, July 16, 1957, 847–49.

158   *Why in the world:* Ibid.

158   *"As long as they":* Ibid.

158   *Well, he certainly had:* Ibid.

159   *Just a few nights back:* Mattie Bell Henley interview; "Negroes Out for 2nd Day; Report Block," *Oak Ridger,* November 29, 1956, 1.

159   *Paul Turner told the Allens:* Boyce and Levy, *This Promise of Change,* 211–17; Cleveland, "Baptist Pastor," 21; United States District Court, *"Bullock,"* December 4, 1956, 37–44, July 16, 1957, 847–49.

159   *Paul had been wrestling:* Roy C. DeLamotte to Paul Turner, September 6, 1956, personal files of Steve Jones, Clinton, TN.

160   *Roy chastised Paul:* Ibid.

160   *white church members had scolded:* Fred and Violet Williams to Paul Turner, September 5, 1956, personal files of Steve Jones, Clinton, TN.

160   *Paul still had refused:* Paul Turner interview; Paul Turner to Frank Clement, November 19, 1956, Lee S. Greene Collection, Knoxville, TN.

160   *Paul tried to find:* Cleveland, "Baptist Pastor," 21; Adamson, "Two Religious Magazines," 12–13.

161   *before he called the Allens:* Cleveland, "Baptist Pastor," 23; Luke 10:30–37 (Revised Standard Version).

161   *about three types of Christians:* "Pastor Points Up Christian Responsibility," *Clinton Courier-News,* December 6, 1956, 3.

161   *one man pulled Paul:* Leo Burnett interview; Trezzvant Anderson, "They're Happy in Clinton, Tenn.," *Pittsburgh Courier,* August 3, 1957, 7.

162   *It would:* Leo Burnett interview.

162   *Paul reached out:* Boyce and Levy, *This Promise of Change,* 211–17; "Beating of Pastor by Mob Arouses Clinton; Carbide Worker Held," *Clinton Courier-News,* December 6, 1956, 1; "Harassment Drives Negro Students Out; Mob Action Closes School, Brings FBI," *Clinton Courier-News,* December 6, 1956, 1; Jim Ryan, "Anderson Board Asks New Federal Action," *Oak Ridger,* December 3, 1956, 1–2; "Racial Question Issue in Election," *Oak Ridger,* December 3, 1956, 1; "Complete Text of Letter to Brownell," *Oak Ridger,* December 3, 1956, 1.

162   *Monday morning, the Black families:* Ibid.

162   *the superintendent phoned:* Ibid.

163   *Oh yes, on a voluntary:* Ibid.

163   *the Allens called Paul:* Ibid.

163   *It was, he:* Ibid.

163   *now it was election day:* Anderson, *The Children of the South,* 19–20; Brittain, "A Case Study," 109; "Beating of Pastor by Mob Arouses Clinton; Carbide Worker Held," *Clinton Courier-News,* December 6, 1956, 1; "Harassment Drives Negro Students Out; Mob Action Closes School, Brings FBI," *Clinton Courier-News,* December 6, 1956, 1; *Clinton Courier-News,* December 6, 1956, 1; "Marshals FBI Told Halt Interference with Clinton School," *Clinton Courier-News,* December 6, 1956, 1; "Seeber Is Mayor; Many Vote," *Clinton Courier-News,* December 6, 1956, 1; Mattie Bell Henley interview; United States District Court, *"Bullock,"* December 4, 1956, 13–44, July 15, 1957, 605–17, July 16, 1957, 655–59, 820.

163   *two white men walking:* Ibid.

163   *"Preacher," Clyde Cook:* Ibid.

163   *"Sir, I do not":* Ibid.

163   *"If a lot of these":* Ibid.

164   *Paul hailed:* Ibid.

164   *Clyde and Alonzo stopped:* Anderson, *The Children of the South,* 19–20; Boyce and Levy, *This Promise of Change,* 211–17; Brittain, "A Case Study," 109; Robert Cain Sr. interview; "Integrated School at Clinton Reopens," *Knoxville News-Sentinel,* December 10, 1956, 1, 2; "Trial of 16 to Be Week of Jan. 28," *Knoxville News-Sentinel,* December 10, 1956, 1, 2; United States District Court, *"Bullock,"* December 4, 1956, 28–31, July 15, 1957, 634–44, July 16, 1957, 655–59, 718–26.

164   *Maurice Soles, the youngest:* Ibid.

164   *Clyde Cook and Alonzo Bullock joined:* Ibid.

164   *Sidney called out:* Ibid.

164   *What do you mean:* Ibid.

164   *"You will see":* Ibid.

164   *More protestors joined:* Ibid.

164   *Don't target me:* Ibid.

164   *I'll do:* Ibid.

164   *He took her to police:* Ibid.

164   *students and their escorts:* Ibid.

165   *If you bring:* Ibid.

165   *"Nigger lover!" others:* Ibid.

165   *substitute teacher stood:* Ibid.

165   *knot of white teens:* Ibid.

165   *segregationists taunted Paul:* Anderson, *The Children of the South,* 19–20; Brittain, "A Case Study," 109; publication unknown, December 5, 1956, pgs. unknown, Anna Holden Papers, Madison, WI; United States District Court, *"Bullock,"* December 4, 1956, 13–27, 37–44, July 16, 1957, 834.

165   *Would you write:* Ibid.

165   *The chief urged:* Anderson, *The Children of the South,* 19–20; Brittain, "A Case Study," 109; publication unknown, December 5, 1956, pgs. unknown, Anna Holden Papers, Madison, WI; United States District Court, *"Bullock,"* December 4, 1956, 13–27, 37–44, July 16, 1957, 834; Tennessee State Library and Archives, "World War II Draft Cards Young Men, 1940–1947," digital image, s.v. "Clyde Cook," Ancestry.com; ibid., digital image, s.v. "Paul Winston Turner," Ancestry.com.

166   *Then: "Watch out!":* Anderson, *The Children of the South,* 19–20; Brittain, "A Case Study," 109; publication unknown, December 5, 1956, pgs. unknown, Anna Holden Papers, Madison, WI; United States District Court, *"Bullock,"* December 4, 1956, 13–27, 37–44, July 16, 1957, 834.

166   *Did someone have a knife?:* Anderson, *The Children of the South,* 19–20; Brittain, "A Case Study," 109; publication unknown, December 5, 1956, pgs. unknown,

Anna Holden Papers, Madison, WI; United States District Court, "*Bullock*," December 4, 1956, 37–44, July 17, 1957, 894; Williams et al., "Clinton and the Law."

166 *"Nothing much I could do"*: Anderson, *The Children of the South*, 19–20; Brittain, "A Case Study," 109; publication unknown, December 5, 1956, pgs. unknown, Anna Holden Papers, Madison, WI; United States District Court, "*Bullock*," December 4, 1956, 37–44, July 17, 1957, 894; Williams et al., "Clinton and the Law"; "'Meddler' at Trial Sentenced to 30 Days," *Knoxville Journal*, December 7, 1956, 1, 9.

166 *Now the preacher:* Anderson, *The Children of the South*, 19–20; Brittain, "A Case Study," 109; publication unknown, December 5, 1956, pgs. unknown, Anna Holden Papers, Madison, WI; United States District Court, "*Bullock*," December 4, 1956, 37–44, July 17, 1957, 894; Williams et al., "Clinton and the Law"; "'Meddler' at Trial Sentenced to 30 Days," *Knoxville Journal*, December 7, 1956, 1, 9.

166 *"Kill the ——":* "Clinton High School Closed," *Oak Ridger*, December 4, 1956, 1–2.

166 *CBS news reporter:* Anderson, *The Children of the South*, 18–20; Brittain, "A Case Study," 109, 227–28; "Beating of Pastor by Mob Arouses Clinton; Carbide Worker Held," *Clinton Courier-News*, December 6, 1956, 1; "Harassment Drives Negro Students Out; Mob Action Closes School, Brings FBI," *Clinton Courier-News*, December 6, 1956, 1; "Cook Fined for Attack on Turner," *Clinton Courier-News*, January 3, 1957, 1, 6; Jerry Hamilton interview; publication unknown, December 5, 1956, pgs. unknown, Anna Holden Papers, Madison, WI; Clinton High School Closed," *Oak Ridger*, December 4, 1956, 1–2; United States District Court, "*Bullock*," December 4, 1956, 37–44, July 17, 1957, 897, 929–30, 953.

166 *"What are they doing":* Anderson, *The Children of the South*, 19–20; Brittain, "A Case Study," 109; "Beating of Pastor by Mob Arouses Clinton; Carbide Worker Held," *Clinton Courier-News*, December 6, 1956, 1; "Harassment Drives Negro Students Out; Mob Action Closes School, Brings FBI," *Clinton Courier-News*, December 6, 1956, 1; "Cook Fined for Attack on Turner," *Clinton Courier-News*, January 3, 1957, 1, 6; publication unknown, December 5, 1956, pgs. unknown, Anna Holden Papers, Madison, WI; United States District Court, "*Bullock*," December 4, 1956, 37–44, July 17, 1957, 929–30, 953; Williams et al., "Clinton and the Law."

166 *she'd save her pastor:* Ibid.

166 *Stop! she cried:* Ibid.

167 *The men ignored her:* Ibid.

167 *two police officers arrived:* Don Cravens, Getty Images; Clinton High School Closed," *Oak Ridger*, December 4, 1956, 1–2; "Federals Poised to Make Clinton Arrests," *Oak Ridger*, December 5, 1956, 1.

167 *officers arrested Clyde Cook:* Anderson, *The Children of the South*, 19–20; Brittain, "A Case Study," 109; "Beating of Pastor by Mob Arouses Clinton; Carbide Worker Held," *Clinton Courier-News*, December 6, 1956, 1; "Harassment Drives Negro Students Out; Mob Action Closes School, Brings FBI," *Clinton*

Courier-News, December 6, 1956, 1; "15 Held; Contempt Is Charged," *Clinton Courier-News*, December 6, 1956, 1, 3; "Cook Fined for Attack on Turner," *Clinton Courier-News*, January 3, 1957, 1, 6; publication unknown, December 5, 1956, pgs. unknown, Anna Holden Papers, Madison, WI; United States District Court, *"Bullock,"* December 4, 1956, 37–44, July 17, 1957, 929–30, 953.

167   *Principal D. J. Brittain Jr. was meeting:* Anderson, *The Children of the South,* 19–20; D. J. Brittain Jr. interview; Brittain, "A Case Study," 109.

167   *I'm here to "get":* Ibid.

167   *The teens scuffled:* Ibid.

168   *Student Council met:* Anderson, *The Children of the South,* 19–20; D. J. Brittain Jr. interview; Brittain, "A Case Study," 109; "Beating of Pastor by Mob Arouses Clinton; Carbide Worker Held," *Clinton Courier-News,* December 6, 1956, 1; "Harassment Drives Negro Students Out; Mob Action Closes School, Brings FBI," *Clinton Courier-News,* December 6, 1956, 1; "Students and Faculty Call for Assistance," *Clinton Courier-News,* December 6, 1956, 4, December 13, 1956, 1; Jerry Shattuck interview; "Student Council Asks for Quick Action," *Oak Ridger,* December 4, 1956, 1; Seivers, "Words of Discrimination," 82; "Tennessee Community in National Spotlight," *Southern School News,* January 1957, 6–7; "The True Face of Clinton," *Time,* December 17, 1956, 21–22.

168   *faculty council met:* "Harassment Drives Negro Students Out; Mob Action Closes School, Brings FBI," *Clinton Courier-News,* December 6, 1956, 1; "Students and Faculty Call for Assistance," *Clinton Courier-News,* December 6, 1956, 4.

168   *on Tuesday afternoon, a delegation:* New York Post, December 6, 1956, pgs. unknown, Anna Holden Papers, Madison, WI; "Clinton High School Closed," *Oak Ridger,* December 4, 1956, 1.

169   *they were electrified:* Anderson, *The Children of the South,* 18–20; "Beating of Pastor by Mob Arouses Clinton; Carbide Worker Held," *Clinton Courier-News,* December 6, 1956, 1; "Harassment Drives Negro Students Out; Mob Action Closes School, Brings FBI," *Clinton Courier-News,* December 6, 1956, 1; Horace V. Wells Jr., "As We See It!" *Clinton Courier-News,* December 6, 1956, 1; "Seeber Is Mayor; Many Vote," *Clinton Courier-News,* December 6, 1956, 1; publication unknown, December 5, 1956, pgs. unknown, Anna Holden Papers, Madison, WI; "Clinton High School Closed," *Oak Ridger,* December 4, 1956, 1–2; "Federals Poised to Make Clinton Arrests," *Oak Ridger,* December 5, 1956, 1.

169   *votes were tallied:* "Lewallen Wins Clinton Race," *Knoxville Journal,* December 8, 1954, 1; "Clinton High School Closed," *Oak Ridger,* December 4, 1956, 1–2.

169   *"I'm going to bed":* Publication unknown, December 5, 1956, pgs. unknown, Anna Holden Papers, Madison, WI; "Clinton High School Closed," *Oak Ridger,* December 4, 1956, 1–2; "Federals Poised to Make Clinton Arrests," *Oak Ridger,* December 5, 1956, 1.

169   *"We would have all":* Jane Turner to her family, December 11, 1956, personal files of Steve Jones, Clinton, TN; "Federals Poised to Make Clinton Arrests," *Oak Ridger,* December 5, 1956, 1.

170 *That very night:* Jo Ann Allen Boyce interview; Anna Theresser Caswell interview; "Blast Rocks Oliver Springs," *Clinton Courier-News,* December 6, 1956, 6; "Federals Poised to Make Clinton Arrests," *Oak Ridger,* December 5, 1956, 1; "Dynamite Blast in Olivers," *Oak Ridger,* December 5, 1956, 1.

170 *Then the Klan:* Ibid.

170 *Herbert, Josephine, and Jo Ann:* Jo Ann Allen Boyce interview; Anna Theresser Caswell interview; "Blast Rocks Oliver Springs," *Clinton Courier-News,* December 6, 1956, 6; "Federals Poised to Make Clinton Arrests," *Oak Ridger,* December 5, 1956, 1; "Dynamite Blast in Olivers," *Oak Ridger,* December 5, 1956, 1; Boyce and Levy, *This Promise of Change,* 221–22.

170 *Josephine Allen was finished:* Sam F. Yette, "Allen Family Gets Out," *Baltimore Afro-American,* December 8, 1956, 1, 15; Jo Ann Allen Boyce interview; Boyce and Levy, *This Promise of Change,* 186–87, 248–49; "CHS Reopens; Students Warned Against Disorder," *Clinton Courier-News,* December 13, 1956, 1; "Ex-Clinton Girl, 16, Finds Peace in L.A.," *Pittsburgh Courier,* December 29, 1956, 7.

171 *"Jo Ann and I":* "Here's Why Jo Ann Allen Didn't Go to Clinton High School This Morning," *Chicago Defender,* December 10, 1956, quoted in Boyce and Levy, *This Promise of Change,* 254–55.

171 *"I'll be glad":* Jo Ann Allen Boyce interview; Boyce and Levy, *This Promise of Change,* 248–53; "CHS Reopens; Students Warned Against Disorder," *Clinton Courier-News,* December 13, 1956, 1; "Ex-Clinton Girl, 16, Finds Peace in L.A.," *Pittsburgh Courier,* December 29, 1956, 7.

171 *she struggled to make eye:* Jo Ann Allen Boyce interview; Boyce and Levy, *This Promise of Change,* 248–53; "CHS Reopens; Students Warned Against Disorder," *Clinton Courier-News,* December 13, 1956, 1; "Ex-Clinton Girl, 16, Finds Peace in L.A.," *Pittsburgh Courier,* December 29, 1956, 7.

SIXTEEN: TICK. TICK. TICK.

172 *man from the telephone: New York Post,* December 6, 1956, pgs. unknown, Anna Holden Papers, Madison, WI; "Federals Poised to Make Clinton Arrests," *Oak Ridger,* December 5, 1956, 1; Jim Ryan, "16 Arrested for Clinton Interference," *Oak Ridger,* December 6, 1956, 1; "School Monday If All Goes Well," *Oak Ridger,* December 6, 1956, 1, 4.

172 *reporters had rushed:* Cleveland, "Baptist Pastor," 22; "Clinton Again in Newsmags Over School," *Clinton Courier-News,* December 13, 1956, 1; "Flood of Letters, Wires Praises, Condemns Baptist Minister Here," *Clinton Courier-News,* December 13, 1956, 1, 4; Bernice Cofer of the Baptist Home Mission Board to Paul Turner, December 7, 1957, personal files of Steve Jones, Clinton, TN.

173 *Black families in Little Rock:* Jone R. Cotton to Paul Turner, July 24, 1956, William and Esther Roberts to Paul Turner, December 6, 1956, personal files of Steve Jones, Clinton, TN.

173 *"We are proud":* Jone R. Cotton to Paul Turner, July 24, 1956, William and

Esther Roberts to Paul Turner, December 6, 1956, personal files of Steve Jones, Clinton, TN.

173   *John Lewis:* Boyce and Levy, *This Promise of Change*, 259–60.

173   *officers' first arrest:* Jim Ryan, "16 Arrested for Clinton Interference," *Oak Ridger*, December 6, 1956, 1; "School Monday If All Goes Well," *Oak Ridger*, December 6, 1956, 1, 4.

174   *They found William:* Jim Ryan, "16 Arrested for Clinton Interference," *Oak Ridger*, December 6, 1956, 1; "School Monday If All Goes Well," *Oak Ridger*, December 6, 1956, 1, 4; "Beating of Pastor by Mob Arouses Clinton; Carbide Worker Held," *Clinton Courier-News*, December 6, 1956, 1; "Harassment Drives Negro Students Out; Mob Action Closes School, Brings FBI," *Clinton Courier-News*, December 6, 1956, 1; "15 Held; Contempt is Charged," *Clinton Courier-News*, December 6, 1956, 1, 3; "Marshals, FBI Told to Halt Interference with Clinton School," *Clinton Courier-News*, December 6, 1956, 1; "16 Racists Ask Single, Jury Trials," *Clinton Courier-News*, December 13, 1956, 1, 4; "Cook Fined for Attack on Turner," *Clinton Courier-News*, January 3, 1957, 1, 6; *New York Post*, December 6, 1956, pgs. unknown, Anna Holden Papers, Madison, WI; "Integration Row Halts as Clinton Is Left Alone," *Knoxville News-Sentinel*, August 31, 1956, 2; "Letter to the Editor," *East Tennessee Reporter*, February 22, 1957, 2.

175   *everyone except for Lawrence:* "Beating of Pastor by Mob Arouses Clinton; Carbide Worker Held," *Clinton Courier-News*, December 6, 1956, 1; "Harassment Drives Negro Students Out; Mob Action Closes School, Brings FBI," *Clinton Courier-News*, December 6, 1956, 1; "15 Held; Contempt is Charged," *Clinton Courier-News*, December 6, 1956, 1, 3; "Marshals, FBI Told to Halt Interference with Clinton School," *Clinton Courier-News*, December 6, 1956, 1; "16 Racists Ask Single, Jury Trials," *Clinton Courier-News*, December 13, 1956, 1, 4; "Cook Fined for Attack on Turner," *Clinton Courier-News*, January 3, 1957, 1, 6; "Kasper Ranked with Subversives," *East Tennessee Reporter*, February 8, 1957, 1, 4; "Suspension of Student Appealed to School Board," *East Tennessee Reporter*, February 15, 1957, 1; "New School Incidents Calmed by Brittain; Threatens Expulsion," *East Tennessee Reporter*, February 15, 1957, 1; "Federal Court Increases Fear in Clinton," *East Tennessee Reporter*, March 1, 1957, 1, 6; *New York Post*, December 6, 1956, pgs. unknown, Anna Holden Papers, Madison, WI.

175   *families and friends:* Ibid.; U.S. Census Bureau, "1940 United States Federal Census," digital image, s.v. "Mary Nell Collins," Ancestry.com.

175   *Journalists and cameramen:* Jim Ryan, "16 Arrested for Clinton Interference," *Oak Ridger*, December 6, 1956, 1; "School Monday If All Goes Well," *Oak Ridger*, December 6, 1956, 1, 4.

175   *In Knoxville, the Clinton defendants:* Emilie E. Powell, "Excitement at Court Akin to Sheer Bedlam," *Knoxville Journal*, December 7, 1956, 1, 4; "16 Racists Ask Single, Jury Trials," *Clinton Courier-News*, December 13, 1956, 1; "Knox Man Jailed for Contempt After Literature Passed," *Clinton Courier-News*, December 13, 1956, 1; "Integrated School at Clinton Reopens," *Knoxville News-Sentinel*, December 10,

1956, 1, 2; "Trial of 16 to Be Week of Jan. 28," *Knoxville News-Sentinel*, December 10, 1956, 1, 2; Jim Ryan, "16 Arrested for Clinton Interference," *Oak Ridger*, December 6, 1956, 1; "School Monday If All Goes Well," *Oak Ridger*, December 6, 1956, 1, 4.

176   *Fifty-eight families:* "92 FBI Agents in Clinton, Dobbs Says," *Knoxville News-Sentinel*, October 1, 1957, 2.

176   *Paul returned:* Anderson, *The Children of the South*, 20; Cleveland, "Baptist Pastor," 21–23; "Says No Color Line at Cross," *Clinton Courier-News*, December 13, 1956, 4; "Clinton Being Featured on TV by Murrow," *Clinton Courier-News*, December 13, 1956, 4; Hechinger, "Clinton and the Law," 5; Williams et al., "Clinton and the Law."

177   *"Either we assert":* Ibid.

177   *"Dear Paul":* "First Baptist Men Honor Their Pastor with Christmas Gift," *Clinton Courier-News*, December 27, 1956, 2; First Baptist Church of Clinton, TN, "Recommendations of the Deacon Board, First Baptist Church," April 21, 1957, First Baptist Church of Clinton, TN: Records 1840–1990; J. H. Turner to Paul Turner, December 4, 1956, December 6, 1956, December 20, 1956, personal files of Steve Jones, Clinton, TN; Dail Skaggs, Mary Jane Martin, and Antoinette Martinez interview; unsigned to Paul Turner, undated, personal files of Steve Jones, Clinton, TN.

177   *Paul also worried about:* Cleveland, "Baptist Pastor," 22; "Flood of Letters, Wires Praises, Condemns Baptist Minister Here," *Clinton Courier-News*, December 13, 1956, 1, 4; "Says No Color Line at Cross," *Clinton Courier-News*, December 13, 1956, 4.

177   *pastor in Knoxville announced:* Charles Trentham interview; James Carty, "Clinton Pastor Gets Call Here," *Tennessean*, September 25, 1958, 25.

177   *D. J. reopened Clinton High:* "Integrated School at Clinton Reopens," *Knoxville News-Sentinel*, December 10, 1956, 1, 2; "Trial of 16 to Be Week of Jan. 28," *Knoxville News-Sentinel*, December 10, 1956, 1, 2; Seivers, "Words of Discrimination," 191–92; "Tennessee Community in National Spotlight," *Southern School News*, January 1957, 6–7.

177   *Eight of the Black teenagers:* Mikki Marlowe, "Staff Report on Clinton High School Student Visit," December 1956, Tennessee Virtual Archive.

178   *the kids and their new friends:* Ibid.; Anna Theresser Caswell interview.

179   *their parents met:* Ibid.

179   *a gaggle of white elementary school:* "Anti-Integration Blast Rocks Clinton Negroes," *Cavalier Daily*, September 28, 1956, 1, 4; "Blast Remains a Mystery to Local Officers," *Clinton Courier-News*, October 4, 1956, 1; "Dynamite, Caps, Fuse Found by Marlow Children," *Clinton Courier-News*, December 20, 1956, 4; Horace V. Wells Jr., "As We See It!," *Clinton Courier-News*, January 3, 1957, 1; publication unknown, December 5, 1956, pgs. unknown, Anna Holden Papers, Madison, WI; "Blast Set Off by Clinton Home," *Tennessean*, September 27, 1956, 1.

179   *at 2:30:* "Seaboard Citizens Council Building Ripped by Blast Shortly After

Meeting," *Clinton Courier-News*, January 3, 1957, 1, 3; publication unknown, December 5, 1956, pgs. unknown, Anna Holden Papers, Madison, WI.

179   *A fourth detonated:* "Seaboard Citizens Council Building Ripped by Blast Shortly After Meeting," *Clinton Courier-News*, January 3, 1957, 1, 3; publication unknown, December 5, 1956, pgs. unknown, Anna Holden Papers, Madison, WI.

179   *John had rented:* "Negro Students Are Still Absent," *Oak Ridger*, November 30, 1956, 1; Clinton High School Closed," *Oak Ridger*, December 4, 1956, 1–2; Federal Bureau of Investigation, "Citizens' Council Movement."

180   *After the explosion:* "John Kasper Is Now 'Big Joke'?" *Baltimore Afro-American*, March 30, 1957, 5.

180   *when he attended:* Federal Bureau of Investigation, "Citizens' Council Movement"; "Guard's Intervention at Clinton Defended," *Knoxville Journal*, March 31, 1957, 14-A; "Atlantan Discredits Kasper Et Al," *Knoxville Journal*, March 31, 1957, 14-A; "KKK Imperial Wizard Visits in Anderson Area," *East Tennessee Reporter*, April 5, 1957, 1, 4.

180   *someone tried to blow up:* "Explosion on Railroad Jars Clinton Again," *Clinton Courier-News*, January 10, 1957, 4.

181   *11:30 p.m.:* "Another Blast Rocks Clinton," *Clinton Courier-News*, January 17, 1957, 1.

SEVENTEEN: ALFRED WILLIAMS

182   *Alfred Williams didn't fit in:* Alabama, "Alabama Deaths and Burials Index," digital image, s.v. "Marie Ralston," Ancestry.com; "Royston, Marie," *Anniston, Alabama, City Directory 1945*, 403; "Royster, Marie Mrs. I," *Anniston, Alabama, City Directory 1948*, 373; Eddie, Maurice, and Charles Soles interview; Maurice Soles interview; U.S. Census Bureau, "1940 United States Federal Census," digital image, s.v. "Marie Royston," Ancestry.com; Alfred Williams interview.

183   *men in the Williams/Royston:* "No Air of Great Joy Among Clinton Folks," *Baltimore Afro-American*, December 11, 1956, 12; Robert Brannon interview; "Negro Boy Expelled by Board," *Knoxville Journal*, February 22, 1957, 7; Eddie, Maurice, and Charles Soles interview; "Williams, Steve," *Anniston, Alabama, City Directory 1929*, 300; Tennessee State Library and Archives, "Tennessee Death Records, 1908–1965," digital image, s.v. "Steve Williams," Ancestry.com; U.S. Census Bureau, "1920 United States Federal Census," digital image, s.v. "Steve Williams," Ancestry.com, "1930 United States Federal Census," digital image, s.v. "Steve Williams," Ancestry.com; Alfred Williams interview.

183   *Alfred had failed:* "Explosion on Railroad Jars Clinton Again," *Clinton Courier-News*, January 10, 1957, 4; "Negro Boy Expelled by Board," *Knoxville Journal*, February 22, 1957, 7; "Reinstatement of Student Sought," *Knoxville News-Sentinel*, February 21, 1957, 9; Eddie, Maurice, and Charles Soles interview; Maurice Soles interview; Alfred Williams interview, "Larry Graham Makes Cage History in Tennessee," *Afro-American*, March 9, 1957, 12.

184   *Alfred had intended:* Staley Opotowsky, "The Battle of Clinton," *Afro Magazine Section*, March 2, 1957, 3–4.

184   *Wednesday, January 9, two effigies:* Brittain, "A Case Study," 173–81; "Two 'Dummies' Hung at School," *Clinton Courier-News*, January 10, 1957, 1; "Boys Caught After Shoe Store Theft," *Clinton Courier-News*, January 10, 1957, 6; "Juveniles Continue Crime Spree," *Clinton Courier-News*, January 17, 1957, 1, 4; "Six Clinton Boys Held in Thefts," *Knoxville Journal*, January 11, 1957, 1, 11; "Gang Builds Up Tension in Clinton," *Knoxville Journal*, February 24, 1957, 1; "Find 2 Effigies Hanging at Clinton High School," *Oak Ridger*, January 10, 1957, 1; "Arrest of 6 in Clinton Solves Several Crimes," *Oak Ridger*, January 11, 1957, 1, 6; Alfred Williams interview.

184   *two different groups:* Ibid.; "School Authorities Make Attempt to Censor News," *East Tennessee Reporter*, March 1, 1957, 1; "Federal Court Increases Fear in Clinton, *East Tennessee Reporter*, March 1, 1957, 1, 6; "Last High School 'Incident' Exaggerated, Brittain Asserts," *East Tennessee Reporter*, March 1, 1957, 1.

185   *police let the girls:* Ibid; "Youth Gets Two Year Sentence," *Clinton Courier-News*, January 24, 1957, 1.

185   *James Dale Patmore, out on:* "Youth Gets Two Year Sentence," *Clinton Courier-News*, January 24, 1957, 1; "Licensed to Wed," *Knoxville News-Sentinel*, June 7, 1945, 11; "Pierce, Fred B.," *Knoxville News-Sentinel*, January 4, 1985, 19; Social Security Administration, "Social Security Applications and Claims Index, 1936–2007," digital image, s.v. "Hazel Ruby Grouse," digital image, s.v. "James Dale Patmore," Ancestry.com; U.S. Census Bureau, "1950 United States Federal Census," digital image, s.v. "Ruby Pierce," Ancestry.com.

185   *Jimmy and three other:* "Jordonia Aide Beaten in Escape Try," *Nashville Banner*, March 2, 1957, 4; "Boy Seized at Clinton Cited Again," *Knoxville Journal*, March 2, 1957, 1, 6; Nellie Kenyon, "Escape Effort Brewed a Week," *Tennessean*, March 2, 1957, 3.

186   *Jimmy told a reporter:* "Jordonia Aide Beaten in Escape Try," *Nashville Banner*, March 2, 1957, 4.

186   *why had he:* Ibid.

186   *No, Jordonia:* Ibid.

186   *"I always have an urge":* Ibid.

186   *In punishment:* Ibid.; "Boy Seized at Clinton Cited Again," *Knoxville Journal*, March 2, 1957, 1, 6; Nellie Kenyon, "Escape Effort Brewed a Week," *Tennessean*, March 2, 1957, 3.

186   *police chief was amazed:* "Juveniles Continue Crime Spree," *Clinton Courier-News*, January 17, 1957, 1, 4; "School Authorities Make Attempt to Censor News," *East Tennessee Reporter*, March 1, 1957, 1; "Federal Court Increases Fear in Clinton, *East Tennessee Reporter*, March 1, 1957, 1, 6; "Last High School 'Incident' Exaggerated, Brittain Asserts," *East Tennessee Reporter*, March 1, 1957, 1.

186   *lawyer connected:* Ibid.

186   *Jimmy Patmore was released:* "Clinton Convict Stabs Guard," *Knoxville Journal*,

December 13, 1961, 18; "Hunger Strikers at Penitentiary Drop to Four," March 20, 1963, 16; "Clinton Convict Stabs Prison Guard," *Knoxville News-Sentinel*, December 12, 1961, 24; "3 'Fasters' Were Charged Here," *Knoxville News-Sentinel*, March 16, 1963, 12.

187   *Thursday, January 31, Alfred:* "Negro CHS Student Is Expelled," *Clinton Courier-News*, February 28, 1957, 8; "Racial Clash in School," *East Tennessee Reporter*, February 8, 1957, 1, 4; "School Board Members Claim Ignorance of Law," *East Tennessee Reporter*, February 22, 1957, 1; "Ward Family Planning to Leave," *East Tennessee Reporter*, February 22, 1957, 4; Maurice Soles interview; Alfred Williams interview.

187   *"There he goes":* "Negro CHS Student Is Expelled," *Clinton Courier-News*, February 28, 1957, 8; "School Board Members Claim Ignorance of Law," *East Tennessee Reporter*, February 22, 1957, 1; "Ward Family Planning to Leave," *East Tennessee Reporter*, February 22, 1957, 4.

187   *"Here I go":* Ibid.

187   *he looked down the intersecting:* Brittain, "A Case Study," 181; "School Board Members Claim Ignorance of Law," *East Tennessee Reporter*, February 22, 1957, 1; "Ward Family Planning to Leave," *East Tennessee Reporter*, February 22, 1957, 4; Jean-Jacques, "Love Overcomes a Young Man's Anger"; Regina Turner Smith interview; Eddie Soles interview; Eddie, Maurice, and Charles Soles interview; Maurice Soles interview; Alfred Williams interview.

187   *Dan Ward—a white:* Ibid.; "Racial Clash in School," *East Tennessee Reporter* February 8, 1957, 1, 4; "Negro Boy Expelled by Board," *Knoxville Journal*, February 22, 1957, 7.

187   *"Get him!":* Ibid.

187   *"I know who":* Ibid.

187   *Alfred noticed the paper boy:* "Racial Clash in School," *East Tennessee Reporter*, February 8, 1957, 1, 4; Alfred Williams interview.

187   *If you come up:* Ibid.

187   *"He waved that knife":* Ibid.

187   *preparing the newspaper's:* "Racial Clash in School," *East Tennessee Reporter*, February 8, 1957, 1, 4; "School Authorities Make Attempt to Censor News," *East Tennessee Reporter*, March 1, 1957, 1; "Federal Court Increases Fear in Clinton, *East Tennessee Reporter*, March 1, 1957, 1, 6; "Last High School 'Incident' Exaggerated, Brittain Asserts," *East Tennessee Reporter*, March 1, 1957, 1.

187   *wasn't the first time:* Ibid.

187   *That's true, a third:* Ibid.

187   *"Something happens":* Ibid.

187   *Regina Turner and Gail Ann Epps had:* Brittain, "A Case Study," 181; "School Board Members Claim Ignorance of Law," *East Tennessee Reporter*, February 22, 1957, 1; "Ward Family Planning to Leave," *East Tennessee Reporter*, February 22, 1957, 4; Jean-Jacques, "Love Overcomes a Young Man's Anger"; Regina Turner

Smith interview; Eddie Soles interview; Eddie, Maurice, and Charles Soles interview; Maurice Soles interview; Alfred Williams interview.

187 *teachers broke up:* Ibid; "Racial Clash in School," *East Tennessee Reporter*, February 8, 1957, 1, 4.

189 *teachers quickly figured:* "Racial Clash in School," *East Tennessee Reporter*, February 8, 1957, 1, 4.

189 *Dan Ward and Jimmy Ray McGill knew:* Ibid.; Brittain, "A Case Study," 181; "School Board Members Claim Ignorance of Law," *East Tennessee Reporter*, February 22, 1957, 1; "Ward Family Planning to Leave," *East Tennessee Reporter*, February 22, 1957, 4; Jean-Jacques, "Love Overcomes a Young Man's Anger"; Regina Turner Smith interview; Eddie Soles interview; Eddie, Maurice, and Charles Soles interview; Maurice Soles interview; Alfred Williams interview.

189 *That's when I hit:* "Racial Clash in School," *East Tennessee Reporter*, February 8, 1957, 1, 4.

189 *wasn't a case:* Ibid.

189 *parents of Dan and Jimmy Ray:* Ibid.; "Suspension of Student Appealed to School Board," *East Tennessee Reporter*, February 15, 1957, 1; "New School Incidents Calmed by Brittain; Threatens Expulsion," *East Tennessee Reporter*, February 15, 1957, 1.

189 *next morning, Assistant Principal Juanita:* "Negro CHS Student Is Expelled," *Clinton Courier-News*, February 28, 1957, 8; "Racial Clash in School," *East Tennessee Reporter*, February 8, 1957, 1, 4; "Suspension of Student Appealed to School Board," *East Tennessee Reporter*, February 15, 1957, 1; "New School Incidents Calmed by Brittain; Threatens Expulsion," *East Tennessee Reporter*, February 15, 1957, 1; "School Authorities Make Attempt to Censor News," *East Tennessee Reporter*, March 1, 1957, 1; "Federal Court Increases Fear in Clinton, *East Tennessee Reporter*, March 1, 1957, 1, 6; "Last High School 'Incident' Exaggerated, Brittain Asserts," *East Tennessee Reporter*, March 1, 1957, 1; Alfred Williams interview.

190 *"Alf stood":* Trezzvant W. Anderson, "Clinton, Tenn. Integration Battleground," *Pittsburgh Courier*, June 22, 1957, 38.

190 *same night as the fight:* "Dynamite Is Shot Thursday on Eagle Bend," *Clinton Courier-News*, February 7, 1957, 1; "Racial Clash in School," *East Tennessee Reporter*, February 8, 1957, 1, 4; "Another Dynamite Charge Set Off in City," *East Tennessee Reporter*, February 8, 1957, 1.

190 *white merchants downtown:* Horace V. Wells Jr., "As We See It!" *Clinton Courier-News*, February 7, 1957, 1, 4.

191 *10:15 on Valentine's:* "Police Press Investigation of Explosion That Rocked Clinton," *Clinton Courier-News*, February 21, 1957, 1, 6; "Police Continue Investigation of Explosion," *Clinton Courier-News*, February 21, 1957, 1; Horace V. Wells Jr., "As We See It!" *Clinton Courier-News*, February 21, 1957, 1; "School Board Members Claim Ignorance of Law," *East Tennessee Reporter*, February 22, 1957, 1; "Dynamite Blast on Foley Hill Routs Residents," February 22, 1957, 1,

6; Harold Jones, "Blast Rips Negro Homes in Clinton," *Knoxville News-Sentinel,* February 15, 1957, 1, 8.

191   *white intruder had pulled:* Ibid.

191   *blast threw pieces:* Ibid.

191   *"Is this happening":* "Police Press Investigation of Explosion That Rocked Clinton," *Clinton Courier-News,* February 21, 1957, 1, 6; "Police Continue Investigation of Explosion," *Clinton Courier-News,* February 21, 1957, 1; Horace V. Wells Jr., "As We See It!" *Clinton Courier-News,* February 21, 1957, 1.

191   *"Somebody will be killed":* "Dynamite Blast on Foley Hill Routs Residents," *East Tennessee Reporter,* February 22, 1957, 1, 6.

192   *men of the Hill demanded:* Harold Jones, "Blast Rips Negro Homes in Clinton," *Knoxville News-Sentinel,* February 15, 1957, 1, 8.

192   *Anderson County school board met:* "School Board Says No to Resolution," *Clinton Courier-News,* February 21, 1957, 1; "School Board Sets Hearing on Expulsion," *Clinton Courier-News,* February 21, 1957, 1; "Negro CHS Student Is Expelled," February 28, 1957, 8; "Suspension of Student Appealed to School Board," *East Tennessee Reporter,* February 15, 1957, 1; "New School Incidents Calmed by Brittain; Threatens Expulsion," *East Tennessee Reporter,* February 15, 1957, 1; "School Authorities Make Attempt to Censor News," *East Tennessee Reporter,* March 1, 1957, 1; "Federal Court Increases Fear in Clinton, *East Tennessee Reporter,* March 1, 1957, 1, 6; "Last High School 'Incident' Exaggerated, Brittain Asserts," *East Tennessee Reporter,* March 1, 1957, 1; "Negro Boy Expelled by Board," *Knoxville Journal,* February 22, 1957, 7.

192   *Juanita Moser, who had suspended:* Ibid.; "Racial Clash in School," *East Tennessee Reporter,* February 8, 1957, 1, 4; "School Board Members Claim Ignorance of Law," *East Tennessee Reporter,* February 22, 1957, 1; "Ward Family Planning to Leave," *East Tennessee Reporter,* February 22, 1957, 4; Alfred Williams interview.

192   *Alfred's witnesses took:* Ibid.

193   *Alfred spoke:* Ibid.

193   *asked Alfred about:* Ibid.

193   *"I shot":* "School Board Members Claim Ignorance of Law," *East Tennessee Reporter,* February 22, 1957, 1; "Ward Family Planning to Leave," *East Tennessee Reporter,* February 22, 1957, 4.

193   *Given everything:* Ibid.

193   *"I couldn't learn":* Ibid.; Alfred Williams interview.

193   *"What do you want":* "School Board Members Claim Ignorance of Law," *East Tennessee Reporter,* February 22, 1957, 1; "Ward Family Planning to Leave," *East Tennessee Reporter,* February 22, 1957, 4.

193   *"I've been going":* "Ibid.; "School Board Says No to Resolution," *Clinton Courier-News,* February 21, 1957, 1; "School Board Sets Hearing on Expulsion," *Clinton Courier-News,* February 21, 1957, 1; "Negro CHS Student Is Expelled," February 28, 1957, 8; "Negro Boy Expelled by Board," *Knoxville Journal,* February 22, 1957, 7; Alfred Williams interview.

193   *school board polled:* "Negro CHS Student Is Expelled," *Clinton Courier-News*, February 28, 1957, 8; "School Board Members Claim Ignorance of Law," *East Tennessee Reporter*, February 22, 1957, 1; "Ward Family Planning to Leave," *East Tennessee Reporter*, February 22, 1957, 4.

193   *"We would rather":* Ibid

193   *"No," Alfred:* Ibid.

193   *His suspension:* Ibid.

EIGHTEEN: A WAR OF NERVES

194   *harassing Bobby:* Brittain, "A Case Study," 173–81; "Juveniles Continue Crime Spree," *Clinton Courier-News*, January 17, 1957, 1, 4; "Another Blast Rocks Clinton," *Clinton Courier-News*, January 17, 1957, 1; "Trial of 16 in Race Violence Delayed," *Knoxville Journal*, January 11, 1957, 1; "Six Clinton Boys Held in Thefts," *Knoxville Journal*, January 11, 1957, 1; "Gang Builds up Tension in Clinton," *Knoxville Journal*, February 24, 1957, 1; "Find 2 Effigies Hanging at Clinton High School," *Oak Ridger*, January 10, 1957, 1; "Arrest of 6 in Clinton Solves Several Crimes," *Oak Ridger*, January 11, 1957, 1, 6.

194   *Wednesday of Valentine's:* "Suspension of Student Appealed to School Board," *East Tennessee Reporter*, February 15, 1957, 1; "New School Incidents Calmed by Brittain; Threatens Expulsion," *East Tennessee Reporter*, February 15, 1957, 1.

195   *He thought it was:* Ibid.

195   *D. J. issued an ultimatum:* Ibid.

195   *Clyde Cook, recently elected:* Federal Bureau of Investigation, "Citizens' Council Movement."

195   *John Gates came:* "Many New Faces to Appear on Clubs in VA. League This Year," *Bristol Herald Courier*, March 21, 1927, 5; "Get-Together Club of Keokee," *The Post*, September 28, 1932, 1; "5 Lee County Men Held in Tennessee," February 24, 1938, 1; U.S. Census Bureau, "1940 United States Federal Census," digital image, s.v. "John Gates," Ancestry.com; Virginia Department of Health, "Birth Records, 1912–2015, Delayed Birth Records, 1732–1911," digital image, s.v. "John Ballard Gates," Ancestry.com.

195   *enlisted in the Army:* "872 Enlisted Here for Army Service," *Bristol Herald Courier*, November 3, 1940, 18; "John Gates, 41, Dies in Hospital at Knoxville," *Clinton Courier-News*, March 20, 1957, 1; "John Gates Jailed Then Placed in Eastern State as Mentally Unbalanced," *East Tennessee Reporter*, March 15, 1957, 1, 6; "18 Lee Youths Enlist in Army," *The Post*, November 7, 1940, 1; "Keokee," *The Post*, July 16, 1942; "Keokee," *The Post*, December 23, 1943, 8; "Keokee," *The Post*, January 13, 1944, 5; "Keokee," *The Post*, February 10, 1944, 8; "Keokee," *The Post*, February 24, 1944, 2.

196   *arrived in Clinton along:* "Goes to Indianapolis," *Bristol Herald Courier*, October 10, 1948, 29; "Social Notes of Keokee Area," April 10, 1949, 25; "Ann's Cafe," *Clinton Courier-News*, August 9, 1956, 2:6; "Kasper Hunted, Gates Arrested by

U.S. Officers," February 28, 1957, 1, 8; "John Gates, 41, Dies in Hospital at Knox-ville," March 20, 1957, 1; "John Gates Jailed Then Placed in Eastern State as Mentally Unbalanced," *East Tennessee Reporter*, March 15, 1957, 1, 6; Federal Bureau of Investigation, "Citizens' Council Movement"; "Blast Rips Segregation Council Headquarters," *Knoxville Journal*, December 30, 1956, 1, 5; "Pastor Describes Attack Blow by Blow," *Knoxville Journal*, July 17, 1957, 1, 3; "Segregationists Meet in Clinton," *Knoxville News-Sentinel*, January 12, 1957, 10; Charles Flowers, "6 Notebooks Filled by Court Reporter," *Knoxville News-Sentinel*, July 17, 1957, 5; "Mob Ruled Clinton Aug. 31, Court Told," *Knoxville News-Sentinel*, July 17, 1957, 1, 5; "Keokee," *The Post*, October 14, 1948, 8; "Keokee," *The Post*, November 5, 1953, 10; United States District Court, *"Bullock,"* July 12, 1957, 432, July 18, 1957, 1096–97, 1112–13.

196   *sharing their stories:* "Racial Clash in School," *East Tennessee Reporter*, February 8, 1957, 1, 4; "Suspension of student Appealed to School Board," *East Tennessee Reporter*, February 15, 1957, 1; "New School Incidents Calmed by Brittain; Threatens Expulsion," *East Tennessee Reporter*, February 15, 1957, 1; "School Authorities Make Attempt to Censor News," *East Tennessee Reporter*, March 1, 1957, 1; "Federal Court Increases Fear in Clinton, *East Tennessee Reporter*, March 1, 1957, 1, 6; "Last High School 'Incident' Exaggerated, Brittain Asserts," *East Tennessee Reporter*, March 1, 1957, 1.

196   *the judge added:* "Kasper Hunted, Gates Arrested by U.S. Officers," *Clinton Courier-News*, February 28, 1957, 1, 8; "School Authorities Make Attempt to Censor News," *East Tennessee Reporter*, March 1, 1957, 1, "Federal Court Increases Fear in Clinton," *East Tennessee Reporter*, March 1, 1957, 1, 6, "Last High School 'Incident' Exaggerated, Brittain Asserts," *East Tennessee Reporter*, March 1, 1957, 1; "Negro Students Are Still Absent," *Oak Ridger*, November 30, 1956, 1; Clinton High School Closed," *Oak Ridger*, December 4, 1956, 1–2.

198   *3:30 in the afternoon:* "Kasper Hunted, Gates Arrested by U.S. Officers," *Clinton Courier-News*, February 28, 1957, 1, 8; "Federal Court Increases Fear in Clinton, *East Tennessee Reporter*, March 1, 1957, 1, 6.

198   *Sure thing:* Ibid.

198   *marshals served John:* Ibid.; "Second Arrest of Kasper Ordered; Clinton Café Operator Is Jailed," *Nashville Banner*, February 26, 1957, 1.

198   *John said, he needed:* Ibid.

198   *stress and shame:* "Gates Breaks Windows at High School," *Clinton Courier-News*, March 14, 1957, 1; "Federal Court Increases Fear in Clinton, *East Tennessee Reporter*, March 1, 1957, 1, 6.

198   *Paul told his congregation:* Ibid.

198   *John Gates sat alone:* Ibid.

199   *Ann decided she needed:* Ibid.

199   *chief of police grabbed:* Ibid.

199   *"Here, John, stop":* Ibid.

199   *I have "the devil":* Ibid.

199   *What did he mean:* Ibid.

199   *It "won't work":* Ibid.

199   *lawmen could see lights:* Ibid.

200   *Hand over:* "John Gates Jailed Then Placed in Eastern State as Mentally Unbalanced," *East Tennessee Reporter*, March 15, 1957, 1, 6.

200   *"I'm already":* Ibid.

200   *Three more officers:* Ibid., "Gates Breaks Windows at High School," *Clinton Courier-News*, March 14, 1957, 1.

200   *John Gates snapped his head:* "John Gates Jailed Then Placed in Eastern State as Mentally Unbalanced," *East Tennessee Reporter*, March 15, 1957, 1, 6; "Gates Breaks Windows at High School," *Clinton Courier-News*, March 14, 1957, 1.

201   *John Gates seemed settled:* Ibid.; Tennessee State Library and Archives, "Death Records, 1908–1965," digital image, s.v. "John B Gates," Ancestry.com.

201   *family with a history:* "Pistol in Drawer Kills Dryden Man," *Richmond News Leader*, August 21, 1956, 4; "Lee Man Slain in Gun Mishap," *Bristol Virginia-Tennessean*, August 21, 1956, 10; "Gun Accident Claims Life of Lee Man," *The Post*, August 23, 1956, 6; "Gates, John B." *Knoxville Journal*, March 20, 1957, 8; "Gun Accident Claims Life of Lee Man," *The Post*, August 23, 1956, 6; U.S. Census Bureau, "1940 United States Federal Census," digital image, s.v. "Octavia Carter," Ancestry.com.

201   *doctors diagnosed John:* "John Gates Jailed Then Placed in Eastern State as Mentally Unbalanced," *East Tennessee Reporter*, March 15, 1957, 1, 6; "John Gates Dies at Eastern State," *East Tennessee Reporter*, March 22, 1957, 1, 4; "John Gates Widow Seeks Answer," *East Tennessee Reporter*, March 29, 1957, 1; "Gates, John B.," *Knoxville News-Sentinel*, March 20, 1957, 32; R. P. Oliver, *Brainwashing in the U.S.A.*, 15–20, quoted in Taylor, "Retribution, Responsibility and Freedom," 66; "Former Keokee Resident Dies in Tennessee," *The Post*, March 21, 1957, 12; Tennessee State Library and Archives, "Death Records, 1908–1965," digital image, s.v. "John B Gates," Ancestry.com.

201   *Bobby was sitting:* "School Board Says No to Resolution," *Clinton Courier-News*, February 21, 1957, 1; "School Board Sets Hearing on Expulsion," *Clinton Courier-News*, February 21, 1957, 1; "School Authorities Make Attempt to Censor News," *East Tennessee Reporter*, March 1, 1957, 1; "Federal Court Increases Fear in Clinton, *East Tennessee Reporter*, March 1, 1957, 1, 6; "Last High School 'Incident' Exaggerated, Brittain Asserts," *East Tennessee Reporter*, March 1, 1957, 1.

202   *Bobby crossed paths:* Bobby Cain interview; "High School Fuss Not Fist Fight, Say Participants," *East Tennessee Reporter*, March 29, 1957, 1.

202   *You shouldn't be:* Ibid.

202   *Bobby shoved:* Ibid.

202   *What did you say:* Ibid.

202   *Bobby reached:* Ibid.

202   *dynamite attempt happened:* "Dynamite Fails to Explode," *Clinton Courier-News*, March 14, 1957, 1.

202   *Alvah Jay McSwain dropped out:* Anderson, *The Children of the South*, 59; Bobby
      Cain interview; Anna Theresser Caswell interview; Bob Gilbert, "10 Years After
      Race Rift, Clinton Blames Outsiders," *Knoxville News-Sentinel*, August 26, 1966,
      1, 13; Green McAdoo Cultural Center, "About the Center"; "Negro Girl Drops
      Out at Clinton," *Knoxville Journal*, May 16, 1957, 1; Jim Elliott, "Luther King
      Featured at Highlander," *Nashville Banner*, August 30, 1957, 6.

203   *John Kasper was finally:* "Kasper Arrested, Released on Bond," *East Tennessee Re-
      porter*, March 29, 1957, 1; "Kasper Out as $7500 Bond Made," *Clinton Courier-
      News*, March 28, 1957, 1.

203   *Three more altercations:* "School Board Members Claim Ignorance of Law," *East
      Tennessee Reporter*, February 22, 1957, 1; "Ward Family Planning to Leave," *East
      Tennessee Reporter*, February 22, 1957, 1; "Racial Clashes Continue at Clinton
      High," *East Tennessee Reporter*, April 12, 1957, 1, 6; "Another CHS Student Ex-
      pected to Withdraw," *East Tennessee Reporter*, April 26, 1957, 1; "Kasper and Six
      Convicted; New Trial Possible," *East Tennessee Reporter*, July 26, 1957, 1; "Ray-
      mond Woods Hasn't Changed, He Tells Reporter," *East Tennessee Reporter*, July
      26, 1957, 1; "Rev. Bullock Refutes 'Smear' News Stories," *East Tennessee Reporter*,
      July 26, 1957, 1.

203   *"that Negro boys sometimes":* "School Authorities Make Attempt to Censor News,"
      East Tennessee Reporter, March 1, 1957, 1; "Federal Court Increases Fear in Clin-
      ton, *East Tennessee Reporter*, March 1, 1957, 1, 6; "Last High School 'Incident'
      Exaggerated, Brittain Asserts," *East Tennessee Reporter*, March 1, 1957, 1; "Racial
      Clashes Continue at Clinton High," *East Tennessee Reporter*, April 12, 1957, 1, 6.

204   *white students acknowledged:* Anderson, *The Children of the South*, 7, 13–14; Mar-
      garet Anderson interview; Boyce and Levy, *This Promise of Change*, 180; Anna
      Theresser Caswell interview; Bobby Cain interview; Maurice Soles interview;
      Gail Ann Epps Upton interview.

204   *Margaret called one:* Anderson, *The Children of the South*, 66, 69; Alfred Williams
      interview.

205   *Margaret asked Regina:* Anderson, *The Children of the South*, 59.

205   *"Do you think":* Ibid.

205   *"I don't know":* Ibid.

NINETEEN: A DESEGREGATED SCHOOL

206   *Bobby Cain would never:* Bobby Cain interview; Bobby and Margo Cain inter-
      view.

206   *Disoriented, Bobby:* Ibid.

206   *In the darkness:* Ibid.

206   *lights came back:* Ibid.

206   *lights died:* Ibid.

207   *three years:* Ibid.; Green McAdoo Cultural Center, "Permanent Exhibition."

207 *lights turned on:* Bobby Cain interview; Bobby and Margo Cain interview; Robert Cain Sr. interview.

207 *summer had come early:* Ibid.; Green McAdoo Cultural Center, "Permanent Exhibition."

207 *administration had crafted:* Ibid.; Anderson, *The Children of the South,* 21; D. J. Brittain Jr. interview; "CHS Graduates 89 Ending Eventful Year," *Clinton Courier-News,* May 23, 1957, 1, 6.

207 *Six days earlier, the valedictorian:* Jerry Shattuck, "As They See It," *Clinton Courier-News,* April 24, 1958, 2:2; "Four Hurt in Crash North of Clinton," *Clinton Courier-News,* May 16, 1957, 1; "Klan Motorcade Interrupted on Broad Street," *East Tennessee Reporter,* May 17, 1957, 1; "Witnesses Place 6 at Scene of Violence," *Knoxville Journal,* July 16, 1957, 2.

208 *state troopers investigating:* Jerry Shattuck, "As They See It," *Clinton Courier-News,* April 24, 1958, 2:2; "Four Hurt in Crash North of Clinton," *Clinton Courier-News,* May 16, 1957, 1; "Klan Motorcade Interrupted on Broad Street," *East Tennessee Reporter,* May 17, 1957, 1; "Witnesses Place 6 at Scene of Violence," *Knoxville Journal,* July 16, 1957, 2.

208 *segregationist protestors would cause:* "Ku Klux Klan Here Saturday," *East Tennessee Reporter,* May 10, 1957, 1; "Klan Motorcade Interrupted on Broad Street," May 17, 1957, 1; Horace V. Wells Jr., "As We See It!" *Clinton Courier-News,* May 16, 1957, 1; "KKK Group Meets Here Burns Crosses," *Clinton Courier-News,* May 16, 1957, 8.

209 *cavalcade ended:* Ibid.

209 *John Kasper couldn't stand:* Horace V. Wells Jr., "As We See It!" *Clinton Courier-News,* May 16, 1957, 1; "KKK Group Meets Here Burns Crosses," *Clinton Courier-News,* May 16, 1957, 8; "Klan Motorcade Interrupted on Broad Street," *East Tennessee Reporter,* May 17, 1957, 1.

209 *D. J. Brittain Jr. had approached:* D. J. Brittain Jr. interview; Anderson, *The Children of the South,* 21; "CHS Graduates 89 Ending Eventful Year," *Clinton Courier-News,* May 23, 1957, 1, 6; Bob Gilbert, "10 Years After Race Rift, Clinton Blames Outsiders," *Knoxville News-Sentinel,* August 26, 1966, 1, 13.

209 *no journalists present:* D. J. Brittain Jr. interview; Anderson, *The Children of the South,* 21; "CHS Graduates 89 Ending Eventful Year," *Clinton Courier-News,* May 23, 1957, 1, 6; Bob Gilbert, "10 Years After Race Rift, Clinton Blames Outsiders," *Knoxville News-Sentinel,* August 26, 1966, 1, 13; Bobby Cain interview; "Graduation at High School Tense But Quiet," *East Tennessee Reporter,* May 24, 1957, 1; "Brittain Learns from Judge Taylor," *East Tennessee Reporter,* May 24, 1957, 2; Helen Fuller interview.

210 *the chase through:* Ibid.

210 *Bobby and his family:* Bobby Cain interview.

210 *Bobby Cain, however:* Ibid.

210 *months between Clinton High:* Ibid.; "Clinton Negro Graduate to Be Honored,"

Knoxville Journal, May 27, 1957, 5; "Tell of Fight for Freedom in the South," *Baltimore Afro-American*, June 4, 1957, 5.

210 *Bobby also gave:* Bobby Cain interview; "Robert E. Cain's College Fund Climbing Slowly," *Pittsburgh Courier*, July 6, 1957, 14; "Cain's Scholarship Fund Goes Over $300 Mark!" *Pittsburgh Courier*, July 20, 1957, 6; "Cain Scholarship Fund Praised by Minister," July 22, 1957, 22; Ms. June, "For Bobby Cain, Clinton 12 Pain Still Fresh," *Tennessee Tribune*, June 7, 2018, https://tntribune.com/for-cain-clinton-12-pain-still-fresh/; Julieta Martinelli, "Graduate of First Integrated Class in the South Talks Desegregation with Teachers," WPLN, July 25, 2017, https://wpln.org/post/graduate-of-first-integrated-class-in-the-south-talks-desegregation-with-tennessee-teachers/.

211 *segregationists arrested:* "Judge Taylor Delays Trials for Sixteen," *Clinton Courier-News*, January 17, 1957, 1, 6; "Kasper Not in Court as Appeal Heard," *Clinton Courier-News*, April 11, 1957, 5; "Attorneys Seek Talks with Students," *Clinton Courier-News*, April 11, 1957, 8; "Judge Taylor to Hear Oral Arguments Today," *Clinton Courier-News*, May 2, 1957, 1, 8; "Kasper, Others Are Given Jury Trials by Judge Taylor," *Clinton Courier-News*, May 9, 1957, 1; "Clinton School Violence Trial Opens; First Witnesses Are Heard After Fight Over Jury," July 11, 1957, 1, 4; "Trial Emphasizes Two Attitudes in Clinton," *Clinton Courier-News*, July 11, 1957, 1, 5; "Witnesses Tell of Violence at Trial of Kasper and 14," *Clinton Courier-News*, July 18, 1957, 1, 6; "Kasper, 6 Others Held Guilty, Announce Plans to Appeal," *Clinton Courier-News*, July 25, 1957, 1, 6; "Four More Defendants Freed on Thursday," *East Tennessee Reporter*, July 19, 1957, 1; "Irwin Refutes Crossno Story; WCC List Read," *East Tennessee Reporter*, July 19, 1957, 1; "Kasper and Six Convicted; New Trial Possible," *East Tennessee Reporter*, July 26, 1957, 1; "Raymond Woods Hasn't Changed, He Tells Reporter," *East Tennessee Reporter*, July 26, 1957, 1; "Rev. Bullock Refutes 'Smear' News Stories," *East Tennessee Reporter*, July 26, 1957, 1; "Back Glances Show Incidents of Interest," *East Tennessee Reporter*, July 26. 1957, 2, 8.

212 *spectators sat intermingled:* Trezzvant Anderson, "Fists Fly Briefly at Trial!" *Pittsburgh Courier*, August 3, 1957, 7; "Clinton School Violence Trial Opens; First Witnesses Are Heard After Fight Over Jury," July 11, 1957, 1, 4; "Trial Emphasizes Two Attitudes in Clinton," *Clinton Courier-News*, July 11, 1957, 1, 5; "Witnesses Tell of Violence at Trial of Kasper and 14," *Clinton Courier-News*, July 18, 1957, 1, 6; "Kasper, 6 Others Held Guilty, Announce Plans to Appeal," *Clinton Courier-News*, July 25, 1957, 1, 6; "Four More Defendants Freed on Thursday," *East Tennessee Reporter*, July 19, 1957, 1; "Irwin Refutes Crossno Story; WCC List Read," *East Tennessee Reporter*, July 19, 1957, 1; "Kasper and Six Convicted; New Trial Possible," *East Tennessee Reporter*, July 26, 1957, 1; "Raymond Woods Hasn't Changed, He Tells Reporter," *East Tennessee Reporter*, July 26, 1957, 1; "Rev. Bullock Refutes 'Smear' News Stories," *East Tennessee Reporter*, July 26, 1957, 1; "Back Glances Show Incidents of Interest," *East Tennessee Reporter*, July 26. 1957, 2, 8.

212 *phalanx of defense:* Carson Brewer, "Clinton Editor Scores Victory on Stand,"

Knoxville News-Sentinel, July 12, 1957, 1; Charles Flowers, "Views Vary on Length of Trial," *Knoxville News-Sentinel,* July 12, 1957, 1; "Bias Charged in Photos of Clinton Riots," *Knoxville News-Sentinel,* July 12, 1957, 1; Charles Flowers, "6 Notebooks Filled by Court Reporter," *Knoxville News-Sentinel,* July 17, 1957, 5; Carson Brewer, "Weakening of Turner Testimony Attempted," *Knoxville News-Sentinel,* July 17, 1957, 1, 5.

212   *women took off:* "Crawford Cuts Catnap to Cross-Examine," *Knoxville Journal,* July 19, 1957, 2; "Brittain Tells of Terror in School Closing," *Knoxville News-Sentinel,* July 15, 1957, 1; Maureen Rickard, "Attorney for Defense Shocks Easily," *Knoxville News-Sentinel,* July 15, 1957, 1.

213   *witnesses were getting:* " 'Filth' Yelled at Pastor," Jury Told," *Knoxville News-Sentinel,* July 16, 1957, 6; Carson Brewer, "Defense Roars Fail to Stir Calm Davis," *Knoxville News-Sentinel,* July 16, 1957, 1, 6; Charles Flowers, "Court Now a Tourist Attraction," *Knoxville News-Sentinel,* July 18, 1957, 16; "Four More Freed in Clinton Trial," *Knoxville News-Sentinel,* July 18, 1957, 16.

213   *spectators swirled:* Carson Brewer, "Clinton Editor Scores Victory on Stand," *Knoxville News-Sentinel,* July 12, 1957, 1; Charles Flowers, "Views Vary on Length of Trial," *Knoxville News-Sentinel,* July 12, 1957, 1; "Bias Charged in Photos of Clinton Riots," *Knoxville News-Sentinel,* July 12, 1957, 1; "Brittain Tells of Terror in School Closing," *Knoxville News-Sentinel,* July 15, 1957, 1; Maureen Rickard, "Attorney for Defense Shocks Easily," *Knoxville News-Sentinel,* July 15, 1957, 1; "Clinton Man Says He Heads K.K.K. Group," *Clinton Courier-News,* July 18, 1957, 6.

213   *He took our picture:* Carson Brewer, "Clinton Editor Scores Victory on Stand," *Knoxville News-Sentinel,* July 12, 1957, 1; Charles Flowers, "Views Vary on Length of Trial," *Knoxville News-Sentinel,* July 12, 1957, 1; "Bias Charged in Photos of Clinton Riots," *Knoxville News-Sentinel,* July 12, 1957, 1.

213   *cameraman apologized:* "Bias Charged in Photos of Clinton Riots," *Knoxville News-Sentinel,* July 12, 1957, 1.

213   *journalists remained:* "Clinton Folk Express Hope for Quiet Now," *Knoxville Journal,* July 24, 1957, 14; "Clinton Reporters Form 'Order of Cockroaches,' " *Knoxville Journal,* July 24, 1957, 14; Carson Brewer, "Clinton Editor Scores Victory on Stand," *Knoxville News-Sentinel,* July 12, 1957, 1; Charles Flowers, "Views Vary on Length of Trial," *Knoxville News-Sentinel,* July 12, 1957, 1; "Bias Charged in Photos of Clinton Riots," *Knoxville News-Sentinel,* July 12, 1957, 1.

214   *testimony wrapped:* "Clinton School Violence Trial Opens; First Witnesses Are Heard After Fight Over Jury," July 11, 1957, 1, 4; "Trial Emphasizes Two Attitudes in Clinton," *Clinton Courier-News,* July 11, 1957, 1, 5; "Witnesses Tell of Violence at Trial of Kasper and 14," *Clinton Courier-News,* July 18, 1957, 1, 6; "Kasper, 6 Others Held Guilty, Announce Plans to Appeal," *Clinton Courier-News,* July 25, 1957, 1, 6; "Kasper Files Appeal, Clinton Co-Defendants Get Probation," *Clinton Courier-News,* November 21, 1957, 1, 6; "Kasper, 6 Others Appeal," *Clinton Courier-News,* May 15, 1958, 3:6; "Four More Defendants Freed on Thursday,"

East Tennessee Reporter, July 19, 1957, 1; "Irwin Refutes Crossno Story; WCC List Read," *East Tennessee Reporter*, July 19, 1957, 1; "Kasper and Six Convicted; New Trial Possible," *East Tennessee Reporter*, July 26, 1957, 1; "Raymond Woods Hasn't Changed, He Tells Reporter," *East Tennessee Reporter*, July 26, 1957, 1; "Rev. Bullock Refutes 'Smear' News Stories," *East Tennessee Reporter*, July 26, 1957, 1; "Back Glances Show Incidents of Interest," *East Tennessee Reporter*, July 26. 1957, 2, 8; Trezzvant Anderson, "They're Happy in Clinton, Tenn.," *Pittsburgh Courier*, August 3, 1957, 7.

214   *July 23 after only:* "Kasper, 6 Others Held Guilty, Announce Plans to Appeal," *Clinton Courier-News*, July 25, 1957, 1, 6; "Kasper Files Appeal, Clinton Co-Defendants Get Probation," *Clinton Courier-News*, November 21, 1957, 1, 6; "Kasper, 6 Others Appeal," *Clinton Courier-News*, May 15, 1958, 3:6; "Kasper and Six Convicted; New Trial Possible," *East Tennessee Reporter*, July 26, 1957, 1; "Raymond Woods Hasn't Changed, He Tells Reporter," *East Tennessee Reporter*, July 26, 1957, 1; "Rev. Bullock Refutes 'Smear' News Stories," *East Tennessee Reporter*, July 26, 1957, 1; "Back Glances Show Incidents of Interest," *East Tennessee Reporter*, July 26. 1957, 2, 8; Trezzvant Anderson, "They're Happy in Clinton, Tenn.," *Pittsburgh Courier*, August 3, 1957, 7; Emilie E. Powell, "Defendants Bitter, Rail at Verdict," *Knoxville Journal*, July 24, 1957, 1, 2; "Senators Told Clinton Decision Shows Fairness of Southern Jury," *Knoxville Journal*, July 24, 1957, 1, 2; "Jury Verdict Reached on First Ballot," *Knoxville Journal*, July 24, 1957, 1; "Kasper, 6 Others Guilty,' " *Knxoville Journal*, July 24, 1957, 1, 2; "Courtroom Stilled by Verdict," *Knoxville Journal*, July 24, 1957, 1, 2.

214   *"We've gotten a rotten":* Emilie E. Powell, "Defendants Bitter, Rail at Verdict," *Knoxville Journal*, July 24, 1957, 1, 2; "Senators Told Clinton Decision Shows Fairness of Southern Jury," *Knoxville Journal*, July 24, 1957, 1, 2; "Jury Verdict Reached on First Ballot," *Knoxville Journal*, July 24, 1957, 1; "Kasper, 6 Others Guilty,' " *Knoxville Journal*, July 24, 1957, 1, 2; "Courtroom Stilled by Verdict," *Knoxville Journal*, July 24, 1957, 1, 2; Julian Granger, "Convicted Kasper and 6 to Appeal," *Knoxville News-Sentinel*, July 24, 1957, 1, 2; "People of Clinton Uncertain, Watchful," *Knoxville News-Sentinel*, July 24, 1957, 1, 2; "Remarks of Sen. Estes Kefauver (Dem, Tenn) on the Clinton, Tennessee, Verdict," July 23, 1957, Estes Kefauver Papers; Webb, "Introduction," in *Massive Resistance*, 5.

215   *gathered at Steve:* Trezzvant Anderson, "They're Happy in Clinton, Tenn.," *Pittsburgh Courier*, August 3, 1957, 7.

215   *"Amen," her husband:* Ibid.

215   *"I think the verdict":* Emilie E. Powell, "Defendants Bitter, Rail at Verdict," *Knoxville Journal*, July 24, 1957, 1, 2; "Senators Told Clinton Decision Shows Fairness of Southern Jury," *Knoxville Journal*, July 24, 1957, 1, 2; "Jury Verdict Reached on First Ballot," *Knoxville Journal*, July 24, 1957, 1; "Kasper, 6 Others Guilty,' " *Knoxville Journal*, July 24, 1957, 1, 2; "Courtroom Stilled by Verdict," *Knoxville Journal*, July 24, 1957, 1, 2; Julian Granger, "Convicted Kasper and 6 to Appeal," *Knoxville*

News-Sentinel, July 24, 1957, 1, 2; "People of Clinton Uncertain, Watchful," *Knoxville News-Sentinel,* July 24, 1957, 1, 2.

215 *sending white parents:* "Clinton Remains Quiet," *Chattanooga Daily Times,* September 5, 1957, 1; "Unsigned Postcards Received at Clinton," *Knoxville Journal,* August 30, 1957, 11; Dudley Brewer, "Complete Calm Reigns at Clinton High," *Knoxville Journal,* September 4, 1957, 9; Julian Granger, "Integrated Clinton School Opens Quietly," *Knoxville News-Sentinel,* September 3, 1957, 1–2; B. F. Middlebrooks, "New Principal Gains Respect with Firm Hand," *Knoxville News-Journal,* September 8, 1957, 7; Trezzvant Anderson, "Peace Reigns in Clinton as School Year Starts," *Pittsburgh Courier,* September 7, 1957, 2.

215 *Shortly before registration:* Ibid.

216 *September 3, 1957:* Sherlock Hope, "Clinton HS Starts Year Peacefully," *Knoxville Journal,* August 28, 1957, 1, 5; "Unsigned Postcards Received at Clinton," *Knoxville Journal,* August 30, 1957, 11; Dudley Brewer, "Complete Calm Reigns at Clinton High," *Knoxville Journal,* September 4, 1957, 9; Julian Granger, "Integrated Clinton School Opens Quietly," *Knoxville News-Sentinel,* September 3, 1957, 1–2; B. F. Middlebrooks, "New Principal Gains Respect with Firm Hand," *Knoxville News-Journal,* September 8, 1957, 7; Trezzvant Anderson, "Peace Reigns in Clinton as School Year Starts," *Pittsburgh Courier,* September 7, 1957, 2; "Schools Overflowing, More Space Needed as 802 Are Enrolled," *Clinton Courier-News,* September 5, 1957, 1, 6.

216 *Only one protestor:* Ibid.; "Clinton Remains Quiet," *Chattanooga Daily Times,* September 5, 1957, 1.

216 *Principal W. D. Human had taken:* D. J. Brittain Jr. interview; "W.D. Human of Morgan County Has Proper Qualifications for Clinton Job," *Knoxville Journal,* May 12, 1957, 46; Dudley Brewer, "Complete Calm Reigns at Clinton High," *Knoxville Journal,* September 4, 1957, 9; "Brasel Elected Morgan Sheriff," *Knoxville News-Sentinel,* August 3, 1956, 8, September 3, 1957, 1–2; Julian Granger, "Integrated Clinton School Opens Quietly," *Knoxville News-Sentinel,* September 8, 1957, 7; Celdon Lewallen interview; Seivers, "Words of Discrimination," 170; United States District Court, *"Bullock,"* December 4, 1956, 12.

217 *new principal promised:* Gail Ann Epps Upton interview.

217 *Tom Powell, a local:* "Clinton Police Probing Mystery Explosion," *Knoxville Journal,* November 2, 1957, 5; "Explosion Plot Bared," *Knoxville Journal,* November 8, 1957, 1; "Probes Dynamite," *Knoxville News-Sentinel,* October 20, 1957, 46; "Catch the Real Culprits," *Tennessee Reporter,* November 8, 1957, 1; "Dynamite Plot Disclosed by Woodward," *Tennessee Reporter,* November 8, 1957, 1; "150 Sticks Dynamite Found Here," *Clinton Courier-News,* October 31, 1957, 1; "Plot to Blow Up Clinton High School Is Revealed," *Clinton Courier-News,* November 7, 1957, 1, 2.

218 *lawmen needed to find:* Ibid.

218 *Edward Cline came:* Ibid.; "Auto Thief Receives Suspended Sentence," *Knoxville*

Journal, October 17, 1946, 22; "Theft Suspect Questioned in Wartburg," *Knoxville Journal,* June 8, 1949, 18; "Kentuckian Sentenced," *Knoxville Journal,* September 28, 1949, 16; "Dr. Grubb Income Tax Case Transferred Here," *Knoxville Journal,* December 2, 1952, 12; "Escapee Picked Up in Kentucky Theft," *Knoxville News-Sentinel,* August 19, 1949, 13; "19 Calves Die in Truck Crash," *Messenger,* September 1, 1951, 8; "Plot to Blow Up Clinton High School Is Revealed," *Clinton Courier-News,* November 7, 1957, 1, 2.

219   *Avon contacted:* Julian Granger, "One Convicted, Two Freed in Dynamite Plot," *Knoxville News-Sentinel,* February 12, 1958, 1, 8; "Cline Convicted in Dynamite Case, Two Co Defendants Freed," *Tennessee Reporter,* February 13, 1958, 1; "Plot to Blow Up Clinton High School Is Revealed," *Clinton Courier-News,* November 7, 1957, 1, 2.

219   *three guys picked:* "Two Youths Held in Clinton Plot," *Knoxville Journal,* November 8, 1957, 23; Curwood Garrett, "Cline Found Guilty in Dynamiting," *Knoxville Journal,* February 12, 1958, 1–2; "Plot to Dynamite Clinton High Bared," *Knoxville News-Sentinel,* November 7, 1957, 1; "Catch the Real Culprits," *Tennessee Reporter,* November 8, 1957, 1; "Dynamite Plot Disclosed by Woodward," *Tennessee Reporter,* November 8, 1957, 1; "Cline Convicted in Dynamite Case, Two Co Defendants Freed," *Tennessee Reporter,* February 13, 1958, 1; "Plot to Blow Up Clinton High School Is Revealed," *Clinton Courier-News,* November 7, 1957, 1, 2.

219   *Then I got:* Ibid.

219   *three men carted:* Ibid.; "Cline Case Taken Under Advisement," *Knoxville Journal,* December 13, 1957, 5.

220   *nineteen-year-old had never:* "Two Youths Held in Clinton Plot," *Knoxville Journal,* November 8, 1957, 23; Curwood Garrett, "Cline Found Guilty in Dynamiting," *Knoxville Journal,* February 12, 1958, 1–2; Julian Granger, "One Convicted, Two Freed in Dynamite Plot," *Knoxville News-Sentinel,* February 12, 1958, 1, 8; "Nolan, Avon," *1955 Clinton City Directory,* 251; "Catch the Real Culprits," *Tennessee Reporter,* November 8, 1957, 1; "Dynamite Plot Disclosed by Woodward," *Tennessee Reporter,* November 8, 1957, 1; "Plot to Blow Up Clinton High School Is Revealed," *Clinton Courier-News,* November 7, 1957, 1, 2.

220   *state legislature had given:* "Two Youths Held in Clinton Plot," *Knoxville Journal,* November 8, 1957, 23; "Suspect in Blast Plan Held," *Knoxville Journal,* December 9, 1957, 1–2; "One Bound for Having Dynamite," *Knoxville Journal,* January 1, 1958, 2; "School Dynamiting Queries Scheduled," *Knoxville Journal,* January 1, 1958, 2; "Ex-Convict Linked to Conspiracy," *Knoxville Journal,* January 3, 1958, 3; Curwood Garrett, "Cline Found Guilty in Dynamiting," *Knoxville Journal,* February 12, 1958, 1–2; "Plot to Dynamite Clinton High Bared," *Knoxville News-Sentinel,* November 7, 1957, 1; "3rd Jailed in Clinton High Dynamite Plot," December 9, 1957, 24; "Officer to Quiz Dynamite Suspect," *Knoxville News-Sentinel,* December 31, 1957, 7; Julian Granger, "One Convicted, Two Freed in Dynamite Plot," *Knoxville News-Sentinel,* February 12, 1958, 1, 8; Wallace Westfeldt, "Dynamite Curb Bill Indorsed by House Group," *Tennessean,* February 23, 1957, 1; "Catch the Real

Culprits," *Tennessee Reporter*, November 8, 1957, 1; "Dynamite Plot Disclosed by Woodward," *Tennessee Reporter*, November 8, 1957, 1; "Officials in Wrangle over Cline Evidence," *Clinton Courier-News*, December 19, 1957, 1.

220   *On February 11, the case:* Curwood Garrett, "Cline Found Guilty in Dynamiting," *Knoxville Journal*, February 12, 1958, 1–2, 10; Julian Granger, "One Convicted, Two Freed in Dynamite Plot," *Knoxville News-Sentinel*, February 12, 1958, 1, 8; "Cline Convicted in Dynamite Case, Two Co Defendants Freed," *Tennessee Reporter*, February 13, 1958, 1; "Cline Draws 2–10 Year Prison Term; Files New Trial Motion," *Clinton Courier-News*, February 13, 1958, 1, 8.

221   *Testimonies and closing statements:* Ibid.

221   *Gail Ann Epps survived:* Boyce and Levy, *This Promise of Change*, 258; Gail Ann Epps Upton interview.

TWENTY: BOOM

222   *4:30 in the morning:* Federal Bureau of Investigation, "FBI File 44–13723: Clinton High School Bombing," June N. Adamson Papers, Knoxville, TN; Drew Pearson, Washington Merry-Go-Round, October 13, 1958, American University Digital Research Archive; Curwood Garrett, "FBI Launches Probe into Major Disaster," *Clinton Courier-News*, October 9, 1958, 1; Horace V. Wells Jr., "Clinton High Picture of Utter Devastation," *Clinton Courier-News*, October 9, 1958, 1, 6; "Pictures Tell Tragic Story of School," *Clinton Courier-News*, October 9, 1958, 5.

222   *the campus had been bustling:* Margaret Anderson interview; Anna Theresser Caswell interview; Federal Bureau of Investigation, "FBI File 44–13723: Clinton High School Bombing," June N. Adamson Papers, Knoxville, TN; Diane Pemberton interview.

222   *First on the scene:* Jack Setters, "'58 Graduate Halts Fire at School," *Nashville Banner*, October 6, 1958, 8; Curwood Garrett, "FBI Launches Probe into Major Disaster," *Clinton Courier-News*, October 9, 1958, 1; Horace V. Wells Jr., "Clinton High Picture of Utter Devastation," *Clinton Courier-News*, October 9, 1958, 1, 6.

223   *on the floor:* Drew Pearson, Washington Merry-Go-Round, October 20, 1958, American University Digital Research Archive.

223   *Anna Theresser Caswell, now:* Margaret Anderson interview; Anna Theresser Caswell interview; Federal Bureau of Investigation, "FBI File 44–13723: Clinton High School Bombing," June N. Adamson Papers, Knoxville, TN; Diane Pemberton interview; Horace V. Wells Jr., "Clinton High Picture of Utter Devastation," *Clinton Courier-News*, October 9, 1958, 1, 6.

223   *teachers and students adapted:* Margaret Anderson interview; Anderson, "The South Learns Its Hardest Lessons"; Diane Pemberton interview; Horace V. Wells Jr., "Clinton High Picture of Utter Devastation," *Clinton Courier-News*, October 9, 1958, 1, 6; "Clinton High Classes Resumed; Welcome Is Extended by Ridgers," *Clinton Courier-News*, October 9, 1958, 1, 5; "Pictures Tell Tragic Story of School," *Clinton Courier-News*, October 9, 1958, 5.

224   *Margaret Anderson didn't want:* Anderson, "Children in a Crucible."

224   *Thursday morning, the substitute:* Margaret Anderson interview; Drew Pearson, Washington Merry-Go-Round, December 12, 1958, American University Digital Research Archive; "Clinton High Classes Resumed; Welcome Is Extended by Ridgers," *Clinton Courier-News*, October 9, 1958, 1, 5.

224   *refitted the elementary:* Margaret Anderson interview; Drew Pearson, Washington Merry-Go-Round, December 12, 1958, American University Digital Research Archive; "Clinton High Classes Resumed; Welcome Is Extended by Ridgers," *Clinton Courier-News*, October 9, 1958, 1, 5; "Hatred Again Hurts School," *Life*, October 20, 1958, 32–33; "Clinton High Classes Resumed; Welcome Is Extended by Ridgers," *Clinton Courier-News*, October 9, 1958, 1, 5; "Band Greets Clinton Students at Linden," *Clinton Courier-News*, October 16, 1958, 4.

224   *Principal W. D. Human and the school:* "Bombed-Out Students, Negroes Included, in Rebuilt Clinton School," *Knoxville Journal*, August 26, 1960, 1, 2; Drew Pearson, Washington Merry-Go-Found, October 5, 1959, American University Digital Research Archive, October 13, 1958, American University Digital Research Archive, October 25, 1958, American University Digital Research Archive; "President Asked for Aid," *Clinton Courier-News*, October 9, 1958, 1, 6; "President Rejects General Aid Policy," *Clinton Courier-News*, October 16, 1958, 1.

225   *FBI arrived:* Federal Bureau of Investigation, "FBI File 44–13723: Clinton High School Bombing," June N. Adamson Papers, Knoxville, TN; "FBI Office in Operation," *Clinton Courier-News*, October 9, 1958, 4; "Agencies Seek Clues in Bombing," *Clinton Courier-News*, October 23, 1958, 1.

225   *local police so badly:* Robert Cain Sr. interview.

226   *federal agents determined:* Drew Pearson, Washington Merry-Go-Round, December 14, 1958, American University Digital Research Archive; "Evidence in Dynamiting Considered Insufficient," *Southern School News*, August 1962, 10; Horace V. Wells interview; Agencies Seek Clues in Bombing," *Clinton Courier-News*, October 23, 1958, 1.

226   *two months, two homes:* Federal Bureau of Investigation, "FBI File 44–13723: Clinton High School Bombing," June N. Adamson Papers, Knoxville, TN; "Negro Buildings Burned," *Southern School News*, January 1959, 7–8.

226   *visited Edward Cline:* "Plea Denied in School Blast Plot," *Knoxville News-Sentinel*, March 4, 1960, 1; "Cline, Held on Dynamite Charge, Seeks Freedom," *Clinton Courier-News*, October 16, 1958, 1.

226   *state pardons and paroles:* "Cline Case Brings Blast and Reply," *Knoxville Journal*, December 14, 1957, 14; "Clinton Plotter Rips Trial Evidence," *Knoxville News-Sentinel*, April 28, 1960, 2; "State Board Denies Parole in Clinton Case," *Southern School News*, May 1963, 3; "Cline's Conviction in Dynamiting Upheld," *Clinton Courier-News*, December 18, 1958, 1.

227   *Pearson decided Clinton High:* "Fountainhead of Vitriol: Columnist Drew Pearson Turns Novelist," *Life*, August 9 1968, 31; Drew Pearson, Washington Merry-Go-Round, October 20, 1958, December 12, 1958, September 29,

1962, American University Digital Research Archive; "The Press: Querulous Quaker," *Time*, December 13, 1948, http://www.time.com/time/magazine/article/0,9171,799488,00.html; "Money, Labor Given," *Southern School News*, January 1959, 7; "Pearson Opens Fund Campaign to Rebuild Clinton High School," *Clinton Courier-News*, October 16, 1958, 1; "Pearson's Plan to Re-Build Clinton High OKed by Board," *Clinton Courier-News*, October 16, 1958, 1, 6; Horace V. Wells Jr., "America Opens Its Heart to Plight of Bombed-Out School; Pearson's Drive in High Gear," *Clinton Courier-News*, October 23, 1958, 1, 8.

227   *Billy Graham joined:* Graham, *Just As I Am*, 201–2; Miller, *Billy Graham and the Rise of the Republican South*, 55–57; Drew Pearson, Washington Merry-Go-Round, November 30, 1958, American University Digital Research Archive; "Billy Graham Accepts Invitation to Preach Here Sunday, Dec. 14," *Clinton Courier-News*, November 27, 1958, 1, 8; Vernon McKinney, "Meeting Held in Clinton to Give the World a Better Understanding of the People Here," *Clinton Courier-News*, December 18, 1958, 1, 6.

228   *Graham began his day:* Drew Pearson, Washington Merry-Go-Round, November 30, 1958, American University Digital Research Archive; "Billy Graham Accepts Invitation to Preach Here Sunday, Dec. 14," *Clinton Courier-News*, November 27, 1958, 1, 8; Vernon McKinney, "Meeting Held in Clinton to Give the World a Better Understanding of the People Here," *Clinton Courier-News*, December 18, 1958, 1, 6; "Money, Labor Given," *Southern School News*, January 1959, 7; James Carty, "Clinton Pastor Gets Call Here," *Tennessean*, September 25, 1958, 25; "Turner Is Called to Nashville," *Clinton Courier-News*, September 25, 1958, 1; "Turner Resigns Pastorate," *Clinton Courier-News*, October 2, 1958; "Thousands Expected on Sunday to See and Hear Billy Graham," *Clinton Courier-News*, December 11, 1958, 1; "Billy Graham Says Love Is Answer to World Problems," *Clinton Courier-News*, December 18, 1958, 1, 6.

228   *meeting opened:* Horace V. Wells interview; Horace V. Wells Jr., "America Opens Its Heart to Plight of Bombed-Out School; Pearson's Drive in High Gear," *Clinton Courier-News*, October 23, 1958, 1, 8; "Contributions Pour in from All over the World as Students, Parents Protest School Bombing," *Clinton Courier-News*, November 6, 1958, 1, 4; "Billy Graham Says Love Is Answer to World Problems," *Clinton Courier-News*, December 18, 1958, 1, 6; "Pearson Presents Gifts of Thousands of Givers," *Clinton Courier-News*, December 18, 1958, 1, 6.

228   *"If God is a God":* Billy Graham, "Billy Graham in Clinton, Tennessee, 1958," June Adamson Papers, Knoxville, TN.; "Billy Graham Says Love Is Answer to World Problems," *Clinton Courier-News*, December 18, 1958, 1, 6.

228   *Because God is loving:* Ibid.

229   *Contributions to rebuild:* Anderson, "The South Learns Its Hardest Lessons"; Drew Pearson, Washington Merry-Go-Round, October 5, 1959, October 13, 1958, October 15, 1958, October 25, 1958, November 5, 1958, November 27, 1958, December 14, 1958, American University Digital Research Archive; Horace V. Wells Jr., "America Opens Its Heart to Plight of Bombed-Out School; Pearson's Drive in

High Gear," *Clinton Courier-News*, October 23, 1958, 1, 8; "Contributions Pour in from All over the World as Students, Parents Protest School Bombing," *Clinton Courier-News*, November 6, 1958, 1, 4.

229   *August 29, 1960:* Anderson, "The South Learns Its Hardest Lessons"; "Clinton Starts Using Its New School Building," *Knoxville Journal*, August 30, 1960, 3; "Clinton High Opens Quietly," *Knoxville News-Sentinel*, August 29, 1960, 17; "Dinner Fetes Clinton High Benefactors," *Knoxville News-Sentinel*, September 25, 1960, 1; Drew Pearson, Washington Merry-Go-Round, September 29, 1960, American University Digital Research Archive; Roberts, *High School*, 68.

229   *next ten years:* James L. Cain interview; Bob Gilbert, "10 Years After Race Rift, Clinton Blames Outsiders," *Knoxville News-Sentinel*, August 26, 1966, 1, 13; Louis Cassels, "Small Gains Since Desegregation Ruling 7 Years Ago," *Press-Courier*, May 17, 1961, 23.

230   *D. J. Brittain Jr. thrived:* D. J. Brittain Jr. interview; "Principal Brittain Given Fellowship," *Clinton Courier-News*, April 4, 1957, 1; "D. J. Brittain Gets $6, School Post," *Clinton Courier-News*, May 1, 1958, 4; Patterson, *American Education* 59; "Former Clinton Principal Receives Award at NYU," *Southern School News*, April 1964, 6.

230   *superintendent of New Jersey's:* D. J. Brittain Jr. interview; Cotton et al., "Desegregation in Ewing Township, New Jersey."

230   *D. J. could not forget:* Steve Jones interview; Henry Quinn interview; Social Security Administration, "Social Security Death Index," s.v. "David J. Brittain," Ancestry.com.

231   *Paul Turner had remained: Baptist Press*: News Service of the Southern Baptist Convention, December 23, 1980, 2–3; Cleveland, "Baptist Pastor," 23; First Baptist, September 28, 1958, Business Meeting, First Baptist Church of Clinton, TN: Records 1840–1990; Harold K. Graves to Paul Turner, July 18, 1957, Edwin O. Kennedy to Paul Turner, April 27, 1957, Edward R. Morrow to Paul W. Turner, March 7, 1957, Liston Pope to Paul Turner, April 30, 1957, personal files of Steve Jones, Clinton, TN; Paul and Jane Turner to First Baptist Church of Clinton, September 28, 1958, First Baptist Church of Clinton, TN: Records 1840–1990; Paul Turner, "P.R. 651 Research Paper," Spring 1968, personal files of Steve Jones, Clinton, TN.

231   *December 18, 1980: Baptist Press*: News Service of the Southern Baptist Convention, December 23, 1980, 2–3; California Department of Health, "Death Certificates," s.v. "Paul Turner," Ancestry.com.

231   *"The Paul Turner":* Grimsley, "Who Pastors Pastors? . . . ," 1–2.

232   *Clinton High School had cost:* Bobby Cain interview; Anna Theresser Caswell interview; Bob Gilbert, "10 Years After Race Rift, Clinton Blames Outsiders," *Knoxville News-Sentinel*, August 26, 1966, 1, 13.

232   *symptoms of what we now:* "Trauma survivors cannot merely forget the past: rather, they are forced to live with a moment of time that curiously has no ending, that has attained no closure, and that can never be 'done,' " memory theorist Proma Tagore explains. "The uniqueness of trauma . . . rests precisely in such latency, that is, its

interruption and reworking of historical time. . . . Because survivors of violence are often unable to experience the traumatic event as it occurs—sometimes as a matter of survival—trauma is rarely felt in the present but rather experienced and communicated belatedly." Tagore, *The Shapes of Silence*, 15.

The question of PTSD among social justice activists is just beginning to be studied. For more information, check out Jane Barry with Jelena Djordjevic's *What's the Point of Revolution If We Can't Dance?*; Ruth Thompson-Miller, Joe R. Feagin, and Leslie H. Picca's *Jim Crow's Legacy: The Lasting Impact of Segregation*; and the Human Rights Resilience Project at the Center for Human Rights and Global Justice. If you are a white antiracist activist (or an ally in any of the other human justice fights), I encourage you to also read Gorski and Erakat's "Racism, Whiteness, and Burnout in Antiracism Movements."

232 *"I really did not"*: Anderson, *The Children of the South*, 64–65; Minnie Ann Dickie Jones interview.

232 *"The thing that I"*: Anderson, *The Children of the South*, 64–65.

TWENTY-ONE: SILENCE, SPREADING

233 *May 17, 2007*: Large Art Company, "The Large Art Company Completes Historic Sculptures in Tennessee"; "Governor's Budget Includes Money for 'Clinton 12' Statues," *Oak Ridger*, May 29, 2006; "Opening/Dedication," Green McAdoo Cultural Center, "Opening/Dedication."

233 *"I never thought"*: Billy Graham, "Billy Graham in Clinton, Tennessee, 1958," June N. Adamson Papers, Knoxville, TN.; "Billy Graham Says Love Is Answer to World Problems," *Clinton Courier-News*, December 18, 1958, 1, 6.

233 *Jo Ann Allen Boyce agreed*: Ibid.; Jo Ann Allen Boyce interview.

234 *Regina Turner's family*: Boyce and Levy, *This Promise of Change*, 269–70; Green McAdoo Cultural Center, "About the Center."

234 *Robert Thacker's family took*: Boyce and Levy, *This Promise of Change*, 270; *Mount Clemens High School 1958*, 27, Ancestry.com; "Robert Lee (Shine) Thacker," 2019, https://www.cobbsfuneralhome.com/obituaries/print?o_id=6737332.

234 *Maurice Soles enlisted*: Boyce and Levy, *This Promise of Change*, 268–69; Green McAdoo Cultural Center, "About the Center"; "Maurice Soles," *Oak Ridger*, December 26, 2011; Maurice Soles interview.

234 *Anna Theresser Caswell finished*: Boyce and Levy, *This Promise of Change*, 267; Anna Theresser Caswell interview; Green McAdoo Cultural Center, "About the Center"; Bria McKamey, "No Color Line at the Cross," *Triangle*, 2015, https://www.bryantriangle.com/presenting-the-winners-of-lit-contest-2015/.

234 *Ronald Hayden, who had*: Boyce and Levy, *This Promise of Change*, 270; Marilyn Hayden interview; Tennessee State Library and Archives, "Death Records, 1908–1965," s.v. "Ronald Gordon Hayden," Ancestry.com.

234 *Gail Ann followed*: Green McAdoo Cultural Center, "About the Center"; Gail Ann Epps Upton interview.

234   *Jo Ann Allen Boyce and:* Green McAdoo Cultural Center, "About the Center."

234   *May 1957, Alvah:* Anna Theresser Caswell interview; *El Companile*, 151, Ancestry.com; Green McAdoo Cultural Center, "About the Center"; Dick Turpin, "3,600 Get Diplomas at Rites in Southland," *Los Angeles Times*, June 10, 1963, 1, 37; Joseph R. Marshall, "White Students at Strife-Torn Clinton Firmly Opposed to Integration Orders," *Lubbock Evening Journal*, September 6, 1956, 12.

235   *Bobby Cain could not:* Bobby Cain interview; Bobby and Margo Cain interview.

235   *stopped talking:* Anna Theresser Caswell interview; Bria McKamey, "No Color Line at the Cross," *Triangle*, 2015, https://www.bryantriangle.com/presenting -the-winners-of-lit-contest-2015/.

235   *deep anger:* Bobby Cain interview; Eddie, Maurice, and Charles Soles interview; Maurice Soles interview; Alfred Williams interview.

235   *only reason Bobby's:* Bobby Cain interview.

237   *2001, Asbury Methodist:* Alan Jones interview.

237   *Reverend Willis told:* Ibid.; Bobby Cain interview.

237   *Alan wanted to celebrate:* Alan Jones interview; Bobby Cain interview; Alan Jones, *Untitled*, painted mural, 2004, Asbury United Methodist Church, Clinton, TN.

237   *May 16, 2004:* Alan Jones interview; Lola Alapo, "Crowd Urged to Commit to Justice," *Knoxville News-Sentinel*, May 17, 2004, A1, A7; Gail Ann Epps Upton interview.

238   *raze Green McAdoo:* Cleo Ellis interview; Marilyn Hayden interview; Alan Jones interview; Steve Jones interview; Wimp Shoopman interview; Jerry Shattuck interview.

238   *In the mid-1990s:* Batson v. Kentucky, 476 U.S. 79 (1986), 107; Carr, Sarah, "Why We Could Soon Lose Even More Black Teachers," *The Hechinger Report*, January 5, 2022. https://hechingerreport.org/why-we-could-soon-lose-even-more -black-teachers/.

238   *Black students carried the weight:* Carr, "Why We Could Soon Lose Even More Black Teachers"; El-Mekki, "To Achieve Educational Justice, We Need More Black Teachers"; Lutz, "The Hidden Cost of Brown v. Board."

239   *Ruling integration had been attained:* Perry, *South to America.*

239   *survey conducted at UC Berkeley:* Frankenberg et al., "Harming our Common Future"; Menendian, Gambhir, and Gailes, "The Roots of Structural Racism Project."

240   *school segregation more than:* Frankenberg et al., "Harming our Common Future"; Menendian, Gambhir, and Gailes, "The Roots of Structural Racism Project"; Frankenberg et al., "Southern Schools."

240   *Pinellas County:* "Failure Factories," *Tampa Bay Times*, 2015–17, https://projects .tampabay.com; Schnur, "Desegregation of Public Schools in Pinellas County, Florida," 26–43.

240   *Cleveland, Mississippi:* McLaughlin, "Mississippi School District Ends Segregation Fight."

240   *New York City, the most:* Cohen, "NYC School Segregation Report Card."

241   *the Nashville Way:* Houston, *The Nashville Way.*

EPILOGUE: FROM THE TOP OF FREEDMAN'S HILL, JULY 2009

245   *A year earlier:* Hohle, *Racism in the Neoliberal Era*; Matt Lakin, "Cross Burner Gets 6 Months in Prison," *Knoxville News-Sentinel*, March 19, 2011, 4.

245   *It was the 1980s:* Meier, Stewart, and England, *Race, Class and Education*, 136; Neil, "New Report Shows Segregation Is Increasing."

246   *"Desegregation involves":* Anderson, "The South Learns Its Hardest Lessons."

BIBLIOGRAPHY

NEWSPAPERS

Afro-American (1956–58)
Baltimore Afro-American (1956–58)
Chicago Defender (1956–58)
Citizens' Council (1956–60)
Clinton Courier-News (1950–60)
Clinton–Knox County Stars and Bars (February 8, 1957)
East Tennessee Reporter (1956–57)
Knoxville Journal (1956–60)
Knoxville News-Sentinel (1956–60)
Nashville Banner (1956–60)
New York Times (1956–60)
Oak Ridger (1954–60)
Southern School News (1955–60)
Tennessee Reporter (1956–58)
Tennessean (1956–60)
Tri-State Defender (1956–60)

ARCHIVAL COLLECTIONS

Adamson, June N. June N. Adamson Papers, 1870–2003, MS 2739. University of Tennessee Special Collections Library, Knoxville, TN.

Anderson County, TN. *Anderson County Records*. Microfilm collection, Tennessee State Library and Archives, Nashville.

"Clinton, TN, Schools." Vertical file. Knox County Archives, Knoxville, TN.

Federal Bureau of Investigation. "KASPER, Frederick John—HQ 67-105095." Digital file. https://archive.org.

First Baptist Church of Clinton, TN. First Baptist Church of Clinton, TN: Records 1840–1990. Microfilm collection, Knox County Archives, Knoxville, TN.

Greene, Lee S. Lee S. Greene Collection, 1930–1986, MS-1391. University of Tennessee Special Collections Library, Knoxville.

Holden, Anna. Papers, 1946–1977. Microfilm collection, Wisconsin Historical Archives, Madison.

National Archives and Records Administration. "Returns from Regular Army Infantry Regiments, June 1821–December 1916." Ancestry.com.

Records of the Selective Service System. "World War II Draft Cards Young Men, 1940–1947." Ancestry.com.

"Segregation Report: The Statements of Asa (Ace) Carter, John Kasper, James Dodrell, Harold McBride, and Kenneth Adams." September 30, 1956. Knox County Archives, Knoxville, TN.

Social Security Administration. "Social Security Applications and Claims Index, 1936–2007." Ancestry.com.

_____. "Social Security Death Index." Ancestry.com.

Tennessee State Library and Archives. "Tennessee Death Records, 1908–1958." Ancestry.com.

_____. "Tennessee State Marriage Index, 1780–2002." FamilySearch.com.

Tennessee Valley Authority. "Family Removal and Population Readjustment Case Files, 1934–1953." Ancestry.com.

Turner, Paul. Papers. Personal files of Steve Jones, Clinton, TN.

United States Court of Appeals. "*Alonzo Bullock et al. v. United States of America v. Frederick John Kasper*, 1957, Case No. 13512 and 13513." United States District Court, Eastern District of Tennessee at Knoxville. National Archives and Records Administration—Southeast Region, Atlanta, GA.

_____. "*Joheather McSwain et al. v. County Board of Education of Anderson County*, 1950, Case No. 1555." United States District Court, Eastern District of Tennessee at Knoxville. Civil Liberties Cases, National Archives and Records Administration—Southeast Region, Atlanta, GA.

_____. "*Joheather McSwain et al. v. County Board of Education of Anderson County*, 1952, Case No. 1555." United States District Court, Eastern District of Tennessee at Knoxville. Civil Liberties Cases, National Archives and Records Administration—Southeast Region, Atlanta, GA.

"U.S., World War II Army Enlistment Records, 1938–1946." Ancestry.com.

PHOTOGRAPHS, TELEVISION PROGRAMS, AND OTHER MEDIA

Associated Press. AP Images, New York. http://www.apimages.com/.

Bettmann Archive. Photographic archive. Getty Images, New York. http://gettyimages .com/.

Corman, Roger. *The Intruder*. Charleston, SC: Roger Corman Productions, 1962.

Jones, Alan. *Untitled*. Painted mural. 2004. Asbury United Methodist Church, Clinton, TN.

Knoxville Journal. Photographic Collection. Knox County Archives, Knoxville, TN.

Life. Photographic archive. Getty Images, New York. http://gettyimages.com/.

_____. Photographic archive. Google Arts and Culture, Mountain View, CA. https:// artsandculture.google.com/entity/clinton/m0_srh?categoryId=place.

Reasoner, Harry, Fred W. Friendly, Arthur D. Morse, Ralph McGill, Leonoir Chambers, S. Ernest Vandiver, and Orval Eugene Faubus. *CBS Reports: The Other Face of Dixie*. "Integration in the South's Public Schools." Aired October 24, 1962, on CBS.

Time. Photographic archive. Getty Images, New York. http://gettyimages.com/.

Williams, Palmer, Edward R. Murrow, Fred W. Friendly, Arthur D. Morse, and Edmund Scott. "Clinton and the Law: A Study in Desegregation." Directed by Don Hewitt. *See It Now.* First broadcast January 6, 1957, on CBS.

ORAL HISTORY INTERVIEWS

Anderson, Margaret. Interview by Rachel L. Martin. Digital recording. Clinton, TN. October 21, 2005. MTSU Center for Historic Preservation, Murfreesboro, TN.

Bolling, David O. Interview by June Adamson. Analog recording. August 29, 1980. University of Tennessee Special Collections, Knoxville.

Boyce, Jo Ann Crozier Allen. Interview by Rachel L. Martin. Digital recording. July 20, 2009. Clinton, TN. In the possession of the interviewer, Nashville, TN.

Brannon, Robert. Interview by Keith McDaniel. Digital recording. March 18, 2011. Oak Ridge, TN. Oak Ridge Public Library, Oak Ridge, TN.

Brewer, Dudley. Interview by June Adamson. Analog recording. July 10, 1979. University of Tennessee Special Collections, Knoxville.

Brittain, D. J., Jr. Interview by June Adamson. Analog recording. 1978. University of Tennessee Special Collections, Knoxville.

Burnett, Leo. Interview by June Adamson. Analog recording. March 20, 1980. University of Tennessee Special Collections, Knoxville.

Byerly, Don and Sue. Interview by Rachel L. Martin. Digital recording. July 20, 2009. Knoxville, TN. In the possession of the interviewer, Nashville, TN.

Cain, Bobby. Interview by Rachel L. Martin. Digital recording. July 18, 2009. Nashville, TN. In the possession of the interviewer, Nashville, TN.

Cain, Bobby, and Margo Cain. Interview by Gwen Smith. Digital recording. June 13, 2007. Nashville Public Library, Nashville, TN.

Cain, James L. Interview by Rachel L. Martin. Digital recording. October 21, 2005. Clinton, TN. MTSU Center for Historic Preservation, Murfreesboro, TN.

Cain, Robert, Sr. Interview by June Adamson. Analog recording. January 20, 1979. University of Tennessee Special Collections, Knoxville.

Caldwell, Ken. Interview by June Adamson. Analog recording. October 29, 1979. University of Tennessee Special Collections, Knoxville.

Caswell, Anna Theresser. Interview by Rachel L. Martin. Digital recording. October 22, 2005. Claxton, TN. MTSU Center for Historic Preservation, Murfreesboro, TN.

Coker, Bettye. Interview by Rachel L. Martin. Digital recording. July 15, 2009. Clinton, TN. In the possession of the interviewer, Nashville, TN.

Copeland, Homer. Interview by Rachel L. Martin. Digital recording. August 17, 2009. Clinton, TN. In the possession of the interviewer, Nashville, TN.

Cowan, Carl. Interview by June Adamson. Analog recording. August 29, 1979. University of Tennessee Special Collections, Knoxville.

Crawford, John C., III. Interview by June Adamson. Analog recording. October 23, 1981. University of Tennessee Special Collections, Knoxville.

Davenport, Shirley and James. Interview by Rachel L. Martin. Digital recording. November 18, 2005. Knoxville, TN. MTSU Center for Historic Preservation, Murfreesboro, TN.

Davis, Eleanor. Interview by June Adamson. Analog recording. September 12, 1978. University of Tennessee Special Collections, Knoxville.

Ellis, Cleo. Interview by Rachel L. Martin. Digital recording. July 23, 2009. Clinton, TN. In the possession of the interviewer, Nashville, TN.

Fuller, Helen. Interview by Rachel L. Martin. Digital recording. October 22, 2005. Clinton, TN. MTSU Center for Historic Preservation, Murfreesboro, TN.

Fulks, Alama. Interview by June Adamson. Analog recording. July 29, 1980. University of Tennessee Special Collections, Knoxville.

Hamilton, Jerry. Interview by Rachel L. Martin. Digital recording. August 19, 2009. Clinton, TN. In the possession of the interviewer, Nashville, TN.

Hayden, Marilyn. Interview by Rachel L. Martin. Digital recording. July 23, 2009. Clinton, TN. In the possession of the interviewer, Nashville, TN.

Hayden, Sara. Interview by Rachel L. Martin. Digital Recording. November 19, 2005. Clinton, TN. MTSU Center for Historic Preservation, Murfreesboro, TN.

Henley, Mattie Bell. Interview by June Adamson. Analog recording. July 12, 1978. University of Tennessee Special Collections, Knoxville.

Henry, Joe. Interview by June Adamson. Analog recording. January 9, 1980. University of Tennessee Special Collections, Knoxville.

Hooper, Fred. Interview by Rachel L. Martin. Digital recording. July 21, 2009. Oliver Springs, TN. In the possession of the interviewer, Nashville, TN.

Hoskins, Steve. Interview by Rachel L. Martin. Digital recording. June 19, 2009. Murfreesboro, TN. In the possession of the interviewer, Nashville, TN.

Humphrey, Steve. Interview by June Adamson. Analog recording. July 25, 1978. University of Tennessee Special Collections, Knoxville.

Iker, Gladys. Interview by June Adamson. Analog recording. March 21, 1980. University of Tennessee Special Collections, Knoxville.

Jones, Alan. Interview by Rachel L. Martin. Digital recording. July 25, 2009. Knoxville, TN. In the possession of the interviewer, Nashville, TN.

Jones, Steve. Interview by Rachel L. Martin. Digital recording. July 23, 2009. Clinton, TN. In the possession of the interviewer, Nashville, TN.

Lewallen, Buford. Interview by June Adamson. Analog recording. March 23, May 23, June 20, 1990. University of Tennessee Special Collections, Knoxville.

Lewallen, Celdon. Interview by Rachel L. Martin. Digital recording. October 22, 2005. Clinton, TN. MTSU Center for Historic Preservation, Murfreesboro, TN.

Lunsford, Hugh. Interview by June Adamson. Analog recording. July 3, 1979. University of Tennessee Special Collections, Knoxville.

McAlduff, Harold. Interview by Rachel L. Martin. Digital recording. October 21, 2005. Oak Ridge, TN. MTSU Center for Historic Preservation, Murfreesboro, TN.

Martin, Gail. Interview by Rachel L. Martin. Digital recording. August 20, 2009. Clinton, TN. In the possession of the interviewer, Nashville, TN.

McIlwain, Milton. Interview by Rachel L. Martin. Digital recording. July 22, 2009. Knoxville, TN. In the possession of the interviewer, Nashville, TN.

McNees, Bob and Elizabeth. Interview by June Adamson. Analog recording. July 21, 1980. University of Tennessee Special Collections, Knoxville.

Michael, W. E. Interview by June Adamson. Analog recording. October 1, 1982. University of Tennessee Special Collections, Knoxville.

Miller, Loye. Interview by June Adamson. Analog recording. March 27, 1979. University of Tennessee Special Collections, Knoxville.

Moore, Diane. Interview by Rachel L. Martin. Digital recording. November 19, 2009. Clinton, TN. MTSU Center for Historic Preservation, Murfreesboro, TN.

Pemberton, Diane. Interview by Rachel L. Martin. Digital recording. October 22, 2005. Clinton, TN. MTSU Center for Historic Preservation, Murfreesboro, TN.

Quinn, Henry. Interview by June Adamson. Analog recording. 1990. University of Tennessee Special Collections, Knoxville.

Rose, Nava Lou Dunnaway. Interview by Rachel L. Martin. Digital Recording. June 22, 2009. Biloxi, MS. In the possession of the interviewer, Nashville, TN.

Rutherford, Geneva. Interview by Rachel L. Martin. Digital recording. August 16, 2009. Clinton, TN. In the possession of the interviewer, Nashville, TN.

Shattuck, Jerry. Interview by June Adamson. Analog recording. February 5, 1979. University of Tennessee Special Collections, Knoxville.

———. Interview by Rachel L. Martin. Digital recording. July 15, 2009. Clinton, TN. In the possession of the interviewer, Durham, NC.

Shoopman, Wimp. Interview by Rachel L. Martin. Digital recording. July 16, 2009. Clinton, TN. In the possession of the interviewer, Durham, NC.

Skaggs, Dail, Mary Jane Martin, and Antoinette Martinez. Interview by June Adamson. Analog recording. August 28, 1979. University of Tennessee Special Collections, Knoxville.

Smith, Regina Turner. Interview by June Adamson. Analog recording. August 7, 1980. University of Tennessee Special Collections, Knoxville.

Soles, Eddie, Maurice, and Charles. Interview by June Adamson. Analog recording. October 15, 1980. University of Tennessee Special Collections, Knoxville.

Soles, Maurice. Interview by Rachel L. Martin. Digital recording. August 19, 2009. Clinton, TN. In the possession of the interviewer, Nashville, TN.

Stansberry, Dr. and Florence. Interview by Rachel L. Martin. Digital recording. October 22, 2005. Clinton, TN. MTSU Center for Historic Preservation, Murfreesboro, TN.

Taylor, Robert L. Interview by June Adamson. Analog recording. July 13, 1978. University of Tennessee Special Collections, Knoxville.

Trentham, Charles. Interview by June Adamson. Analog recording. August 14, 1979. University of Tennessee Special Collections, Knoxville.

Turner, Paul. Interview by June Adamson. Analog recording. 1980. University of Tennessee Special Collections, Knoxville.

Upton, Gail Ann Epps. Interview by June Adamson. Analog recording. October 1, 1982. University of Tennessee Special Collections, Knoxville.

_____. Interview by Rachel L. Martin. Digital recording. August 20, 2009. Sweetwater, TN. In the possession of the interviewer, Nashville, TN.

Weals, Vic. Interview by June Adamson. Analog recording. October 5, 1979. University of Tennessee Special Collections, Knoxville.

Weaver, Eugene. Interview by June Adamson. Analog recording. January 6, 1980. University of Tennessee Special Collections, Knoxville.

Wells, Horace V. Interview by June Adamson. Analog recording. May 8, 1990. Clinton, TN. University of Tennessee Special Collections, Knoxville.

West, C. Van. Interview by Rachel L. Martin. Digital recording. June 19, 2009. Murfreesboro, TN. In the possession of the interviewer, Nashville, TN.

West, David Earl. Interview by Rachel L. Martin. Digital recording. July 20, 2009. Knoxville, TN. In the possession of the interviewer, Nashville, TN.

Williams, Alfred. Interview by Rachel L. Martin. Digital recording. October 22, 2005. Clinton, TN. MTSU Center for Historic Preservation, Murfreesboro, TN.

Willis, Orville. Interview by June Adamson. Analog recording. July 10, 1978. University of Tennessee Special Collections, Knoxville.

Woodward, Mae. Interview by June Adamson. Analog recording. July 21, 1980. University of Tennessee Special Collections, Knoxville.

ARTICLES AND ESSAYS

Academy of American Poets, The. "Ezra Pound." http://www.poets.org/poet.php/prm PID/161.

Acosta, Anna M., Pedro L. Moro, Susan Hariri, and Tejpratap S. P. Tiwari. "Diphtheria." CDC, August 2021. https://www.cdc.gov/vaccines/pubs/pinkbook/dip.html.

Adamson, June N. "Few Black Voices Heard: The Black Community & the Desegregation Crisis in Clinton, TN, 1956." *Tennessee Historical Quarterly* 53 (1994): 30–41.

_____. "Two Religious Magazines Report on South's First Public School Desegregation." For presentation at the Seventy-Fourth Annual AEJMC Convention. Boston, August 7–10, 1991.

Anderson, Margaret. "Children in a Crucible." *New York Times*, November 2, 1958. http://proquest.umi.com.

_____. "The South Learns Its Hardest Lessons." *New York Times*, September 11, 1960. http://proquest.umi.com.

"Back to School." *Time*, September 10, 1956. http://content.time.com.

Balloch, Jim, and Jamie Satterfield. "'I Am Proud of My Heritage': Former Student Defends Confederate Flag." *Knoxville News-Sentinel*, August 12, 2008. http://www.knoxnews.com/.

Blair, Carol, and Neil Michel. "Reproducing Civil Rights Tactics: The Rhetorical Performances of the Civil Rights Memorial." *Rhetoric Society Quarterly* 30, no. 2 (Spring 2000): 31–55.

Brill, Andrew. "*Brown* in Fayetteville: Peaceful Southern School Desegregation in 1954."

Arkansas Historical Quarterly 65, no. 4 (Winter 2006): 337–59. https://www.jstor .org/stable/40028090.

Butcher, Jamie. "Religion, Race, Gender, and Education: The Allen School, Asheville, North Carolina, 1885 to 1974." *Appalachian Journal* 33, no. 1 (Fall 2005): 78–109. https://www.jstor.org/stable/40934774.

Carr, Sarah. "Why We Could Soon Lose Even More Black Teachers." *The Hechinger Report*, January 5, 2022. https://hechingerreport.org/why-we-could-soon-lose-even -more-black-teachers/.

"Celebrating Elvis Presley's First Appearance on the Ed Sullivan Show (September 9, 1956)." *Graceland Blog*, September 9, 2020. https://www.graceland.com/blog/posts /elvis-presleys-first-appearance-on-the-ed-sullivan-show.

Cleveland, Mary L. "A Baptist Pastor and Social Injustice in Clinton, TN." *Baptist History & Heritage* 14 (1979): 15–19.

"Cover Story." *Metro Pulse*, August 24, 2006. http://www.metropulse.com/news/2006 /aug/24/cover_story-2006-34/.

Dailey, Jane. "Sex, Segregation and the Sacred after *Brown*." *Journal of American History* 91, no. 1 (June 2004): 119–44.

Dykeman, Wilma. "Clinton, Tennessee: A Town on Trial." *New York Times Magazine*, October 26, 1958.

Dykeman, Wilma, and James Stokely. "Courage in Action in Clinton, TN." *Nation*, December 22, 1956, 531–33.

———. "On the Road with John Kasper." *New Republic* 139, no. 22 (December 1, 1958): 13–14.

———. " 'The South' in the North." *New York Times Magazine*, April 17, 1960. http:// proquest.umi.com.

El-Mekki, Sharif. "To Achieve Educational Justice, We Need More Black Teachers." *EdSurge*, September 9, 2021. https://www.edsurge.com/news/2021-09-09-to-achieve -educational-justice-we-need-more-black-teachers.

Eriksson, Katherine, and Gregory T. Niemesh. "Death in the Promised Land: The Great Migration and Black Infant Mortality." *SSRN*, 2016, 16. https://papers.ssrn.com /sol3/papers.cfm?abstract_id=3071053.

Fitzpatrick, Cara, Lisa Gartner, and Michael LaForgia. "Failure Factories." *Tampa Bay Times*, 2015–17. https://projects.tampabay.com/projects/2015/investigations/pin ellas-failure-factories/.

"Former Pastor, Prof, Found Dead in Home." *Baptist Press*: News Service of the Southern Baptist Convention, December 23, 1980, 2–3.

Friend, Craig Thompson. "From Southern Manhood to Southern Masculinities: An Introduction." In *Southern Masculinity: Perspectives on the South Since Reconstruction*, edited by Craig Thompson Friend, vii–xxvi. Athens: University of Georgia Press, 2009.

Gorski, Paul C., and Noura Erakat. "Racism, Whiteness, and Burnout in Antiracism Movements: How White Racial Justice Activists Elevate Burnout in Racial Justice Activists of Color in the United States." *Ethnicities*, March 21, 2019. https://doi .org/10.1177/1468796819833871.

"Governor's Budget Includes Money for 'Clinton 12' Statues." *Oak Ridger*, May 29, 2006. http://nl.newsbank.com/.

Green McAdoo Cultural Center. "About the Center." https://www.greenmcadoo.org /about-the-center.

———. "Opening/Dedication." http://www.greenmcadoo.com/grandopening.html.

Grimsley, Roger. "Who Pastors Pastors? ..." *The Voice of St. Luke's Cumberland Presbyterian Church* 7, no. 47 (December 20, 1980): 1–2.

"Guide to Declarations of Martial Law in the United States." Brennan Center. https:// www.brennancenter.org/our-work/research-reports/guide-declarations-martial-law -united-states.

Hall, Jacquelyn Dowd. "The Long Civil Rights Movement and the Political Uses of the Past." *Journal of American History* 91, no. 4 (2005): 1233–63.

Hamburger, Robert. "'For Us the Living:' Visits to Civil Rights Museums." *Southern Cultures* 14:3 (Fall 2008): 52–67.

Hays, Gabrielle, and Madison Stacey. "And Her Name Is Adaline." *10News*, February 22, 2020. https://www.wbir.com/article/features/her-name-is-adaline.

Hechinger, Fred M. "Clinton and the Law." *Herald Magazine*, January 20, 1957, 5.

Herman, George R. "A Bad Day at Douglas Army Airfield." *Arizona Historical Society* 36, no. 4 (Winter 1995): 367–92.

Hoffschwelle, Mary S. "Public Education in Tennessee." *Trials, Triumphs and Transformations: Tennesseans' Search for Citizenship, Community, and Opportunity*. Murfreesboro: Middle Tennessee State University, 2014. https://dsi.mtsu.edu/trials.

Hofstadter, Richard. "Reflections on Violence in the United States." In *American Violence: A Documentary History*, edited by Richard Hofstadter and Michael Wallace, 3–46. New York: Knopf, 1970.

Janssen, Richard F. "Clinton Aftermath: Integrated Tennessee School Opens Calmly but Tensions Persist." *Wall Street Journal*, September 3, 1958. http://proquest.umi.com.

Jean-Jacques, Johanne. "Love Overcomes a Young Man's Anger." *Clinton Courier-News*, June 4, 2006. http://www.greenmcadoo.org/alfred.html.

Jones, Robert W., Jr. "Howard James Sochurek (1924–1994)." *Veritas* 3, no. 2 (2007). https://arsof-history.org/articles/v3n2_montagnard_sb_sochurek.html.

Large Art Company. "The Large Art Company Completes Historic Sculptures in Tennessee." 2007. http://largeart.com/press/Custom-Commission-Bronze-Sculpture -Clinton-12-Green-McAdoo.aspx.

Leonard, Ira M. "Think Piece: Violence is the Engine of U.S. History (Part I)." *Black Commentator*, June 30, 2005. http://www.blackcommentator.com/144/144_think_ violence_1.html.

Lowenstein, Nancy J., Stephen F. Enloe, John W. Everest. James H. Miller, Donald M. Ball, and Michael G. Patterson. "History and Use of Kudzu in the Southeastern United States." *Forestry & Wildlife*, March 8, 2022. https://www.aces.edu/blog/topics /invasive-species/the-history-and-use-of-kudzu-in-the-southeastern-united-states/.

Lutz, Mallory. "The Hidden Cost of *Brown v. Board*: African American Educators' Resistance to Desegregating Schools." *Online Journal of Rural Research & Policy* 12, no. 4

(2017). https://newprairiepress.org/cgi/viewcontent.cgi?article=1085&context}=
ojrrp.

McLaughlin, Elliott C. "Mississippi School District Ends Segregation Fight." CNN,
March 14, 2017. https://www.cnn.com/2017/03/14/us/cleveland-mississippi-school
-desegregation-settlement/index.html.

McMillan, George. "The Ordeal of Bobby Cain." *Collier's*, November 23, 1956, 68–69.
http://historymatters.gmu.edu/d/6254/.

McMillen, Neil R. "Organized Resistance to School Desegregation in Tennessee." *Tennessee Historical Quarterly* 30 (1971): 315–28.

Martin, Rachel Louise. "The Brave and Tragic Trail of Reverend Turner." *Narratively*
(January 2015). https://narratively.com/the-brave-and-tragic-trail-of-reverend-turner/.

——. "Let Me Tell You About Coal Creek." *Oxford American* (Summer 2019). https://
main.oxfordamerican.org/magazine/item/1757-let-me-tell-you-about-coal-creek.

——. "The Clinton 12." *US of America*, (February 2018): 224–29.

Menendian, Stephen, Samir Gambhir, and Arthur Gailes. "The Roots of Structural Racism Project." *Belonging*, June 21, 2021. https://belonging.berkeley.edu/roots-structural
-racism.

"Mid-Content Refinery Strike." In Oklahoma Historical Society, *Encyclopedia of Oklahoma History and Culture*. https://www.okhistory.org/publications/enc/entry.php?entry
=MI005.

Moore, Scotty. "Elvis' 1955 Martin 9-28." 2003. http://scottymoore.net/55D28.html.

Neil, Marcus-Alexander. "New Report Shows Segregation Is Increasing." The Leadership Conference, January 26, 2009. http://www.civilrights.org/archives/2009/01/030
-school-segregation.html.

Newsom, Moses. "Mixed Schools 'Old Hat' to One Junior in Clinton." *Chicago Defender*, September 13, 1956, 10.

Ogletree, Charles J. "All Deliberate Speed." Center for American Progress, April 12,
2004. https://www.americanprogress.org/article/all-deliberate-speed/.

Orfield, Gary. "Schools More Separate: Consequences of a Decade of Resegregation." Boston: Harvard Civil Rights Project, 2007. http://www.eric.ed.gov/PDFS
/ED459217.pdf. http://www.civilrights.org/education/resegregation/american82
17s-schools8212increasingly-separate-and-unequal.html; http://www.csmonitor.com
/USA/Society/2008/0125/p01s01-ussc.html.

Orfield, Gary, and Chungmei Lee. "Why Segregation Matters: Poverty and Educational
Inequality." Cambridge, MA: The Civil Rights Project, Harvard University, 2005.
http://civilrightsproject.ucla.edu/research/k-12-education/integration-and-diver
sity/why-segregation-matters-poverty-and-educational-inequality/orfield-why-segre
gation-matters-2005.pdf.

Orfield, Gary, and John T. Yun. "Resegregation in American Schools." Cambridge, MA:
The Civil Rights Project, Harvard University, 1999. http://w3.uchastings.edu/win
gate/PDF/Resegregation_American_Schools99.pdf.

Pearson, Drew. Washington Merry-Go-Round. American University Digital Research
Archive. https://auislandora.wrlc.org/islandora/object/pearson%3A1.

"Photography of Howard Sochurek." *Life*. https://www.life.com/photographer/howard
-sochurek/.

Poetry Foundation. "Ezra Pound." http://www.poetryfoundation.org/bio/ezra-pound.

Pounds, Jessie. "Clinton 12 Recall Emotions of Desegregation." *Knoxville News-Sentinel*,
February 28, 2009. http://www.knoxnews.com/news/2009/feb/28/clinton-12-recall
-emotions-of-desegregation/.

"The Press: The Southern Front." *Time*, September 17, 1956. http://www.time.com
/time/magazine/article/0,9171,893568-1,00.html.

Ramsey, Sonya. " 'We Will Be Ready Whenever They Are': African American Teachers'
Responses to the *Brown* Decision and Public School Integration in Nashville, Tennessee, 1954–1966." *Journal of African American History* 90, no. 1-2 (2005): 29–51.

Schnur, James Anthony. "Desegregation of Public Schools in Pinellas County, Florida."
Tampa Bay History 13 (Spring/Summer 1991): 26–43. https://digitalcommons.usf
.edu/cgi/viewcontent.cgi?article=4002&context=fac_publications.

Smith, Courtland. "An Interpretative History of the First Ten Years." In *Alive in the
Spirit: Essays on the First Fifty Years of the Olin T. Binkley Memorial Baptist Church*,
1–3. Chapel Hill, NC: self-published, 2008.

Smith, David Ray. "McSwain Sisters Tell the Story That Predated the Clinton 12." *Historically Speaking*, September 2, 2006. http://smithdray1.net/historicallyspeaking
/2006/9-2-06%20McSwain%20Sisters.pdf.

Stoecker, Jen, and Carroll Van West. "Pearl High School (Martin Luther King Magnet)
Nashville." *Southern Places*. Murfreesboro: Middle Tennessee State University James
E. Walker Library, 2005. https://digital.mtsu.edu/digital/collection/p15838coll4
/id/625.

Tagore, Proma. *The Shapes of Silence: Writing by Women of Colour and the Politics of Testimony*. Montreal: McGill-Queen's University Press, 2009.

Taylor, E. L. (Stacey) Hebden. "Retribution, Responsibility and Freedom: The Fallacy
of Modern Criminal Law from a Biblical-Christian Perspective." *Law and Contemporary Problems* 44, no. 2 (Spring 1981): 51–82.

Titus, Julia. "Allen High School History." 1962. http://toto.lib.unca.edu/findingaids
/mss/blackhigh/hbh_schools/allen_high_school.htm.

United States Court of Appeals. "Appeal from the United States District Court for
the Eastern District of Tennessee at Knoxville. No. 06-00450—Thomas A. Varlan,
District Judge." *Defoe et al. v. Spiva et. al*. Cincinnati, OH: United States Court of
Appeals for the Sixth Circuit, 2010. http://www.ca6.uscourts.gov/opinions.pdf/10a
0358p-06.pdf.

United States District Court. "Filing 323: Memorandum and Order." *Defoe et al. v. Spiva
et al*. Knoxville: United States District Court, Eastern District of Tennessee at Knoxville, 2009. http://docs.justia.com/.

———. "Filing 429: Memorandum Opinion." *Defoe et al. v. Spiva et al*. Knoxville: United
States District Court, Eastern District of Tennessee at Knoxville, 2009. http://docs
.justia.com/

———. "First Amended Complaint." *Shreeve et al. v. Obama et al*. Chattanooga: United

States District Court, Eastern District of Tennessee at Chattanooga, 2010. http:// www.libertylegalfoundation.net/.

———. "Memorandum of Facts and Law in Support of Defendants' Response to Motion of Summary Judgement." *Tommy Defoe v. The Anderson County School Board*. Chattanooga: United States District Court, Eastern District of Tennessee at Chattanooga, 2007. http://web.knoxnews.com/pdf/081208flag_school.pdf.

U.S. Department of Energy. *Environmental Assessment, Proposed Changes to the Sanitary Sludge Land Application Program on the Oak Ridge Reservation*, DOE/EA-1042, 1996. https://www.energy.gov/sites/default/files/EA-1042-FEA-1997.pdf.

———. "Introduction to the Oak Ridge Reservation." *Oak Ridge Reservation Annual Site Environmental Report—2013*, August 2014. https://doeic.science.energy.gov/aser /aser2013/Chapter%201_Introduction%20to%20the%20Oak%20Ridge%20Res ervation.pdf.

Vanlandingham, K. Elizabeth. "Sites of Resistance: History, Memory and Community." *Carson Newman Studies* 15, no. 1 (Fall 2014): 5–18. https://classic.cn.edu/libraries/ tiny_mce/tiny_mce/plugins/filemanager/files/library/Carson_Newman_Studies /v15n1_2014.pdf.

Vervack, Jerry J. "The Hoxie Imbroglio," *Arkansas Historical Quarterly* 48, no. 1 (Spring 1989): 17–33. https://www.jstor.org/stable/40027804.

Walker, Anders. "*Blackboard Jungle*: Delinquency, Desegregation and the Cultural Politics of *Brown*." *Columbia Law Review* 110, no. 7 (November 2010): 1911–53.

Walker, Hunter. "This Is What It's Like to Get Tear-gassed." *Business Insider*, August 14, 2014. https://www.businessinsider.com/this-is-what-its-like-to-get-tear -gassed-2014-8.

Watts, Trent. "Introduction: Telling White Men's Stories." In *White Masculinity in the Recent South*, edited by Trent Watts, 1–29. Baton Rouge: Louisiana State University Press, 2008.

Weeks, Lee. "Southeastern's 2nd President, Olin T. Binkley, Dies at 91." Baptist Press, August 27, 1999. http://www.bpnews.net/bpnews.asp?id=457.

Wells, Horace V., Jr. " 'Imported' Racism Poisons a Town." *Washington Post and Times Herald*, September 23, 1956. http://proquest.umi.com.

West, Carroll Van. "The Civil Rights Movement in Clinton and Its Relationship to Green McAdoo School." *Southern Places*. Murfreesboro: Middle Tennessee State University James E. Walker Library, 2005. https://digital.mtsu.edu/digital/collec tion/p15838coll4/id/552/.

———. "Description, Green McAdoo School." *Southern Places*. Murfreesboro: Middle Tennessee State University James E. Walker Library, 2005, https://digital.mtsu.edu /digital/collection/p15838coll4/id/541/rec/1.

BOOKS, PAMPHLETS, AND DISSERTATIONS

Adamson, June. "The Lit Stick of Dynamite: Clinton, Tennessee, Faces Brown v. Board of Education." Oak Ridge, TN: published by the author, 1999.

Anderson, Margaret. *The Children of the South*. New York: Farrar, Straus and Giroux, 1966.

Anderson, Susan Willoughby. "The Past on Trial: The Sixteenth Street Baptist Church Bombing, Civil Rights Memory and the Remaking of Birmingham." PhD dissertation, University of North Carolina at Chapel Hill, 2008.

Armada, Bernard John. "The Fiery Urgency of Now: Public Memory and Civic Transformation of at the National Civil Rights Museum." PhD dissertation, Pennsylvania State University, 1999.

Arnow, Harriette Simpson. *Seedtime on the Cumberland*. East Lansing: Michigan University Press, 2013.

Ayers, Edward L. *The Promise of the New South: Life after Reconstruction*. New York: Oxford University Press, 1992.

Ayers, William, and Therese Quinn. Foreword to *Refusing Racism: White Allies and the Struggle for Civil Rights* by Cynthia Stokes Brown, ix–xii. New York: Teachers College Press, 2002.

Baker, Bruce E. *What Reconstruction Meant: Historical Memory in the American South*. Charlottesville: University of Virginia Press, 2007.

Bal, Mieke, Jonathan V. Crewe, and Leo Spitzer. *Acts of Memory: Cultural Recall in the Present*. Hanover, NH: Dartmouth College, 1999.

Barclay, Joanne Sarah. "Uncivil War: Memory and Identity in the Reconstruction of the Civil Rights Movement." M.A. thesis, University of North Carolina at Chapel Hill, 2005.

Barry, Jane, and Jelena Djordjevic. *What's the Point of Revolution If We Can't Dance?* New York: Urgent Action Fund, 2008.

Bartley, Numan V. *The Rise of Massive Resistance: Race and Politics in the South during the 1950's*. Baton Rouge: Louisiana State University Press, 1969.

Bell, Augusta Grove. *Circling Windrock Mountain: Two Hundred Years in Appalachia*. Knoxville: University of Tennessee Press, 1998.

Blee, Kathleen, M. *Inside Organized Racism: Women in the Hate Movement*. Berkeley: University of California Press, 2002.

———. ed. *No Middle Ground: Women and Radical Protest*. New York: New York University Press, 1998.

Boyce, Jo Ann Allen, and Debby Levy. *This Promise of Change: One Girl's Story in the Fight for School Equality*. New York: Bloomsbury, 2019.

Brittain, D. J., Jr. "A Case Study of the Problems of Racial Integration in Clinton, Tennessee, High School: A Study Concerned with the Problems Faced by School Officials in the Racial Integration of a Public Secondary School in Compliance with a Federal Court Order." PhD dissertation, New York University, 1960.

Brown, Richard Maxwell. *Strain of Violence: Historical Studies of American Violence and Vigilantism*. New York: Oxford University Press, 1975.

Brundage, William Fitzhugh. *The Southern Past: A Clash of Race and Memory*. Cambridge, MA: Belknap Press, 2005.

Burlein, Ann. *Lift High the Cross: Where White Supremacy and the Christian Right Converge*. Durham, NC: Duke University Press, 2002.

Butchart, Ronald E. *Schooling the Freed People: Teaching, Learning, and the Struggle for Black Freedom, 1861–1876*. Chapel Hill: University of North Carolina Press, 2010.

Bynum, Jamie. *The Uprising of '34*. West Georgia Textile Heritage Trail. https://westgatextiletrail.com/feature-stories/the-uprising-of-34/.

Cahn, Susan K. *Sexual Reckonings: Southern Girls in a Troubling Age*. Cambridge, MA: Harvard University Press, 2007.

Chadwick, Janie Farmer. "A Comparative Study of Graduates of Clinton High School Who Had Attended Anderson County and Clinton City Elementary Schools." M.S. thesis, University of Tennessee, 1962.

Chappell, David L. *A Stone of Hope: Prophetic Religion and the Death of Jim Crow*. Chapel Hill: University of North Carolina Press, 2004.

Cohen, Daniel. "NYC School Segregation Report Card: Still Last, Action Needed Now." Civil Rights Project, June 10, 2021. https://www.civilrightsproject.ucla.edu/news/research/k-12-education/integration-and-diversity/nyc-school-segregation-report-card-still-last-action-needed-now.

Coles, Robert. *Children of Crisis*. Vol. 2, *Migrants, Sharecroppers, Mountaineers*. New York: Little, Brown, 1973.

———. *The Desegregation of Southern Schools: A Psychiatric Study*. New York: Anti-Defamation League of B'nai B'rith, 1963. http://catalog.hathitrust.org/api/volumes/oclc/6067539.html.

Coskren, T. Dennis, and Helen B. Hay. *Field Trip Guides for Geological Society of America Annual Meeting*. Lexington: University of Kentucky, 1984.

Cotton, Oscar D., Brian Estrada, Eileen Goldstein, Bonnie Smith, and Robert Young. "Desegregation in Ewing Township, New Jersey: A Case Study." New York: Columbia University Teachers College, 1974. http://www.eric.ed.gov:80/PDFS/ED117279.pdf.

Cox, Earnest Sevier. "The School Situation at Clinton, Tennessee: An Essay." Clinton, TN: Sn, c. 1956.

Courier-News. Clinton, an Identity Rediscovered. Clinton, TN: Courier-News, 1985.

Curry, Constance. *Silver Rights*. Chapel Hill, NC: Algonquin Books, 1995.

D'Angelo, Raymond. *The American Civil Rights Movement: Readings and Interpretations*. Guilford, CT: McGraw-Hill/Dushkin, 2001.

Daniel, Julia. *The Crozier Family History: The Happiness of Being Together*. Oliver Springs, TN: published by the author, 1993. https://dla.acaweb.org/digital/collection/Tusculum/id/3076.

Daniel, Pete. *Lost Revolutions: The South in the 1950s*. Chapel Hill: University of North Carolina Press, 2000.

Darnell, Riley C. *Tennessee Blue Book, 2007–2008*. Nashville, TN: Department of State Publications, 2007. http://www.state.tn.us/sos/bluebook/05-06/43-past_cons.pdf.

Davis, Doug. *Gifts Given: Family, Community, and Integration's Move from the Courtroom to the Schoolyard*. Bloomington, IN: iUniverse, 2012.

Diehl, Huston. *Dream Not of Other Worlds: Teaching in a Segregated Elementary School, 1970.* Iowa City: University of Iowa Press, 2007.

Dragon Digital image. Ancestry.com.

Dragon 1957, The. Digital image. Ancestry.com.

DuBois, W. E. B. *Black Reconstruction in America, 1860–1880.* New York: Free Press, 1999.

Dunaway, Wilma A. *Slavery in the American Mountain South.* New York: Cambridge University Press, 2003.

Edkins, Jenny. *Trauma and the Memory of Politics.* New York: Cambridge University Press, 2003.

Faulkner, William. *Requiem for a Nun.* London: Chatto & Windus, 1919. https://archive.org/details/in.ernet.dli.2015.149792.

Federal Bureau of Investigation. "National States Rights Party: Monographs and Attorney General's Letter." Washington, DC: Federal Bureau of Investigation, 1966.

Fielder, George F., Jr. *Archaeological Survey with Emphasis on Prehistoric Sites of the Oak Ridge Reservation.* Oak Ridge, TN: Oak Ridge National Laboratory, 1974. https://www.nrc.gov/docs/ML1805/ML18054A475.pdf.

Fine, Benjamin. *1,000,000 Delinquents.* Cleveland: World, 1955.

Frankenberg, Erica, Jongyeon Ee, Jennifer B. Ayscue, and Gary Orfield. "Harming Our Common Future: America's Segregated Schools 65 Years after *Brown*." Civil Rights Project, May 10, 2019. https://www.civilrightsproject.ucla.edu/research/k-12-education/integration-and-diversity/harming-our-common-future-americas-segregated-schools-65-years-after-brown/Brown-65-050919v4-final.pdf.

Frankenberg, Erica, Genevieve Siegel Hawley, Jongyeon Ee, and Gary Orfield. "Southern Schools: More Than Half a Century after the Civil Rights Revolution." Civil Rights Project, May 2017. https://www.civilrightsproject.ucla.edu/research/k-12-education/integration-and-diversity/southern-schools-brown-83-report/Brown63_South_052317-RELEASE-VERSION.pdf.

Gardner, Eric. *Unexpected Places: Relocating Nineteenth-Century African American Literature.* Jackson: University Press of Mississippi, 2009.

Goff, James R., Jr. *Close Harmony: A History of Southern Gospel.* Chapel Hill: University of North Carolina Press, 2002.

Goodspeed Publishing Company. *History of Tennessee: From the Earliest Time to the Present; Together with an Historical and a Biographical Sketch from Twenty-Five to Thirty Counties of East Tennessee, Besides a Valuable Fund of Notes, Original Observations, Reminiscences, Etc. Etc., 1887.* Reprint, with added material by Silas Emmett Lucas, Jr. Greenville, SC: Southern Historical Press, 1980.

Gordy, Sondra Hercher. "Teachers of the Lost Year, 1958–1959: Little Rock School District." Ed.D. dissertation, University of Arkansas, 1996.

Gore, Dayo F., Jeanne Theoharis, and Komozi Woodard, eds. *Want to Start a Revolution?: Radical Women in the Black Freedom Struggle.* New York: New York University Press, 2009.

Graham, Billy. *Just As I Am: The Autobiography of Billy Graham.* San Francisco, CA: Harper San Francisco, 1997.

Hendrickson, Robert C., with Fred J. Cook. *Youth in Danger: A Forthright Report by the Former Chairman of the Senate Subcommittee on Juvenile Delinquency.* New York: Harcourt, Brace, 1956.

Herd, Valerie Marie Hulett. "The Desegregation of Clinton High School: Then and Now." M.A. thesis, University of Tennessee, 1995.

Hill, Lance. *The Deacons for Defense: Armed Resistance and the Civil Rights Movement.* Chapel Hill: University of North Carolina Press, 2006.

Hill, Stephanie A. *Clinton.* Charleston: Arcadia, 2011.

Hohle, Randolph. *Racism in the Neoliberal Era: A Meta History of Elite White Power.* New York: Routledge, 2017.

Holden, Anna, Bonita Valien, and Preston Valien. *Clinton, Tennessee: A Tentative Description and Analysis of the School Desegregation Crisis.* Field Reports on Desegregation in the South. New York: Anti-Defamation League of B'nai B'rith, 1957.

Hoskins, Katherine B. *Anderson County.* Memphis, TN: MSU Press, 1979.

_____. *Anderson County Historical Sketches.* Clinton, TN: Courier-News, 1987.

Houston, Benjamin. *The Nashville Way: Racial Etiquette and the Struggle for Social Justice in a Southern City.* Athens: University of Georgia Press, 2012.

Kasper, John. *Charlottesville Attack.* Charlottesville, VA: Seaboard White Citizens Council, c. 1956.

_____. *Jail NAACP, Alien, Unclean, Unchristian, BLAST Irreverent, Ungodly LEADERS, HANG 9 SUPREME COURT SWINE (This Year Domine '56) BANISH LIARS Destroy REDS (ALL Muscovite Savages, Rooseveltian Dupes) EXPOSE BERIA'S 'Psycho-politics' DEATH TO USURERS.* Washington, DC: Seaboard White Citizens' Council, 1956.

_____. *Segregation or Death.* Washington, DC: Seaboard White Citizens' Council, 1958.

Kimmel, Michael S. Foreword to *Home-Grown Hate: Gender and Organized Racism,* edited by Abby L. Ferber. New York: Routledge, 2004.

Ladino, Robyn Duff. *Desegregating Texas Schools: Eisenhower, Shivers, and the Crisis at Mansfield High.* Austin: University of Texas Press, 1996.

Lait, Jack, and Mortimer Lee. *U.S.A. Confidential.* New York: Crown, 1952.

League of Women Voters of Oak Ridge. *Anderson County, TN, a Handbook.* Oak Ridge: published by the author, 1974.

Locke, Laura. *Let Me Tell You about Coal Creek: My Life, and the History of the Black Citizens of Coal Creek, (now Lake City) Tennessee.* DeQuincy, LA: Classy Expressions, 2000.

Madison, James H. *Indiana through Tradition and Change: A History of the Hoosier State and Its People, 1920–1945.* Indianapolis: Indiana Historical Society, 1982.

Margolick, David. *Elizabeth and Hazel.* New Haven, CT: Yale University Press, 2011.

Marsh, Alec. *John Kasper and Ezra Pound: Saving the Republic.* New York: Bloomsbury, 2015.

McMillen, Neil. *The Citizens' Council: Organized Resistance to the Second Reconstruction, 1954–1964.* Urbana: University of Illinois Press, 1971.

Meier, Kenneth J., Joseph Stewart Jr., and Robert E. England. *Race, Class and Education:*

The Politics of Second-Generation Discrimination. Madison: University of Wisconsin Press, 1989.

Messerschmidt, James W. *Nine Lives: Adolescent Masculinities, the Body and Violence*. Boulder, CO: Perseus Book Groups, 2000.

Miller, Steven P. *Billy Graham and the Rise of the Republican South*. Philadelphia: University of Pennsylvania Press, 2009.

Mills, Cynthia, and Pamela H. Simpson. *Monuments to the Lost Cause: Women, Art and the Landscapes of Southern Memory*. Knoxville: University of Tennessee Press, 2003.

Nashville, Tennessee, City Directory, 1949. St. Louis, MO: R.L. Polk, 1950.

National Park Service. *Geology and History of the Cumberland Plateau*. Oneida, TN: Big South Fork National River and Recreation Area, 2022. https://www.nps.gov/biso/planyourvisit/upload/webgeo.pdf.

1952 Clinton City Directory. Chillicothe, OH: Mullin-Kille, 1952.

1955 Clinton City Directory. Chillicothe, OH: Mullin-Kille, 1952.

Nisbett, Richard E., and Dov Cohen. *Culture of Honor: The Psychology of Violence in the South*. Boulder, CO: Westview Press, 1996.

Patterson, Homer L. *American Education*, vol. 59. Mount Prospect, IL: Educational Directories, 1962.

Perry, Imani. *South to America: A Journey Below the Mason-Dixon to Understand the Soul of a Nation*. New York: HarperCollins, 2022.

Presbyterian Church in the U.S.A. Committee on Freedmen. *Fifth Annual Report of the General Assembly's Committee on Freedmen, of the Presbyterian Church, in the United States of America*. Pittsburgh: James A. McMillin, 1870.

Purcell, Violet Rhea. *Hello, Central*. Clinton, TN: Courier-News, 1984.

Ramsey, Sonya. *Reading, Writing and Segregation: A Century of Black Women Teachers in Nashville*. Urbana: University of Illinois Press, 2008.

Ritterhouse, Jennifer. *Growing Up Jim Crow: How Black and White Southern Children Learned Race*. Chapel Hill: University of North Carolina, 2006.

Roberts, Gene, and Hank Klibanoff. *The Race Beat: The Press, The Civil Rights Struggle, and the Awakening of the Nation*. New York: Vintage Books, 2006.

Roberts, Snyder E. *History of Clinton Senior High School, 1806–1971*. Clinton, TN: Distributive Education Department, 1971.

Scheibach, Michael. *Atomic Narratives and American Youth: Coming of Age with the Atom, 1945–1955*. Jefferson, NC: McFarland, 2003.

Schrum, Kelly. *Some Wore Bobby Sox: The Emergence of Teenage Girls' Culture, 1920–1945*. Girls' History and Culture Book Series. New York: Palgrave Macmillan, 2004.

Seeber, Clifford R. *Good Morning, Professor*. Self-published, 1977.

———. "A History of Anderson County, Tennessee." M.A. thesis, University of Tennessee, 1928.

Seivers, Lana Carmen. "Words of Discrimination, Voices of Determination: Reflections on the Desegregation of Clinton High School." Ed.D. dissertation, University of Tennessee, 2002.

Shumate, Robert N. "The Effect of Social Classes on the Community and Schools of Clinton, Tennessee." M.A. thesis, University of Tennessee, 1956.

Sims, Anne Elizabeth. "Magnet Mills: The Southern Textile Industry in Clinton, Tennessee." M.A. thesis, East Tennessee State University, 1983.

Sokol, Jason. *There Goes My Everything: White Southerners in the Age of Civil Rights, 1945–1975.* New York: Random House, 2007.

Tagore, Proma. *The Shapes of Silence: Writing by Women of Colour and the Politics of Testimony.* Montreal: McGill-Queen's University Press, 2009.

Tennessee Federation for Constitutional Government. *Tyranny at Oak Ridge: An Account of How Integration Was Forced upon Certain Public Schools in Disregard of the Laws, Customs and Educational Policies of the State of Tennessee and despite the Protest of Citizens; How Integration by Federal Fiat Has Affected the Educational and Other Arrangements at Oak Ridge; and a Narrative of Events in Anderson County and East Tennessee.* Nashville, TN: published by the author, 1956.

Thompson-Miller, Ruth, Joe R. Feagin, and Leslie H. Picca. *Jim Crow's Legacy: The Lasting Impact of Segregation.* New York: Rowman & Littlefield, 2015.

U.S. Commission on Civil Rights. *Civil Rights, U.S.A.: Public Schools, Southern States, 1962: Staff Reports.* Washington, DC: U.S. Commission on Civil Rights, 1962.

United States Patent Office. *Official Gazette of the Patent Office* 645:1. Washington, DC: Department of Commerce, 1951.

Volunteer 1942. Digital image. Ancestry.com.

Walker, Alice. *In Search of Our Mothers' Gardens: Womanist Prose.* New York: Harvest Book, 1983.

Weaver, Mary. *One Hundred Years, a Story of the First Baptist Church, Clinton, Tennessee.* Clinton, TN: Courier-News, 1940.

Webb, Clive, ed. *Massive Resistance: Southern Opposition to the Second Reconstruction.* New York: Oxford University Press, 2005.

Wells, Horace V., Jr. *The Days before Yesterday: My Life Sixty Years as an Editor.* Clinton, TN: Courier-News, 1991.

Wendt, Simon. *The Spirit and the Shotgun: Armed Resistance and the Struggle for Civil Rights.* New Perspectives on the History of the South. Gainesville: University Press of Florida, 2007.

Woodward, C. Vann. *Origins of the New South, 1877–1913: A History of the South.* With a critical essay on recent works by Charles B. Dew. Baton Rouge: Louisiana State University Press, 1971.

Wray, Matt. *Not Quite White: White Trash and the Boundaries of Whiteness.* Durham, NC: Duke University Press, 2006.

Zhang, Aimin. *The Origins of the African American Civil Rights Movement, 1865–1956.* New York: Routledge, 2002.

INDEX

ABOUT THE AUTHOR

Rachel Louise Martin, PhD, is a historian and writer whose work has appeared in outlets like the *Atlantic* and *Oxford American*. The author of *Hot, Hot Chicken*, a cultural history of Nashville hot chicken, and *A Most Tolerant Little Town*, the forgotten story of the first school to attempt court-mandated desegregation in the wake of *Brown v. Board*, she is especially interested by the politics of memory and by the power of stories to illuminate why injustice persists in America today. She lives in Nashville, Tennessee.